Iustitia Dei

IUSTITIA DEI

A HISTORY OF
THE CHRISTIAN DOCTRINE OF
JUSTIFICATION

VOLUME I
FROM THE BEGINNINGS TO 1500

ALISTER E. McGRATH
LECTURER IN CHRISTIAN DOCTRINE AND ETHICS
WYCLIFFE HALL, OXFORD

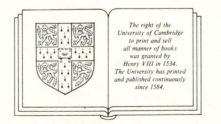

*The right of the
University of Cambridge
to print and sell
all manner of books
was granted by
Henry VIII in 1534.
The University has printed
and published continuously
since 1584.*

CAMBRIDGE UNIVERSITY PRESS

CAMBRIDGE
LONDON   NEW YORK   NEW ROCHELLE
MELBOURNE   SYDNEY

Published by the Press Syndicate of the University of Cambridge
The Pitt Building, Trumpington Street, Cambridge CB2 1RP
32 East 57th Street, New York NY 10022, USA
10 Stamford Road, Oakleigh, Melbourne 3166, Australia

First published 1986

Printed in Great Britain at
the University Press, Cambridge

British Library cataloguing in publication data
McGrath, Alister E.
Iustitia Dei: a history of the Christian doctrine of justification
Vol. 1: From the beginnings to 1500
1. Justification – History of doctrines
I. Title
234'.7'09   BT764.2

Library of Congress cataloguing in publication data
McGrath, Alister E., 1953–
Iustitia Dei
Bibliography: v. 1, p.
Includes index.
Contents: v. 1. From the beginnings to 1500.
1. Justification – History of doctrines. I. title.
BT764.2.M43   1986   234'.7'09   85-31339
ISBN 0 521 30887 9

In memory of
STEPHEN CHARLES NEILL
1900–1984

Contents

Contents

Preface

> But pardon, gentles all,
> The flat unraised spirits that hath dar'd
> On this unworthy scaffold to bring forth
> So great an object: can this cockpit hold
> The vasty fields of France? or may we cram
> Within this wooden O the very casques
> That did affright the air at Agincourt?
>
> Henry V, *Chorus* 8–14

The history of the development of the Christian doctrine of justi-fication has never been written. It is this deficiency which the present volumes seek to remedy. It will be evident, however, that the vast scope of the subject under consideration has resulted in certain inevitable restrictions being placed upon the material here presented. A full treatment of the subject would not be confined to the historical and theological aspects of the matter, but would also deal with the related juristic, semantic, political, moral and metaphysical issues which have shaped the Christian discussion of justification down the ages. It is hoped, however, that the significance of this shortcoming will greatly be diminished by judicious use of the vast body of scholarly material available in the learned literature. Inevitably, pressure upon space means that the established results of scholarship must frequently be referred to, rather than reproduced. In effect, the present study is a bibliographical essay which records, correlates, and where possible extends, the present state of scholarly work on the development of the Christian doctrine of justification. It is not merely a catalogue of the doctrines of justification associated with theologians of alleged importance to the development of that doctrine, but is an attempt to record its continuous development within the western theological tradition.

It is customary to present an *apologia* for a work which may appear to cover much familiar ground. The following considerations suggest that a new study of the development of the Christian doctrine of justification is necessary. First, there has been no major study of the development of the doctrine since the classic study of Albrecht Ritschl, *Die christliche Lehre von der Rechtfertigung und Versöhnung*, published in 1870. The value of that work, now a century old, is greatly reduced by Ritschl's moralist presuppositions, which seriously prejudice his analysis at points, particularly in the case of the young Luther. Secondly, Ritschl's work deals with the development of the doctrine from the eleventh century to the nineteenth, restricting its discussion of the post-Reformation period to its development within German Protestantism. It will therefore be clear that his work requires extension to include the first ten centuries of Christian history, post-Reformation Roman Catholic theology, and later nineteenth- and twentieth-century developments. Thirdly, the vast scholarly undertakings which have given the modern period the magnificent critical editions denied to Ritschl (such as the Weimar Luther edition) have also cast new light on the theology of the medieval period, calling into question most of Ritschl's conclusions. There is an urgent need to correlate these findings and to reappraise the development of the doctrine of justification in the medieval period accordingly. Fourthly, the new interest in ecumenism makes an informed discussion of the development of the doctrine of justification essential. It is thus hoped that the present volumes will at least serve to introduce the subject to a wider circle than would otherwise be the case.

The importance of the present study is twofold. First, the historical study of the development of any Christian doctrine from its origins to the present day is inherently significant, in that it illustrates the factors which have influenced the development of doctrine in general. The doctrine of justification, like other doctrines, was discussed in terms of certain semantic, ontological and juristic assumptions, which were questioned, criticised and replaced as the development of Christian theology proceeded. The development of the doctrine of justification is thus a paradigm for the study of ideological interaction in the development of doctrine, illustrating how theological and secular concepts were related as theologians responded to the cultural situation of their period.

The study is also of theological importance. The theological situation today demands both a *restatement* and a *reinstatement* of the Christian doctrine of reconciliation. The essential prerequisite of any attempt to interpret, reinterpret or restate that doctrine is a due appreciation of the historical origins and subsequent development of the concept. It is clearly futile to develop or defend theories of reconciliation which originally rest upon some manifestly incorrect interpretation of a Hebrew root, which represent a recent distortion of an older and more considered doctrine, or which represent a response to a particular cultural situation which no longer pertains today. Of the several concepts employed in the Christian articulation of the reconciliation effected between God and his world through Christ, the most important is that of *justification*. The present study is thus offered as a means to this end.

The first volume deals with the development of the doctrine in the patristic and medieval periods up to about 1500. On account of the strong degree of continuity within the western theological tradition up to this point, it is possible to treat the subject in a systematic manner at this stage, identifying both the main lines of development and schools of thought within the period. This approach cannot be sustained in the second volume, on account of the radical discontinuity within the western tradition in the sixteenth century arising from the Reformation, and the equally great discontinuity within European Protestantism in the late eighteenth century accompanying the Enlightenment. As a result, the approach adopted to the material in the second volume is necessarily episodic, rather than thematic.

Thomas Aquinas once reminded Siger of Brabant that 'the purpose of the study of philosophy is not to learn what others have thought, but to learn what is true'. The study of the history of doctrine is not an end in itself, nor can historical method be allowed to pass for theological method. Any theologian who takes his responsibilities towards God and his church seriously must consider the detailed study of the development of the Christian doctrine of justification essential to his task. The peculiar importance of Christian doctrine of justification lies in its constituting the essential form of the Christian proclamation down the ages. While the present study will clearly be of interest to the student of the history of idea, it is of particular importance to the theologian, for it documents the historical forms taken by the proclamation of the justification of sinful man, the essence of the gospel, down the ages. We are not the first to proclaim the gospel of the justification of sinful man in Christ, nor will we be the last. The Christian gospel will continue to be proclaimed, and it is the task of the theologian to assist the community of faith as it seeks to articulate the Christian faith in the face of secular views of legitimation and salvation. The present study documents how previous generations attempted an identical task with a seriousness which we must make our own.

Finally, the debt owed by the present writer to the labours of previous generations of scholars must be fully acknowledged. If the present work represents an improvement upon the attempts of others to survey the same field, it is because, like a man contemplating a vast landscape, by standing upon their shoulders, I have been able to see further.

We are like dwarves sitting upon the shoulders of giants. We see more, and things that are more distant, than they did, not because our sight is superior or because we are taller than they, but because they raise us up, and by their great stature add to ours.

John of Salisbury, *Metalogicon* III, 4

Oxford   Pentecost 1985

Acknowledgements

One of the greatest pleasures of scholarship is to be able to acknowledge the assistance which others so generously rendered. I owe sincere thanks to Fr Fergus Kerr O.P., Professor Oliver O'Donovan and Fr Edward Yarnold S.J., who read an earlier draft of this work and made invaluable comments upon it. I also owe thanks to many others, who assisted me in various ways: Fr M. D. Chenu, O.P., Fr Cassian Reel O.F.M.Cap., Beryl Smalley, Peter Southwell and Fr Adolar Zumkeller O.E.S.A. Of the many libraries which were used during the course of this work, I particularly wish to acknowledge the invaluable assistance of the staff of the Bodleian Library, Oxford and Cambridge University Library. I also owe a considerable debt to Merton College, Oxford and St John's College, Cambridge for academic research awards which permitted me to undertake the present work, and Wycliffe Hall, Oxford, for providing me with the facilities to complete it. Finally, I wish to thank the officers of Cambridge University Press, particularly Dr Robert Williams, for their encouragement and support during the closing stages of this work.

This book is dedicated in affectionate memory of a much-loved scholar and bishop, who took considerable personal interest in the final stages of this project.

1. Prolegomena

§1 The subject defined

The nature and significance of the Christian doctrine of justification are best appreciated when the nature of Christianity is considered. The central teaching of the Christian faith is that reconciliation has been effected between God and sinful man through Jesus Christ, and that this new relation between God and man is a present possibility for those outside the church, and a present actuality for those within its bounds. Although the manner in which this relationship is conceived and proclaimed generally reflects the contemporary cultural context, the assertion that a *new relationship* – however this is articulated – is thus possible is essentially independent of cultural considerations. It will therefore be clear that the question of how the saving action of God towards mankind in Christ may be appropriated by the individual is of central significance. The Christian doctrine of justification is not, however, merely concerned with the question of what man must do if he is to enter into a relationship with God through Christ, but also with establishing its presuppositions and consequences.

The Christian doctrine of justification, which forms the subject of the present study, thus constitutes the real centre of the theological system of the Christian church, encapsulating the direct and normative consequences of the historical revelation of God to mankind in Jesus Christ. There never was, and there never can be, any true Christian church without the doctrine of justification, for the community of faith cannot exist without proclaiming, in word and sacrament, the truth of what God has done for man in Christ. It is this truth which called the church into being, and it is this truth which must be expressed in her life and doctrine. In the Christian doctrine of justification, we are concerned with the turning of the godless man against his godlessness; with his transformation from man *without*

I

God to man *with* God, *for* God and *before* God; with his transition from *homo peccator* to *homo iustus*. The doctrine defines the conditions under which man's broken relationship with God may be restored, and the nature of that transition itself. Without the recognition of the *necessity*, the *possibility* and the *actuality* of such a transition, there can be no community of faith – and it is in this sense that the *articulus iustificationis* is the *articulus stantis et cadentis ecclesiae*.[1]

The Christian faith is centred upon the person of Jesus Christ. The centrality of the mystery of the person of Christ to her faith is ultimately an expression of his church's conviction that God was in Christ reconciling the world to himself. The creeds of Christendom may not explicitly state a doctrine of reconciliation, but its thread runs throughout their fabric. *Qui propter nos homines et propter nostram salutem descendit de coelis!* Wherever the church commemorates, celebrates and proclaims the passion of her redeemer and the benefits which she thereby receives, she rehearses her faith in the reconciliation he accomplished on her behalf, and which called her into being. Who Christ is becomes known in his saving action; who man is becomes known through his being the object of that saving action. The doctrine of justification thus encapsulates the essence of the Christian faith and proclamation, locating the essence of Christianity in the saving action of God towards mankind in Jesus Christ. The fundamentally soteriological orientation of the patristic Trinitarian and Christological debates demonstrates the centrality of the concept of reconciliation, however expressed, to the positive articulation of the Christian message. Indeed, the dissociation of these dogmas from their soteriological contexts results in their becoming abstract to the point of irrelevance.

The *concept of justification* and the *doctrine of justification* must be carefully distinguished. The *concept* of justification is one of many employed within the Old and New Testaments, particularly the Pauline corpus, to describe God's saving action towards his people. It cannot lay claim to exhaust, nor adequately characterise in itself, the richness of the biblical understanding of salvation in Christ. The *doctrine* of justification has come to develop a meaning quite independent of its biblical origins, and concerns the *means by which man's relationship to God is established*. The church has chosen to subsume its discussion of the reconciliation of man to God under the aegis of justification, thereby giving the concept an emphasis quite absent from the New Testament. The 'doctrine of justification' has come to bear a meaning within dogmatic theology which is quite independent of its Pauline origins, so that even if it could be shown that it plays a minimal role in Pauline soteriology, or that its origins lie in an anti-Judaising polemic quite inappropriate to the theological circumstances of today, its significance would not be diminished as a result. That it was justification, rather than some other soteriological metaphor, which was singled out in this manner may be regarded as an accident of history, linked to several developments.

1. The rise in Pauline scholarship during the theological renaissance of the twelfth century, and particularly the use of Pauline commentaries as vehicles of theological speculation.

2. The generally high regard for classical jurisprudence within the western church.

3. The semantic relationship between *iustitia* and *iustificatio*, which allowed the theologians of High Scholasticism to find in the cognate concept of justification a means of rationalising the divine dispensation towards mankind in terms of justice.

4. The emphasis placed upon an already important concept by Luther's theological difficulties concerning how the statement 'God is just' could be gospel, so that the Reformation came to be perceived to be inextricably linked with the doctrine of justification.

5. The discussion of the reconciliation of man to God under the aegis of the doctrine of justification by the Council of Trent in its sixth session.

The history of the doctrine of justification has its sphere within the western church alone. The Orthodox emphasis upon the economic condescension of the Son leading to man's participation in the divine being is generally expressed in the concept of deification (θεοποίη-σις or θέωσις) rather than justification.[2] Three factors may be identified which account for this development.

1. The different understandings of the operation of the Holy Spirit associated with the western and eastern churches. The west has tended to subordinate the work of the Holy Spirit to the concept of grace, which is interposed between God and man. The Orthodox stress upon the immediacy of the divine, and the direct encounter of man with the Holy Spirit naturally leads to this encounter being expressed in terms of deification.[3]

2. The concept of deification is particularly suited to a marriage with neo-Platonism, a marriage particularly associated with the mystical works of pseudo-Dionysius, whose use of neo-Platonist concepts to articulate his theology of redemption resulted in a philosophical Christianity of a profundity quite unparalleled in the

west. It was only when his works became available in Latin translation that the theologians of the west began to respond to his influence[4] – by which time, a western theological tradition of a very different cast had already become firmly established. The great theologians of the medieval period, such as Thomas Aquinas, may have modified their doctrines of justification to accommodate his insights, but they were already constrained by tradition to the category of justification, rather than deification.

3. The eastern church never developed the interest in Roman law which is so characteristic of the early theologians of the Latin west which, coupled with the character of the Latin language itself (see §2) led to the western commitment to justification as *the* fundamental soteriological metaphor. It may therefore be noted that the astonishing use of the concept of justification in the works of Cyril Lucaris (1572–1638) merely illustrates his unusual relationship with the Reformed church of his day,[5] rather than any inherent trends within Orthodox theology itself. The great schism between east and west finds expression at a far deeper level than the mere politics of the matter might suggest.

The present study is therefore concerned with the attempts of the western church to analyse the presuppositions and consequences of her proclamation of salvation in Christ from the earliest of times to the present day.

§2 The conceptual foundations of the Christian doctrine of justification

'I am not ashamed of the gospel, for it is the power of God for salvation to everyone who has faith . . . for in it the righteousness of God is revealed' (Romans 1.16–17). For Paul, the revelation of the righteousness of God *is* the gospel.[1] But what is this tantalising 'righteousness of God'? As the present study will make clear, the interpretation of the 'righteousness of God' within the western theological tradition has been accompanied by the most intractable difficulties. The concept of *justification* is inextricably linked with that of *righteousness*, both semantically and theologically.[2] Central to the Christian understanding of the economy of salvation is the conviction that God is righteous, and acts in accordance with that righteousness in the salvation of mankind. It is clear, however, that this conviction raises certain fundamental questions, not least that of which concept of 'righteousness' can be considered appropriate to a discussion of the divine dispensation towards mankind. The relationship between God and man, according to the Christian understanding, may be characterised in three propositions:

1.   God is righteous.
2.   Man is a sinner.
3.   God justifies man.

The quintessence of the Christian doctrine of justification is that these three propositions do not constitute an inconsistent triad. God, in his righteousness, justifies the sinner. The proclamation of this justification to those outside the church has always been accompanied by speculation within the church as to how it is possible for God, being righteous, to justify sinners in the first place. It is therefore of considerable importance to consider the various understandings of the concept of 'righteousness' or 'justice' which have been employed in the articulation of the doctrine of justification.

Modern theological vocabularies contain a host of Hebrew, Greek and Latin words, most of which possess, in their original contexts, a richness and depth of meaning which cannot possibly be conveyed by the mere translation of the word into English. Such an enterprise involves not merely the substitution of a modern word for the original, but the transference of the latter from its own proper conceptual framework to one in which its meaning is distorted. This problem has long been recognised. Jesus ben Sira, presumably in an attempt to divert attention from the absence of a Hebrew original, complained that 'things originally spoken in Hebrew do not have the same force when they are translated into another language ... with the law, the prophets and the rest of the writings, it makes no small difference when they are read in their original language' (Ecclesiasticus, prologue). The conceptual foundations of the Christian doctrine of justification may be sought in the Old Testament, in a milieu quite different from that of western Europe, where it received its systematic articulation. The transference of the concept from this Hebraic matrix to that of western Europe has significant consequences, which we shall explore in the present section.

The primary source for Christian theological speculation is Holy Scripture: indeed, Christian theology may be regarded as an extended commentary upon the biblical material. It is therefore evident that Christian theology will contain a number of important concepts originating from a Hebraic context, and that the transference of these concepts from their original context may result in a shift in meaning with unacceptable theological consequences. In particular, it must be pointed out that the equation of Hebraic and western concepts of 'righteousness' is frequently implicit in theological works, so that western concepts of justice are employed in the articulation of the Christian doctrine of justification. A study of the classic western understandings of justice suggests that these are essentially *secular* and *practical*, and therefore quite unsuited to a discussion of the 'righteousness of God'. The present section, dealing with the Hebrew, Greek and Latin understandings of 'righteousness', is therefore intended as a prolegomenon to the study of the doctrine of justification. Although not strictly a part of the history of the doctrine itself, the question exercised such an influence over the subsequent discussion of justification that its omission at this stage is impossible.

The etymology of the terms ṣedeq and ṣᵉdāqâ is generally accepted to be obscure, and it is quite possible that the original meaning of the grapheme ṣdq is lost beyond recovery. Recent theories of the historical background of the Hebrew language have tended to divide the Hamito-Semitic languages into two groups: the archaic southern Cushitic and Chadic languages, and the more progressive northern group of languages, including the Semitic languages, the Berber languages of north Africa, and ancient Egyptian and Coptic.[3] The triliteral root is a conspicuous feature common to all the languages of the northern group, and it is possible to argue that at every level – whether semantic, grammatical or phonological – features of these languages are theoretically derivable from a common source. When the etymology of the grapheme ṣdq is examined, using other ancient near eastern languages as models, a spectrum of possible meanings emerges, of which the most fundamental appears to be that of *conformity to a norm*.[4] This observation is confirmed by the fact that the dominant sense of the terms ṣedeq and ṣᵉdāqâ appears to be that of 'right behaviour' or 'right disposition'.[5] That similar understandings of 'righteousness' were common in the ancient world is demonstrated by the close semantic association between the ideas of 'righteousness' and 'truth' in the Aryan ṛtá- and Iranian aša.[6]

The validity of such an appeal to etymological considerations has been criticised by Barr,[7] who illustrates the alleged inadequacy of the tool with reference to the English word 'nice'. The etymology of the word indicates that it derives from the Latin *nescius*, presumably *via* the Old French *nice*, thereby suggesting that its meaning should be 'silly' or 'ignorant' – which is clearly of little use in determining its late twentieth century usage. Barr neglects, however, to point out that etymological considerations *can* give an indication of the *early* meaning of a term, despite the connotations it may develop later as a consequence of constant use. Whilst the derivation of 'nice' from 'nescius' does not allow its modern meaning to be established, it is perfectly adequate to allow its *sixteenth*-century meaning to be established, it then bearing the sense of 'silly' or 'ignorant'. As the enterprise in question is to establish the meaning of the term in texts of widely varying age, etymological arguments are perfectly accept-able in an attempt to establish its *early* meaning: the later meaning of the term, of course, cannot be determined by such considerations, as nuances not originally present make their appearance. Thus in later Hebrew, ṣᵉḏāqâ came to mean 'almsgiving', a meaning which cannot be derived from etymological considerations alone. Here, as else-where, the semantic connection between a grapheme and the meaning of a word appears to have eventually become so strained as to have almost snapped completely. However, as we shall indicate below, this later meaning of the word ṣᵉḏāqâ can be understood on the basis of its etymology.

The *oldest* meaning of ṣᵉḏāqâ, as judged by its use in the Song of Deborah (Judges 5.1–31), appears to be 'victory'.[8] This meaning appears to be retained in some later texts,[9] although it is clear that the nuances associated with the term have altered. In this early passage, which contains many unusual grammatical forms and rare words, God is understood to have demonstrated his 'righteousness' by defending Israel when her existence was threatened by an outside agency. Underlying this understanding of *iustitia Dei* is the concep-tual framework of the covenant: when God and Israel mutually fulfil their covenant obligations to each other, a state of righteousness can be said to exist – i.e., things are ṣaddîq, 'as they should be'. Thus Israel's triumphant victories over her enemies were seen as proofs of the ṣidqôt 'ᵃḏoñay,[10] the *iustitiae Dei* of the Vulgate. Even where the term 'righteousness' is not found, it seems that a clear connection is understood to exist between God's activity as a judge and Israel's victory over her neighbours.[11]

At this stage in the history of Israel, the 'righteousness' of the covenant does not appear to have been considered to have been under threat from within Israel itself, but merely from external agencies. However, with the establishment of Israel came the rise of prophecy, and the threat posed to the covenant relationship from within Israel herself became increasingly apparent. This insight was expressed by the prophets in terms of the *conditional election* of Israel as the people of God. For the prophets, ṣᵉdāqâ was effectively that condition or state which was required of Israel if her relationship with God was to continue.[12] Although there are many instances where ṣᵉdāqâ can be regarded as corresponding to the concept of *iustitia distributiva*, which has come to dominate western thinking on the nature of justice (despite the rival claims of *iustitia commutativa*), there remains a significant number which cannot. An illustration of this may be found in the Old Testament attitude to the poor, needy and destitute. As we have noted, ṣᵉdāqâ refers to the 'right order of affairs' which is violated, at least in part, by the very existence of such unfortunates. In his ṣᵉdāqâ, God must deliver them from their plight – and it is *this* aspect of the Hebrew concept of ṣᵉdāqâ which has proved so intractable to those who attempted to interpret it solely as *iustitia distributiva*. It is clear that this aspect of the Hebraic understanding of 'righteousness' cannot be understood in terms of an impartial judge who administers justice according to which party has broken a universally accepted law.

It is to the genius of Cremer that we owe the fundamental insight that ṣᵉdāqâ, in its basic sense, refers to an actual relationship between two persons, and implies behaviour which corresponds to, or is consistent with, whatever claims may arise from or concerning either party to the relationship. The relationship in question is that presupposed by the covenant between God and Israel, which must be considered as the ultimate norm to which ṣᵉdāqâ must be referred. The Hebrew concept of ṣᵉdāqâ stands in a class of its own – a class which Cremer brilliantly characterised as *iustitia salutifera*.[13]

The strongly soteriological overtones of the term ṣᵉdāqâ can be illustrated from a number of passages in which 'righteousness' and 'salvation' are practically equated, particularly from Deutero-Isaiah:

> I will bring my ṣᵉdāqâ near, it is not far away,
> And my salvation will not be delayed.[14]

This is not, it must be emphasised, to say that 'righteousness' and 'salvation' are treated as being synonymous: rather, they are regarded as being inextricably linked on account of the covenant relationship between God and Israel. Semantic and theological considerations combine to give the Old Testament concept of the 'righteousness of God' such strongly soteriological overtones, which the western concept of *iustitia distributiva* cannot convey. The later meaning of ṣᵉdāqâ in post-bibilical Hebrew ('almsgiving') can thus be seen as the development of a trend already evident in passages such as Psalm

112.9 and Daniel 4.27 (Aramaic 4.24: although this section of the book of Daniel is written in Aramaic, rather than Hebrew, the same word is used in each language). The 'right order of affairs' is violated by the existence of the poor and needy; it is therefore a requirement of ṣᵉḏāqâ that this be remedied by the appropriate means. Thus the sense which ṣᵉḏāqâ assumes in the Targums and Talmud ('bene-volence' in general, or 'almsgiving' in particular) can be seen to represent a natural development of the soteriological nuances which had been associated with the term from the earliest of times, rather than the final rupture of the semantic connection between a word and its root.[15]

The difficulties attending the translation of the Old Testament into any second language, whether modern English or Hellenistic Greek, are well illustrated by the application of semantic field theory. The *semantic field*[16] of a word includes not merely its synonyms, but also its antonyms, homonyms and homophones. As such, it is much broader than the *lexical field*, which may be defined very precisely in terms of words which are closely associated with one another. The enormous size of such semantic fields may be illustrated from the associative field of the French word *chat*, which is estimated to consist of some two thousand words.[17] The translation of a word into a different language inevitably involves a distortion of the semantic field, so that certain nuances and associations present in the original cannot be conveyed in a translation, and new nuances and associ-ations not already present make their appearance. The word chosen to translate the original will itself have a well-established semantic field, so that an alien set of associations will be imposed upon the word in question. This difficulty is well illustrated in the two non-contiguous semantic transitions of importance to our study, ṣᵉḏāqâ → *iustitia*, and haṣdîq → *iustificare*, whether these proceed directly, or indirectly through the Greek of the Septuagint (LXX). We shall consider these semantic transitions individually.

1. ṣᵉḏāqâ → δικαιοσύνη → *iustitia*

The considerable influence of Greek philosophy and culture upon Christian thought in its formative period has been well documen-ted.[18] This influence is also mediated through the LXX, whose origins date from the beginning of the third century BC.[19] The term δικαιοσύνη had by then acquired a generally Aristotelian sense, so that by δικαιοσύνη we may understand something very similar to *iustitia distributiva*.[20] Aristotle's ethical thinking is to be set in the context of the political community, the πόλις, so that 'righteousness' is defined teleologically, in terms of the well-being which it brings to the political community as a whole. Lower beings, such as the animals, and higher beings, such as the gods, were excluded from any discussion of δικαιοσύνη precisely because they were not members of the contracting political community. The sphere of δικαιοσύνη is defined as that of the πόλις, so that the concept of the 'righteousness of God' has no immediate practical significance.

It is evident that this understanding of 'righteousness' is quite different from that signified by the Hebrew word ṣᵉḏāqâ. In particular, δικαιοσύνη is a secular concept incapable of assuming the soteriological overtones associated with the Hebrew term. Whilst the translators of the LXX appear to have attempted consistency in this translation of Hebrew terms,[21] they were unable to accommodate the meaning of ṣᵉḏāqâ by the simple substitution of δικαιοσύνη in every case. Of particular interest is the translation of ṣdq in the construct form (e.g., at Leviticus 19.36, Deuteronomy 25.15 and Ezekiel 45.10). The Hebrew has the sense of 'accurate' – i.e., in the case of Leviticus 19.36, the weights are 'as they are intended to be' – accurate. Thus the στάθμια δίκαια of the LXX are clearly nothing more than accurate weights. Similarly, the 'sacrifices of righteousness' (Deuteronomy 33.19; Psalm 4.6; 51.21) appear to be nothing more than 'correct sacrifices' – i.e., those which are 'in order' under the cultic circumstances, rather than ethically or forensically 'righteous'. The basic meaning of the ṣdq-group as 'conformity to a requirement' is well illustrated by the use of ṣdq in the construct form – a meaning for which there was no satisfactory Greek equivalent. While the δικ-lexical group appears to have been considered capable of translating the ṣdq-group in the majority of cases, the soteriological connotations of ṣᵉḏāqâ were occasionally so strong that it could not be translated by δικαιοσύνη, the translators being forced to use ἐλεημοσύνη.[22] This would be expected to have at least one very significant consequence for the Greek reader of the Old Testament, unfamiliar with its Hebrew original: here he might encounter a reference to God's δικαιοσύνη, there to his ἐλεημοσύνη – and yet the same Hebrew word, ṣᵉḏāqâ, might lie behind both. The reader, unaware that the same Hebrew word was being 'translated' in each case, might conceivably set God's 'righteousness' and 'mercy' in opposition, where no such tension is warranted on the basis of the text itself.

For the first fifteen hundred years of her existence, the western church's theologians depended mainly upon Latin translations of the bible, chiefly the Vulgate, for their theological deliberations. As most theologians of the period did not have access to the original Hebrew version of the Old Testament – assuming, of course, that they knew Hebrew[23] – their interpretation of *theologoumena* such as *iustitia Dei* and *iustificare* would ultimately be based upon the Latin version of the bible available to them. It is therefore of importance to consider the difficulties attending the translation of essentially Hebraic concepts, such as 'justification', into a Latin linguistic and conceptual framework. By the second century A.D., the Latin term *iustitia* had acquired well-established juristic connotations which were to exert considerable influence over future theological interpretation of such *theologoumena*. The Ciceronian definition of *iustitia* as *reddens unicuique quod suum est* had become normative. Iustitia virtus est, communi utilitate servata, suam cuique tribuens dignitatem.[24] In effect, the Ciceronian definition encapsulates the western concept of *iustitia distributiva*, the 'due' of each man being established through the *iuris consensus*, and embodied in *ius*. The tension between this concept of 'righteousness' and that of the Old Testament will be evident.

The most important book of the Old Testament, as judged by its influence upon the development of the Christian doctrine of justification, is the Psalter, the subject of major commentaries by Augustine, Peter Lombard and Luther, to name but three. The Vulgate, as we know it, contains Jerome's translation of the Hebrew books of the Old Testament, with the *exception* of the Psalter. The Psalter found in the Vulgate is the *Psalterium Gallicum*, Jerome's second revision of the Old Latin Psalter, itself based upon Origen's recension of the LXX version.[25] His later *Psalterium iuxta hebraicam veritatem* never gained general acceptance. The difference between the two Psalters may be illustrated from their translations of Psalm 24.5 (Vulgate 23.5):

Psalterium Gallicum:
accipiet benedictionem a Domino et *misericordiam* a Deo salvatore suo.
Psalterium iuxta hebraicam veritatem:
accipiet benedictionem a Domino et *iustitiam* a Deo salutari suo.
Here the Gallic Psalter follows the LXX, and the *Psalterium iuxta hebraicam veritatem* the original Hebrew.

Although it is clear that considerable confusion could potentially have arisen through such translations, two important factors served to greatly reduce this possibility.

1. The Vulgate itself is not consistent in its translation of the LXX.

Thus the LXX ἐλεημοσύνη, translating ṣᵉdāqâ, is translated as
iustitia at Psalm 35.24 and elsewhere. The reasons for this inconsistency are not clear.

2. The two passages in the Psalter which appear to have exercised
the greatest influence over western conceptions of *iustitia Dei* are
Psalm 31.1 (Hebrew and Vulgate: 30.2) and 71.2 (Vulgate: 70.2).[26]
In both these passages, the Psalmist appeals to God, in his righteousness, to deliver him:

> In you, O Lord, do I take refuge,
> Let me never be put to shame.
> *In your righteousness* deliver me and rescue me.

In both cases, the LXX translated ṣᵉdāqâ as δικαιοσύνη, and the
Vulgate thence as *iustitia*. The strongly soteriological sense of *iustitia*
could thus be appreciated, as is borne out by the study of the exegesis
of such passages in the early medieval period.

2. haṣdîq → δικαιοῦν → *iustificare*

The Hebrew term haṣdîq, usually translated 'to justify', cannot bear
the negative sense 'to condemn' or 'to punish', its primary sense
apparently being 'to vindicate', 'to acquit', or 'to declare to be in the
right'.[27] The difficulty faced by the LXX translators was that the
corresponding Greek verb δικαιοῦν differed from haṣdîq in two
important respects.

1. In its classical usage, δικαιοῦν with a *personal* object almost
invariably seems to be applied to someone whose cause is *unjust*, and
thus bears the meaning of 'to do justice to' – i.e., 'to punish'.
Although it is possible to adduce occasional classical references in
which δικαιοῦν may conceivably be interpreted as assuming a
positive sense – i.e., to 'right an injustice suffered'[28] – it may be
emphasised that this is extremely unusual. In general, the classical
usage of δικαιοῦν is such that it is highly unusual to find it applied,
with a personal object, in the sense of 'to justify – and yet it is this
positive sense which constitutes the *norm* for the Septuagintal use of
the verb. Indeed, there are no known occurrences of δικαιοῦν in a
negative sense in any part of the Septuagint for which there exists a
Hebrew original.[29] It is therefore clear that the Septuagintal usage of
the term represents a significant shift away from the classical meaning
of the term towards that of the corresponding Hebrew term – a shift
which might prove stultifying to a Greek reader of the Old Tes-

tament, not familiar with the Hebrew original. No example of the classical use of δικαιοῦν can be adduced from the LXX, and the normal meaning it assumes in the LXX can only be adduced in a few isolated and controversial passages in classical Greek literature.

2. In classical Greek, δικαιοῦν with a personal object *applied to a person whose cause is unjust* invariably assumes the negative meaning 'to punish'. The Septuagintal use of the verb in an identical context demands that it assumes a *positive* meaning – i.e., 'to justify', 'to declare to be in the right', or 'to acquit'. For example, Isaiah 5.22–3 (LXX) follows both the wording of the Massoretic text very closely, giving the following translation: οὐαὶ ... οἱ δικαιοῦντες τὸν ἀσηβῆ ἕνεκεν δώρων καὶ τὸ δίκαιον τοῦ δικαίου αἴροντες. The substance of the complaint is that certain men are, for the sake of financial considerations, δικαιοῦντες τον ἀσηβῆ. This complaint does not make sense if the classical sense of δικαιοῦν (e.g., as it is encountered at Ecclesiasticus 42.2) is presumed to apply: if the unjust are punished – i.e., have 'justice done to them' – there can be no cause for complaint. The complaint does, however, make sense if the term is presumed to have a Hebraic background, in that the substance of the complaint is then that certain men have been bribed to declare the guilty to be innocent. It is clear that the term δικαιοῦν, although of classical Greek provenance, has assumed a Hebraic meaning as a consequence of its being used to translate the ṣdq-words. The Greek reader of the Old Testament, unfamiliar with the Hebraic background to such material, would find passages such as the above highly perplexing. The *locus classicus* for the secular Greek use of the verb is Book V of Aristotle's *Nicomachean Ethics*, in which the passive form of δικαιοῦν, (δικαιοῦσθαι) is clearly and unequivocally understood to be the antithesis of ἀδικεῖσθαι and the passive equivalent of the active δικαιοπραγεῖν, as may be seen from the statement ἀδυνατον γὰρ ἀδικεῖσθαι μὴ ἀδικοῦντος, ἢ δικαιοῦσθαι μὴ δικαιοπρα-γοῦντος.[30] It is clear that the passive meaning of the verb is 'to have justice done to one'. If this classical Aristotelian understanding of δικαιοῦσθαι is applied to the Septuagintal translation of Isaiah 43.26, an apparent absurdity results. Israel is there invited to confess her sins, ἵνα δικαιῶθῃς. It is not clear why this should move Israel to confess her sins, as in the classical sense of the verb, her punishment will follow as a matter of course. Of course, if it is assumed that the verb has taken on the meaning of haṣdîq, the meaning becomes clear and comprehensible: Israel is invited to confess her sins, in order that she may be acquitted of them. A similar

conclusion must be drawn in the case of Micah 6.11 (LXX), εἰ δικαιωθήσεται ἐν ζυγῷ ἄνομος καὶ ἐν μαρσίππῳ στάθμια δόλου; in which it is clear that the rhetorical question expects an answer *in the negative*.

It is therefore clear that, under the influence of the Hebrew original, the Septuagintal verb δικαιοῦν came to assume a meaning quite distinct from its classical origin. Furthermore, such a meaning must have become widespread and accepted within Greek-speaking Judaism – otherwise, the Septuagint would have been incomprehensible at points. It is clear that this inherent difficulty reflects the quite different semantic fields of the ṣdq- and δικ-words.

A difficulty of a quite different nature arose in the translation of terms such as haṣdîq or δικαιοῦν into Latin. The verb *iustificare*, employed for this purpose, was post-classical, and thus required interpretation. The general tendency among Latin-speaking theologians was to follow Augustine of Hippo (see §4) in interpreting *iustificare* as *iustum facere*. Augustine's etymological speculations have been the object of derision for some considerable time – for example, his impossible derivation of the name *Mercurius* from *medius currens*.[31] His explanation of the origins of the term *iustificare* is, however, quite plausible, for it involves the acceptable assumption that *-ficare* is the unstressed form of *facere*. While this may be an acceptable interpretation of *iustificare* considered in isolation, it is not an acceptable interpretation of the verb *considered as the Latin equivalent of* δικαιοῦν. This point may be developed with reference to the related case of the Greek and Latin understandings of the concept of 'merit'.[32]

Whilst Tertullian has frequently been singled out as the thinker who shackled the theology of the western church to a theology of 'works' and 'merit', there are reasons for supposing that whatever blame is due may be more fairly attributed to the Latin language itself. In Greek, 'merit' tends to be treated as a quality, so that it is essentially adjectival. Thus 'merit' is essentially a matter of estimation. The Latin term *meritum*, however, is a participial form of *mereri*, itself a deponent form of *mereo*, derived from the Greek verb μερόμαι – 'to receive one's share'. The transferred meaning of this thus becomes 'to deserve' or 'to be worthy of something'. There is, however, no Greek verb which bears quite this sense, for desert is treated essentially as a matter of estimation, rather than a quality in itself. The 'estimation' in question cannot be transferred to its object. The Latin approach to the question, however, involves the identification of the quality of the object which occasioned such an estimation. In other words, the Greek verb refers to something outside the person in question (i.e., the estimation in which he is held by others, and which cannot be treated as a quality), whereas the Latin refers to the qualities of the person in question (i.e., what it is about him that has caused the estimation in which he is held by others). Thus the nearest Greek equivalents to *mereri* are probably the passive form ἀξιοῦσθαι or the periphrastic ἄξιος εἶναι – but in each case, the reference is still to the estimatiion in which the individual is held, rather than to his 'merit'. It is of considerable interest to note that the Latin *meritum* and its cognates derive from the Greek μερόμαι rather than ἀξιοῦσθαι. The Latin notion of 'merit' clearly refers to the *right* of the individual to the particular estimation in which he is held by others, or the reward which results from this. This is clearly stated by Hilary of Poitiers: '*Mereri* is predicable of the person whose own act is the origin of the acquisition of merit for himself.'[33] This observation goes some considerable way towards explaining why the Greek-speaking church never developed a theology of 'merit' in a manner comparable to that of the Latin west.

If this illustration of the relationship between ἀξιοῦσθαι and *mereri* is applied to the related case of δικαιοῦσθαι and *iustificari*, it would appear that the Greek verb has the primary sense of being *considered* or *estimated* as righteous, whereas the Latin verb denotes *being* righteous, the reason why one is *considered* righteous by others. Although the two are clearly related, they have quite distinct points of reference.

'Messieurs, l'Angleterre est une île'. Jules Michelet prefaced his lectures on British history by pointing to a single geographical factor which had such a decisive influence upon his subject, and which was all too easily overlooked. As we begin our study of the development of the Christian doctrine of justification, it is necessary to observe that the early theologians of the western church were dependent upon Latin versions of the bible, and approached their texts and their subject with a set of presuppositions which owed more to the Latin language and culture than to Christianity itself. The initial transference of a Hebrew concept to a Greek, and subsequently to a Latin, context point to a fundamental alteration in the concepts of 'justification' and 'righteousness' as the gospel spread from its Palestinian source to the western world. Viewed theologically, this transition resulted in a shift of emphasis from *iustitia coram Deo* to *iustitia in hominibus*. This shift in emphasis and reference from God to man is inevitably accompanied by an anthropocentricity in the discussion of justification which is quite absent from the biblical material. The subsequent development of the theology of justification within the western church would be concerned with the elucidation of this *iustitia in hominibus* – i.e., with questions such as: what was the nature of this righteousness within man, how did it get there, and where did it come from? These questions are largely the result of a changed linguistic and conceptual framework resulting from the transference of originally Hebraic concepts to the western Latin-speaking world. The shifts in meaning we have noted for the non-contiguous semantic transitions ṣᵉdāqâ → δικαιοσύνη → *iustitia* and haṣdîq → δικαιοῦν → *iustificare* must be regarded as being of decisive importance in the shaping of the western discussion of justification. As we begin the study of the development of the doctrine of justification within the western church, it must be appreciated that the Latin language itself has had a far greater influence upon that development than has been generally appreciated.

2. The fountainhead: Augustine of Hippo

Introduction

The theology of the medieval period may be regarded as thoroughly Augustinian, a series of footnotes to Augustine, in that theological speculation was essentially regarded as an attempt to defend, expand, and where necessary modify, the Augustinian legacy. The doctrine of justification is of particular significance in this respect, in that the medieval period witnessed a decisive shift in emphasis away from speculation concerning the *person* of Christ to speculation concerning the *work* of Christ. While the patristic period witnessed considerable interest in the question of who Christ *was*, the medieval period recognised the need to amplify the somewhat unsatisfactory patristic replies to the question of what Christ *did*. An awareness of the leading features of Augustine's doctrine of justification is therefore an essential prerequisite to a correct understanding of the medieval discussion of the doctrine of justification. In the present chapter, we propose to indicate the main features of Augustine's soteriology, after considering the early confusion on the matter within the pre-Augustinian tradition.

§3 The pre-Augustinian tradition

The patristic era is that of the exploration, and where possible reduction, of the tension existing between the need to retain a traditional *corpus* of belief as the *regula fidei*,[1] and the need to expand and develop that *corpus* in the face of opposition from both within and without the Christian community. The earlier patristic period represents the age of the exploration of concepts, when the proclamation of the gospel within a pagan culture was accompanied by an exploitation of both Hellenistic culture and pagan philosophy as vehicles for theological advancement. This tentative exploration of the conceptual world is particularly well illustrated by the rise and subsequent decline of the Logos-Christology. The use of such concepts in Christian theology was not, however, without its risks: it was not sufficient merely to baptise Plato and Plotinus, for the tension which existed between the essentially Hebraic concepts which underlie the gospel and the Hellenism of the medium employed in its early formulation and propagation remains unresolved. Whilst it is evident that some form of adaptation may be necessary in order to give the gospel more immediate impact on its introduction to an alien culture, it is equally evident that such an adaptation may result in both compromise and distortion of the characteristic and distinctive elements of the gospel. An excellent example of the influence of a Hellenistic milieu upon Christian theology is provided by the doctrine of the ἀπάθεια of God,[2] which clearly demonstrates the subordination of a biblical to a philosophical view of God.

Part of the fascination of the patristic era to the scholar lies in the efforts of its theologians to express an essentially Hebraic gospel in a Hellenistic milieu: the delights of patristic scholarship must not, however, be permitted to divert our attention from the suspicion voiced by the Liberal school in the last century – that Christ's teaching was seriously compromised by the Hellenism of its earliest adherents.[3] The early history of the development of the Christian doctrine of justification lends support to such a suspicion. In particular, it can be shown that two major distortions were introduced into the *corpus* of traditional belief within the eastern church at a very early stage, and were subsequently transferred to the emerging western theological tradition. These are:

1. The introduction of the non-biblical, secular Stoic concept of αὐτεξουσία or *liberum arbitrium* in the articulation of the human response to the divine initiative in justification.

2. The implicit equation of ṣeḏāqâ, δικαιοσύνη and *iustitia*, linked with the particular associations of the Latin term *meritum* noted earlier (p. 15), inevitably suggested a correlation between human moral effort and justification within the western church.

The subsequent development of the western theological tradition, particularly since the time of Augustine, has shown a reaction against both these earlier distortions, and may be regarded as an attempt to recover a more biblically orientated approach to the question of justification. The *pre*-Augustinian theological tradition, however, may be regarded as having taken a highly questionable path in its articulation of the doctrine of justification in the face of pagan opposition. The Pelagian controversy may be regarded as having highlighted the two points noted above, although not in the precise form in which they are there stated, so that considerable attention was subsequently paid to their more precise formulation. It is therefore advisable to follow late medieval theological scholarship in drawing a distinction between the *modus loquendi theologicus* prior and subsequent to the Pelagian controversy.[4]

The history of early Christian doctrine is basically the history of the emergence of the Christological and Trinitarian dogmas. Whilst the importance of soteriological considerations, both in the motivation of the development of early Christian doctrine and as a normative principle during the course of that development, is generally conceded,[5] it is equally evident that the early Christian writers did not choose to express their soteriological convictions in terms of the concept of justification. This is not to say that the fathers avoid the term 'justification': their interest in the concept is, however, minimal, and the term generally occurs in their writings as a direct citation from, or a recognisable allusion to, the epistles of Paul, generally employed for some purpose other than a discussion of the concept of justification itself. Furthermore, the few occasions upon which a specific discussion of justification can be found generally involve no interpretation of the matter other than a mere paraphrase of a Pauline statement. Justification was simply not a theological issue in the pre-Augustinian tradition. The emerging patristic understanding of matters such as predestination,[6] grace and free will[7] is somewhat confused, and would remain so until controversy forced a full discussion of the issue upon the church. Indeed, by the end of the fourth century, the Greek fathers had formulated a teaching on human free will based upon philosophical rather than biblical foundations. Standing in the great Platonic tradition, heavily influenced by Philo, and reacting against the fatalisms of their day, they taught that man was utterly free in his choice of good or evil. It is with the Latin fathers that we observe the beginnings of speculation on the nature of original sin and corruption, and the implications which this may have for man's moral faculties.[8]

'It has always been a puzzling fact that Paul meant so relatively little for the thinking of the church during the first 350 years of its history. To be sure, he is honored and quoted, but – in the theological perspective of the west – it seems that Paul's great insight into justification by faith was forgotten.'[9] In part, the early patristic neglect of the Pauline writings may reflect uncertainty concerning the extent of the New Testament canon.[10] As the Pauline epistles came to be accorded increasing authority within the church, so their influence upon theological debate increased correspondingly. Thus the end f the period of oral tradition (c. 150) may be considered to mark a return to Paulinism in certain respects, so that writers such as Irenaeus of Lyons may be regarded as representing the gospel more accurately than Ignatius of Antioch.[11] It must also be appreciated, however, that the early fathers do not appear to have been faced with a threat from Jewish Christian activists teaching justification by works of the law, such as is presupposed by those Pauline epistles dealing with the doctrine of justification by faith in most detail (e.g., Galatians). The only patristic work which appears to presuppose this specific threat is the tract *de his qui putant se ex operibus iustificari*[12] of Mark the Hermit (fl. c. 431), probably dating from the early fifth century. The main external threat to the early church, particularly during the second century, appears to have been pagan or semi-pagan fatalisms, such as Gnosticism, which propagated the thesis that man is neither responsible for his own sins, nor for the evil of the world. It is quite possible that the curious and disturbing tendency of the early fathers to minimise original sin and emphasise the freedom of fallen man[13] is a consequence of their anti-Gnostic polemic. Whilst it is true that the beginnings of a doctrine of grace may be discerned during this early period,[14] its generally optimistic estimation of the capacities of fallen humanity has led many scholars to question whether it can be regarded as truly Christian in this respect.

The pre-Augustinian theological tradition is practically of one voice in asserting the freedom of the human will. Thus Justin Martyr rejects the idea that all human actions are foreordained on the grounds that this eliminates human accountability.[15] This argument is supplemented by an appeal to scriptural texts apparently teaching man's freedom of action, such as Deuteronomy 30.19: 'I have set before you life and death, the blessing and the curse; therefore choose life, that you may live.' It must be pointed out, of course, that Justin's defence of the free will is not in any way specifically *Christian*, in any way linked to the Incarnation, for example. With the obvious exception of the use of biblical quotations, Justin's anti-fatalist arguments can be adduced from practically any of the traditional pagan refutations of astral fatalisms, going back to the second century B.C.[16] Furthermore, the biblical quotations which Justin does employ can be shown to be predominantly from the Old Testament, and traditionally used in *Jewish* refutations of such fatalisms. Thus

Philo of Alexandria had earlier used an anti-fatalist argument practically identical to Justin's, down to the citation from Deuteronomy 30.19.[17]

Whilst Justin's defence of the freedom of the will does not appear to have been occasioned by Gnosticism, its rise appears to have had a profound effect upon his successors. While there is still uncertainty concerning the precise nature of Gnosticism, it may be noted that a strongly fatalist or necessitarian outlook appears to be characteristic of the chief Gnostic systems.[18] Far from recognising the limitations of man's free will, many early fathers enthusiastically proclaimed its freedom (ἐλευθερία) and self-determination (αὐτεξουσία): ἐλεύθερον γὰρ καὶ αὐτεξούσιον ἐποίησεν ὁ θεος ἄνθρωπον.[19] The introduction of the *secular* concept of self-determination (αὐτεξουσία) into the theological vocabulary of Christendom is of particular significance, particularly in view of its later application in the Macarian homilies.[20] There man's self-determination is proclaimed to be such that he can apply himself either to good or evil.[21] God cannot be said to force the free will, but merely to influence it.[22] While God does not wish man to do evil, he cannot compel him to do good.[23] John Chrysostom's defence of the power of the human free will was so convincing that it was taken up by many Pelagian writers: 'good and evil do not originate from man's nature itself, but from the will and choice alone'.[24] This localisation of the origin of sin in the misuse of the human free will was a theological commonplace by the fourth century.[25] The patristic discussion of human freedom received significant development by the Cappadocians. Gregory of Nyssa distinguished two types of freedom: structural freedom, by which Adam was able to communicate with God and all of his creation; and functional freedom, by which man has freedom of choice. The former was lost at the Fall, but by proper use of the latter, man is able to regain it.[26] Nemesius of Emesa may be regarded as having developed this idea along Aristotelian lines, thus providing an important link between the latter patristic and early scholastic understandings of human freedom.[27] Nemesius' distinction between the *voluntarium* and *involuntarium*, and his emphasis upon the role of *consilium* in decision-making, leads to his insistence that the human reason itself is the basis of man's freedom.

The western theological tradition was somewhat slower to develop than the eastern, and in the course of that development, the theological vocabulary of the east became current in the west. This necessitated the translation of Greek theological terms into Latin, with inevitable shifts in their meanings as a result. It is almost certain to that the western theological tradition owes much of its vocabulary to Tertullian. Thus it is due to his influence that the term *persona* came to translate ὑπόστασις, despite the rival claims of *substantia*.[28] And it is the same writer who introduced to the west the Latin term which would not become the equivalent of αὐτεξουσία – *liberum arbitrium*.[29] It may be noted that αὐτεξουσία concerns ἐξουσία, 'authority-to-act', and has at best remote associations with the concepts of 'will' or 'choice'. The idea of 'will' (*voluntas*) may, indeed, be argued only to have become fully articulated when the Latin language became the normal vehicle of Christian philosophical expression. The weakness of Pauline influence in the early church may be illustrated from the fact that two non-Pauline, non-biblical terms (αὐτεξουσία and *liberum arbitrium*) came to be introduced into the early Christian discussion of man's justification before God. While the introduction of the equally non-biblical term ὁμοούσιος in the fourth century occasioned considerable protest,[30] no objections appear to have been raised to the introduction of the term αὐτεξουσία to refer to man's autonomy in justification. Yet, like the ἀπάθεια of God, the 'self-determination' of the human free will is not so much a Christian idea, as a philosophical idea of its early Hellenistic milieu. Whereas Christian theology has had to wait until the twentieth century for a convincing critique of the former, Augustine's penetrating theological critique of the latter was not long delayed.

The earliest known Latin commentary upon the Pauline epistles is that of Ambrosiaster.[31] Most modern commentators on this important work recognise that its exposition of the doctrine of justification by faith is grounded in the contrast between Christianity and Judaism: there is no trace of a more universal interpretation of justification by faith meaning freedom from a law of works – merely freedom from the Jewish ceremonial law. The Pauline doctrine of freedom from the works of the law is given a specific historical context by Ambrosiaster, in the Jewish background to Christianity. In other respects, Ambrosiaster is more akin to Pelagius than to Augustine. The Pelagian controversy had yet to break, and much of Ambrosiaster's teaching seems strange in the light of that controversy. Like many of his contemporaries, for example, he appears to be obsessed with the idea that man can acquire merit before God, and the associated idea that certain labours are necessary to attain this.[32] Similar ideas have often been detected in the writings of Tertullian, leading some commentators to suggest that his theology is merely a republication of that of Judaism,[33] others charging him with uniting Old Testament legalism with Roman moralism and jurisprudence.[34] His most debatable contribution to the developing western tradition on justification, his introduction of the term *liberum arbitrium* aside, is his theology of merit. For Tertullian, the man who performs good works can be said to make God his debtor: bonum factum deum habet debitorem, sicuti et malum: quia iudex omnis remunerator est causae.[35] The understanding of the 'righteousness of God' as *reddens unicuique quod suum est* underlies this teaching. A similar tendency can be detected in his teaching that man can 'satisfy' his obligation to God on account of his sin through penance.[36] Indeed, Tertullian has exercised a certain fascination over legal historians, who have noted his introduction of legal terms such as *meritum* and *satisfactio* into theology with some interest.[37] The concept of a divine obligation to man thus makes its appearance in the western theological tradition in a somewhat naïve form, and once more it is due to the religious genius of Augustine that the concept was subjected to penetrating criticism.

For the first three hundred and fifty years of the history of the church, her teaching on justification was inchoate and ill-defined. There had never been a serious controversy over the matter, such as those which had so stimulated the development of Christology over the period. The patristic inexactitude and naïveté on the question merely reflects the absence of a controversy which would force more precise definition of the terms used. If the first centuries of the western theological tradition appear be characterised by a 'works-righteousness' approach to justification, it must be emphasised that this was quite innocent of the overtones which would later be associated with it. This 'works-righteousness' ceased to be innocent and ingenuous in the system of Pelagius and his followers, and came to threaten and obscure the gospel as the message of the free grace of God. It is therefore to Augustine of Hippo that we turn for the first definitive statements of the western doctrine of justification.

§4 Augustine of Hippo

According to Isidore of Seville (c. 560–636), the following cautionary lines were written above the cupboard which housed the works of Augustine in the Seville library:

> Mentitur, qui te totum legisse fatetur,
> An quis cuncta tua lector habere potest?[1]

It is certain that no writer, other than those of scripture, has exercised so great an influence over the development of western Christian thought as Augustine of Hippo. This influence is particularly associated with, although by no means restricted to, the theological renaissance of the twelfth century, and the Reformation of the sixteenth. Anselm of Canterbury spoke for the theological tradition of the west when he equated orthodoxy with conformity to the writings *catholicorum patrum et maxime beati Augustini*.[2] *All* medieval theology is 'Augustinian', to a greater or lesser extent. It is, however, remarkable that although much attention has been paid in the literature to Augustine's doctrine of *grace*, there is a virtual absence of studies dealing with his doctrine of *justification*. This *lacuna* is all the more astonishing when the significance of Augustine's understanding of justification to his social and political thought is considered. The significance of Augustine's doctrine of justification to the present study relates to its subsequent influence upon the medieval period and beyond. Augustine's doctrine of justification is the first discussion of the matter of major significance to emerge from the twilight of the western theological tradition, establishing the framework within which the future discussion of the justification of man before God would be conducted.

It is important to appreciate that Augustine's doctrine of justification underwent significant development. For example, prior to his elevation to the see of Hippo Regis in 395, Augustine appears to have held precisely the same opinion which he would later condemn – the Massilian attribution of the *initium fidei* to the human free will. Some thirty years after his consecration, Augustine conceded that his earlier works, particularly his *Expositio quarundam propositionum ex epistula ad Romanos* (394), should be corrected in the light of his later insights concerning the doctrine of grace.[3] When did Augustine change his mind on this crucial matter? Fortunately, we have his own answer to this question: it was 'in the first of two books written to Simplicianus',[4] written in late 396 or early 397. This work is generally regarded as containing the key to Augustine's changed views on justification.[5] In view of the fact that the Pelagian controversy would not break out until early the following century, it is important to appreciate that Augustine appears to have developed his new understanding of justification – which would henceforth bear the epithet 'Augustinian' – in a non-polemical context. It is not correct to suppose that Augustine's doctrine of justification is merely a reaction against Pelagianism.

Prior to 396, Augustine appears to have seen the spiritual life as an ascent to perfection.[6] This understanding of the Christian life is particularly well expressed in his early conviction that man can take the initiative in this spiritual ascent to God by believing in him, and calling upon God to save him.[7] Augustine was forced to reappraise this youthful opinion in 395, when his Milanese acquaintance Simplicianus posed a series of questions relating to predestination. Why did God hate Esau? Augustine appears to have avoided issues such as this up to this point, but was now obliged to consider the question – and as a result, he appears to have abandoned his earlier attempts to uphold the unrestricted freedom of the will. Among the important changes in his thinking on justification as a result of his reflections on Romans 9.10–29, the following may be noted.

1. Man's election is now understood to be based upon God's eternal decree of predestination.[8] Augustine had earlier taught that man's temporal election of God is prior to God's eternal election of man.

2. Man's response of faith to God's offer of grace is now understood to be in itself a gift of God.[9] Augustine abandons his earlier teaching that man's response to God depends solely upon his unaided free will.

3. While conceding that man's free will is capable of many things, Augustine now insists that it is compromised by sin, and incapable of leading to man's justification unless it is first liberated by grace.[10] In view of the fact that Augustine's teaching on justification altered so radically at this point, and that he is generally regarded as having worked within the same basic conceptual framework for the next thirty years,[11] it is clearly important to exclude any writings prior to his elevation to the episcopacy[12] from our analysis of his mature doctrine of justification, which henceforth would be known as the 'classic Augustinian theology of grace'.[13] We begin our analysis of this theology by considering one of its most difficult aspects – Augustine's teaching on the *liberum arbitrium*.

Luther's 1525 treatise *de servo arbitrio* derives its title from a phrase used in passing by Augustine in the course of his controversy with the Pelagian bishop Julian of Eclanum.[14] In selecting this phrase, Luther appears to claim the support of Augustine for his radical doctrine of the *servum arbitrium*. A consideration of Augustine's background, however, suggests that it is improbable that he held such a doctrine. He had been engaged in anti-Manichaean polemic for some time, defending the catholic teaching against its fatalist opponents. *De libero arbitrio* (388–95) was written against precisely such necessitarian teachings (e.g., that evil is natural, and not the work of the human free will). Although Augustine would later modify his earlier views on the nature of man's *liberum arbitrium*,[15] it is important to appreciate that the central thesis of the existence of such a *liberum arbitrium* was neither rejected nor radically altered.

In many respects, Pelagianism may be regarded as the antithesis of Manichaeism: whereas the latter rejected the existence of free will, the former exaggerated its role in justification. Augustine's first anti-Pelagian work, *de peccatorum meritis et remissione* (411), opened the attack against Pelagianism with the assertion that it attributed too much to man's *liberum arbitrium*, and thereby effectively denied the need for special grace. It must be stressed that Augustine does not refute the error by *denying* man's free will. Augustine insists that the need for grace can be defended without denying man's *liberum arbitrium*. His discussion of human freedom in justification proceeds upon the assumption that both grace and free will are to be affirmed, the problem requiring resolution being their precise relationship. God has given man free will, without which he cannot be said to live well or badly,[16] and it is on the basis of his use of this *liberum arbitrium* that he will be judged.[17] Grace, far from *abolishing* man's free will, actually *establishes* it.[18] How can this be so?

Augustine, reacting against the Pelagian exaggeration of fallen man's abilities, maintained that man possesses *liberum arbitrium* and denied that he possesses *libertas*.[19] The sinner has free will, but it is unable to function properly, and thus to allow him freedom. 'The free will taken captive (*liberum arbitrium captivatum*) does not avail, except for sin; for righteousness it does not avail, unless it is set free and aided by divine action.'[20] By *libertas*, Augustine means the power to choose and accomplish good – a power which fallen human nature does not possess. However, this loss of *libertas* does not imply the loss of *liberum arbitrium*. The human will cannot be likened to a scale, in whose balance-pans the arguments for and against a possible course of action are carefully weighed before any action is taken (i.e., *libertas indifferentiae*), as Julian of Eclanum insisted to be the case. While Augustine allows that the scales in question really do exist, and are capable of operating, he argues that the balance-pans are loaded on the side of evil, yielding a judgement invariably biased towards evil. Although Adam possessed *liberum arbitrium* before the Fall, man's free will is now compromised by sin, so that it is now *liberum arbitrium captivatum*. The free will is not lost, nor is it non-existent: it is merely incapacitated, and may be healed by grace.[21] In justification, the *liberum arbitrium captivatum* becomes the *liberum arbitrium liberatum* by the action of healing grace. Hence the possibility of not sinning cannot exist in fallen man, although Augustine is at pains to point out that this does not exclude man's natural freedom. God would not command us to do something unless there was free will by which we could do it.[22] Augustine's ethics presuppose that man's destiny is determined by merit or demerit, which in turn presuppose – at least for Augustine – free will. Thus Augustine's doctrine of *liberum arbitrium* is to be sharply distinguished from Luther's doctrine of *servum arbitrium*: 'If there is no such thing as God's grace, how can he be the saviour of the world? And if there is no such thing as free will, how can he be its judge?'[23] Augustine's concept of *liberum arbitrium captivatum* resolves the dialectic between grace and free will without denying the reality of either.

For Augustine, man's *liberum arbitrium captivatum* is incapable of either desiring or attaining justification. How, then, does faith, the fulcrum about which justification takes place, arise in the individual? According to Augustine, the act of faith is itself a divine gift, in which God acts upon the rational soul in such a way that it comes to believe. Whether this action on the will leads to its subsequent assent to justification is a matter for man, rather than God. Qui fecit te sine te, non te iustificat sine te.[24] Although God is the origin of the gift which man is able to receive and possess, the acts of receiving and possessing themselves can be said to be man's.

To meet Pelagian evasions, Augustine drew a distinction between *operative* and *cooperative* grace (or, more accurately, between operative and cooperative modes of gratuitous divine action: Augustine does not treat them as distinct species). God *operates* to initiate man's justification, in that he is given a will capable of desiring good, and subsequently *cooperates* with that good will to perform good works, to bring that justification to perfection. God operates upon the bad desires of the *liberum arbitrium captivatum* to allow it to will good, and subsequently cooperates with the *liberum arbitrium liberatum* to actualise that good will in a good action. Man's justification is therefore an act of divine mercy, in that he does not desire it (because the *liberum arbitrium captivatum* is incapable of desiring good) nor does he deserve it (because of his sin and lack of merit). On account of the Fall, man's free will is weakened and incapacitated, though not destroyed. Thus man does not wish to be justified, because his *liberum arbitrium captivatum* is incapable of desiring justification;

however, once restored to its former capacities by healing grace, it recognises the goodness of what it has been given. God thus cures man's illness, of which the chief symptom is the absence of any desire to be cured. This apparent contradiction has, of course, been criticised for failing to respect man's free will.[25] In response to this, it must be pointed out that the divine justification of the sinner in the manner outlined above does not in any way compromise man's free will, understood as *liberum arbitrium liberatum*, nor his *libertas*: the only 'free will' which is compromised is the *liberum arbitrium captivatum*, itself a crippled parody of the real thing. The compromise of the *liberum arbitrium captivatum* is necessary in order that the *liberum arbitrium liberatum* may be restored.

Once justified by divine action, the sinner does not at once become a perfect example of holiness. Man needs to pray to God continually for his growth in holiness and the spiritual life, thereby acknowledging that God is the author of both. God *operates* upon man in the *act* of justification, and *cooperates* with him in the *process* of justification.[26] Once justified, the sinner may begin to acquire merit – but only on account of God's grace. Merit is seen to be a divine, rather than a human work. Thus it is clearly wrong to suggest that Augustine excludes or denies merit;[27] while merit *before* justification is indeed denied, its reality and necessity *after* justification is equally strongly affirmed.[28] It must be noted, however, that Augustine understands merit as a gift from God to the justified sinner,[29] and does not adopt Tertullian's somewhat legalist approach to the matter.[30] *Hominis bona merita, Dei munera.* Eternal life is indeed the reward for merit – but merit is itself a gift from God, so that the whole process must be seen as having its origin in the divine liberality, rather than in man's works.[31] If God is under any obligation to man on account of his merit, it is an obligation which God has imposed upon himself, rather than one which is imposed from outside, or is inherent in the nature of things. Fidelis Deus, qui se nostrum debitorem fecit, non aliquid a nobis accipiendo, sed tanta nobis promittendo.[32] The classic Augustinian statement on the relation between eternal life, merit and grace is the celebrated *dictum* of Epistle 194: 'When God crowns our merits, he crowns nothing but his own gifts.'[33] The possibility of a preparation of grace, whether meritorious or not, such as that associated with the Franciscan school in the medieval period, cannot be adduced from the mature writings of Augustine, although traces of such a doctrine may be found in his writings prior to 396.[34]

Central to Augustine's doctrine of justification is his understanding of the 'righteousness of God', *iustitia Dei*.[35] The righteousness of God is not that righteousness by which he is himself righteous, but that by which he justifies sinners.[36] The righteousness of God, veiled in the Old Testament and revealed in the New, and supremely in Jesus Christ, is so called because, by bestowing it upon man, God makes him righteous.[37] How is it possible for God, being just, to justify the ungodly? Augustine shows relatively little interest in this question, giving no systematic account of the work of Christ.[38] Instead, he employs a series of images and metaphors to illustrate the purpose of Christ's mission. Of these, the most important is generally agreed to be his demonstration of the divine love for man, *ad demonstrandum erga nos dilectionem Dei*.[39] Other metaphors and images which he uses to express his understanding of Christ's work include mediation,[40] sacrifice,[41] deliverance from the power of Satan,[42] or an example to be imitated.[43] It must be emphasised that it is manifestly an imposition upon Augustine's theology to develop a systematic account of the work of Christ, for the bishop is primarily concerned with the question of *how* God justifies man, rather than how God *is able* to justify him. Like Luther, he employs a wide range of images and metaphors to illustrate the nature of Christ's mission, and declines to commit himself exclusively to any one of these.

As noted above, God's prevenient grace prepares man's will for justification. Augustine understands this grace to be intimately involved with the sacrament of baptism: however, while he insists that there can be no salvation without baptism (or, more accurately, without what baptism represents) it does not follow that every baptised sinner will be justified, or finally saved. The grace of final perseverance is required if a Christian is to persevere in faith until the end of his life. It is clear that this raises the question of predestination: God may give the regenerate faith, hope and love, and yet decline to give them perseverance.[44]

While Augustine occasionally appears to understand grace as an impersonal abstract force, there are many points at which he makes a clear connection between the concept of grace and the operation of the Holy Spirit. Thus regeneration is itself the work of the Holy Spirit.[45] The love of God is shed abroad in our hearts by the Holy Spirit, which is given to us in justification. The appropriation of the divine love to the person of the Holy Spirit may be regarded as one of the most profound aspects of Augustine's doctrine of the Trinity.[46] *Amare Deum, Dei donum est*.[47] The Holy Spirit enables man to be inflamed with the love of God and the love of his neighbour – indeed,

the Holy Spirit himself *is* love.[48] A man who has faith and not love –
and this is perfectly possible, given Augustine's strongly intellectualist concept of faith – is nothing. Faith can exist without love, but is of
no value in the sight of God.[49] God's other gifts, such as faith and
hope, cannot bring us to God unless they are accompanied or
preceded by love.[50] The motif of *amor Dei* dominates Augustine's
theology of justification, just as that of *sola fide* would dominate that
of one of his later interpreters. Faith without love is of no value. So
how does Augustine understand those passages in the Pauline corpus
which speak of justification *by faith* (e.g., Romans 5.1)? This question
brings us to the classic Augustinian concept of 'faith working through
love', *fides quae per dilectionem operatur*, which would dominate
western Christian thinking on the nature of justifying faith for the
next thousand years. The process by which Augustine arrives at this
understanding of the nature of justifying faith illustrates his desire to
do justice to the total biblical view on the matter, rather than a few
isolated Pauline gobbets. In *de Trinitate*, Augustine considers the
difficulties arising from I Corinthians 13.1–3,[51] which stipulate that
faith without love is useless. He therefore draws a distinction between
a purely intellectual faith (such as that 'by which even the devils
believe and tremble' (James 2.19)) and true justifying faith, by
arguing that the latter is faith *accompanied by love*. Augustine finds
this concept conveniently expressed within the Pauline corpus at
Galatians 5.6: 'In Christ Jesus neither circumcision nor uncircum-
cision avails anything, but *faith that works through love*.'[52] Although
this is open to a Pelagian interpretation, this is excluded by Augustine's insistence that both the faith and love in question are gifts of God
to man rather than man's natural faculties. Augustine tends to
understand faith primarily as an adherence to the Word of God,
which inevitably introduces a strongly intellectualist element into his
concept of faith,[53] thus necessitating its supplementation with *caritas*
or *dilectio* if it is to justify man.[54] Faith alone is merely assent to
revealed truth, itself adequate to justify.[55] It is for this reason that it is
unacceptable to summarise Augustine's doctrine of justification as
sola fide iustificamur – if any such summary is acceptable, it is *sola
caritate iustificamur*.[56] For Augustine, it is love, rather than faith,
which is the power which brings about the conversion of man. Just as
cupiditas is the root of all evil, so *caritas* is the root of all good. Man's
personal union with the Godhead, which forms the basis of his
justification, is brought about by love, and not by faith.[57]

Augustine understands the verb *iustificare* to mean 'to make righteous', an understanding of the term which he appears to have held throughout his working life.[58] In arriving at this understanding, he appears to have interpreted -*ficare* as the unstressed form of *facere*, by analogy with *vivificare* and *mortificare*. Although this is a permissible interpretation of the *Latin word*, it is unacceptable as an interpretation of the *Hebrew concept* which underlies it (see §2). The term *iustificare* is, of course, post-classical, having been introduced through the Latin translation of the bible, and thus restricted to Christian writers of the Latin west. Augustine was thus unable to turn to classical authors in an effort to clarify its meaning, and was thus obliged to interpret the term himself. His establishment of a relationship between *iustificare* and *iustitia* is of enormous significance, as will become clear.

Augustine has an all-embracing understanding of justification, which includes both the *event* of justification (brought about by operative grace) and the *process* of justification (brought about by cooperative grace). Augustine himself does not, in fact, distinguish between these two aspects of justification: the distinction dates from the sixteenth century. However, the importance of Augustine to the controversies of that later period make it necessary to interpret him in terms of its categories at this point. The renewal of the divine image in man, brought about by justification, may be regarded as amounting to a new creation, in which sin is rooted out and the love of God planted in the hearts of men in its place, in the form of the Holy Spirit. God's new creation is not finished once and for all in the event of justification, and requires perfecting,[59] which is brought about by cooperative grace collaborating with the *liberum arbitrium liberatum*. Whilst *concupiscentia* may be relegated to the background as *caritas* begins its work of renewal within man, it continues to make its presence felt, so that renewed gifts of grace are required throughout man's existence, as sin is never totally overcome in this life.[60]

Man's righteousness, effected in justification, is regarded by Augustine as *inherent* rather than *imputed*, to use the vocabulary of the sixteenth century.[61] A concept of 'imputed righteousness', in the later Protestant sense of the term, would be quite redundant within Augustine's doctrine of justification, in that man is *made righteous* in justification. The righteousness which man thus receives, although originating from God, is nevertheless located within man, and can be said to be *his*, part of his being and intrinsic to his person. An element which underlies this understanding of the nature of justifying righteousness is the Greek concept of deification, which makes its appearance in the later Augustinian soteriology.[62] By charity, the Trinity itself comes to inhabit the soul of the justified sinner,[63] although it is not clear whether Augustine can be said to envisage a 'state of grace' in the strict sense of the term – i.e., a habit of grace, created within the human soul.[64] It is certainly true that Augustine speaks of the real interior renewal of the sinner by the action of the Holy Spirit, which he later expressed in terms of participation in the divine substance itself. However, it seems most prudent to state that Augustine's theological vocabulary was not sufficiently developed to allow us to speak of his teaching 'created grace' in the later sense of the term. The later Augustine frequently uses phrases which are strongly reminiscent of the Cappadocians – e.g., *Deus facturus qui homines erant, homo factus est qui Deus erat*[65] – and frequently places the concepts of adoptive filiation and deification side by side in his discussion of justification. There is thus a pronounced element of participation in Augustine's later understanding of the nature of justifying righteousness, even if it is not possible to speak of a 'state of grace' in the strict sense of the term. God has given man the power both to receive and participate in the divine being.[66] By this participation in the life of the Trinity, the justified sinner may be said to be deified.[67] Augustine's understanding of adoptive filiation is such that the believer does not merely receive the *status* of sonhood, but *becomes* a son of God. A real change in man's *being*, and not merely his *status*, is envisaged in his justification, so that he *becomes* righteous and a son of God, and is not merely *treated as if he were* righteous and a son of God.

For Augustine, justification includes both the beginnings of man's righteousness before God and its subsequent perfection, the event and the process, so that what late became the Reformation concept of 'sanctification' is effectively subsumed under the aegis of justification. Although Augustine is occasionally represented, on the basis of isolated passages, as understanding justification to comprise merely the remission of sins, it is clear that he also understands it to include the ethical and spiritual renewal of the sinner through the internal operation of the Holy Spirit. Justification, according to Augustine, is fundamentally concerned with 'being made righteous'. But what does he understand by *iustus* and *iustitia*? With this question, we come to the relation between Augustine's doctrine of justification and his ethical and political thought.

According to Augustine, the *iustitia* of an act is to be defined both in terms of the substance of the act itself (*officium*) and its inner motivation (*finis*). The correct motivation for a righteous action can only come about through operative grace and the interior action of the Holy Spirit within the believer. Righteousness, itself regarded as a gift of the Holy Spirit, consists both in the possession of a good will (effected by operative grace) and in having that potentiality actualised through cooperative grace. It will therefore be clear that Augustine understands *iustitia* participationally, rather than relationally.[68] Everyone who is incorporated into Christ can perform an action which is *iustus*.[69] In other words, Augustine defines *iustitia* in such a manner that, by definition, only Christians may perform good actions. This is well illustrated by his famous example of the two men,[70] one of whom does not hold a 'true and catholic faith in God', yet leads a morally blameless life, and another, who holds such a faith and yet leads a morally inferior existence. Which is the superior in the sight of God? For Augustine, it is the latter, on account of his faith, even though the former may be superior morally. Had the former faith, he would be the superior in the sight of God. This example illustrates the difference between the inherent moral value of an act itself (*officium*), and the inner motivation which establishes the theological foundation for the righteousness of an act (*finis*). A correct inner motivation is only possible through *fides quae per dilectionem operatur*. It may be noted that Augustine does *not* deny pagans the ability to perform morally good acts, as some have represented him as doing. These works are good, considered as *officium* – i.e., they are good *coram hominibus*, but not *coram Deo*. The moral and meritorious realms are scrupulously distinguished by Augustine. Pagans may practise continency, temperance, even *caritas humana*[71] – yet these are not virtues *coram Deo*.[72] The *virtutes impiorum* are *iustae* in terms of their *officium*, but have no value in obtaining felicity.[73] In itself, such an act may be good – but if performed outside the specific context of faith, it is sterile or even sinful.[74] The crucial distinction between the *virtutes impiorum* and *virtutes piorum* lies in justification, by which God makes godly those who were once ungodly (*ex impio pius fit*). Thus Augustine's moral theology (i.e., his theology of *iustitia*, applied to the individual) can be seen to be closely related to his doctrine of justification. The bridge between the moral and the meritorious, between the human and the divine estimation of an act, lies in the justification of the ungodly.

Augustine's political theology (i.e., his theology of *iustitia*, applied to the community) is of considerable inherent interest, and is also closely associated with his doctrine of justification. *De civitate Dei* (413–26) contains a critique of the Ciceronian understanding of the basis of social justice of decisive importance to our study. It is only within the city of God that the true divine justice, effected through justification, may be found.[75] Augustine's concept of *iustitia* within the *civitas Dei* is based on his concept of God as *iustissimus ordinator*, who orders the universe according to his will.[76] The idea of *iustitia* involved can approach that of a physical ordering of all things, and is also reflected in the right ordering of human affairs, and man's relationship to his environment.[77] For Augustine, *iustitia* is practically synonymous with the right ordering of human affairs in accordance with the will of God.[78] It may be noted that Augustine's quasi-physical understanding of justice reflects his hierarchical structuring of the order of being: *iustitia* is essentially the ordering of the world according to the order of being, itself an expression of the divine will. God created the natural order of things, and therefore this natural order of things must itself reflect *iustitia*. Thus God created man as he ought to be – i.e., he created man *in iustitia*, the correct order of nature. By choosing to ignore this ordering, man stepped outside this state of *iustitia*, so that his present state may be characterised as *iniustitia*. Justification is therefore essentially a 'making right', a restoration of every facet of the relationship between God and man, the rectitude of which constitutes *iustitia*. *Iustitia* is not conceived primarily in legal or forensic categories, but transcends them, encompassing the 'right-wising' of the God–man relationship in its many aspects: the relationship of God to man, of man to his fellows, and of men to their environment. Justification is about 'making just' – establishing the rectitude of the created order according to the divine intention. Although it is clear that justification has legal and moral ramifications, given the wide scope of Augustine's concept of *iustitia*, it is not primarily a legal or moral concept.

It is therefore clear that the interpretation of *iustitia* is dependent upon its particular context. What is *iustum* in the case of the relationship between God and man may not be *iustum* in the case of man's relationship to his fellows, so that the analogical predication of human concepts of *iustitia* to God cannot be regarded as inherently justifiable. This point is particularly well illustrated by Augustine's critique of the Ciceronian definition of *iustitia* as *reddens unicuique quod suum est*, 'giving to each his due'.[79] While Augustine is prepared to use this secular definition at points,[80] it is clear that his own concept of *iustitia* is grounded firmly in the divine will. In the course of his controversy with Julian of Eclanum, Augustine found it necessary to counter the application of a secular concept of justice to rationalise the divine dispensation towards mankind.[81] Julian defined justice in terms of God rendering to each man his due, without fraud or grace, so that God would be expected to justify those who merited his grace on the basis of their moral achievements. This approach yielded a doctrine of the justification of the *godly*, whereas Augustine held the essence of the gospel to be the justification of the *ungodly*. In countering Julian's concept of *iustitia Dei*, Augustine appealed to the parable of the labourers in the vineyard (Matthew 20.1–16) to demonstrate that *iustitia Dei* primarily refers to God's fidelity to his promises of grace, irrespective of the merits of those to whom the promise was made (see further §6).

Augustine's fundamental concept of *iustitia* is that of the submission of the individual's whole being to God. While this theme of submission to God may reflect the neo-Platonist notion of the acceptance of the established order of the universe, it is possible that Augustine's understanding of *iustitia* within the *civitas Dei* is based upon ideas similar to those to be found in the *Divinae Institutiones* of Lactantius (c. 250–317). The political theology developed by Lactantius was particularly suited to the new Christian empire, then developing under Constantine. Here *iustitia* is practically equated with *religio*: 'justice is nothing other than the pious and religious worship of the one God'.[82] This definition could be interpreted as an extension of the Ciceronian understanding of *iustitia* as 'rendering to each his due' to include man's proper obligation to God, whose chief part is worship. In *de civitate Dei*, Augustine subjected Cicero's classic definition of the *res publica*[83] by making *iustitia* an essential element of the *iuris consensus*: where there is no true *iustitia*, there is no true *ius*. Whereas Cicero taught that *iustitia* was based on *ius*, arising from the *iuris consensus*, Augustine argued that *ius* itself must be regarded as based on *iustitia*. Thus for Augustine there can be no *res publica* without there being true *iustitia* within the community – i.e., a right ordering of all its relationships in accordance with the divine purpose.[84] Where this justice does not exist, there is certainly no 'association of men united by a common sense of right and a community of interest' (as Cicero had defined the *res publica*). It is only in the *civitas Dei* that true justice exists: in the city of men, only vestiges of this true justice may be found. It is clear that Augustine understands all human *ius*, in so far as it is just, to derive ultimately from an eternal divine law: 'there is nothing just or legitimate in temporal law save what men have derived from the eternal law'.[85] Whilst God's law is eternal and unchanging, the positive laws which govern men's relationships may vary from place to place, and yet still reflect that divine law.[86] Although it is only in the regenerate that *vera iustitia* is possible, through their justification, there remain some *vestigia supernae iustitiae* even in the unjustified, and it is such vestiges which form the basis of human ideas of justice as they find their expression in human legal and political institutions. Without such vestiges, Augustine insists, there could be no justice of any sort among men.[87]

The student of Augustine's doctrine of justification can only admire the astonishing comprehensiveness of its scope. Quid est enim aliud, iustificati, quam iusti facti, ad illo scilicet qui iustificat impium, ut ex impio fiat iustus?[88] Augustine's discussion of *iustitia*, effected only through man's justification, demonstrates how the doctrine of justification encompasses the whole of Christian existence from the first moment of faith, through the increase in righteousness before God and man, to the final perfection of that righteousness in the eschatological city. Justification is about 'being made just' – and Augustine's understanding of *iustitia* is so broad that this could be defined as 'being made to live as God intends man to live, in every aspect of his existence', including his relationship with God, with his fellow men, and the relationship of his higher and lower self (on the neo-Platonic anthropological model favoured by Augustine). That *iustitia* possesses legal and moral overtones will thus be evident – but this must not be permitted to obscure its fundamentally *theological* orientation. By justification, Augustine comes very close to understanding the restoration of the entire universe to its original order, established at creation, an understanding not very different from the Greek doctrine of cosmic redemption. The ultimate object of man's justification is his 'cleaving to God', a 'cleaving' which awaits its consummation and perfection in the new Jerusalem, which is even now being established. Aeterno creatori adhaerantes, et nos aeternitate afficiamur necesse est.

3. The development of the doctrine in the medieval period

Introduction

The terms 'medieval' and 'Middle Ages' are modern, signifying the period of transition between the intellectual glories of antiquity and those of the modern period. Although phrases similar to 'medieval' are encountered in the medieval period itself, their meaning is quite distinct from the modern sense of the term. Thus Julian of Toledo uses the phrase 'middle age' (*tempus medium*) in an Augustinian sense to refer to the period between the incarnation and the second coming of Christ.[1] The question as to when the 'Middle Ages' can be said to have begun has vexed historians for some time, and the answers given to this question depend upon the criterion used in its definition. The practically simultaneous suppression of the Athenian Platonic academy and the establishment of Montecassino in 529 are regarded by many as marking, although not in themselves causing, the transition from late antiquity to the medieval period. For the purposes of the present study, the medieval period is regarded as having been initiated through Alaric's conquest of Rome in 410, with the resulting gradual shift in the centres of intellectual life from the Mediterranean world to the northern European world of Theodoric and Charlemagne, and later to the abbey and cathedral schools of France, and the universities of Paris and Oxford. While Augustine's world was that of the *imperium Romanum*, that of his later interpreters would be the courts and monasteries of northern Europe.[2]

Associated with this shift in the intellectual centres of Europe was a related shift in the method employed by the theologians of the medieval period. The accumulated body of tradition associated with the world of antiquity – which included both pagan philosophy and patristic theology – was assimilated and incorporated into the emerging theological literature. Prosper of Aquitaine's *Liber sententiarum ex operibus Augustini* may be regarded as an early example of this phenomenon.[3] The medieval period was characterised by its attempts to accumulate biblical and patristic material considered to be relevant to particular issues of theological interpretation, and by its attempt to develop hermeneutical methods to resolve the apparent contradictions encountered in this process.[4] These collections of patristic 'sentences' appear to have been modelled upon the codifications of the canonists, who initially grouped their collected decretals chronologically, and later according to subject.[5] An examination of such collections of patristic 'sentences' suggests that they were largely drawn from the works of Augustine. The most famous such collection, the *Sententiarum libri quattuor* of Peter Lombard, has been styled an 'Augustinian breviary', in that its thousand citations from Augustine comprise four-fifths of the work.[6] The high regard in which Augustine was held during the theological renaissance of the late eleventh and twelfth centuries ensured that the framework of the medieval discussion of justification was essentially Augustinian. The theology of the period may be regarded as a systematic attempt to restate and reformulate Augustine's theology to meet the needs of the new era then developing.[7] The development of the doctrine of justification during the medieval period may be considered primarily as the systematisation, clarification and conceptual elaboration of Augustine's framework of justification, where possible restating the dogmatic content of his works in the accepted categories of the day.

The period saw the concept of justification developed as the metaphor most appropriate for the articulation of the soteriological convictions of the western church. Associated with this development were two factors of particular importance, which we shall consider before turning to the development of the doctrine of justification during the period.

1. The transference of the discussion of the salvation of mankind from the *mythological* to the *moral* or *legal* plane.

2. The earlier medieval use of Pauline commentaries as vehicles for theological development, which inevitably led to Pauline concepts, such as justification, being incorporated into the *modus loquendi theologicus* of the later medieval period.

The early patristic discussion of the redemption of mankind in Christ frequently took the form of the portrayal of a cosmic battle between God and the devil, with its *locus* in the cross of Christ. This theme would later pass into the medieval tradition in the notion of the 'Harrowing of Hell'.[8] Associated with the image of a cosmic battle fought between God and the devil over man are several concepts which indicate the crude realism of its mythology – for example, the ideas of the devil possessing rights over man (the *ius diaboli*), of God entering into a transaction with the devil, or of God deceiving the devil.[9] The theological renaissance of the late eleventh century saw this structure being subjected to a devastating theological criticism, particularly by Anselm of Canterbury, largely on account of the conviction that *iustitia Dei*, the 'righteousness of God', necessarily entailed that God acted righteously in all his actions, including the redemption of mankind (see §6). This fundamental conviction led to the medieval construction of theories of redemption in which emphasis was laid upon the moral or legal propriety of both the redemption of mankind in the first place, and the means subsequently employed by God in this redemption. It is possible to argue that it is with Anselm's insights that the characteristic thinking of the western church on the means of the redemption of mankind may be said to begin.[10] The emphasis which is then laid upon the moral or legal character of God inevitably leads to increased interest in the precise nature of *iustitia Dei*, and the question of how *iustitia Dei* and *iustitia hominis* are correlated. The recognition of the cognate relationship between *iustitia*, *ius* and *iustificatio* served to further enhance the importance of the concept of justification as a soteriological metaphor.

The importance of the influence of Pauline commentaries to the development of theology during the earlier medieval period has been well documented,[11] and it is possible to demonstrate that the development of the various theological schools of the period may be illustrated with reference to this literary genre. These commentaries are known to have been of particular importance in the early systematisation of theology during the medieval period:[12] a survey of the commentaries on Romans alone – the most important of the Pauline epistles, judged from the standpoint of the development of the doctrine of justification – suggests that practically every theologian of note during the early medieval period used such a commentary for both the positive statement and development of his own characteristic theological positions.[13] It was therefore inevitable that these theological positions would be influenced, to a greater or lesser extent, by the Pauline material with reference to which they were developed and expounded. The discussion of questions such as the salvation of the Old Testament patriarchs, and the relation between faith and works, are but two examples of pertinent theological questions which such theologians were thus obliged to discuss with reference to the concept of justification. Thus the distinction between *iustificatio per legem* and *per fidem* was frequently used by these theologians in connection with *heilsgeschichtlich* questions such as the salvation of Abraham,[14] usually discussed with reference to Romans 4.4, whilst the discussion of the relation between faith and works would often involve discussion of the apparent differences on the matter between Paul and James[15] – again, with explicit reference to the concept of justification. Thus the early use of such Pauline commentaries as vehicles for positive theological articulation and development assisted the establishment of justification as *the* most important soteriological concept, precisely because it was used by Paul in connection with those soteriological issues which attracted the attention of the theologians of the period. By the time the later *Commentaries on the Sentences* and *Summae* had replaced these commentaries, the influence of the Pauline material upon which the earlier commentaries were based was so great that it had made an indelible impression upon the emerging medieval theological vocabulary. Furthermore, the tendency of early medieval systematic works other than Pauline commentaries to use a *heilsgeschichtlich* format in presenting their material,[16] which necessitated a careful distinction between the times of the law and gospel, naturally led to an appeal to the Pauline concepts of *iustificatio per legem* and *per fidem* in an attempt to clarify the difference between the two periods. In other words, the actual systematic presentation of theology itself during the early medieval period may be regarded as having further enhanced the importance attached to the metaphor of justification by medieval theologians.

The present chapter documents the development of particular aspects of the doctrine of justification during the medieval period, and illustrates how Augustine's basic insights into the framework of the doctrine of justification were preserved, while being developed to meet the needs of the new era in theology which was dawning.

§5 The nature of justification

What is signified by the word 'justification'?[1] As noted previously (§§2, 4), the Latin term *iustificatio* is post-classical, and almost entirely restricted to theological contexts. The Vulgate uses the term to translate the Greek δικαίωσις, although the plural *iustificationes* is occasionally encountered,[2] when the term is used to translate δικαιώματα. Augustine's interpretation of *iustificare* as *iustum facere* (see

§4), based on the assumption that *-ficare* was the unstressed form of *facere*, was universally accepted during the medieval period, almost certainly reflecting the considerable esteem in which the opinions of the bishop were held. Although *iustificare* is occasionally interpreted as *iustum habere*,[3] it is clear that this is intended to refer to *iustificatio coram hominibus* rather than *coram Deo*.[4] The characteristic medieval understanding of the nature of justification may be summarised thus: justification refers not merely to the beginning of the Christian life, but also to its continuation and ultimate perfection, in which the Christian is made righteous in the sight of God and the sight of men through a fundamental change in his nature, and not merely his status. In effect, the distinction between justification (understood as an external pronouncement of God) and sanctification (understood as the subsequent process of inner renewal), characteristic of the Reformation period, is excluded from the outset. This fundamental difference concerning the *nature* of justification remains one of the best *differentiae* between the doctrines of justification associated with the medieval and Reformation periods.[5]

An examination of the early vernacular works appears to confirm this conclusion concerning the ubiquity of the Augustinian interpretation of the significance of 'justification'. The most convenient vernacular works to study in this respect are the Old English homilies of Wulfstan (d. 1023) and Ælfric (c. 955–1020),[6] and the Gothic Bible, the *Vulfila*. Wulfstan does not, in fact, mention the term 'justification' in his homilies, and it is with the latter works that we are chiefly concerned. The Old English church was generally able to express Christian ideas by giving new meanings to existing words in the vernacular, or by forming new compounds of words already in use.[7] Occasionally, this seems to have been impossible, with the result that 'loan words' were introduced – for example, *dēofol* (for the Latin *diabolus*) and *biscop* (for the Gallo-Roman *ebescobu* – cf. Latin *episcopus*). The theological vocabulary of Old English frequently had recourse to literal translations of Latin words – for example, *gecyrrednyss* for the Latin *conversio*. The subsequent disappearance of most of these words may be attributed to the Norman Conquest of 1066. Thus *hæl* (salvation), *ærist* (resurrection) and others disappeared, whilst *God*, *heofon* and *hel* remained. The Old English terms for 'justification' and its cognates appears to have suffered the former fate, *gerihtwīsung* being replaced with the Middle English *iustification* and *gerihtwisian* with *iustifien*, both presumably derived from the Old French *justification* and *justifier*. This disappearance may be illustrated from the translation of Psalm 143.2 from a fourteenth century vernacular source, where the Romance theological term seems out of place among its Anglo-Saxon neighbours:

> Lorde, they seruaunt dragh neuer to dome,
> For non lyuyande to the is justyfyet.[8]

Ælfric regularly translates *iustificatio* by *gerihtwīsung*,[9] and in this he follows what appears to be a traditional interpretation of the Latin text.[10] It is clear that the Old English term is an interpretation, rather than a mere translation, of the original Latin term. A factitive, rather than declarative, interpretation of the term is indicated by the fact that Ælfric uses the phrase *rihtwise getealde* to mean 'reckoned righteous',[11] so that the most appropriate contemporary translation of *gerihtwīsung* would appear to be 'putting right', or 'rightwising'. A similar interpretation can be adduced from the Gothic version,[12] traditionally held to have been translated directly from the Greek by the Arian bishop Ulphilas (d. 383). Although the value of this source is seriously diminished by its fragmentary character,[13] it is clear that the factitive interpretation of δικαιοῦσθαι can be demonstrated in the Gothic version of the Pauline epistles. Thus δικαιοῦν, as it occurs in Galatians 2.16, is translated as *raihts wairthan*,[14] which clearly bears the sense of 'becoming righteous'.[15] It may be noted, however, that δικαιοῦν is not translated regularly as *raihts wairthan* in the Gothic version of the gospels – for example, it is translated as the comparative *garaithoza* at Luke 18.14. This interesting interpretation arises through misreading δεδικαιωμένος as the comparative form of δικαίος, and ἤ as 'than', as is indicated by the following *thau*.

The systematic discussion of the *inner structure* of justification dates from the beginning of the twelfth century, with the formulation of the *processus iustificationis*. This discussion is an important development in the history of the doctrine of justification, as it marks an attempt to correlate the process of justification with the developing sacramental system of the church. Its beginnings may, however, be discerned at a much earlier period in the history of doctrine. Thus Augustine distinguished three aspects of the justification of the ungodly:

Iustificatio porro in hac vita nobis secundum tria ista confertur: prius, lavacro regenerationis, quo remittuntur cuncta peccata; deinde, congressione cum vitiis, a quorum reatu absoluti sumus; tertio, dum nostra exauditur oratio, qua dicimus, *Dimitte nobis debita nostra.*[16]

Bruno the Carthusian also distinguished three aspects of the process of justification.[17] A more detailed discussion of the inner structure of justification may be found in Hervaeus of Bourg-Dieu's comments on Romans 3.20: the recognition of sin is followed by the operation of healing grace, which leads to a love for righteousness:

Per legem enim cognitio peccati; per fidem impetratio gratiae contra peccatum; per gratiam sanatio animae a vitio peccati; per animae sanitatem libertas arbitrii; per liberum arbitrium, iustitiae dilectio; per iustitiae dilectionem legis operatio.[18]

The sequential ordering of the process, with one element leading to another in a causal sequence, foreshadowed the twelfth-century discussion of the *processus iustificationis*.

Initially, the theologians of the twelfth century envisaged the *processus iustificationis* as consisting of three elements. Peter Manducator defined the sequence as follows: tria enim sunt, in quibis iustificatio consistit, scilicet primarie gratie infusio, cordis contritio, peccati remissio.[19] As a study of twelfth-century works indicates, the terminology of the *processus iustificationis* is still fluid, and although the threefold structure appears fixed, its elements were still not clearly defined. For example, the *processus* is elsewhere defined as consisting of *gratiae infusio, liberi arbitrii cooperatio, et consummatio*.[20] Occasionally, a threefold scheme is encountered which omits any reference to the infusion of grace, such as *peccati desertio, propositum non peccandi de cetero, dolor de peccato preterito*.[21] Nevertheless, it is clear that a threefold process, which is initiated through the infusion of grace and terminates in the remission of sin, was widely accepted as normative. Although it must be conceded that the *processus* does not in itself represent an important advance, in that the three elements involved had long been recognised as closely inter-related, it does represent an important advance in the *systematic discussion of justification*, in that the three elements are now linked as the 'process of justification'.

Although the threefold scheme appears to have gained considerable acceptance in the twelfth century, it was a fourfold scheme of the inner structure of justification which would finally become accepted as normative. The threefold *processus* recognised a single notion of the *liberum arbitrium*, which subsequently came to be divided into two components: a movement of the free will towards God, and a movement of the free will away from sin. As stated by Peter of Poitiers, the scheme has the following form:

Sciendum est autem quod ad iustificationem impii quatuor occurunt: infusio gratiae, motus surgens ex gratia et libero arbitrio, contritio, peccatorum remissio. Nullum istorum prius est aliquo eorumdem tempore, sed tamen naturaliter praecedit gratiae infusio et per ordinem sequuntur alia tria, non tempore, sed natura. Sciendum est autem quod quodlibet istorum quatuor dicitur iustificatio, nec unum potest esse in homine sine aliis tribus.[22]

The infusion of grace thus initiates a chain of events which eventually leads to justification: if any of these events may be shown to have taken place, the remaining three may also be concluded to have taken place. The fourfold *processus iustificationis* differs from the threefold scheme in including a dual, rather than a single, motion of the human free will, otherwise retaining the same overall structure. It was taken up by the first Summist, William of Auxerre, in the form *infusio gratiae, motus liberi arbitrii, contritio, peccatorum remissio*,[23] and was accepted in this form by the doctors of the early Dominican and Franciscan schools.[24] The inclusion of *contritio* in the *processus* is of no small significance, as it greatly assisted the correlation of the *processus* with the sacrament of penance in the thirteenth century (see §8).

The justification of the fourfold *processus iustificationis* within the early Dominican school is of particular interest, as it demonstrates the considerable influence of Aristotelian physics upon theological speculation within that school.[25] Albertus Magnus defined justification as a *motus* from sin to grace and rectitude.[26] Having already applied the Aristotelian theory of motion, as stated in the celebrated maxim of Aristotelian physics, *omne quod movetur ab alio movetur*, to a physical *motus* such as free fall, or a theological problem of *motus* such as the existence of God,[27] the same principle is applied to the analysis of the inner structure of the *motus* of justification. The explicit application of the Aristotelian theory of generation to the transition from nature to grace leads to a fourfold *processus iustificationis*, with a dual motion of the free will. This application of Aristotelian physics to the *motus* of justification is particularly associated with Thomas Aquinas. Having stated the *processus iustificationis* to be:

1.   the infusion of grace;
2.   the movement of the free will directed towards God through faith;
3.   the movement of the free will directed against sin;
4.   the remission of sin;

Thomas now justifies this on the basis of Aristotelian physics. By nature, the movement of the mover must come first, followed by the disposition of the matter, or the movement of that which is to be moved, followed by the final termination of the motion when the objective of the movement has been achieved.[28] Thus the infusion of grace must precede the remission of sin, as the infusion of grace is the efficient cause of that remission. Thus the *motus* which is justification ends in the remission of sin, which may be considered as the *terminus* of the infusion of grace.[29] As every movement may be said to be defined by its *terminus*, justification may thus be said to consist of the remission of sin.[30]

Some commentators have misunderstood Thomas' occasional definition of justification solely in terms of the remission of sin, representing him as approaching a forensic concept of justification. It will be clear that this is a serious misunderstanding. Where Thomas defines justification as *remissio peccatorum*, therefore, he does not exclude other elements – such as the infusion of grace – from his definition, for the following reasons. First, justification is thus defined without reference to its content, solely in terms of its *terminus*. Such a definition is adequate, but not exhaustive, and should not be treated as if it were. Second, Thomas' understanding of the *processus iustificationis* means that the occurrence of any one of the four elements necessarily entails the occurrence of the remaining three. The definition of *iustificatio* as *remissio peccatorum* therefore expressly *includes* the remaining three elements.

Having established that the remission of sin is the final element in the *processus iustificationis*, Thomas argues that the element intervening between the initial (i.e., *infusio gratiae*) and the final (i.e., *remissio peccatorum*) elements must be the disposition of the object of justification – i.e., the *motus mobilis*, the movement of that which is to be moved. As justification is *motus mentis*, this disposition must refer to the human free will, which precedes justification itself by nature.[31] This consideration leads to a definition of justification as *quidam motus quo humana mens movetur a Deo a statu peccati in statum iustitiae*,[32] and allows a threefold *processus iustificationis* to be established: *infusio gratiae, motus liberi arbitrii, remissio peccatorum*. Tradition had by now, however, established a dual motion of the free will in justification, in faith and contrition,[33] so that it was necessary to resolve the *motus mobilis* into two elements. Thomas achieves this by applying a further axiom of Aristotelian physics – that 'in movements of the soul, the movement to the principle of understanding or to the end of the action comes first'[34] – to the *motus animi* of justification. Thus a movement of the *liberum arbitrium* towards God must precede its motion against sin, as the former is the cause of the latter.[35] This teaching, found in the *Summa Theologiae*, is of particular interest, as it represents an abandonment of his earlier teaching, that there should be no intermediates between the influence of grace and the remission of sin.[36]

In justification, according to Thomas, man is translated from a state of corrupt nature to one of habitual grace; from a state of sin to a state of justice, with the remission of sin.[37] But how is this state of justice to be conceived? As noted earlier (§4), Augustine's understanding of *iustitia* embraces practically the entire ordering of the universe, so that justification can be understood as the restoration of man to his correct place in the hierarchy of being, including the establishment of the correct relationship between the various existential strata within man, on the basis of the neo-Platonist anthropological model favoured by Augustine. Thomas' discussion of the question involves a crucial distinction between the *virtue* of justice, and the *supernatural habit* of justice, infused by God. *Iustitia acquisita*, the virtue of acquired justice,[38] may be considered either as particular justice, which orders man's actions relating to his fellow men, or as legal justice, as defined by Aristotle.[39] *Iustitia infusa*, however, on the basis of which man is justified, comes from God himself, through grace.[40] Failure to appreciate this distinction will lead to the quite untenable conclusion that Thomas teaches justification purely through self-endeavour or moral attainment. Justification is concerned with justice in the sight of God, *iustitia quae est apud Deum*.[41] *Iustitia infusa* is that justice which is infused into man by God, by which man's higher faculties are submitted to God. In essence, it may be noted that Thomas' concept of infused justice is very similar to Aristotle's notion of metaphorical justice,[42] which refers primarily to a rectitude of order within man's interior disposition. It is this infused justice, and this justice alone, which is the basis of man's justification.

The characteristically Augustinian understanding of justification as the restoration of man to his proper place in the created hierarchy of being is reflected in Thomas' discussion of why justification is properly named after justice, rather than faith or love. Although both faith and love are involved in justification,[43] and although their supernatural habits are infused in its course, Thomas insists that the transformation which is called 'justification' is properly named after justice alone on account of the all-embracing character of the latter, which refers to the entire rectitude of order of the human soul, with all its faculties. Faith and love refer only to specific aspects of this order, whereas justice embraces man's higher nature in its totality.[44]

It may be noted at this point that Thomas' understanding of justification as a *motus mentis* reflects his intellectualist understanding of human nature; if the higher nature is subordinate to God, it will be enabled to restrain the lower nature. Man's intellect is restored through justifying faith, so that he is able to avoid *mortal* sin; although the higher nature subsequently restrains the lower, it is unable to overcome it entirely, so that man is still unable to avoid *venial* sin after justification.[45] Thus even the man who is in a state of grace cannot be said to be free from sin. Thomas' exposition of Romans 7 is of particular interest in this respect, as he clearly understands the chapter to refer to the Christian constituted in grace.[46] Justification is about 'being made just': the precise nature of this 'making just' is, however, carefully defined in terms of the rectitude of the human mind so that it, acting as a secondary cause, may bring all that is subordinate to it into conformity with the exemplar established for it by God. The *event* of the infusion of the habit of justice must therefore be followed by the *process* of the submission of the lower to the higher nature; in this understanding of the dual nature of justification, Thomas remains faithful to the teaching of Augustine.

Thomas' understanding of justification as a *motus mentis* allows him to apply the Aristotelian theory of motion to its presuppositions, as well as its interior structure, and is of particular interest in relation to his discussion of the need for a disposition towards justification on the part of the sinner.[47] The early Franciscan school, however, developed a more psychological approach to justification, reflecting an Augustinian illuminationist epistemology which is not characteristic of the Dominican school. The general features of the early Franciscan teaching on the nature of justification may be found in Bonaventure's *Itinerarium mentis in Deum*, which develops a hierarchical concept of justification which clearly reflects the influence of Dionysius. The three fundamental operations of grace in justification are the *purification*, *illumination* and *perfection* of the soul.[48] Christ performed three acts which re-established and reordered man's supernatural life towards God: he purged our guilt, enlightened us by his example, and perfected us by enabling us to follow in his footsteps. The Christian is required to respond to these in three hierarchical acts by which he can appropriate their benefits. These three aspects of the justification of the sinner correspond to the 'Three Ways' which are so characteristic of Bonaventure's spirituality, distinguished by their goals rather than their relation in time. The *stimulus conscientiae* motivates the way of purification, the *radius intelligentiae* the way of illumination, and the *igniculus sapientiae* the way of unity with God. From the moment of its first infusion, sanctifying grace takes over the substance and faculties of the soul, setting each in its respective place, and ordering the soul that it may be conformed to God.[49] The process of justification involves the destruction of the passions which threaten the development of man's new life, so that man can rediscover the image of God within himself. Thus the soul, reconstituted by grace, can begin its ascent towards the goal of supernatural perfection. It will be clear that Bonaventure's understanding of the nature of justification differs from that of Thomas only in emphasis: both understand justification as the establishment of rectitude within man's higher nature, whether this be considered as *mens* or *anima*. Bonaventure's teaching was developed by his Italian disciple Matthew of Aquasparta, who discussed justification in terms of six stages: the hatred of sin and the love of good; regeneration; the reforming and reordering of man's nature; the generation of virtues; conversion to, and union with, God; and remission of sin.[50] His emphasis upon the regeneration of the sinner and his ultimate union with God point to a psychological approach to justification more characteristic of Bonaventure than Thomas.

The medieval statements concerning the nature of justification demonstrate that justification is universally understood to involve a real change in its object, so that regeneration is subsumed under justification. As John of La Rochelle pointed out, unless justification did produce a real change in man, it would appear to serve no useful purpose:

Homo est iustificatus. Si nihil ponitur in eo, nulla mutatio fit a parte ipsius, nec est proximus bono aeterno quam prius; si ponitur aliquid, id dico esse gratiam.[51]

This statement is of particular interest, as it involves the appeal to the reality of a change in man arising through his justification in the refutation of the earlier opinion, gratia ponit nihil in anima.[52] Whilst justification was universally understood to involve the regeneration of man, the opinion that an *ontological* change is thereby effected within man is particularly associated with the period of High Scholasticism and the development of the concept of created grace. The earlier medieval theologians expressed the change effected in justification in terms of a particular presence of God in his creature, which did not necessarily effect an ontological change. Thus the *Summa Fratris Alexandri*, written after 1240, developed the Augustinian concept of the indwelling of God in his creatures by declaring that God is present in all his creatures, but that only some (i.e., those who are justified) may be said to possess him. All creatures can participate in God – only the justified can be said to actually possess that divine presence. The *Summa* conceives a special presence of God in the justified, such that an ontological change occurs in the soul. The presence of God in the justified sinner necessarily results in *created* grace – a created grace which can be conceived as a conformity of the soul to God.[53] This special presence of God in the souls of the justified must be distinguished from the general presence of God in the world, and from the unique union between God and man achieved in the hypostatic union. In this, the *Summa* makes an important advance on Peter Lombard's discussion of the divine presence in all creatures; in angels and the souls of the justified through indwelling grace, and in Christ *non per adoptionis sed per gratiam unionis.*[54]

The later medieval period saw the rise of the opinion particularly associated with the *via moderna* according to which the relationship between God and man was to be understood *covenantally* rather than *ontologically.*[55] Although this opinion involves the linking of justification with the extrinsic denomination of the divine acceptation, the *de facto* necessity of a habit of grace in justification continued to be maintained. Although the ultimate reason for man's acceptation lies in the divine decision to accept, the fact remains that *de potentia Dei ordinata* the infusion of grace, the indwelling of the Holy Spirit, and the divine acceptation coincide. The rejection of the metaphysical necessity of such a habit of grace must be carefully distinguished from the assertion of its *de facto* necessity within the context of the covenant which governs the divine dispensation towards mankind. The necessity of a habit of created grace in justification is radically contingent, a *necessitas consequentiae* rather than a *necessitas consequentis*; however, as theology is concerned with the articulation of the divine dispensation towards mankind as it now pertains, man's justification before God must be considered to involve an ontological change within him. *De potentia Dei ordinata* the habit of created grace is the middle term between sinful man and his acceptation by God in justification: it need not have been so, but the fact remains that it is so. The essential contribution of the *via moderna* to the medieval understanding of the nature of justification is its emphasis upon the *contingent* nature of the ontological change which occurs within man in justification. It is only by confusing the actual divine dispensation *de potentia ordinata* with a hypothetical dispensation *de potentia absoluta* that any continuity with the Reformation understandings of the nature of justification may be maintained.

Associated with the *via moderna* in particular is the weakening of the link between the elements of the *processus iustificationis*. As noted above, the four elements of the process were regarded as essentially aspects of the one and the same transformation, causally linked by their very nature (*ex natura rei*). From the time of Duns Scotus onwards, this view was subjected to increasing criticism. The infusion of grace and the remission of sin came increasingly to be seen as fundamentally distinct, coexisting and causally related only through the divine ordination (*ex pacto divino*). One may take place without the other. Scotus states four reasons why the remission of sin and the infusion of grace cannot be regarded as aspects of one and the same change (i.e., justification):[56]

1. The remission of sin is multiple, as God forgives each committed sin individually, whilst the infusion of grace is single.
2. Infusion of grace can occur without remission of sin, and *vice versa*. Thus God infused grace into Adam in his state of innocence without remitting his sin, as he did also with the good angels.
3. There is no necessary correlation between sin and grace as opposites.
4. Sin cannot be regarded simply as the privation of grace, which would be necessary if justification were regarded as the transition from a privation to its corresponding quality.

Furthermore, Scotus points out that infusion of grace is a *real* change in man, whilst the remission of sin is a *mutatio rationis*, an ideal change within the divine mind and not within man himself. As the concepts of the infusion of grace and the remission of sin have totally different points of reference, they cannot be allowed to be causally related as in the traditional *processus iustificationis*. Since their relationship does not derive from the nature of the elements themselves, it must derive from the divine will – i.e., it is arbitrary. Without in any way challenging the *de facto* relationship of the elements of the *processus iustificationis*, Scotus demonstrated that this relationship was itself radically contingent, the consequence of divine ordination rather than the nature of the entities themselves. This point, which relates to the nature of the causal processes involved in justification, will be developed further in our discussion of the rôle of supernatural habits in justification (see §13).

The medieval concept of justification includes the renovation as well as the forgiveness of the sinner: in iustificatione animarum duo concurrunt, scilicet remissio culpae et novitas vitae per gratiam.[57] Although some theologians appear to define justification solely as the remission of sins,[58] it must be pointed out that this is a consequence of their use of Aristotelian categories in their discussion of justification: as a *motus* may be defined by its *terminus*, justification may be defined as the remission of sins. The entire medieval discussion of justification proceeds upon the assumption that a *real* change in the sinner is effected thereby. This observation is as true for the *via moderna* as it is for the earlier period.[59] It is quite untenable to suppose that the Reformation distinction between justification and regeneration can be adduced from the medieval period, when it is clear that the universal opinion is that such a distinction is excluded from the outset. Indeed, the *modernus* Gabriel Biel explicitly contrasts a forensic justification before a secular judge with justification as transformation in relation to God, the spiritual judge.[60] In the later medieval period, the *de facto* necessity of a habit of created grace in justification is maintained, even by those theologians who otherwise stood closest to the Reformers.[61] As we have insisted, the notional distinction between *iustificatio* and *regeneratio* provides one of the best *differentiae* between Catholic and Protestant understandings of justification, marking the Reformers' complete discontinuity with the earlier western theological tradition. From its beginning to its end, the medieval period saw justification as involving a real change in the sinner – an understanding which precludes the Reformation distinction between *iustificatio* and *regeneratio* from the outset.

§6 The righteousness of God

What is signified by the 'righteousness of God', and how is it manifested? What does it mean to affirm that God is 'righteous'? The importance of these questions was emphasised by the patristic exegesis of Romans 1.17,[1] in which Paul practically equates *iustitia Dei* with the gospel. An examination of the medieval exegesis of Romans 1.17 indicates that there was an early consensus among Pauline exegetes that *iustitia Dei* was to be understood as referring primarily to God's righteousness as demonstrated in the justification of the ungodly, *iustificatio impii*, in accordance with his promises of mercy. In general, two main lines of interpretation may be distinguished in the early medieval period.

1. A subjective understanding of the construction *iustitia Dei* – i.e., *iustitia Dei* is the righteousness by which God is himself righteous.

This interpretation, which appears to stem from Ambrosiaster, emphasises the maintenance of the divine integrity in justification. God, having promised to give salvation, subsequently gives it, and as a result is deemed to be 'righteous' – i.e., faithful to his promises. The 'righteousness of God' is therefore demonstrated in his faithfulness to his promises of salvation: iustitia est Dei, quia quod promisit dedit, ideo credens hoc esse se consecutum quod promiserat Deus per prophetas suos, iustum Deum probat et testis est iustitiae eius.[2] The gospel is therefore understood to manifest the divine righteousness in that God is shown to have fulfilled the Old Testament promises, made in the prophets and elsewhere, of salvation for his people.

2. An objective interpretation of the construction iustitia Dei – i.e., iustitia Dei is the righteousness whose origin is God, given to the sinner in his justification, rather than the righteousness by which God is himself just. This interpretation, which appears to stem from Augustine (see §4), treats the construction iustitia Dei as an example of genitivus auctoris: iustitiam Dei vocat gratiam, non qua ipse iustificatur, sed qua hominem induit.[3]

In both cases, the 'righteousness of God' is understood to refer to his gracious act of justification, rather than to a divine property which stands over and against man. In the case of the subjective interpretation of the construction, iustitia Dei is understood to refer to the general framework within which the justification of man takes place (i.e., the promises of the Old Testament), whereas the objective interpretation of the construction refers to the immediate means by which that justification takes place (i.e., the 'righteousness' which God bestows upon the sinner, in order that he may be 'made just'). It will be clear that the two interpretations of the construction iustitia Dei are complementary rather than mutually exclusive, and it is not uncommon to find both interpretations within the same work. Iustitia Dei is thus understood to be set in a soteriological context, referring to the salvation of mankind, whether as a consequence of God's faithfulness to his promises of mercy, or of the bestowal of divine righteousness upon the sinner.

It can, however, be shown that a third interpretation of the concept existed in the earlier medieval period, apparently corresponding to a form of popular Pelagianism. Iustitia Dei is here understood to refer to the divine attribute by which God rewards man according to his just deserts. God, in his righteousness, will reward those who act justly and punish those who act unjustly – thereby justifying the godly, and punishing the ungodly. Iustitia enim tua est, ut qui fecerit voluntatem tuam, transeat a morte in vitam, per quam et ego nunc eripi deprecor.[4] This corresponds to what might be called a 'popular catholic' understanding of justification, according to which justification is understood to be dependent upon man's efforts to emulate the example which is set him in Christ. While the early exponents of this theology of justification insisted that man cannot justify himself,[5] it may be pointed out that the orthodoxy of this position is superficial. As justification is defined as the *divine* judgement that man is righteous, it follows as a matter of course that man is not competent to pronounce this judgement himself, and thereby usurp the place of God. Justification is God's judgement upon man, made upon the basis of whether he has emulated the *iustitia Dei* revealed to man in Christ – i.e., the divine standard of righteousness, which man must imitate. Pelagius' interpretation of the concept of the 'righteousness of God' is of particular interest in this respect, as it is taken to refer to the righteousness which God gives to man in Christ *as his example*, so that his justification may be attributed to his own moral efforts to imitate *iustitia Dei, per exemplum Christi*, through the free and autonomous exercise of *liberum arbitrium*. A similar, although more developed, understanding of *iustitia Dei* can be found in the writings of Julian of Eclanum.[6] God deals with man in equity, totally impartially, considering only his merits and demerits in justification, reddentem sua unicuique sine fraude sine gratia, id est sine personarum acceptione.[7] In effect, Julian applies a *quid pro quo* understanding of justice to the divine dealings with men – an understanding of *iustitia* which found its classic expression in the Ciceronian definition of *iustitia* as habitus animi, communi utilitate conservata, suam cuique tribuens dignitatem (see §§2, 4). For Julian, God rewards man according to his merits – otherwise, God is made guilty of a gross injustice. Julian singles out several aspects of Augustine's theology of grace for particular criticism on the basis of this understanding of *iustitia Dei* – for example, his understanding of the nature of original sin, and the doctrine of the justification of the *ungodly*. If God is to reward man *sine personarum acceptione*, he must reward them on the basis of what they *have done*, rather than on the basis of who *they are* – i.e., they must be rewarded on the basis of merit. This Ciceronian understanding of *iustitia Dei* had earlier been criticised by Augustine (see §4), who pointed out that the Parable of the Labourers in the Vineyard (Matthew 20.1–10) gave a more reliable insight into the divine justice than Julian's Ciceronian analogy. Every man was rewarded with his denarius, irrespective of the period he actually spent working: although the workers had no claim to the denarius in terms of the work they had performed, they *did* have a claim on account of the promise made to them by the owner of the vineyard. By analogy, man has no claim to grace on the basis of his works (i.e., on a *quid pro quo* basis), but such a claim on the basis of the obligation of God to fulfil his promise.

JULIAN: Est igitur procul dubio iustitia, sine qua deitas non est; quae si non esset, deus non esset; est autem Deus, est itaque sine ambiguitate iustitia. Non est autem aliud quam virtus omnia continens et restituens suum unicuique sine fraude sine gratia; consistit autem maxime in divinitatis profundo.

AUGUSTINE: Definisti esse iustitiam virtutem omnia continentem et restituentem suum unicuique sine fraude sine gratia. Proinde videmus eam sine fraude restituisse denarium eis, qui per totum diem in opere vineae laboraverant; hoc enim placuerat, hoc convenerat, ad hanc mercedem se fuisse conductos negare non poterant. Sed dic mihi, quaeso te: quomodo eis sine gratia tantundem dedit, quit una hora in illo opere fuerunt? An amiserat fortasse iustitiam? Cohibe itaque te potius; neminem quippe fraudat divina iustitia, sed multa donat non merentibus gratia.[8]

This criticism of the predication of the Ciceronian concept of *iustitia* to God would be continued by the theologians of the early medieval period. Thus Remigius of Auxerre pointed out that human concepts of justice involved the rendering of good for good, and evil for evil – yet God rendered good for evil when he justified sinful man.[9] If God's dealings with men are to be rationalised on the basis of justice, human ideas of justice must give way to those of God. A somewhat different approach to the question may be found in Atto of Vercelli's gloss on Romans 1.17. Here the legal category of justice is retained, along with a Ciceronian interpretation of *iustitia* – but it is interpreted in terms of Christ's obedience to the law:

Iustitia enim Dei in eo revelatur ex fide in fidem. Iustitia dicitur, quasi iuris status. Iustitia ergo est, cum unicuique proprium eius tribuitur: unde et iustus dicitur, eo quod ius custodiat. Iustitia autem Dei Christus est, quae revelatur in eo.[10]

In effect, this marks a development of Ambrosiaster's approach to *iustitia Dei*, in that God's faithfulness to his promise of mercy is now expressed in legal terms – i.e., 'faithfulness' is interpreted in terms of 'keeping the law'. It may, however, be emphasised that while the earlier medieval period is characterised by its conviction that God's righteousness is somehow grounded in his promise of mercy, there is no real attempt to establish the precise relationship between *iustitia*

Dei and *misericordia Dei*: most theologians were content merely to affirm that God, in his righteousness, was faithful to his promises.[11]

The theological renaissance of the late eleventh and twelfth centuries[12] saw the 'righteousness of God' being discussed in terms of two separate, although clearly related, questions:

1. What concept of *iustitia* is appropriate to characterise God's dealings with men?
2. How is it possible, given the limitations of human language, to speak of God being 'righteous' in the first place?

We shall consider these questions separately.

The first major discussion of the first point is due to Anselm of Canterbury. It must be pointed out that Anselm's soteriology has frequently been criticised as 'legalist', typical of the Latin 'impulse to carry religion into the legal sphere'.[13] This misguided and discredited criticism of Anselm, however, brings us to the very point which confronted Anselm as he began his attempt to defend the rationality of the incarnation of the son of God: what was the relationship between the 'righteousness of God' and the ideas of 'righteousness' taken from 'ordinary human life'?

God is wholly and supremely just.[14] How can he then give eternal life to one who deserves eternal death? How can he justify the sinner? This is the central question with which Anselm is concerned in *Cur Deus homo* (1098). Earlier, Anselm had wrestled with substantially the same problem in the *Proslogion* (1079):

Verum malis quomodo parcis, si es totus iustus et summe iustus? Quomodo enim totus et summe iustus facit aliquid non iustum? Aut quae iustitia est merenti mortem aeternam dare vitam sempiternam? Unde ergo, bone Deus, bone bonis et malis, unde tibi salvare malos, si hoc non est iustum, et tu non facis aliquid non iustum?[15]

Initially, Anselm locates the source of God's mercy in his *bonitas*, which may be contrasted with his *iustitia*. He then proceeds to argue, however, that despite the apparent contradiction between the divine *misericordia* and *iustitia*, God's mercy must somehow be grounded in his justice. Anselm resolves this dilemma by arguing that God is just, not because he rewards according to merit, but because he does what is appropriate to him as the highest good, *summum bonum*: ita iustus es non quia nobis reddas debitum, sed quia facis quod decet te summe bonum.[16] The explicit criticism of the Ciceronian definition of *iustitia* as *reddens unicuique quod suum est* will be evident. A similar pattern may be seen in *Cur Deus homo*, where Anselm notes various interpretations of the concept of *iustitia*, before selecting that which is most appropriate for his purposes: *iustitia hominis*, which pertains under law;[17] *iustitia districta*, beyond which 'nothing more strict can be imagined' – Anselm presumably therefore understands *iustitia hominis* as *iustitia aequitatis*[18] – and supreme justice, *summa iustitia*.[19] The concept of justice which Anselm selects as most appropriate to characterise God's dealings with men is, as in the *Proslogion*, justice understood as action directed towards the highest good. As that highest good includes the redemption of fallen mankind, the salvation of man may be regarded as an act of divine justice. In the course of the discussion, however, it becomes clear that Anselm understands the concept of *rectitudo* to underlie that of *iustitia*, and to determine its basic meaning.

According to Anselm, justice is a 'rectitude of will served for its own sake (*rectitudo voluntatis propter se servata*)'.[20] Similarly, truth must be defined in terms of rectitude: non aliud ibi potest intelligi veritas quam rectitudo, quoniam sive veritas sive rectitudo non aliud in eius voluntate fuit quam velle quod debuit.[21] The relationship between rectitude, truth and justice could be expressed as follows:

rectitudo
→ *veritas* (i.e., metaphysical rectitude)
→ *iustitia* (i.e., moral rectitude)

Anselm clearly assumes that the three concepts are closely linked: habes igitur definitionem iustitiae, si iustitia non est aliud quam rectitudo. Et quoniam de rectitudine mente sola perceptibili loquimur, invicem sese definiunt veritas et rectitudo et iustitia.[22] The concepts of 'truth' and 'righteousness' had, of course, been long recognised to have close conceptual connections,[23] and Anselm may be regarded as establishing the conceptual foundation of both to be 'rectitude'. *Iustitia* has as its fundamental sense the moral rectitude of the created order, established by God at creation, and in itself reflecting the divine will and nature. This moral ordering of the universe extends to the relationship between man and God, and man and his fellow men. Anselm appears to use the term *rectitudo* to describe the basic God-given ordering of the universe, and employs the term *iustitia* in a number of derivative senses, each of which may be traced back to the fundamental concept of rectitude. God's moral governing of the universe clearly involves both the divine regulation of the affairs of men, and also the self-imposed regulation by which

God governs his dealings with men – and it is not possible to argue that the laws governing each are the same. In its fundamental sense, *iustitia* merely refers to rectitude; it remains to be seen what form this ordering may take with respect to the various aspects of creation. The justice which regulates the affairs of men (e.g., the Ciceronian and Justinian principle of *reddens unicuique quod suum est*) cannot be considered to be identical with the justice which regulates God's dealings with man.

Man was created in a state of *iustitia originalis*, which was forfeited at the Fall. It may be noted that the concept of 'original justice' is understood by Anselm to refer to the initial moral rectitude of man within the created order. For Anselm, the basic requirement of *iustitia* is that rational creatures be subject to God,[24] which merely amounts to a statement of the place of man in the hierarchical moral ordering of creation. This moral ordering of creation, itself an expression of the divine will, allots a specific place to man, with a concomitant obligation that he submit his rational nature to God. This moral ordering of the universe was violated by man at the Fall, so that man's present state is that of *iniustitia*, understood as the privation of *iustitia* rather than as a positive entity in itself. The essence of original sin is the inherited lack of moral rectitude in the will of fallen man.[25] Man's violation of the moral order of creation means that he is no longer capable of submitting his rational nature to God – and therefore that he is incapable of redeeming himself. If man is to be redeemed, a divine act of redemption is required *which must itself be consonant with the established moral order of the universe*. God, having created the moral order of the universe as an expression of his nature and will, is unable to violate it himself in the redemption of mankind.

This important point is made with particular clarity at that point in *Cur Deus homo* at which Anselm considers the question of why God cannot simply forgive sins as an act of mercy.[26] For Anselm, God's freedom in will and action is limited by his own nature. God is not free to do anything which violates his own nature, since this involves a contradiction. Thus what is *iustum* cannot become *iniustum* simply because God wills it, as such an alteration involves a radical change in the divine nature itself. God's character as *summa iustitia* is expressed in the moral order of creation, and the free forgiveness of sins through mercy alone would violate this ordering. God's attributes are essential to his being, and not mere accidents which he may change at will. Anselm's theological insight is that the divine attributes must coexist within the limiting conditions which they impose upon each other. Thus the rectitude of the established moral order requires that God redeem man in such a way that his own nature as *summa iustitia* is not contradicted.

In a very brief, but highly significant, review of the accounts traditionally given of the redemption of mankind in Christ, Anselm makes it clear that he is not satisfied with their failure to explain *why* God chose to redeem man – at best, they were merely descriptions of *how* God redeemed man, offering no explanation for why God should choose to redeem man in the first place, nor the particular mode of redemption selected. Anselm therefore presents an account of the redemption of mankind, based on *iustitia*, which demonstrates:

1.   that the redemption of mankind is necessary *as a matter of justice*;
2.   that this redemption is effected in a manner that is consonant with the divinely established moral ordering of the universe.

We shall consider these points individually.

If *iustitia Dei* is understood as a *lex talionis*, or in the Ciceronian sense of *reddens unicuique quod suum est*, it is clearly impossible, in Anselm's view, to consider God's act of redemption as an act of justice. It is for this reason that Anselm does not employ these concepts of justice in his soteriology. For Anselm, the moral ordering of the universe was violated by the sin of man, so that the present state of affairs is that of a privation of justice – i.e., *iniustitia*. As whatever is unjust is a contradiction of the divine nature, it is therefore imperative that the moral rectitude of the created order be restored. God, as *summa iustitia* is therefore obliged, by his very nature (since to permit a state of injustice to continue indefinitely is tantamount to a contradiction of his nature) to restore the rectitude of the created order by redeeming fallen man – *as an act of justice*.

Anselm prefaces his discussion of the method by which God redeemed mankind by considering the rival theory of the *ius diaboli*, the 'devil's rights'. This theory may be illustrated from the tract *de redemptione humana*, attributed to Bede,[27] in which it is argued that, while the death of Christ is a free act of divine love, the choice of the means employed to effect man's deliverance from the devil is necessarily dictated by the fact that the devil is *justly* entitled to punish sinners. The origins of this teaching may be traced back to Gregory the Great, who taught that the devil had acquired a legal right over sinners as a consequence of the Fall, but had no such right over anyone who was sinless. Christ therefore assumed the form of man in order to deceive his opponent, who naturally assumed that he, like the rest of humanity, was a sinner. As the devil thus brought about the crucifixion of the sinless Christ contrary to justice his own legitimate power over sinners was justly abolished.[28] This theory makes its appeal to justice – but it is a very different concept of justice to that employed by Anselm. For Anselm, justice relates to the moral ordering of creation, which the devil himself, as a rational creature, is subject to. The devil clearly violated this order in his seduction of man, and cannot be regarded as having any *just* claim over man. Himself a rational creature, the devil is obliged to submit his rational nature to God – only if he were not part of God's creation, and could therefore stand aloof from its moral ordering, could the devil claim any 'right' over man. By his own violation of *iustitia*, the devil had lost any claim to *ius* over man. Anselm therefore dismisses the theory of the work of Christ which had been current for so long, and with it, an unacceptable concept of *iustitia Dei*: non video quam vim habeat.

Anselm's own theory may be stated as a series of propositions, if the numerous digressions are ignored. When this is one, the centrality of the concept of *iustitia* to his argument becomes apparent:

1. Man was created in a state of original justice for eternal felicity.
2. This felicity requires the perfect and voluntary submission of man's will to God – i.e., *iustitia*.
3. Man's present state is that of *iniustitia*.
4. Either this must result in man's being deprived of eternal felicity, or else the situation must be rectified by an appropriate satisfaction.
5. This satisfaction must exceed the act of disobedience.
6. Man cannot offer to God anything other than the demands of *iustitia*, and on account of his present *iniustitia*, he cannot even do that.
7. Therefore God's purpose in creating man has been frustrated.
8. But this is unjust, and poses a contradiction to the divine nature.
9. Therefore a means of redemption must exist if justice is to be reestablished.
10. Man cannot redeem himself, being unable to make the necessary satisfaction for sin.
11. God could make the necessary satisfaction.
12. Since only God can, and only man ought to, make the necessary satisfaction, it must be made by a God-man.
13. Therefore the incarnation is required as an act of justice.

The importance of justice at this stage in the argument is often overlooked. The 'syllogism' – Aristotle, it must be recalled, had yet to be rediscovered! – which demonstrates the 'necessity' of the incarnation may be stated thus:

A.   Only man ought to make satisfaction for sin – but he cannot.

B.   Only God can make the necessary satisfaction – but he is under no obligation to do so – indeed, he ought not to do so.

It is clear that this primitive 'syllogism' could lead to two conclusions.

1.   A God-man both cannot and ought not to make such a satisfaction.

2.   Only a God-man both can and ought to make such a satisfaction.

From a purely dialectical standpoint, the work in question could equally well be entitled *Cur Deus non homo*. However, as justice demands that man's predicament be resolved, Anselm feels himself justified in drawing the second conclusion, and overlooking the first.

The weak point in Anselm's soteriology is generally considered to be his theory of satisfaction,[29] which we do not propose to discuss further. The essential point, however, is that Anselm considers, presumably on the basis of the established satisfaction-merit model of the penitential system of the contemporary church, that the payment of a satisfaction by the God-man would be regarded by his readers as an acceptable means of satisfying the demands of moral rectitude without violating the moral order of creation. For our purposes, this aspect of Anselm's soteriology is subsidiary, the main element being his development of *iustitia Dei* as action directed towards the highest good, and thus embracing the redemption of mankind. Anselm's soteriology is dominated by the understanding of justice as moral rectitude, and it marks a decisive turning point in the medieval discussion of the 'righteousness of God'.

The theory that the devil has rights over man, which God was obliged to respect, continued to influence theologians for some time after Anselm's death. Thus the school of Laon, marked by its extreme theological conservatism, taught that the devil had gained just possession of man because man had freely enslaved himself to the devil as a consequence of his sin. God is therefore obliged to respect the *ius diaboli*.[30] The theological justification provided for the incarnation by the school of Laon is that it is only God who has the *ability* and only man who has the *obligation* to overcome the devil: by logic similar to that employed by Anselm of Canterbury, the necessity of the incarnation is then deduced. The devil has no *ius* over the God-man, and by his abuse of his legitimate power, the devil forfeits his *ius* over man.[31]

This position was subjected to a penetrating theological critique by Peter Abailard. While in no way denying that the devil exercised *potestas* over man *de facto*, Abailard insisted that this power was not acquired or administered *de iure*. By seducing man, the devil acquired no rights over man: diabolus in hominem quem seduxit nullum ius seducendo acquisierit.[32] If the devil has any power over sinful man, he possesses it solely by divine permission, in that God has allotted him the function of captor of sinful man in the economy of salvation. Outside the realm of this divine permission, the devil has no rights over man. As the devil does not possess even this limited *potestas* by an absolute right, God is at liberty to withdraw it. A similar position is adopted by Hugh of St Victor, who argues that although man is justly punished by the devil, his dominion over man is held unjustly: iniuste ergo diabolus tenet hominem, sed homo iuste tenetur.[33] The school of Abailard, as might be expected, upheld their master's teaching that the devil had *potestas* over man *de facto* but not *de iure*.[34] Bernard of Clairvaux, an opponent of Abailard on so many matters, concedes that the devil's power over man may be said to be just in that it derives from God, but unjust in that it was usurped by the devil.[35] The classic position characteristic of the later twelfth century is summarised in the teaching of Peter of Poitiers: the devil has no right to punish man, but on account of his sin, man deserves to be placed under his power.[36]

The significance of the critique of the *ius diaboli* lies in the concept of *iustitia* employed to characterise God's dealings with the devil. If *iustitia* is understood to entail the respect of established *ius* – i.e., the situation as it exists *de facto* – then God is obliged to respect the dominion of the devil over man. If *iustitia* is conformity to the divine will, the devil has no *de iure* rights over man, having abused the limited and conditional rights which some theologians were prepared to allow him in the context of the economy of salvation. The general rejection of the *ius diaboli* by the theologians of the twelfth century is therefore of considerable significance in the development of the articulation of the 'righteousness of God'.

A further theological development of significance is associated with Peter Abailard. Throughout his writings, there is an analogical predication to God of the definition of *iustitia* taken directly from Cicero: iustitia virtus est, communi utilitate servata, suam tribuens dignitatem.[37] In effect, it is this concept of *iustitia* which underlies Abailard's rejection of the *ius diaboli*: the devil, by insisting upon more than his due, stepped outside the boundaries of *iustitia*. Although Augustine had earlier subjected the theological application of the Ciceronian concept of *iustitia* to a penetrating critique (see §4), most theologians of the late twelfth century returned to the Ciceronian concept of *iustitia* to clarify the apparently related concept of *iustitia Dei*. The widespread use of the concept within the Abailardian school[38] suggests the influence of Abailard in this respect. While Godfrey of Poitiers followed Stephen Langton in distinguishing three aspects of the term *iustitia*, he appears to have introduced a significant innovation – the opinion that *iustitia reddit unicuique quod suum est* is attributed to *Augustine*.[39] William of Auxerre, the first Summist, distinguished the specifically theological use of the term from its ordinary sense,[40] noting that justice and mercy were not opposed in the former case. Simon of Hinton also reproduces the Ciceronian definition, again attributing it to Augustine.[41] The application of this concept of *iustitia* to the specific matter of justification may be illustrated from the *de virtutibus* of John of La Rochelle:

iustitia est sua cuique tribuens, Deo, sibi, et proximo. De hac etiam dicitur Matth. VI: primum querite regnum Dei et iustitiam eius. Hec est iustitia generalis que iustificatur impius, cuius sunt due partes: declinare a malo et facere bonum. Huius etiam iustitie generalis partes sunt latria, dulia et obedientia.[42]

It will be clear that the justification of man is seen as an act of divine justice, rendering to man his due for his efforts to avoid evil and do good. This understanding of *iustitia Dei* is clearly closely linked to a doctrine of merit, by which the divine justification of man may be rationalised on the basis of justice, understood as *reddens unicuique quod suum est*. It will also be evident that this approach requires reference to the divine equity as much as to the divine justice – i.e., God justifies those who merit it *sine gratia sine fraude sine personarum acceptione*.

A somewhat different approach to the matter is found in the works of Hugh of St Victor. His discussion of justification involves the distinction between *iustitia potestatis* and *iustitia aequitatis*. The former, also referred to as *iustitia secundum debitum facientis*, is such that the agent (i.e., God) is permitted to do anything within his power, provided that it is not unjust. The latter, or *iustitia secundum meritum patientis*, is that which relates to man as the object of the divine justification, and is such that he is permitted to have whatever he is entitled to, irrespective of whether he wants it.[43] Applying these concepts of justice to man's justification, Hugh argues that God is able to justify man justly, although it may reasonably be pointed out that Hugh's definitions of justice lead to the conclusion that whatever God wills for man is just, whether justification or condemnation, by virtue of the power of the divine will.[44]

The middle of the thirteenth century saw the introduction of the Aristotelian concept of justice into the theology of the western church. Thus Albertus Magnus' commentary on Book III of the *Sentences* appears to demonstrate familiarity with Book V of the *Nicomachean Ethics*,[45] while his commentary on Book IV (1249) makes use of a translation of this work for the first time.[46] While this introduction allowed a classification of the various senses which the term *iustitia* could bear, it does not appear to have had a significant effect on the medieval discussion of the 'righteousness of God'. The basic concepts employed remain the same, despite differences in terminology. Of far greater importance is the emergence of a clear distinction between the *intellectualist* and *voluntarist* approaches to the question of *iustitia Dei*, which may be illustrated from the works of Thomas Aquinas and Duns Scotus respectively.

Thomas rejected the opinion that *iustitia Dei* is merely an arbitrary aspect of the divine will. To assert that *iustitia* ultimately depends upon the will of God amounts to the blasphemous assertion that God does not operate according to the order of wisdom.[47] Underlying *iustitia* is *sapientia*, discernable to the intellect, so that the ultimate standard of justice must be taken to be right reason.[48] This intellectualism is particularly evident in Thomas' discussion of the rationale of the salvation of mankind in Christ. For Thomas, the deliverance of mankind through the death of Christ is the most appropriate mode of redemption, and can be established as such on rational grounds. After listing the five reasons which lead to this assertion, Thomas concludes: et ideo convenientius fuit quod per passionem Christi liberaremur, quam per solam Dei voluntatem.[49] Underlying this point is Thomas' critique of a voluntarist interpretation of *iustitia Dei*, according to which God's justice demanded Christ's passion as a *necessary* satisfaction for human sin: iustitia Dei exigebat ut homo a peccato liberaretur, Christo per passionem suam satisfaciente. Thomas argues that human sin counts as *culpa*, and as such must be treated as coming under private, rather than public, law. If God is considered as judge (*iudex*), then he is not at liberty to remit an offence (*culpa*) without satisfaction, as the offence in question has been committed against a higher authority (e.g., the king), on whose behalf the judge is obliged to act. However, as God is the supreme and common good of the universe (*supremum et commune bonum totius universae*), it follows that the *culpa* in question has not been committed against some higher authority than God, but against God himself. And just as it is perfectly acceptable for an individual to forgive an offence against himself without satisfaction, so God may forgive the sinner without the *necessity* of satisfaction.[50] An interpretation of *iustitia Dei* which insists upon the absolute necessity of satisfaction – and Thomas appears to have Anselm of Canterbury in mind – is to be rejected in favour of one by which satisfaction is recognised to be most appropriate to right reason, and *universally* recognised as such by rational beings.

This point becomes clearer when the voluntarist interpretation of *iustitia Dei* is considered. Although the origins of this approach are especially associated with Duns Scotus,[51] it would find its most thorough development in the soteriology of the *via moderna*. Gabriel Biel insists upon the priority of the divine will over any moral structures by declaring that God's will is essentially independent of what is right or wrong; if the divine will amounted to a mere endorsement of what is good or right, God's will would thereby be subject to created principles of morality. What is good, therefore, is only good if it is accepted as such by God:

Nihil fieri dignum est nisi de tua benignitate et misericordia voluntate dignum iudicare volueris, neque enim quia bonum aut iustum est aliquid, ipsum Deus vult, sed quia Deus vult, ideo bonum est et iustum. Voluntas nanque divina non ex nostra bonitate, sed ex divina voluntate bonitas nostra pendet, nec aliquid bonum nisi quia a Deo sic acceptum.[52]

The divine will is thus the chief arbiter and principle of justice, establishing justice by its decisions, rather than acting on the basis of established justice. Morality and merit alike derive from the divine will, in that the goodness of an act must be defined, not in terms of the act itself, but in terms of the *divine estimation of that act*. Duns Scotus had established the general voluntarist principle, that every created offering to God is worth precisely whatever God accepts it for: dico, quod sicut omne aliud a Deo, ideo est bonum, quia a Deo volitum, et non est converso; sic meritum illud tantum bonum erat, pro quanto acceptabatur.[53] The consequences of this principle for the doctrine of merit will be explored in §10. Applying this principle to the passion of Christ and the redemption of mankind, Scotus points out that a good angel could have made satisfaction in Christ's place, had God chosen to accept his offering as having sufficient value: the merit of Christ's passion lies solely in the *acceptatio divina*.

A further development of the medieval discussion of the 'righteousness of God' is also accepted with Duns Scotus. This development is essentially grammatical, and concerns the distinction between *univocity* and *equivocity*: a term is strictly univocal when it signifies the things it represents by means of one concept and one grammatical mode of signification.[54] The earlier medieval theologians had distinguished two main senses of the term *iustitia* – *iustitia distributiva* and *condecentia bonitatis*[55] – permitting *iustitia* and *misericordia* to be correlated within the context of the economy of salvation. The *locus classicus* for this interpretation of the 'righteousness of God' was due to Thomas Aquinas: misericordia non tollit iustitiam, sed est quaedam iustitiae plenitudo.[56] This approach to the matter was precluded by Scotus' insistence upon the univocity of *iustitia*: in Deo non est nisi unica iustitia ... Nullam iustitiam habet nisi ad reddendum suae bonitati vel voluntati, quod eam condecet.[57] Scotus' Aristotelian interpretation of *iustitia Dei*, linked with his insistence upon the univocity of the term, led to a hiatus being imposed between *iustitia* and *misericordia*:[58] the 'righteousness of God' cannot find its expression in man's justification, which must now be seen as an aspect of the divine mercy.[59]

One of the most significant developments in relation to the medieval understanding of the 'righteousness of God' took place within the *via moderna*, and is of particular importance in relation to the developing theology of the young Luther.[60] Gabriel Biel's doctrine of justification is based upon the concept of a *pactum* between God and man (see §11) which defines the conditions which man must meet if he is to be justified, as well as emphasising the divine reliability. The present order of salvation, although radically contingent, is nevertheless totally reliable and strictly immutable.[61] Thus God, having freely and of his *liberalitas* determined to enter into such a binding contract with man, is now obliged to respect the terms of that covenant; deus dat gratiam facienti quod in se est necessitate immutabilitatis et ex suppositione quia disposuit dare immutabiliter gratiam facienti quod in se est.[62]

The establishment of such a reliable moral framework within which justification takes place allows Biel to resolve a difficulty which had previously impeded theologians from applying the Ciceronian definition of *iustitia* directly to God. The Ciceronian, Justinian and Aristotelian concepts of *iustitia* are based upon the notion of a contracting community, the *res publica* or πόλις, which establishes the *iuris consensus*. The direct application of such concepts of *iustitia* to God was rendered problematical by the absence of a theological equivalent to this contractual framework. The postulation of a *pactum* between God and man eliminates this difficulty, the *pactum* effectively functioning as the *iuris consensus* which is required if *iustitia Dei* is to be defined in terms of *reddens unicuique quod suum est.* Furthermore, studies of the medieval discussion of the concept of the divine self-limitation (as expressed in the *pactum*) have demonstrated how the theologians of the period found the terminology of Canon Law – particularly *iustitia* – to be an ideal vehicle for its articulation.[63] Under the terms of the covenant (*pactum*), God is obliged to reward the man who does *quod in se est* with grace *as a matter of justice*, in that he is rendering to him that to which he is entitled. The *pactum* determines *quod suum est*, and specifies the conditions upon which the *viator* may receive it. Biel is able to correlate the divine justice and divine mercy by pointing out that the present order of salvation, to which God is now irrevocably committed as a matter of justice, is ultimately an expression of the divine mercy. *Stante lege*, God is necessarily obliged to reward the *viator* who does *quod in se est* with *quod suum est* – i.e., justifying grace. In his mercy, God established an order of justice to which he is presently and irrevocably bound. Failure on the part of God to honour the pactum would result in his being unjust, which is inconceivable: ita etiam quod stante sua promissione qua pollicitus est dare vitam eternam servantibus sua mandata, non posset sine iniusticia subtrahere eis premia repromissa.[64] It is therefore up to the individual, knowing the divine will, to conform himself to it if he wishes to be justified.[65] It is therefore clear that Biel understands *iustitia Dei* to refer to equity within the context of the *pactum*, by which God has established his dealings with men upon a reliable basis.

It is this understanding of the 'righteousness of God' which is reproduced by Martin Luther in the earlier part of his *Dictata super Psalterium* (1513–15), as may be judged from his scholion on Psalm 9.9 (Vulgate: 10.9):

Iustitia autem dicitur redditio unicuique quod suum est. Unde prior est equitas quam iustitia et quasi prerequisita. Et equitas meriti distinguit, iustitia premiae reddit. Sic Dominus iudicat orbem terrae in equitate (quia omnibus idem est, vult omnes salvos fieri) et iudicat in iustitia, quia reddit unicuique suum premium.[66]

Luther here reproduces the key aspects of Biel's understanding of *iustitia Dei: iustitia* is understood to be based upon divine equity, which looks solely to man's merits in determining his reward within the framework established by the covenant: hinc recte dicunt doctores, quod homini facienti quod in se est, Deus infallibiliter dat gratiam.[67] Luther's theological breakthrough is intimately connected with his discovery of a new meaning of the 'righteousness of God',[68] and it is important to appreciate that his earlier works are characterised by the teaching of the *via moderna* upon this matter.

The second question concerning the 'righteousness of God' raises the whole issue of the analogical nature of theological language. How is it possible to speak of God being 'righteous' (*iustus*)? As we noted earlier (§2), the biblical material upon which the medieval commentators based their exegesis contained a Hebraic concept of the 'righteousness of God', *iustitia salutifera*, which bore little resemblance to the concept of *iustitia distributiva* characteristic of western European thought. As such, it was difficult to argue from human to divine justice, a point which was frequently emphasised by early biblical commentators with reference to the problem of the 'transference of meaning'.[69] Peter Abailard thus urged extreme caution when employing terms borrowed from their everyday context (*translata a consuetis significationis*) in statements concerning God,[70] although he appears to have overlooked his own principle when analogically predicating human concepts of justice to God, as we noted above.

This use of human concepts of justice, applied analogically to God, was criticised by several theologians of the twelfth century, most notably by Alan of Lille. According to Alan, every term which is predicated of God is necessarily transferred from its proper meaning (*transfertur a sua propria significatione*). Recognising that God can only be described as *iustus* by an indirect transference of the term from its proper signification, Alan insists that this transference be understood to refer solely to the word (*nomen*) thus transferred, and not to its signification (*res*):

Deus est iustus, hoc nomen *iustus* transfertur a sua propria significatione ad hoc ut conveniat Deo, sed res nominis non attribuitur Deo.[71]

In other words, the statement 'Deus est iustus' contains the term *iustus* transferred from a particular human context – but the term cannot be allowed to bear precisely the same meaning in this statement as it assumes in that specific human context. Even though the same term *iustus* is predicated by God in the statement 'Deus est iustus' as in the analogical statement 'Socrates est iustus', it cannot be allowed to bear the same signification in each case. On account of its transference from its proper context, the word acquires a 'borrowed meaning'[72] which, although analogous to its original meaning, is not identical with it. Thus divine justice is not the same as human justice, so that the statement 'Deus est iustus' cannot be allowed to have the same point of reference as 'Socrates est iustus'. This leads to the inevitable conclusion that, since the 'borrowed meaning' of *iustus* is unknown, and almost certainly unknowable, the statement 'Deus est iustus' has no meaning. If we do not know precisely what meaning the term *iustus* assumes in the statement 'Deus est iustus', we cannot know what the statement means.[73] Most theologians of the twelfth century thus preferred, like the Benedictine Hugh, Archbishop of Rouen, to seek refuge in the divine incomprehensibility: Deus enim semper est id quod est, qui determinari seu describi vel diffiniri non potest, quia incomprehensibilis est.[74]

The question of how God may be described as *iustus* raises the related question of how his attributes may be discussed. What does it mean to speak of God's wisdom, righteousness, etc.? The rise of the Ockhamist epistemology in the late fourteenth century led to the existence of such attributes being called into question.[75] Henry of Ghent maintained the reality of such divine attributes. If the mental distinction between essence and attributes in God rested upon a comparison with reference to the same qualities in creatures, the existence of the divine attributes would come to be dependent upon creatures – which Henry considered impossible. Therefore the divine attributes must be considered to differ by an internal relation of reason, independent of any intellectual comparison with the same qualities among creatures. Godfrey of Fontaines, however, argued that the basis of the distinction between the divine attributes must be considered to lie in creatures, rather than in God himself. Godfrey, like most of his contemporaries, accepted that the distinction between the divine attributes was purely mental, but insisted that the distinction must originate outside the mind. Whilst Henry located the origin of this distinction in God himself, Godfrey located it within creatures. The distinction between the attributes must rest upon a comparison within the intellect between God himself and the diversity which exists in his creatures, as otherwise God, being supremely simple, would only be conceived as one. The divine attributes, therefore, are contained virtually within the divine essence as the source of all perfection, and are known only by comparison with what approximates to them – i.e., by the recognition on the part of the human intellect of a similarity between God and creature in respect of the quality involved. As such forms and qualities in creatures owe their existence and origin to the divine ideas and their perfection in God, the existence of such a similarity, albeit only to a limited and determinate extent, is to be expected.

By contrast, William of Ockham rejected both opinions. The

distinction between the divine attributes on the part of the human intellect owes nothing either to any such distinction in God himself, nor to any comparison with himself or anything else. According to Ockham, God's attributes, such as his *iustitia*, *misericordia*, etc., cannot be said to correspond to anything real within God himself, but arise purely and simply from the multiplicity of acts of human cognition involved.[76] Thus *iustitia Dei* cannot be allowed to have any real existence within God, as it is a consequence purely of the act of cognition on the part of the human intellect. The only distinction that may be allowed among the divine attributes is that they are different concepts within the human mind: they do not denote a formal distinction within God, nor do they correspond to any distinction *in* him, or *in relation to* him. The concepts involved are neither *really* nor *formally* identical with the divine essence. The fact that such conceptual distinctions are known by the human intellect cannot be allowed to impose such a distinction upon the object of the intellect, so that any diversity which may be posited among the divine attributes cannot be allowed to correspond to a diversity within God himself, but merely to concepts which are distinguished by the intellect. God, as supremely simple, is either apprehended totally, or not at all, and as a consequence his attributes are merely the product of the human intellect. Whereas God is real, his attributes are not (unless, of course, concepts are allowed to be real). The essence of Ockham's important criticism of the real existence of the divine attributes is that they are not founded in being. A twofold distinction must therefore be made:[77]

1. The divine attributes, taken absolutely for the perfection which is God himself.
2. The divine attributes, taken as concepts which can be predicated of God.

If the attributes of God are understood as in (1), there is no real distinction between them; if they are understood as in (2), the attributal distinction is purely mental, and has no foundation in reality. Either way, it makes little sense to speak of *iustitia Dei*, and still less to speak of a tension between *iustitia* and *misericordia* in God.

Ockham's critique of the divine attributes does not appear to have had any real significance upon the later medieval discussion of *iustitia Dei*, which tended to proceed on the assumption that a real distinction could be drawn between *iustitia* and *misericordia Dei*. The problem of defining that 'righteousness', however, proved to be intractable. The medieval period can be characterised by its insistence that God's mercy, righteousness and truth were simultaneously manifested in his salvation of mankind, a point often made in connection with the Christological exegesis of Psalm 85.10 (Vulgate: 84.11):

> Misericordia et veritas obviaverunt sibi,
> Iustitia et pax osculatae sunt.

The theologians of the medieval period were convinced that God's righteousness was expressed in the manner in which he chose to redeem mankind in Christ. The difficulties associated with this understanding of the 'righteousness of God', particularly in connection with the correlation of *iustitia Dei* and *iustitia hominis* were never, however, fully resolved.

§7 The subjective appropriation of justification

The medieval theological tradition followed Augustine of Hippo in insisting that man has a positive role to play in his own justification. Augustine's celebrated *dictum* 'Qui fecit te sine te, non te iustificat sine te'[1] virtually achieved the status of an axiom[2] in the medieval discussion of justification. The definition of the precise nature of this human rôle in justification was, however, the subject of considerable disagreement within the medieval theological schools. The development of the various traditional positions on the question, which forms the subject of the present section, is conveniently discussed under three headings:

1. the nature of the human free will;
2. the necessity and nature of the proper disposition for justification;
3. the origin, application and interpretation of the axiom *facienti quod in se est Deus non denegat gratiam*.

Before considering these three aspects of the appropriation of justification, it is necessary to make two observations. First, it is impossible to discuss the medieval understandings of the subjective appropriation of justification without reference to the rôle of the sacraments in justification, to be discussed in the following section (§8). Second, the medieval discussion of the appropriation of justification is not conducted in terms of the concept of justification *by faith*. Justifying faith is universally understood to be a gift of God bestowed upon man as a consequence of his disposition towards justification. In effect, the possibility of justifying faith being a human work is excluded from the outset. The medieval discussion of the appropriation of justification is primarily concerned with establishing the conditions upon which justifying grace and faith are bestowed upon the individual by God. In the present section, the three aspects of the question of the subjective appropriation of justification identified above will be considered individually.

1 The nature of the human free will

The influence of Augustine upon the medieval discussion of justification is probably at its greatest in connection with the relation between grace and free will. Although the term *liberum arbitrium* is pre-Augustinian and un-biblical (§3), Augustine succeeded in imposing an interpretation upon the term which allowed a profoundly biblical understanding of human bondage to sin and need for grace to be maintained, while simultaneously upholding the reality of human free will. This understanding of the nature of the human free will would be clarified in the course of a series of controversies immediately succeeding Augustine's death, in addition to two during his lifetime – the Pelagian and Massilian controversies.

In essence, Pelagianism must be seen as a reforming movement in the increasingly corrupt world of the later Roman empire, especially critical of the growing tendency to see in Christianity an almost magical way of obtaining salvation in the next world without undue inconvenience in the present. It was primarily against this moral laxity that Pelagius and his supporters protested,[3] apparently unaware that their chief theological opponent shared precisely the same concern. Augustine's account of the origin of the Pelagian controversy relates how Pelagius was outraged by the much-cited prayer from his *Confessions*, 'Give what you command, and command what you will.'[4] To Pelagius, these words suggested that man was merely a puppet wholly determined by divine grace, thereby encouraging moral quietism of the worst order. For Pelagius, moral responsibility presupposed freedom of the will: I ought, therefore I can. The fundamental doctrine of Pelagius' theological system is the unequivocal assertion of the autonomous and sovereign character of the human *liberum arbitrium*: in creating man, God gave him the unique privilege of being able to accomplish the divine will by his own choice, setting before him life and death, and bidding him choose the former – but permitting the final decision to rest with man

71

himself. Pelagius found particularly offensive the suggestion that man's *liberum arbitrium* was diseased, compromised or handicapped in any way, so that it has an inherent bias towards evil-doing. While Pelagius conceded that Adam's sin had disastrous consequences for his posterity, he insisted that these arose by *imitation*, rather than by *propagation*. There is no congenital fault in man, and no special or general influence upon him to perform evil or good. God, having created man, is unable to exert any influence upon him, except through external non-coercive means (i.e., *gratia ab extra*). In part, the confusion surrounding Augustine's controversy with Pelagius arises from the fact that Pelagius appears to understand by *grace* what Augustine understands by *nature*. Thus when Augustine and Pelagius agree that man stands in need of grace, the latter merely means *general* grace, given in the endowment of nature, enabling man to perform God's will with his natural faculties.

The real *locus* of the Pelagian controversy lies in Augustine's doctrine of prevenient grace. Pelagius understands grace as *gratia ab extra*, an external, non-coercive grace of knowledge such as the Decalogue or the example of Christ. A man can, if he so chooses, fulfil the Law of Moses without sinning. It is this concept of grace which ultimately leads to the harsh doctrine of *impeccantia*: as the Law *can* be fulfilled, so it *must* be fulfilled. This 'theology of example' may be seen in both Pelagius' emphasis upon the need for *imitatio Christi* and in the assertion that it is by the *example* of Adam's sin that his posterity is injured. The Pelagian analysis of volition in terms of *posse, velle, esse* is particularly well suited to an exemplarist soteriology: the external example demonstrates the *posse*, thereby stimulating the *velle*.

The Massilian controversy appears to have arisen over Augustine's doctrine of predestination. The term 'semi-Pelagian' is a seriously misleading anachronism which has no place in this discussion.[5] The term 'Massilian' is used by Augustine himself, and eliminates the unjustified comparison with Pelagianism implicit in the term 'semi-Pelagianism'. Augustine described the Massilians as holding doctrines which 'abundantly distinguished them from the Pelagians', which appears to amount to a rejection of Prosper of Aquitaine's description of them as the *reliquiae Pelagianorum*. He notes their chief error to lie in their teaching on predestination.[6] The same cannot be said of Faustus of Riez, who asserted that man's free will was capable of taking the initiative in his salvation. If the term 'semi-Pelagian' is merited by any Massilian, it is by Faustus. Vincent of Lérins appears to have formulated his canon within the specific context of his refutation of Augustine's predestinarianism. The nature of truly catholic doctrine is that it is *quod ubique, quod semper, quod ab omnibus creditum est.*[7] As Augustine's doctrine of predestination failed to conform to this triple test of ecumenicity, antiquity and consent, it cannot be regarded as catholic. A more positive approach to Augustine's teachings is found in the writings of John Cassian. Like Vincent, he rejected the Pelagian doctrine of the free will, apparently accepting Augustine's theology of grace in its entirety, with the specific exception of his doctrines of predestination and irresistible grace.[8] In particular, it may be noted that he appears to have grasped and upheld the Augustinian concept of the dialectic between the *liberum arbitrium captivatum* and *liberatum*: 'He is truly free who has begun to be your prisoner, O Lord.'[9] Cassian's emphasis upon the reality of the human free will has its context in monastic asceticism, with its characteristic emphasis upon the need for exertion in the spiritual life. Cassian wrote primarily for monks, who may be regarded as having been initiated into the Christian life. It may therefore be assumed that when Cassian speaks of grace, he intends *cooperative,* rather than *operative* grace to be understood (to use Augustine's terms). If Cassian appears to be a 'synergist', it is because, like Augustine, he asserts the synergy of grace and free will *after* justification. Furthermore, it may be pointed out that Cassian's emphasis upon *prayer* as a means for improving the spiritual condition is a sign of the *importance* he attaches to grace, rather than of his *rejection* of its necessity, as some have supposed.

The Synod of Jerusalem (July 415) and the Synod of Diospolis (December 415) led to mild censure of Pelagianism, with the influence of Augustine much in evidence. Neither of these Synods can be considered to be significant in comparison with the Council of Carthage (418),[10] whose canons would receive wide acceptance in the catholic church, and feature prominently in medieval discussions of the nature of the Pelagian error. Of these canons, the most important is the fifth, which teaches the impotence of the human free will unless aided by grace, and the further necessity of grace to enable man to fulfil the commandments of the law.[11] The Council of Ephesus (431) condemned both Nestorianism and Pelagianism (this latter in the form associated with Caelestius), although the council does not appear to have recognised the close theological connection between the heresies so ably summarised in Bishop Gore's *dictum,* 'The Nestorian Christ is the fitting saviour of the Pelagian man.'[12]

The most specific attack upon Pelagianism to be found in a fifth century authoritative source is that of the *Indiculus de gratia Dei* (431), usually regarded as the work of Prosper of Aquitaine. Its chapters explicitly reject the Pelagian understandings of the nature of grace and the capabilities of man's free will. A man cannot rise from the depths of Adam's sin unless the grace of God should lift him up.[13] Even after justification, man requires God's grace if he is to persevere.[14] The most important statement of the document relates to the effects of grace upon free will: the *Indiculus* makes it clear that grace *liberates* rather than *abolishes* man's *liberum arbitrium*.[15]

The definitive pronouncement of the early western church on the Pelagian and Massilian controversies may be found in the Second Council of Orange (529). The Council declared that to teach that the 'freedom of the soul' remained unaffected by the Fall was Pelagian.[16] The Faustian doctrine of the *initium fidei* – i.e., that man can take the initiative in his own salvation – was explicitly rejected: not only the *beginning*, but also the *increase* of faith, are alike gifts of grace.[17] While the Council declared that man's *liberum arbitrium* is injured, weakened and diminished, its existence was not questioned.[18] Although the Council declined to teach the doctrines of double predestination and irresistible grace, it must be pointed out that it is questionable whether these may be considered as authentically *Augustinian*, in that they are not *explicitly taught by Augustine*, even though they may appear to *follow logically* from his teaching. If the epithet 'Augustinian' is understood to mean 'conforming to doctrines explicitly taught by Augustine after 396', it may be asserted that Orange II endorses an Augustinian doctrine of justification.

Although it might therefore appear that the medieval period was thus bequeathed an accurate and definitive account of Augustine's teaching on justification, three factors conspired to generate considerable confusion over this matter. It is a curious and unexplained feature of the history of doctrine that the canons of Orange II appear to have been unknown from the tenth to the middle of the sixteenth centuries.[19] The theologians of the medieval period thus did not have access to this definitive statement of an Augustinian doctrine of justification, and appear to have been unaware of its existence. Second, much of Pelagius' work was mistakenly ascribed to Jerome during the medieval period, with the inevitable result that Jerome and Augustine were thought to have radically different theologies of justification. For example, Peter Lombard found himself in some difficulty as he tried to reconcile Augustine's opinion concerning man, *posse peccare et non posse non peccare etiam damnabiliter*, with the affirmation *hominem semper et peccare et non peccare posse*, which he attributes to Jerome's *Explanatio fidei catholicae ad Damasum*.[20] In fact, the Lombard is unwittingly citing from Pelagius' *Libellus fidei ad Innocentium*! Third, many pseudo-Augustinian works were in circulation in the medieval period, frequently teaching a doctrine of justification which owed more to Pelagius or Faustus of Riez than to Augustine.[21] An excellent example is provided by Pelagius' *Libellus fidei*, which we have already noted to have been attributed by some (e.g., Peter Lombard) to Jerome: elsewhere, this same Pelagian work is attributed to Augustine as *Sermo* 191! A further example is provided by the famous maxim *si non es praedestinatus, fac ut praedestineris* ('If you are not predestined, endeavour to be predestined'), to be discussed in §12. Although fourteenth century source-critical studies achieved a certain degree of resolution of these difficulties, the fact remains that the great theological renaissance of the twelfth century would take place without access to the authentically Augustinian teaching of the sixth century church on the relation between grace and free will. This point is of particular importance in connection with the development of the teaching of Thomas Aquinas on the *initium fidei*, which will be discussed further below.

Despite these circumstances, the twelfth century witnessed considerable agreement on the issues of grace and free will. The profession of faith, composed by Leo IX in 1053, contained a clear statement of the relationship between the two: grace precedes and follows man, yet in such a manner that it does not compromise his free will.[22] Anselm of Canterbury defined free will as the power (*potestas*) of preserving the *rectitudo voluntatis*: man, though fallen, still possesses this *potestas*, and can therefore be said to possess *libertas arbitrii*. However, no power is capable of actualising its potential unaided,[23] and if the *potestas* of the human free will is to be reduced to *actus* it must be actualised by God's general or special *concursus*. In effect, Anselm's definition of free will is such that a positive answer to the question of whether man can justify himself is excluded from the outset: as only God can convert *potestas* to *actus*, so only God can justify.

This concept of the divine actualisation of *potestas* found its expression in the thirteenth century doctrine of the *concursus simultaneus*. There was, however, considerable confusion concerning the precise means by which potency was reduced to act: according to some, the agent involved was the Holy Spirit, whilst others considered it to be actual or habitual grace.[24] Later, the axiom *omnis actus perfectus a forma perfecta* would be employed in the discussion of the question.[25] Underlying these developments, however, is the basic conviction, expressed by Peter Lombard in his *Sentences*, that man's *liberum arbitrium* cannot do good unless it is first liberated (*liberatum*) and subsequently assisted by grace.[26] The subsequent confusion concerning the precise nature of the *concursus* unquestionably reflects a corresponding prior confusion concerning the nature of grace itself, so characteristic a feature of early scholasticism (see §9).

The medieval ignorance of the canons of Orange II is of particular importance in relation to the evaluation of the 'Pelagianism' of the teaching on man's *liberum arbitrium* associated with the *via moderna*. We shall illustrate this with reference to Gabriel Biel. The relevance of Gabriel Biel's doctrine of *liberum arbitrium* to the development of Luther's doctrine of *servum arbitrium* has been emphasised,[27] as it is now generally accepted that Luther's *Disputatio contra scholasticam theologiam* (1517) is specifically directed against Biel, rather than against 'scholastic theology' in general.[28] Following the common teaching of the *via moderna*, Biel declines to distinguish man's intellect and will, so that *liberum arbitrium*, *libertas* and *voluntas* are regarded as being essentially identical. This approach to the question leads to a strong assertion of the freedom of the will, as *libertas* is regarded as a corollary of rationality. That the will is free is evident from experience, and requires no further demonstration.[29] For Biel, free will is the power of the soul which allows the *viator* to distinguish and choose between good and evil, by which he is distinguished from other animals.[30] The theological consequences of Biel's doctrine of *liberum arbitrium* may be stated as follows:[31]

1.   The human free will may choose a morally good act *ex puris naturalibus*, without the need for grace.[32]

2.   Man is able, by the use of his free will and other natural faculties, to implement the law *quoad substantiam actus*, but not *quoad intentionem praecipientis*.[33] In other words, man is able to fulfil the external requirements of the law by his own power, but is unable to fulfil the law in the precise manner which God intended.

3.   *Ex puris naturalibus* the free will is able to avoid mortal sin.[34]

4.   *Ex puris naturalibus* the free will is able to love God above everything else.[35]

5.   *Ex suis naturalibus* the free will is able to dispose itself towards the reception of the gift of grace.[36]

It is this final aspect of Biel's teaching on the capacities of fallen man's free will which has claimed most attention, and has frequently given rise to charges of Pelagianism or 'semi-Pelagianism'.[37] These charges are quite without foundation. As Biel himself makes clear, his discussion of man's rôle in his own justification must be set within the context of the divine *pactum*. The requirement of a minimum response on man's part of the divine offer of grace is totally in keeping with the earlier Franciscan school's teaching, such as that of Alexander of Hales or Bonaventure. Biel has simply placed his theology of a minimum human response to the divine initiative in justification on a firmer foundation in the theology of the *pactum* thereby safeguarding God from the charge of capriciousness. Biel's modern critics' surprise at the absence of contemporary criticism of his teaching as Pelagian[38] simply reflects the fact that, by the standards of the time, Biel's doctrine of justification would not have been considered Pelagian. The sole legitimate criteria by which the 'Pelagianism' of Biel's doctrine of justification may be judged are the canons of the Council of Carthage – the only criteria which medieval doctors then possessed, for reasons we have already noted. Biel's high regard for the tradition of the church is such that he accepts whatever the church defined as being *de fide*. Biel's attitude to tradition is such that, had he known of the decrees of Orange II, he would have incorporated their substance into his doctrine of justification as *determinationes ecclesiae*.[39] If Biel's theology is to be stigmatised as 'Pelagian' or 'semi-Pelagian', it must be appreciated that he suffered from an historical accident which affected the entire period up to the Council of Trent itself. If orthodoxy is to be determined with reference to *known authoritative pronouncements of the church*, orthodoxy would undergo a radical change with the rediscovery of these canons. Those who were orthodox by the standards of 1500 – among whom we may number Gabriel Biel! – may no longer have been so by 1550. Biel himself is aware of the decrees of the Council of Carthage, and makes frequent reference to Canon 5 in particular, which he states thus: 'Qui dixerit, quod sine gratia possumus mandata Dei implere per liberum arbitrium, anathema sit.'[40] Biel's careful distinction between the implementation of the law *quoad substantiam actus* and *quoad intentionem praecipientis* ensures his conformity to the teaching of this canon.

It is clear that the charge of 'Pelagianism' or 'semi-Pelagianism' brought against Biel stands or falls with the definition employed. If it is taken to mean that the *viator* can take the initiative in his own justification, the very existence of the *pactum* deflects the charge: God has taken the initiative away from man, who is merely required to

77

respond to that initiative by the proper exercise of his *liberum arbitrium*. However, neither the Pelagian nor Massilian controversies operated with so sophisticated a concept of causality as that employed by the theologians of the *via moderna*, expressed in the *pactum*-theology, so that the application of epithets such as 'Pelagian' to Biel's theology of justification must be regarded as historically unsound. In terms of the historical controversies themselves, Biel must be regarded as totally innocent of both errors.

In general, although the assertion that man possesses the freedom to respond to the divine initiative in justification is characteristic of the medieval period, this consensus was accompanied by widespread disagreement as to the precise nature of the freedom in question, and whether it could be regarded as given in nature or acquired through grace. This point becomes particularly clear in the medieval discussion of the axiom *facienti quod in se est Deus non denegat gratiam*, to which we shall shortly return. Our attention now turns to the medieval opinions concerning a disposition for justification.

2 The necessity and nature of the proper disposition for justification

What happens before the sinner is justified? Is justification preceded by a preparation on the part of the sinner to receive the gift which God subsequently gives him? And if this is the case, is God *obliged* to bestow the gift in question upon the sinner on account of his having prepared himself to receive it? The twelfth century saw a growing conviction that a preparation was required of man for justification. Peter of Poitiers used a domestic analogy to illustrate the rôle of such a preparation for justification. A man may clean out his house and decorate it in order to receive an important guest, so that all will be ready when he arrives. This preparation, however, does not necessitate the arrival of the guest, which depends only upon the guest's love for his host.[41]

The necessity of a preparation or disposition for justification was insisted upon by both the early Franciscan and Dominican schools, although, as we shall demonstrate, for very different reasons. The pre-Bonaventuran Franciscan school demonstrates a certain degree of uncertainty on the question, partly due to a related uncertainty in relation to the concept of created grace. Alexander of Hales may have seemed to limit man's rôle in justification to not resisting grace,[42] but his teaching was developed by John of La Rochelle in a significant direction. John insists upon the need for a disposition for justification

78

in man, in that the recipient of uncreated grace – i.e., the Holy Spirit – is unable to receive it unless his soul has first been prepared for it. The need for such a disposition does not result from any deficiency on the part of God. John draws a distinction between sufficiency on the part of the agent (i.e., God) and on the part of the recipient in justification. God is all-sufficient in justification, but the recipient of uncreated grace must first be disposed for its reception by created grace.[43] Odo Rigaldi likewise distinguished between the gift of the uncreated grace of the Holy Spirit and the disposition of the human soul towards the reception of this gift by created grace.[44] It may be noted that Odo appears unclear as to what created grace actually *is* – he seems to regard it as a hybrid species.[45] This unclarity was resolved by the *Summa Fratris Alexandri*[46] in what appears to have been the first systematic discussion of the nature of created grace. The *Summa* begins by considering the concept of uncreated grace,[47] which transforms the human soul in justification: gratia ponit aliquid in anima. If uncreated grace did not alter the soul in justification, there would be no difference between the justified and the unjustified sinner. Uncreated grace may therefore be considered as the *forma transformans* and created grace as the *forma transformata*.[48] This important interpretation of the nature of created grace points to its being a quality of the soul – i.e., a *disposition*, rather than a *substance*. The Holy Spirit can be said to dwell in the souls of the justified as in a temple: this is impossible unless there is something within the soul which, although not itself the temple, is capable of transforming the soul into such a temple capable of receiving the Holy Spirit.[49] This interpretation of the nature and function of created grace is closely linked with the anthropology of the early Franciscan school, according to which the human soul is not naturally capable of receiving grace. In order for the human soul to receive grace, it must first be disposed to receive it. By contrast, the early Dominican school maintained that *anima naturaliter est gratiae capax*, reflecting a quite different understanding of man's pristine state. The disposition of the human soul for the reception of uncreated grace is understood by the *Summa* to be a quality of the soul brought about by the action of grace, and which may be termed *created grace*. It will, however, be clear that there was still uncertainty as to whether *gratia creata* was to be considered as the *disposition towards the reception of uncreated grace* or the *result of the reception of uncreated grace*.

This basic teaching of the early Franciscan school was developed along psychological lines by Bonaventure.[50] Human nature is sufficiently frail that it is simply incapable of receiving the gift of sanctifying grace unless it is prepared beforehand.[51] This disposition towards justification is effected with the assistance of prevenient grace, *gratia gratis data*, and cannot be effected by the unaided free will.[52] The transition from nature to grace is effected by prevenient grace disposing the human soul to receive the supernatural gift of habitual grace.[53] Matthew of Aquasparta reports the opinion that a preparation for justification is useless and unnecessary, since grace is given to man according to his natural aptitudes and capacities.[54] This opinion is to be rejected, he argues, as being improbable and contrary to experience: man cannot prepare himself for justification without *gratia gratis data*, which moves and excites the will to detest sin and desire justification.[55] Following Bonaventure, Matthew emphasises the frailty of human nature: just as a man cannot look at the sun until he has become accustomed to its brilliance by appropriate preparation, so the free will cannot prepare itself for the light of grace unless itself moved by grace.[56] In effect, actual grace is conceived as a medium between the states of nature and supernature: it is impossible to proceed directly from one to the other, and *gratia gratis data* provides the intermediate position by which the transition may be effected.[57] Richard of Middleton distinguished between a *proximate* and a *remote* disposition towards justification.[58] Man may dispose himself towards his own justification by virtue of his own powers: this disposition, however, is remote, and not an immediate disposition towards justification, which may only be effected through actual grace exciting and illuminating man's mind.[59] It is clear that Richard understands actual grace to refer primarily to a special supernatural motion directly attributable to the Holy Spirit.[60] Unlike habitual grace, no disposition is required for actual grace. Thus Roger of Marston emphasised that the gift of actual grace is the first gift by which God prepares the human will for grace, and does not itself require any preparation for justification.[61]

In general, the strongly Augustinian illuminationism of the early Franciscan school led to a theology of justification in which the necessity of a disposition or preparation towards justification was maintained on the grounds of the frailty of the unaided human intellect. Just as man's intellect was incapable of attaining and comprehending divine truth unless illuminated directly by God,[62] so man's will was incapable of desiring or attaining justification unless similarly illuminated (see §15).

The early Dominican school also taught the need for a disposition for justification, but for quite different reasons. The axiom *naturaliter est anima gratiae capax* is particularly associated with the early Dominican school,[63] and on the basis of this anthropology there would appear to be no *prima facie* case for the necessity of a disposition towards the reception of grace. If man's soul is naturally capable of receiving grace, there would seem to be no compelling reason to posit such a necessity. The early Franciscan school, it will be recalled, posited the necessity of such a disposition on the grounds that a transformation of the natural state of the human soul was required in order for it to be *capax gratiae*. It is therefore important to observe that the theologians of the school, particularly Thomas Aquinas, deduced the necessity of such a disposition *on the basis of the Aristotelian analysis of motion*.[64] Grace, being a form, exists as a disposition in the subject who receives it. Application of the Aristotelian theory of generation to this results in the deduction of a stage of preparation. Albertus Magnus did not develop this question at any length,[65] and it is with Thomas Aquinas that its full statement may be found.

In his *Commentary on the Sentences* (1254–7), Thomas considers the question *utrum homo possit se praeparare ad gratiam sine aliqua gratia*.[66] His answer involves distinguishing two understandings of grace, either as the arousal of man's will through divine providence, or as a habitual gift in the soul.[67] In both cases, a preparation for grace is necessary, in that justification, being a *motus*, requires premotion on the basis of the Aristotelian theory of generation. Omne quod movetur ab alio movetur. Grace, being a form, exists as a disposition in the subject who receives it. How can the human free will be prepared to receive the gift of habitual grace? Thomas points out that the preparation cannot take the form of a second habitual gift, as this would merely result in an infinite regression of habitual gifts: some gratuitous gift of God is required, moving the soul from within.[68] Whilst man is converted to his ultimate end by the prime mover (God) he is converted to his proximate end (i.e., the state of justification itself) by the motion of some inferior mover.[69]

In the *Commentary on the Sentences*, Thomas had treated the premotion required for justification as being external and natural – the examples which he provides of such premotions include admonition by another person, or physical illness.[70] In the later *Quaestiones disputatae de veritate* (1256–9), however, Thomas acknowledges an internal means of premotion, *divinus instinctus secundum quod Deus in mentibus hominum operatur*,[71] although it appears that his most characteristic position remains that man can naturally dispose himself towards the reception of grace. The *Summa contra Gentiles* (1258–64) is generally regarded as marking a turning point in Thomas' teaching on the nature of the preparation for justification. It appears that the pseudo-Aristotelian *Liber de bona fortuna* first came to Thomas' attention during this period,[72] as it is cited for the first time at III, 89 and frequently thereafter.[73] In this work, Thomas described the 'errors of the Pelagians' as lying in the assertion that the beginning of man's justification is the work of man, whilst its consummation is the work of God.[74] The crucial statement which marks Thomas' changed views on the question is the following: 'Matter does not move itself to its own perfection; therefore it must be moved by something else.'[75] Therefore, man cannot move himself to receive grace, but is moved by God to receive it.[76] The *Quodlibetum primum*, dating from the second Paris period, attributes the beginnings of man's justification to an internal operation of God, by which God acts on the will internally to cause it to do good.[77] The essential difference between Thomas' early and mature opinions on the question, as determined from the *Commentary on the Sentences* and the *Summa Theologiae* respectively, is that whilst in both he asserted the need for premotion for the *motus mentis* of justification, the early opinion that the 'inferior mover' causing the premotion was man himself was rejected in favour of the later opinion that the 'inferior mover' was God himself. Man's preparation for justification is thus understood to be a divine work, so that no preparation is required for man's justification which God himself does not provide.[78] The preparation for grace in man is the work of God as the prime mover and of the free will as the passive entity which is itself moved.[79] Thomas' discussion of the justification of man therefore proceeds along thoroughly Aristotelian lines, pre-supposing that there are two unequal stages in the process: the *praemotio* (i.e., the preparation for justification as the proximate end), and the *motus* itself (i.e., the movement from the natural to the supernatural planes, with the infusion of supernatural justice). We have already emphasised the rôle of Aristotelian physics in Thomas' deduction of the *processus iustificationis* (see §5). It may be noted that Thomas understands the priority of the premotion over the motion to be *by nature* and not *in time*: the two may coincide temporally, as in the case of the conversion of Paul.[80]

The later medieval period saw the need for a human disposition towards justification accepted as axiomatic. The disputed aspects of the matter related primarily to the question of whether this disposition was itself a work of grace, or a purely human act performed without the aid of grace. Thus Luther's mentor Johannes von Staupitz affirmed the necessity of a proper disposition for justification, even though he stressed the moral impotence of fallen man and taught gratuitous election *ante praevisa merita*.[81] This brings us to the question of the *nature* of the disposition towards justification, which was practically invariably discussed in terms of the axiom *facienti quod in se est Deus denegat gratiam*. It is to this axiom that we now turn.

3 The axiom 'facienti quod in se est Deus non denegat gratiam'

This axiom is probably best translated as: 'God will not deny grace to the man who does his best.'[82] The essential principle encapsulated in the axiom is that man and God have their respective rôles to play in justification; when man has fulfilled his in penitence, God will subsequently fulfil his part. The theological principle underlying the axiom may be shown to have been current in the early patristic period – for example, it is clearly stated by Irenaeus: 'If you offer to him (i.e., God) what is yours, that is faith in him and subjection, you shall receive his, and become a perfect work of God.'[83] The medieval period saw this axiom become a dogma, part of the received tradition concerning justification. The final verbal form of the axiom can be shown to have been fixed in the twelfth century,[84] an excellent example being provided by the *Homilies* of Radulphus Ardens:

Est ergo, acsi dicat Dominus: Facite, quod pertinet ad vos, quia facio, quod pertinet ad me. Ego facio, quod amicus, animam meam pro vobis ponendo; facite et vos, quod amici, me diligendo et mandata mea faciendo.[85]

It may, of course, be pointed out that the logic underlying Radulphus' version of the axiom is that man should do *quod in se est* because Christ has already done *quod in se est*. In other words, Christ has placed man under an obligation to respond to him. This logic was, however, generally inverted, to yield the suggestion that God's action was posterior, rather than prior, to man's. The idea that man could, by doing 'what lies within him' (*quod in se est*) place *God* under an obligation to reward him with grace is particularly well illustrated from the works of Stephen Langton[86] and others influenced by him. The use of *debere* by an anonymous twelfth century writer in this connection is of significance: si homo facit, quod suum est, Deus debet facere, quod suum est.[87] A slightly different approach to the matter is based on James 4.8: 'Draw near to God, and he will draw near to you.' This was interpreted by some twelfth century theologians, such as Robert Pullen, to mean that man, by drawing near to God, placed God under an obligation to draw near to man.[88]

The relationship between the human penitential preparation for justification and the divine justification of man which followed it was the subject of considerable discussion among twelfth century theologians. In general, the possibility of the preparation for grace being the efficient cause of justification was rejected: most theologians appear to have adopted a solution similar to that of Alan of Lille. According to Alan, man's preparation for justification could be likened to opening a shutter to let sunlight into a room. The act of penitence was the *causa sine qua non* and the *occasio*, but not the *causa efficiens*, of justification:

(Poenitentia) est tamen causa sine qua non, quia nisi homo poeniteat, non dimittitur a Deo peccatum. Sic sol domum illuminat quia fenestra aperitur, non tamen apertio fenestrae est causa efficiens illuminationis, sed occasionalis tantum, sed ipse sol est causa efficiens illuminationis.[89]

In effect, man's preparation for justification may be regarded as the removal of an obstacle to grace (*removens prohibens*). This analysis was placed upon a firmer basis by Hugh of St Cher, who distinguished three aspects of the remission of sin: actus peccandi desertio, maculae sive culpae deletio, reatus solutio. The act of sinning is an obstacle to grace, and man, by ceasing to perform acts of sin, removes this obstacle and thus prepares the way for grace to be infused into his soul:

Desertio actus peccandi habilitat hominem, quo facto ingreditur gratia. Actus enim peccandi obstaculum est gratie. Et loquitur Ambrosius sicut communiter dicitur, quod ille qui aperit fenestram, intromittit solem, id est facit aliquid, quo facto sol ingreditur.[90]

Although only God is able to forgive sin, man is able to set in motion a series of events which culminate in forgiveness of sins by the act of ceasing to perform acts of sin, which lies within his own powers. Man does what is asked of him, and God subsequently does the rest.

The origins of the interpretation of the axiom characteristic of the early Franciscan school can be found with John of La Rochelle. Man cannot dispose himself adequately for grace, so that the required disposition must be effected by God. God will, however, effect this disposition, if man does *quod in se est*. John uses Alan of Lille's analogy of the opening of a shutter to illustrate this point: the opening of the shutter permits the light of the sun to dispel darkness, just as the act of doing *quod in se est* permits the grace of God to dispel sin. Although man does not have the power to dispel darkness, he does have the power to initiate a course of action which has this effect, by opening a shutter and thus remove the obstacle to the sun's rays; similarly, although man does not have the ability to destroy sin, he can remove the obstacles to divine grace, which then effects the required destruction of sin.[91] God continually bestows grace through his generosity, and by doing *quod in se est*, man removes any obstacles in the path of that grace.[92] Odo Rigaldi similarly teaches that grace is given to the man who disposes himself to receive it by doing *quod in se est* – for example, by attrition. The subsequent gift of grace transforms this to contrition, which leads to the remission of sins.[93] Whilst this disposition towards grace cannot be considered to be meritorious in the strict sense of the term (i.e., *de condigno*), it can be considered meritorious *de congruo* (see §10).[94] The *Summa Fratris Alexandri* considers the case of the good pagan, who is ignorant of the Christian faith, and argues that if he does *quod in se est* – which is clearly understood as a purely natural act – God will somehow enlighten him, in order that he may be justified.[95] Man prepares himself for justification by receiving the *dignitas congruitatis* which arises from the proper use of his natural faculties of reason or free will.[96] Similarly, Bonaventure argues that, although *gratia gratis data* stirs the will, it remains within the power of the human free will to respond to or reject this excitation. Bonaventure frequently stresses that God does not justify man without his consent,[97] giving grace in such a way that the free will is not coerced into accepting it.[98]

The interpretation of the axiom within the early Dominican school is somewhat confused, as Thomas Aquinas presents radically different interpretations of the axiom in the *Commentary on the Sentences* and the *Summa Theologiae*. In the *Commentary*, Thomas concludes his discussion of the question *utrum homo possit se praeparare ad gratiam sine aliqua gratia* with a *prima facie* Pelagian interpretation of the axiom: man can prepare himself for justification by virtue of his own natural abilities, unaided by grace.[99] This disposition is meritorious *de congruo*.[100] Thomas emphasised that God is continuously offering his grace to man, and anyone who does *quod in se est* necessarily receives it.[101] In effect, this represents a further development of Alan of Lille's analogy of the opening of a shutter. Philip the Chancellor had earlier applied the Aristotelian categories of material and formal causality to the sun and the opening of the shutter respectively, so that the formal (i.e., the immediate) cause of justification is the human preparation for justification, understood as the removal of obstacles to grace. Thomas is thus able to formalise his causal scheme in Aristotelian terms, further enhancing the Aristotelian cast of his discussion of the doctrine of justification.

Critics of Thomas' early teaching on justification, particularly within the early Franciscan school, pointed out that he allowed a purely natural disposition towards justification, which was clearly contrary to the teaching of Augustine.[102] It is therefore important to appreciate that his mature teaching, as expressed in the *Summa Theologiae* (1266–73), is significantly different. Later commentators frequently emphasised these differences: for example, several fifteenth-century manuscripts refer to *conclusiones in quibus sanctus Thomas videtur contradicere sibi ipso*, or *articuli in quibus Thomas aliter dixit in Summa quam in scriptis sententiarum*, or – more diplomatically! – *articuli in quibus frater Thomas melius in Summa quam in scriptis sententiarum dixit*.[103] Whilst Thomas continues to insist upon the necessity of a preparation for justification, and continues to discuss this in terms of man's doing *quod in se est*, he now considers that this preparation lies outside man's purely natural powers. As he now understands the matter, man is not even capable of his full *natural* good, let alone the *supernatural* good required of him for justification. The preparation for justification is itself a work of grace,[104] in which God is active and man passive. For Thomas, the axiom *facienti quod in se est* now assumes the meaning that God will not deny grace to the man who does his best, in so far as he is moved by God to do this: Cum dicitur homo facere quod in se est, dicitur hoc esse in potestate hominis secundum quod est motus a Deo.[105] It is highly significant that Thomas does not follow the early Franciscan school in applying the axiom to the good pagan in the *Summa*, even where it would be expected at IIa–IIae q. 10 a. 1.[106] Thomas now understands *quod in se est* to mean 'doing what one is able to do when aroused and moved by grace', thus marking a significant departure from his earlier interpretation of the concept. A similar interpretation of *quod in se est* is encountered in the writings of Peter of Tarantaise.[107]

A further development may be noted in relation to Thomas' teaching on the meritorious character of the disposition towards justification. In the *Commentary*, Thomas allows that such a disposition is meritorious *de congruo*.[108] In the later *de veritate*, however, we find an unequivocal assertion that there are no merits save *de*merits prior to justification,[109] a view which finds fuller expression in the *Summa Theologiae*. Although Thomas is prepared to allow that a justified sinner can merit *de congruo* the first grace for another person,[110] he is not prepared to allow the individual's preparation for his own justification to be deemed meritorious, even in this weak sense of the term.[111] Significantly, Peter of Tarantaise – who reproduces Thomas' interpretation of *quod in se est* – declines to follow him in this matter, teaching that the preparation for justification is meritorious *de congruo*.[112] It is thus clear that there was some confusion within the early Dominican school upon this matter.

An examination of the writings of later medieval theologians of the Augustinian Order reveals a lack of agreement concerning the interpretation of the axiom. Thomas of Strasbourg states that the man who does *quod in se est* cannot be regarded as preparing himself for justification: man's rôle in his own justification lies in his consenting to the divine action which is taking place within him.[113] In this he is followed, as in so many other matters, by Johannes von Retz.[114] Thomas is, however, prepared to allow that this disposition towards justification is meritorious *de congruo*.[115] Retz' rejection of the possibility of a purely *natural* disposition for grace is of interest, as it proceeds upon Aristotelian presuppositions. Justification involves a transition from form to matter. Just as a natural form is converted to natural matter by a natural agent, so the conversion of a supernatural form to supernatural matter requires the action of a supernatural agent moving the soul – i.e., divine grace.[116] While the theologians of the Augustinian Order continued the common teaching of the necessity of a disposition towards justification, the older Augustinian theologians were prepared to allow this disposition was meritorious *de congruo*, whereas the theologians of the *schola Augustiniana moderna* tended to exclude this possibility. Thus Thomas Bradwardine, Gregory of Rimini, Johannes Klenkok, Angelus Dobelin, Hugolino of Orvieto and Johannes Hiltalingen of Basel rejected the opinion that the disposition for justification was meritorious *de congruo*.[117] A similar position is associated with Luther's mentor at Wittenberg, Johannes von Staupitz,[118] although his regent of studies at Erfurt, Johannes de Paltz, allowed that such a disposition was meritorious *de congruo*.[119]

The theologians of the *via moderna* adopted a much more positive attitude to the axiom *facienti quod in se est*. Underlying this attitude is the theology of the *pactum*, by which a distinction is to be made between the inherent value of a moral act and its ascribed value under the terms of the covenant between God and man. Just as in today's economic system, paper money has a much greater ascribed value than its inherent value on account of the covenant on the part of the issuing agency or bank to pay the bearer the equivalent sum in gold upon request, so in the Middle Ages the king appears to have been regarded as entitled to issue 'token' coinage, often made of lead, which had a negligible inherent value, but which would be redeemed at its full ascribed value at a later date.[120] In the meantime, the ascribed value of the coins was vastly greater than their inherent value, on account of the promise of the king expressed in the covenant regulating the relationship between the *valor impositus* and *valor intrinsecus*. Such analogies from the economic system of the period lent themselves particularly well to illustrate the important distinction, characteristic of the *via moderna*, between the moral and the meritorious value of an act. Just as a major discrepancy could arise within an economic system between *bonitas intrinseca* and *valor impositus*, given a firm and binding contract on the part of the king, so a similar discrepancy could arise between the moral value of an act (i.e., its *bonitas intrinseca*) and its meritorious value (i.e., *valor impositus*), given a comparable covenant on the part of God. Although human acts have negligible inherent value in themselves by God's absolute standards, he has entered into a *pactum* with man by virtue of which such acts have a much greater contracted value – sufficient to merit the first grace *de congruo*. Just as a king might issue a small leaden coin with negligible inherent value, and a considerably greater ascribed value which permitted it to purchase goods, so man's moral acts, although in themselves incapable of meriting grace, have a much greater contracted value adequate for this purpose.

The essential point emerging from this analysis of the context in which the characteristic interpretation of the axiom *facienti quod in se est* associated with the *via moderna* is set is this: man's disposition cannot be said to cause his justification on account of its own nature (*ex natura rei*), but only on account of the value ascribed to it by God (*ex pacto divino*). This point is made by Ockham, again using the illustration of the king and the small lead coin.[121] A similar analogy is used by Robert Holcot, who pointed out that a small copper coin may buy a loaf of bread, despite the much greater inherent value of the latter.[122] Failure on the part of God to honour his contractual obligation by rewarding the man who did *quod in se est* with grace would amount to a contradiction of the divine nature.[123] While God is not bound by absolute necessity (i.e., *necessitas consequentis*) to act in this way, he has imposed upon himself a conditional necessity (i.e., *necessitas consequentiae*) which he is bound to respect.[124] Gabriel Biel interprets the axiom *facienti quod in se est* to mean that God is under obligation to give the first grace to the man who desists from sin. However, this does not mean that man is capable of remitting his own sin. As Biel emphasises, the link between doing *quod in se est* and the remission of sin is provided by the covenant, rather than the nature of the entities in themselves. Alan of Lille and the early Franciscan school illustrated the axiom with reference to a shutter and the rays of the sun, as noted above: implicit in this analogy is an *ontological* concept of causality (see §§7, 9). The nature of the entities (i.e., the shutter and the sun's rays) is such that the removal of the obstacle permits the sunlight to enter the room. Biel and the *via moderna* operated with a concept of *covenantal* causality, by which the relationship between man's action and the divine response is a consequence of the divine ordination, rather than the nature of the entities in themselves. By the *pactum*, God has graciously ordained that such an act may be accepted as worthy of grace. Biel reproduces the earlier Franciscan teaching, by which man's disposition towards justification may be regarded as removing an obstacle in the path of divine grace:

Anima obicis remotione ac bono motu in deum ex arbitrii libertate elicito primam gratiam mereri potest de congruo. Probatur: quia actum facientis quod in se est Deus acceptat ad tribuendum gratiam primam, non ex debito iustitiae, sed ex sua liberalitate; sed anima removendo obicem, cessando ab actu et consensu peccati et eliciendo bonum motum in Deum tamquam in suum principium et finem, facit quod in se est; ergo actum remotionis obicis et bonum motum in Deum acceptat Deus de sua liberalitate ad infundendum gratiam.[125]

Following the general teaching of the Franciscan schools, Biel holds this disposition towards justification as meritorious *de congruo*. Although man is able to remove an obstacle to grace, Biel insists that it is God, and God alone, who remits sin – but by virtue of the *pactum*, man is able to act in such a manner as to oblige God to respond thus.[126]

The pastoral significance of the axiom may be illustrated with reference to the sermons of Johannes Geiler of Keisersberg, cathedral preacher at Strasbourg from 1478 to 1510.[127] In his exposition of the Lord's Prayer, Geiler stresses that if a man's prayer is to be heard, he must do *quod in se est*. Each of the seven petitions of the Lord's Prayer presupposes that man is already doing what lies within his powers. Thus man prays to God that he might be given his daily bread

– but this presupposes that man does *quod in se est* by cultivating the fields.[128] The same principle is elaborated with reference to Matthew 6.26, which refers to the birds of the air being fed by their heavenly father. Geiler observes that this does not mean that the birds sit on their branches all day, doing nothing: they too must do *quod in se est*, going out early in the morning looking for food.[129] It is therefore only to be expected that Geiler should apply the same principle to man's justification, for which he considers preparation to be essential: 'Fools expect to have this gold without paying for it – that is, without a disposition for grace.'[130] Just as the wind does not enter into a sail until the sailsman first turns the sail directly into the wind, so the wind of the Holy Spirit only enters a soul which has been prepared to receive it. Man must therefore dispose himself towards the reception of grace by doing *quod in se est*.[131] The pastoral orientation of Geiler's sermons is evident from the fact that the axiom is usually expressed in the imperative form: fac quod in te est!

The use of the axiom remained a commonplace in the early sixteenth century, and is encountered in the earlier writings of Martin Luther.[132] Luther's continuity with the *via moderna* is particularly evident in the *Dictata super Psalterium* (1513–15), and may be illustrated from his comments on Psalm 114.1 (Vulgate: 113.1):

Hinc recte dicunt doctores, quod homini facienti quod in se est deus infallibiliter dat gratiam et licet non de condigno sese possit ad gratiam praeparare, quia est incomparabilis, tamen bene de congruo propter promissionem istam dei et pactum misericordiae.[133]

In this, as in so many other respects, the young Luther demonstrated his close affinity with the theology of justification associated with the *via moderna*.

The discussion of the subjective appropriation of justification presented in the above section may have conveyed the impression that the theologians of the medieval period understood justification in purely individualist terms, teaching that justification is solely concerned with the individual *viator* and his status *coram Deo*. This is, in fact, not the case. The medieval discussion of justification proceeds upon the basis of certain explicit presuppositions concerning the community within which this justification takes place. Justification takes place within the sphere of the church, being particularly associated with the sacraments of baptism and penance, so that it is impossible to discuss the medieval understanding of the subjective appropriation of justification without reference to the relationship between justification and the sacraments. The present section, therefore, may be regarded as having dealt with the individualist aspects of the appropriation of justification; the following section, which considers the relation between justification and the sacraments, may be considered to deal with the communal aspects of the appropriation of justification.

§8 Justification and the sacraments

The systematic development of sacramental theology is a major feature of the medieval period, particularly between the years 1050–1240.[1] Associated with this development is the specific linking of justification with the *sacramenta mortuorum*, baptism and penance, and hence with the sacramental system of the church. The earlier medieval writers, such as Cassiodorus and Sedulius Scotus, had identified baptism as the justifying sacrament.[2] The ninth century, however, saw the Anglo-Irish system of private penance become widespread in Europe, with important modifications to the theology of penance following in its wake. Although earlier writers considered that penance could only be undertaken once in a lifetime, as a 'second plank after a shipwreck' (*tabula secunda post naufragiam*),[3] this opinion was gradually abandoned, rather than refuted, as much for social as for pastoral reasons. Thus the eighth-century bishop Chrodegang of Metz recommended regular confession to a superior at least once a year,[4] whilst Paulinus of Aquileia advocated confession and penance before each mass. Gregory the Great's classification of mortal sins became incorporated into the penitential system of the church during the ninth century,[5] so that private penance in the presence of a priest became generally accepted.[6] Penitential books began to make their appearance throughout Europe, similar in many respects to those which can be traced back to sixth-century Wales.[7] The spread of the practice in the Carolingian church appears to have been due to the formidable influence of Alcuin, who has greater claim than any to be considered the founder of the Carolingian renaissance.[8] It is therefore of considerable significance that Alcuin specifically links penance with justification: non dubitamus circa fidem iustificari hominem per poenitentiam et conpunctionem.[9] Associated with this correlation between justification and penance is a maxim which represents a conflation of Ezekiel 18.21 and 33.12: in quacumque hora conversus fuerit peccator, vita vivet et non morietur.[10] The essential feature of this development is that justification is understood to *begin* in baptism, and *to be continued* in penance. A further development of this idea may be found in the works of Rabanus Maurus, who became the leading proponent of private confession in the Frankish church after Alcuin: justification is here linked, not merely with penance, but with sacerdotal confession.[11] The relationship between justification, baptism and penance was defined with particular clarity in the ninth century by Haimo of Auxerre:

Redemptio nostra qua sumus redempti, et per quam iustificamur, passio Christi est quae, iuncta baptismo, iustificat hominem per fidem: et postmodum per poenitentiam. Ita enim illa duo mutuo sunt coniuncta, ut unum sine altero hominem non possit iustificare.[12]

The possibility of constructing a totally sacramental economy of salvation was demonstrated by Bruno of Cologne in the late eleventh century. Like most of his contemporaries, Bruno defined grace in non-ontological terms, understanding it as the remission of sin:

determinat quidem Paulus gratiam Dei, quotquot peccata sint, in baptismo omnia dimittere, sed postquam iustificati sunt, si iterum peccant, non sicut prius ex gratia, sed merito poenitentiae dimittentur peccata.[13]

The emerging understanding of the *processus iustificationis* (see §5) further assisted the integration of justification within the sacramental system of the church. Of particular significance in this respect is the occasional inclusion of a fifth element in the traditional fourfold *processus iustificationis* to allow the direct correlation of justification with the temporal remission of sin.[14]

The relationship between justification and the sacraments of baptism and the sacraments of baptism and penance was to preoccupy most, if not all, of the theologians of the twelfth century. How can infants or imbeciles, who are incapable of any rational act, be justified by baptism?[15] No general solution to the problem may be said to have emerged during the period, at least in part due to the fact that there was a general failure to distinguish between habit, act and virtue. Anselm of Canterbury taught that infants are treated *quasi iusti* on account of the faith of the church.[16] In this, he was followed by Bernard of Clairvaux, who noted that, as it was impossible to please God without faith, so God has permitted children to be justified on account of the faith of others.[17] This was given some theological justification by Peter Manducator, who argued that as children are contaminated by the sins of another (i.e., Adam) in the first place, it is not unreasonable that they should be justified by the faith of others.[18] Peter Abailard was sceptical as to whether an infant was capable of an act of faith: given that this possibility appeared to be excluded, he derived some consolation from the idea that infants who die before maturity are given a perception of the glory of God at their death, so that charity may be born within them.[19] Gilbert de la Porrée is typical of the many who declined to speculate on the mysterious operation of the Holy Spirit, which none could fathom.[20]

The origins of the generally-accepted solution to this difficulty date from the closing years of the twelfth century, with the introduction of the Aristotelian concept of the *habitus*. Thus Alan of Lille, one of the more speculative theologians of the twelfth century, distinguished between *virtus in actu* and *virtus in habitu*.[21] An infant may be given the habit of faith in baptism as the *virtus fidei in habitu*, which will only be manifested as the *virtus fidei in actu* when the child reaches maturity and becomes capable of rational acts. The lack of agreement which characterised the twelfth century is well illustrated from the letter of Innocent III, dated 1201, in which he declined to give any definite positive statements on the effects of baptism, merely noting two possible opinions: (1) that baptism effects the remission of sins; (2) that baptism effects the infusion of virtues as habits, to be actualised when maturity is reached.[22]

Although baptism had been recognised as a sacrament from the earliest of times,[23] the same recognition had not always been extended to penance. Hugh of St Victor had defined a sacrament as a 'physical or material object admitted to the perception of the external senses, representing a reality beyond itself by virtue of having been instituted as a sign of it, and containing within it some invisible and spiritual grace, in virtue of having been consecrated'.[24] It is clear that this definition of a sacrament, which insists upon the presence of a physical element, leads to the exclusion of penance from the list of sacraments. Peter Lombard's definition of a sacrament[25] is therefore as interesting for what it does *not* say as for what it does, as no reference is made to the need for a 'physical or material element from without'. It is this decisive omission which allowed the Lombard to include penance among the seven sacraments – an inclusion which is of major significance to the development of the doctrine of justification within the sphere of the western church.

The necessity of sacerdotal confession for the remission of sins in penance was insisted upon by many of the earlier medieval theologians. Honorius of Autun,[26] Hervaeus of Bourg-Dieu[27] and Bruno of Asti[28] all use the Pentateuchal leper-cleansing ritual to illustrate the need for sacerdotal confession: the sinner's faults are only cleansed when they are confessed before a priest. Just as baptism effects the remission of *original* sin, so confession effects the remission of *actual* sin.[29] This distinction leads to the obvious conclusion that regular confession is to be encouraged, in order to receive absolution. Such exhortations to confession were generally accompanied with an appeal to texts such as Isaiah 45.22, Joel 2.12 or Zechariah 1.3: convertimini ad me, ait Dominus exercituum, et convertar ad vos.[30] It must be emphasised, however, that these exhortations to confession are set within the context of the reconciliation of a lapsed believer, a justified sinner who wishes to be restored to fellowship within the church, and are not capable of a Pelagian interpretation. They refer to the restoration of justification, rather than its inception – i.e., the second rather than the first justification, to use the terms of a later period. The use of such texts, and the maxim *in quacumque hora*, noted above, indicates a growing awareness of the association of the recovery of justification with the sacrament of penance, which involves the confession of sin, penance and absolution. It may be noted, however, that there was no general agreement upon the necessity of *sacerdotal* confession: in the twelfth century, for example, the Abailardian school rejected its necessity, whilst the Victorine school insisted upon it.[31]

The integration of justification within the context of the sacrament of penance was greatly assisted by two developments. First, the general acceptance of Peter Lombard's *Sentences* as the basis of theological discussion during the thirteenth century led to justification being discussed with reference to the *locus* of distinction seventeen of the fourth book of the *Sentences* – i.e., within the specific context of the sacrament of penance. Second, the development of the *processus iustificationis* (see §5) had led to contrition and remission of sins being identified as its third and fourth elements respectively – both of which could be correlated with the sacrament of penance. The justification of the sinner was therefore explicitly linked with the sacramental system of the church. This connection may be regarded as having been unequivocally established through the decrees of the Fourth Lateran Council (1215), which laid an obligation upon believers to confess their sins to their priest annually:

Omnis utriusque sexus fidelis, postquam ad annos discretionis pervenerit, omnia sua solus peccata saltem semel in anno fideliter confiteatur proprio sacerdoti, et iniunctam sibi poenitentiam pro viribus studeat adimplere.[32]

The early discussion of penance involved the distinction of three elements: contritio cordis, confessio oris, satisfactio operis.[33] It seems

94

that the earlier medieval discussion of the matter led to the greatest emphasis being placed upon the third element, satisfaction – an observation which is of considerable importance in connection with Anselm of Canterbury's understanding of the incarnation of the Son of God. For Anselm, the satisfaction-merit model provided by the penitential system of the church of his time provided a suitable paradigm for the divine remission of sin through the death of Christ, which his readers would have accepted as just.[34] By the early twelfth century, however, the emphasis appears to have shifted from satisfaction to contrition, with increasing emphasis being placed upon the inner motivation of the penitent, rather than on his external achievements made as satisfaction for sin. Thus Peter Abailard defined *poenitentia* in purely psychological terms: dolor animi super ea, in quo deliquit, cum aliquem scilicet piget in aliquo excessisse.[35] His respect for tradition is such, however, that he does not deny the *de facto* necessity of both confession and satisfaction, subject to qualification on account of possible mitigating circumstances.[36] This contrition-ism was developed by Peter Lombard, who stressed that contrition was the sole precondition for forgiveness: the function of the priest in the sacrament of penance was purely declarative, in that he merely certifies that the penitent has been justified and reconciled to the church.[37]

The precise relationship between justification and penance was the subject of considerable debate during the twelfth century. Peter of Poitiers drew attention to a possible misinterpretation of the relationship between the two: as man can lose the first grace through sin, and subsequently have it restored through penance, it might appear that the first grace can be merited by penance. Peter rejected this interpretation on the basis of its failure to recognise that man can only *regain* the first grace in this manner: it is only the man who has already received *gratia prima* who can be justified again by penance.[38] Simon of Tournai argued that whilst prayers and alms qualify man for becoming good, they cannot be said to make man good in themselves – man only becomes good through the grace of God.[39] Penance, apart from grace, does not justify. Alan of Lille similarly emphasised the unmerited character of grace in his discussion of the relation between justification and penance: the true efficient cause of justification is not penance,[40] as might be thought, but the gracious will of God.[41] Penance is merely the *occasio* and *conditio sine qua non* of justification (see §7). However, it will be clear that the location of any type of cause of justification within the penitent is of significance, in that it naturally leads to the discussion of the nature of the act or disposition required of the penitent if justification is to occur. It is for this reason that the establishment of the triple order of *contritio cordis*, *confessio oris* and *satisfactio operis* within the sacramental system of the church[42] is of such importance, as it allows the necessary steps for the justification of the penitent to be definitely established, in order that the penitent may be assured that he *has* been justified. The psychological aspects of the sacrament of penance must not be overlooked.

The classic medieval representation of the three steps leading to penitential justification may be found in Dante Aligheri's *Purgatorio*. As the poet awakes from his dream, he finds that he has been carried up to the gate of purgatory, before which lie three steps which he must first climb:

> Là ne venimmo; e lo scaglion primaio
> bianco marmo era sì pulito e terso,
> ch'io mi specchiai in esso qual io paio.
> Era il secondo tinto più che perso,
> d'una petrina ruvida ed arsiccia
> crepata per lo lungo e per traverso.
> Lo terzo, che di sopra s'ammassiccia,
> porfido mi parea sì fiammeggiante
> come sangue che fuor di vena spiccia.[43]

The three steps represent the three penitential elements, which Dante presents in the different order of confession, contrition and satisfaction. As the poet faces the first step of polished white marble, he sees himself reflected as he really is, and so is moved to recognise, admit and confess his sin. The second step is black, cracked in the shape of a cross, symbolising the contrite heart, whilst the third, redder than blood spurting from a vein, symbolises Christ's atoning death, to which must be added the satisfaction of the penitent if it is to be made complete.

The most important criticism of the 'contritionist' understanding of penance, associated with Peter Lombard, is due to Duns Scotus. If contrition is required as a necessary disposition for the reception of sacramental grace, the role of the *sacrament* of penance is called into question. If justification through the sacrament of penance is contingent upon an antecedent disposition of contrition, the sacrament can no longer be said to be effective *ex opere operato*, but only *ex opere operantis*.[44] The alternative, according to Scotus, is 'attritionism'. Attrition is essentially repentance for sin based on fear of punishment, whilst contrition is a repentance for sin grounded in a love for

God.[45] According to Scotus, the sinner may be justified in two possible ways:

1. He may be attrite to a sufficient degree to merit grace *de congruo*.
2. He may be attrite to a minimal extent (*parum attritus*) which, although inadequate to merit justifying grace *de congruo*, is sufficient to effect justification *ex pacto divino*, as mediated through the sacrament of penance.

It will be clear that the first alternative is of major importance, as it allows the possibility of *extrasacramental justification*. If the attrition is of sufficient intensity, God informs it by grace, converting it to contrition *directly* by the extrinsic denomination of the *acceptatio divina* (see §10, 13) and thereby effectively bypassing the sacrament of penance. In the second alternative, Scotus defines the concept of *parum attritus* as not placing an obstacle in the path of sacramental grace (*non ponere obicem*) through the avoidance of mortal sin – a teaching which has frequently been criticised for its moral laxism.[46] This device allows the *ex opere operato* efficacy of the sacrament of penance to be maintained. Whereas Thomas Aquinas integrated contrition within the sacrament of penance, thus effectively excluding the possibility of extrasacramental justification, Scotus allows for this possibility by means of an attrition of sufficient intensity to merit *de congruo* its conversion to contrition, and thus to merit the first grace. It may be noted that the two modes of penitential justification are essentially the same, the difference lying in the fact that they are mediated through different secondary causes. Both presuppose, and are based upon, the divine acceptation.

Scotus' doctrine of the *parum attritus* appears to challenge the medieval consensus concerning the inability of the *viator* to know with absolute certainty whether he is in a state of grace: if he can assure himself that he is *parum attritus*, he may rely upon the *ex opere operato* efficacy of the sacrament to assure himself that he is in a state of grace.[47] Although Scotus does indeed state that a greater degree of certitude may be achieved by this mode of justification than by the extrasacramental mode,[48] he does not retract or qualify his specific magisterial rejection of the possibility of certitude of grace made elsewhere.[49] It must therefore be assumed that Scotus did not intend to teach the absolute certitude of grace in this matter.

Scotus' position was criticised by many of his contemporaries and successors, particularly by Gabriel Biel.[50] Biel insisted that justification by perfection attrition (i.e., Scotus' extrasacramental mode of justification) must always be taken as implying the intention of confession, and is therefore implicitly linked with the sacrament of penance.[51] In this, Biel appears to be reverting to a principle established by the early Franciscan school, that the intention to confess (*propositum confitendi*) is an integral element in the definition of true penance: a man cannot be truly penitent if he does not wish to confess his sins to a priest. Biel does not exclude the possibility of *pre*-sacramental justification, but declines to allow that this may be considered to be 'extra-sacramental', a second path to justification apart from the sacrament of penance.[52] It will be evident, however, that Biel's emphasis upon the need for contrition in penance lays him open to the same charge which Scotus earlier directed against Peter Lombard – that sacramental efficacy is thence defined *ex opere operantis* rather than *ex opere operato*. Biel himself avoids this difficulty by stating that the *viator* is able, through the use of his own natural faculties, to elicit an act of love of God for his own sake, on the basis of which the infusion of *gratia prima* takes place. It must be emphasised that this act of love of God for his own sake is to be set within the context of the sacrament of penance, even though Biel observes that it is not necessary, in principle, for justification and sacramental absolution to coincide in time: man's reconciliation to the church *must* be effected through the sacrament of penance, which is therefore necessarily implicated in justification. In effect, Biel appears to be saying that man's presacramental justification must be declared *in foro ecclesiae* by sacramental absolution before it can be deemed to be justification.[53] Like the earlier Franciscan school, Biel anchors justification to the sacrament of penance by means of the *propositum confitendi*.[54] A further criticism which Biel directs against Scotus' doctrine of the *modus meriti de congruo* (as he terms Scotus' extrasacramental mode of justification) is that it is based upon an act of attrition, whose intensity, degree and duration are unknown to anyone, and are not specified by Holy Scripture: as such, it is therefore impossible to be sure that the correct act has been performed for the correct duration.[55] Biel rejects the idea of a fixed duration and intensity on the part of the penitent, insisting upon the need for *amor amicitie super omnia propter Deum* in its place. It will be clear that this doctrine is essentially an extension of Biel's interpretation of *facienti quod in se est* from the *first* justification to the *second* justification. *De potentia ordinata* God is obliged to reward the man who does *quod in se est* with grace, an obligation which exists as much in regard to the sacrament of penance as to the bestowal of the first grace. As Biel pointed out, we do penance, not so that God 'would change his judgement in response to our prayer, but so that by our prayer we might acquire the proper disposition and be made capable of obtaining what we request'.[56]

An attack of a somewhat different type was, however, developed during the fifteenth century, with potentially significant consequences for the sacramental economy of salvation. The Vulgate translated the inauguration of Christ's preaching, 'Repent (μετανοεῖτε), for the kingdom of God is at hand' (Mark 1.14), as follows: 'Do penance (*poenitentiam agite*), for the kingdom of God is at hand.' The double reference of the Latin *poenitentia* (i.e., it can mean 'repentance' or 'penance') served to establish a link between the sinner's inward attitude of attrition and the sacrament of penance. The rise of the new critical philology in the Quattrocento called this link into question. Thus Lorenzo Valla challenged the Vulgate translation of New Testament texts such as the above.[57] In this, he was followed by Desiderius Erasmus, whose *Novum instrumentum omne* (1516) reproduced Valla's challenge to the Vulgate translation of μετανοεῖτε. Thus in the 1516 edition, Erasmus translated the Greek imperative as *poeniteat vos* ('be penitent'), and in the 1527 edition as *resipiscite* ('change your mind'), further weakening the link between the inward attitude of repentance and the sacrament of penance. The full significance of this philological development would, however, only be appreciated in the first phase of the Reformation of the sixteenth century, and did not pose a serious challenge to the correlation of justification and the sacraments in the late medieval period.

In conclusion, it may be stated that the medieval period saw the justification of the sinner firmly linked to the sacramental life of the church, a sound theological link having been established between justification and the sacraments.[58] This linking of justification to the sacramental system of the church has profound theological and pastoral consequences, of which the most important is the tendency to assert *iustificatio extra ecclesiam non est*.[59] Although the theologians of the medieval period were aware that God was not bound by the sacraments, the tendency to emphasise the reliability of the established order of salvation, of which the sacramental system is part, can only have served to convey the impression that the sinner who wishes to be reconciled to God must, *de facto*, seek the assistance of a priest. The explicit statement of the sacramental economy of salvation may be regarded as complete by the thirteenth century, and to have survived the only serious theological attack to be made upon it during the medieval period. The Psalmist exhorted his people to 'enter his gates by confession': the theology of the medieval period ensured that the only manner in which God's gates could be entered was through the sacraments of baptism and penance.[60]

§9 The concept of grace

The earlier medieval writers tended to conceive grace primarily in Augustinian terms, including elements such as the restoration of the divine image, the forgiveness of sins, regeneration and the indwelling of the Godhead.[1] In the present section, we are particularly concerned with three aspects of the development of the concept of grace which are of importance to the overall scheme of the development of the doctrine of justification. These are:

1. The development of the concept of the supernatural in the articulation of the nature and the effects of grace.
2. The distinction between *gratia gratis data* and *gratia gratum faciens*.
3. The distinction between operative and cooperative grace.

We shall consider these points individually. Before this is possible, however, a serious difficulty in terminology must be noted. The terms *gratia gratis data* and *gratis gratum faciens*, used extensively in this section, and elsewhere in this study, are conventionally translated as *actual grace* and *sanctifying grace*. These translations are, in fact, anachronisms, dating from the post-Tridentine period. *Gratia gratis data* is probably better translated as *prevenient grace*, although even this is not totally satisfactory. In view of the widespread tendency to translate *gratia gratis data* as 'actual grace', and the absence of any generally accepted alternative, however, we feel we have no alternative but to continue this practice, having drawn attention to its deficiencies.

The emergence of the concept of the supernatural[2] is associated with the late twelfth century. The theologians of the earlier medieval period had generally been content to assert that grace is a gift of God, which cannot be merited, and appealed to the cognate relationship of the terms *gratia*, *gratis* and *gratuita* in support of this contention. It will be clear that his discussion of the nature of grace merely postponed the inevitable question which could not be ignored: what is the relation of God's grace to his other gifts? Grace is indeed the free gift of God – but are *all* of God's gifts to be identified as his grace? In other words, is the characteristic feature of grace to be located purely in the fact that it is freely bestowed by God? The eleventh and twelfth century discussions of this question made it clear that a careful and systematic distinction between *naturalia* and *gratuita* was required if confusion was to be avoided.[3] The distinction which required elucidation was between *datum* (i.e., that which is already given in nature) and *donum* (i.e., the subsequent and additional gift of grace). As we have noted, confusion over precisely this point prevailed during the Pelagian controversy (see §7).

The first instance of a systematic distinction between *datum* (i.e., nature) and *donum* (i.e., grace) may be found in the ninth century, with Scotus Erigena.[4] Scotus makes a clear distinction between the natural and supernatural orders: donum gratiae neque intra terminos conditae naturae continetur neque secundum naturalem virtutem operatur, sed superessentialiter et ultra omnes creatas naturales rationes effectus suos peragit.[5] Of particular importance in this respect is Scotus' explicit reference to *gratia supernaturalis* in this context.[6] Phrases indicating that the realm of grace was increasingly conceived in supernatural terms – e.g., *supra naturam* or *ultra naturam* – are encountered with increasing frequency in the following centuries.[7] The first major step towards the definition of the concept of the supernatural may be regarded as having been taken by Simon of Tournai, who argued that the *datum* is the purely natural, whilst the *donum* is the purely spiritual:

Datis autem subsistit homo, quod est et qualis est naturaliter; donis vero qualis est spiritualiter. Ex datis ergo contrahit naturalem; ex donis, spiritualem.[8]

This attempt to define the nature of grace in terms of the dialectic between the natural and the spiritual did not, however, really meet the problem. Similar remarks may be made concerning Peter of Poitiers' attempt to define the distinction between *naturalia* and *gratuita* in terms of their origins:

Naturalia dicunt illa quae habet homo a nativitate sua, unde dicuntur naturalia, ut ratio, ingenium, memoria, etc. Gratuita sunt illa quae naturalibus superaddita sunt, ut virtutes et scientiae; unde etiam dicuntur gratuita, quia a Deo homini per gratiam conferuntur.[9]

Whilst it is impossible to point to any single theologian who may be credited with making the crucial distinction between nature and supernature in defining the essence of grace, it would seem that if anyone is entitled to this claim, it is Praepositinus of Cremona.

Standing at the dawn of the thirteenth century, Praepositinus argued that there must be a higher order than nature itself, and deduced its existence from considerations such as the following. Reason is the highest thing in nature, yet faith must be considered to transcend reason. Therefore faith must be regarded as transcending the natural, being itself something which is beyond nature (*supra naturam*).[10] This distinction can also be applied to the virtues. For example, in his polemic against the teaching of Hugh of St Victor, William of Auxerre distinguished a purely natural *amor amicitiae erga Deum* from a meritorious love for God.[11] On the basis of such considerations, William argued for two distinct orders of being. Even though there is a tendency here to define grace purely in terms of the meritorious, it is clear that significant progress towards the classic definition of supernature has been made. The turning point in achieving this definition appears to have been due to Philip the Chancellor, who distinguished the natural order from the 'more noble' supernatural order: to the former belong reason and natural love, to the latter faith and charity.[12] This important distinction allowed justification to be resolved into a twofold operation.

1. The natural: grace operates on the will, effecting its moral goodness.

2. The supernatural: grace effects the meritoriousness of human acts, raising them from the purely natural plane to that of the supernatural.

In one sense, it could be argued that this is not a new development at all, for these effects of justification had been generally accepted since the time of Augustine. Philip's achievement, however, is to distinguish the two aspects of justification in terms of two levels of being, thereby removing much of the confusion surrounding the matter. Whilst the theologians of the earlier twelfth century tended to define grace in terms of merit, the theologians of the closing years of the century generally regarded merit as the consequence of the transference of an act from the natural (i.e., morally good) to the supernatural (i.e., meritorious) plane, in a transition effected by grace. This distinction, once made, became generally accepted: thus Thomas Aquinas stated that 'when someone is said to have the grace of God, what is meant is something supernatural (*quiddam supernaturale*) in man which originates from God'.[13]

The earlier medieval period was characterised by confusion concerning the various manners in which grace could be understood. Peter Lombard drew a distinction between *gratia gratis dans* (i.e., the uncreated grace which is God himself) and *gratia gratis data* (i.e., the grace of justification).[14] This latter concept, however, was clearly ill-defined, and it became a task of priority to clarify what was meant by the term. Bonaventure noted the general tendency to conceive grace in the broadest of terms, and demonstrated the advantages of restricting the term to *gratis gratis data* and *gratum faciens*.[15] The distinction between *gratia gratis data* and *gratia gratum faciens* appears to have been established by the dawn of the thirteenth century, although confusion in relation to the terms employed is frequently encountered. In broad terms, *gratia gratum faciens* came to be understood as a supernatural habit within man, while *gratia gratis data* was understood as external divine assistance, whether direct or indirect. Initially, this clarification took place by cataloguing the senses in which *gratia gratis data* could be understood. For example, Albertus Magnus distinguishes the following eight senses of the term:[16]

1. rational nature and its powers;
2. natural moral goodness;
3. Adam's supernatural gifts prior to the Fall;
4. imperfect movements towards salvation;
5. inspiration, thaumaturgy and similar gifts;
6. the assistance of the angels;
7. the indelible character received in the sacraments of baptism and confirmation;
8. the divine *concursus*.

Although Bonaventure concludes that the divine *concursus* should be excluded from this list,[17] the concept of *gratia gratis data* is still conceived in the broadest of terms:

Vocatur hic gratia gratis data, quidquid illud sit, quod superadditum est naturalibus, adiuvans aliquo modo et praeparans voluntatem ad habitum vel usum gratiae, sive illud gratis datum sit habitus, sicut timor servilis, vel pietas aliquorum visceribus inserta ab infantia, sive sit etiam aliquis actus, sicut aliqua vocatio vel locutio, qua Deus excitat animam hominis, ut se requirat.[18]

It would seem that the general concept which underlies Bonaventure's catalogue of instances of *gratis gratis data* is that of anything which prepares or disposes man towards the gift of *gratia gratum faciens*. A similar degree of ambiguity is evident from the earlier writings of Thomas Aquinas. Thus Thomas uses the term *gratia gratis data* in a flexible manner, apparently regarding the concept as being beyond meaningful definition.[19] In contrast, the concept of *gratia gratum faciens* appears to have been relatively well characterised by this point.[20] Further confusion, however, existed concerning the distinction between operative and cooperative grace,[21] an important feature of Augustine's theology of justification (see §4). We shall illustrate this point with reference to the developing insights of Thomas Aquinas on this matter.

It is important to appreciate that Thomas Aquinas' understanding of both the nature and the operation of grace underwent considerable development during his lifetime. In his early discussion of grace in the *Commentary on the Sentences*, Thomas poses the following question, to answer it in the negative: utrum gratia sit multiplex in anima?[22] The reply given to this question illustrates his early confusion concerning the concept of actual grace. A distinction may be made between grace and the virtues: if grace is to be identified with these, it must follow that there are many graces, which is impossible. Although it might appear that the distinctions between prevenient and subsequent, operative and cooperative grace seem to point to the multiplicity of grace, these distinctions in fact merely reflect the various effects of the one grace. In other words, the distinction between *gratia praeveniens* and *subsequens*, *operans* and *cooperans*, are purely notional and not real. Grace produces in us a number of effects, and the multiplicity of the effects of grace does not necessitate the deduction of a multiplicity of graces. The effect of operative grace is to produce a good will within man, and that of cooperative grace to actualise this good will in a good performance – which amounts to an exact restatement of the teaching of Augustine on this matter. Thus internal acts are to be attributed to operative grace, and external acts to cooperative grace. This understanding of grace may be summarised as follows:

Gratia
- *formaliter*
  - *operans* (making man acceptable to God)
  - *cooperans* (making man's deeds acceptable to God)
- *effective*
  - *operans* (making man's will desire good)
  - *cooperans* (actualising man's good will in good deeds)

This simple division of grace, based simply upon the distinction between the formal and effective aspects of operative and cooperative grace, is of particular significance in that the entire analysis of the nature of grace proceeds without reference to *gratia gratis data*!

In his discussion of the matter in the later *de veritate*, a slightly different question is posed: utrum in uno homine sit una tantum gratia gratum faciens?[23] In his answer to this question, Thomas makes an important and explicit distinction between *gratia gratis data* and *gratia gratum faciens*, the former being more a loose catalogue of various possibilities rather than a precise catalogue, and is hence evidently multiple. *Gratia gratum faciens*, however, is something quite different. If this type of grace is understood as referring to every aspect of the divine will, such as good thoughts or holy desires, it is clearly multiple. This simple admission of the multiplicity of *gratia gratum faciens* represents a clear and significant development in Thomas' theology of grace. In his earlier *Commentary on the Sentences*, Thomas had insisted upon the simplicity of *gratia gratum faciens*, whilst conceding the multiplicity of its effects. The multiplicity of the division of graces is purely notional, reflecting the effects of the one *gratia gratum faciens*. Thomas now appears to introduce a distinction between the habitual gifts of grace, and grace understood as the effects of the gratuitous will of God. This more complex division may be summarised as follows:

$$
\text{Gratia}
\begin{cases}
\text{understood as a gratuitous} \\
\text{effect of the divine will}
\begin{cases}
\textit{operans} \text{ the justification} \\
\qquad \text{of man} \\
\\
\textit{cooperans} \text{ making man's deeds} \\
\qquad \text{acceptable to God}
\end{cases} \\
\\
\text{understood as a habit,} \\
\text{within the human soul}
\begin{cases}
\textit{operans} \text{ making man's will} \\
\qquad \text{desire good} \\
\\
\textit{cooperans} \text{ actualising man's} \\
\qquad \text{good will in good} \\
\qquad \text{deeds}
\end{cases}
\end{cases}
$$

Here the distinction between formal and efficient causality is retained, but is transferred from the distinction between the external and internal operation of grace (see above) to the distinction between *operation* and *cooperation*. Thus, on the basis of Thomas' statements in *de veritate*, the habitual gift of grace may be said to act as follows:

$$\textit{Gratia} \text{ (understood as a habit)} \begin{cases} \textit{formaliter} \rightarrow \textit{operans} \\ \\ \textit{effective} \rightarrow \textit{cooperans} \end{cases}$$

This has the important consequence of excluding the possibility of operative grace acting *efficiently*, which Thomas had upheld in the *Commentary on the Sentences*. It is clear, however, that the distinction between the formal and efficient causality of habitual grace leads to consequences which are merely distinct at the *notional* level, whilst the distinction between formal and efficient causality in the case of grace, understood as an effect of the divine will, leads to consequences which are distinct *in fact*. This clearly marks a significant departure from the Augustinian understanding of the distinction between operative and cooperative grace – indeed, it seems that Thomas is so dissatisfied with Augustine's understanding of the concepts that he practically abandons them. Whereas Augustine taught that operative grace excites the will to desire good, and that cooperative grace subsequently actualises this good will in good deeds, Thomas now explicitly teaches that *cooperative* grace both excites the will to good desires and also externalises this in external action. This opinion would, however, soon be abandoned.

Thomas' mature discussion of the nature and divisions of grace, as presented in the *Summa Theologiae*, is of particular interest. Thomas' attempt to correlate Augustine's teaching on the relation between good will and good performance, which first appeared in the *Commentary on the Sentences*, only to be rejected in *de veritate*, makes its reappearance in the *Summa Theologiae*, although in a significantly modified form. The Augustinian distinction between operative and cooperative grace, originally introduced in a polemical context to meet the Pelagian distinction between good will and good performance, was simply inadequate to convey the metaphysical aspects of the matter which Thomas considered to be important. Thomas introduces the distinction between *actus interior voluntatis* and *actus exterior voluntatis* to express the substance of Augustine's earlier distinction.[24] Grace is now understood either as a habit or a motion, both of which may be either operative or cooperative. Such is man's frailty that, once in a state of habitual grace, he requires a continual and unfailing supply of actual graces (note the deliberate use of the plural) if he is to grow in faith and charity. The new understanding of the divisions of grace may be represented as follows:

Gratia {
  Motus {
    operans: moves the will to interior action
    cooperans: moves the will to exterior action
  Habitus {
    operans: justifies man
    cooperans: functions as the principle of meritorious action

Habitual grace is *operative*, in so far as it heals man's wounded nature and justifies him, rendering him acceptable to God; and *cooperative*, in so far as it is the basis of man's meritorious action. Grace, understood as *motus*, operates on man's will in order that it may will good – in this matter, God is active and the free will passive. Grace, understood as *motus*, then cooperates with the will to achieve the good act itself. In this matter, the will is active, and may be said to cooperate with grace. The most important point which may be noted concerning this new interpretation of the nature and divisions of grace is that actual grace is now assigned a definite role in man's justification.

It is clear that Thomas' changing views on the nature and divisions of grace are complex and difficult to follow. It is therefore important to identify any underlying factors which may explain the leading features of these changes. The decisive alteration which appears to underlie Thomas' changing views on the nature and divisions of grace appears to be his growing pessimism concerning man's natural faculties, which we noted earlier (§7) in relation to Thomas' teaching on the nature and necessity of man's preparation for justification. In his early period, Thomas regarded a preparation for justification as necessary, yet possible without the assistance of grace. As such, the concept of *gratia gratis data* had no significant role to play in man's justification. In his later period, Thomas taught that the beginning of man's conversion must be seen as an internal operation of grace,[25] thus necessitating the implication of *gratia gratis data* prior to man's justification. Further, in his early period, Thomas appears to have regarded man's natural capacities to be such that, once justified, no further assistance in the form of grace was required: *gratia gratum faciens* alone is treated as being *gratia operans et cooperans*.[26] Thomas cited with approval Averroës' statement to the effect that the possession of a habit allows the will to be transformed to action spontaneously.[27] Thomas, while conceding that man is far from perfect, appears to have considered this deficiency to be remedied by the possession of habitual grace. This conclusion is confirmed by two additional considerations. First, the further interference of God in man's life is to be rejected as amounting to a violation of man's dignity. Second, the mere external action of God would not bring about any permanent change in man. Divine action may make a particular action good, but it fails to bring about any fundamental alteration within man himself. Man would remain as deficient after this external intervention as he was before it, and so a means of grace is to be rejected in favour of an internal change within man, which is articulated in terms of the habitual gift of *gratia gratum faciens*. Thomas' discussion of the same point in *de veritate* suggests that he is no longer content with this understanding of the nature of habitual grace. No matter how perfect the habit may be, man is sufficiently frail that he requires the continual assistance of further divine graces functioning as *gratia cooperans*[28] – i.e., acting on man who is already in a state of habitual grace. No habit or set of habits is sufficiently efficacious to make man's operation truly good,[29] as God alone is capable of perfect action. Thomas makes it clear that he now regards man as requiring actual grace before and after his conversion: the internal change wrought within him by the habit of created grace requires further supplementation by external graces.

It is thus fair to suggest that Thomas' developing understanding of the divisions of grace reflects his new insights into man's impotence, which we noted earlier in relation to man's disposition for justification (see §7).

The development of the concepts of *gratia gratis data* and *gratia gratum faciens* in the later medieval period is shrouded in obscurity at present, as it is not clear how the precise relationship between the habit of created grace and the extrinsic denomination of the divine acceptation was understood in the fourteenth and fifteenth centuries.[30] We shall return to this question in connection with the related question of the formal principle of justification, to be discussed in §13. We conclude the present section by summarising the classic Thomist understanding of the nature and divisions of grace, as stated in the *Summa Theologiae*. Grace may be defined according to whether it is *actual* or *habitual*, and according to whether it *operates* upon man, or *cooperates* with him. Actual grace, *gratia gratis data*, may be conceived as a series of transient effluxes of divine power or influence, given over and above the realm of nature, which impinge upon man's will in order to incline it or assist it to particular actions.

The earlier distinction between *prevenient* and *subsequent* grace must therefore be understood to apply only to *actual* grace. Quite distinct from this is habitual or sanctifying grace, *gratia gratum faciens*, which takes the form of a permanent habit of the soul, infused into man by God, and which may be considered to amount to a participation by man in the divine being. Although permanent in the individual who has been justified, the habit may be lost by mortal sin, and must be regained in penance. The combination of these categories leads to four main categories of grace:

Actual operative: this grace inclines man's will to desire good, and operates without the need for a response from man.

Actual cooperative: this grace assists the renewed will to actualise its good intentions in the form of external actions, and requires the cooperation of the will.

Habitual operative: this is the formal principle of justification within the Thomist understanding of the process.

Habitual cooperative: this is the formal principle of merit within the Thomist system, and requires man's cooperation.

It is to the question of merit that we now turn.

§10 The concept of merit

The medieval discussion of merit may be regarded as based upon Augustine's celebrated maxim: si ergo Dei dona sunt bona merita tua, non Deus coronat merita tua tanquam merita tua, sed tanquam dona sua.[1] When God crowns man's merits, he merely crowns his own gifts to man, rather than some attribute of man which it is obliged to acknowledge, respect and reward. The early Latin fathers, prior to the Pelagian controversy, do not appear to have considered merit to involve any real claim on the part of man to divine reward on the basis of his efforts.[2] Merit appears to have been understood simply as a divine gift to the justified sinner, relating to the bestowal of eternal life, rather than of the first grace, and based upon divine grace rather than upon divine justice or an obligation arising from the nature of merit in itself. Non debendo enim sed promittendo debitorem se Deus fecit.[3] Despite the semantic associations of the Latin term *meritum* (see §2), the early use of the term appears to have been quite innocent of the overtones of 'works-righteousness' which would later be associated with it.

The theological renaissance of the eleventh and twelfth centuries saw several developments of decisive importance in connection with the concept of merit. Of these, the most significant is the shift in the context in which merit was discussed. For Augustine, the purpose of man's temporal existence was 'to win the merit by which we may live in eternity'.[4] The context in which Augustine's doctrine of merit is set is clearly that of the final gaining of eternal life, rather than of man's initial justification. When God 'crowns his merits', he does so, not by *justifying* man, but by bestowing upon him *eternal life*. For Augustine, merit both presupposes and expresses grace. The eleventh and twelfth centuries, however, saw the question of merit discussed within a quite different context – the gratuity of *gratia prima*. Is man capable of meriting his initial justification? The fact that this question was universally answered in the negative[5] is at least in part a consequence of the Augustinian background to the early medieval discussion of merit, in that merit is *per definitionem* a consequence of grace.

The Augustinian interpretation of merit as *gratis pro gratia* can be illustrated from many works of the eleventh and twelfth centuries,[6] but is particularly associated with Gilbert de la Porrée (sometimes referred to as 'Gilbert of Poitiers') and his school,[7] among whom we may number Cardinal Laborans, Odo of Ourscamp, Alan of Lille and Radulphus Ardens. The axiom 'Christus solus meruit' is of particular importance in this connection, as it summarises the opinion, characteristic of the *Porretani*, that only Christ may be said to merit anything in the strict sense of the term.[8] The systematisation of theological discourse during the twelfth century, however, led to a growing realisation that the strict sense of merit as *meritum debitum* was quite inadequate to deal with the spectrum of meanings of the term if the utter gratuity of justification and the necessity of a human disposition or preparation for justification were to be simultaneously upheld (see §7). It can be shown that a distinction came to be drawn between the concepts of *merit* and *congruity*: while man cannot be said to merit justification by any of his actions, his preparation for justification could be said to make his subsequent justification 'congruous' or 'appropriate'. Thus a manuscript source of the late twelfth century makes a clear distinction between the two concepts' digno, dico, non dignitate meriti, sed dignitate congrui.[9] The sense which is clearly intended here is that of a congruity which cannot be considered meritorious in the strict sense of the term. This concept of merit appears to have found its most important application in connection with the question of whether Mary can be said to have merited to bear the saviour of the world.[10] The answer given to this question was that Mary could not be thought of as having merited this distinction in the strict sense of the term, although it was appropriate or congruous that she should have been favoured in this manner. The concept of *meritum congruitas* or *meritum interpretativum* thus passed into general circulation, being understood as a form of merit in the weakest sense of the term. This distinction between merit in the strict sense of the term and it its weaker sense of 'propriety' passed into the theological vocabulary of the thirteenth century as the concepts of *meritum de condigno* and *meritum de congruo*. Although these precise terms can be shown to have been used occasionally in the late twelfth century,[11] they do not always bear precisely the same meaning as they would in later periods. Furthermore, the concept of congruous merit, which was initially used chiefly in connection with the question of the propriety of Mary's bearing the saviour of the world came to be used increasingly in a quite distinct context – that of the meritorious character of man's disposition towards justification (see §7). Thus whenever a theologian of the twelfth century concedes merit prior to justification, the 'merit' in question is not merit in the strict sense of the term, but *meritum de congruo*.[12]

The concept of congruous merit has been the subject of considerable criticism on the part of Protestant historians.[13] For Adolf von Harnack, the concept represented the total disintegration of the Augustinian doctrine of grace. It is, of course, possible to sustain this extravagant thesis with reference to certain theologians of the *via moderna*. Thus Durandus of St Pourçain appears to have regarded *meritum de congruo* as *meritum ante gratiam*:[14] the sole difference between *meritum de congruo* and *meritum de condigno* is that the former exists prior to grace, and the latter subsequent to it. However, an analysis of the origins of the concept, and the intentions which underlie it, conspire to invalidate such criticism. In particular, three points may be noted.

1. The pastoral intention of the concept cannot be overlooked.[15] Although man has no claim to justification on the basis of divine justice, he may look towards the divine generosity and kindness for some recognition of his attempts to amend his life in accordance with the demands of the gospel. It may be pointed out that the concept of a disposition towards justification which is meritorious *de congruo* is particularly associated with the Franciscan Order and the school of theology which came to be associated with it. The pastoral emphasis upon God's kindness towards sinful mankind finds its appropriate expression in the concept of congruous merit.

2. The human activity, which counts as the disposition towards justification, must be regarded as being already set within the context of grace.[16] Even in the later *via moderna*, the axiom *facienti quod in se est Deus non denegat gratiam* (see §7) is always understood as an expression of and a consequence of divine grace. Those theologians who taught that man could prepare himself for justification in a manner which was meritorious *de congruo* invariably insisted that this be understood as a consequence of divine grace. Man's justification must be seen as a divine *gift*, rather than as a divine *reward*.

3. The theologians of the period explicitly taught that man required the assistance of actual grace before he is capable of disposing himself *proximately* towards justification, although they might concede that man is capable of disposing himself *remotely* towards justification through the proper exercise of his natural unaided faculties. Those theologians who held that a proximate disposition towards justification was meritorious *de congruo* thus presupposed the implication of *gratia gratis data* (and not merely the *concursus generalis*) in effecting this necessary disposition.

The concept of condign merit was employed to express the notion of a self-imposed obligation upon the part of God to reward man's efforts. The notion of obligation, which is essential to the concept of merit *de condigno*, may be detected in the early twelfth century. Peter the Chanter explicitly implicated the notion of obligation in his definition of merit: mereri est de indebito debitum facere.[17] In this, he was followed by Alan of Lille, who listed four elements essential to true merit, the fourth being of particular importance:

Ad hoc enim, ut aliquis proprie dicatur aliquid mereri, quattuor concurrunt: ut opus quod agit eius proprie sit; ut apud alium mereatur; ut apud talem qui potestatem habet remunerandi; ut de indebito fiat debitum.[18]

The notion of *de indebito debitum facere* is taken up by theologians of the early thirteenth century, such as Stephen Langton[19] and Godfrey of Poitiers,[20] and is stated with particular clarity by William of Auvergne, who defines merit thus:

meritum ergo proprie et rectissima diffinitione obsequium est retributionis obligatorium, hoc est quod recipientem sive illum, cui impenditur, retributionis efficit debitum.[21]

Merit may therefore be defined as an act performed by man which places God under obligation to him. It must be pointed out, however, that this obligation on the part of God is usually understood to arise as a consequence of his gracious decision to allow himsef to be placed under obligation to man in this manner.[22] A similar definition of merit may be shown to have characterised the writers of the early Franciscan school, such as Odo Rigaldi[23] and Bonaventure,[24] as well as the first Summist, William of Auxerre.[25]

The introduction of Aristotelian physics had a pronounced and profound effect upon the early Dominican school. We have already noted the considerable influence of Aristotelian physics upon Thomas Aquinas' teaching upon the nature of justification (see §5) and the necessity of a disposition for justification (see §7). It can be shown that Aristotelian considerations also exercised a considerable influence upon the early Dominican school's teaching on merit. Roland of Cremona defined merit thus: mereri est motum ex virtute gratuita et libero arbitrio elicere in via militiae; et aliquem mereri sibi est motum virtutis pro se elicere.[26] The essence of merit is here understood to lie in its being a *motus* intermediate between man's initial state and the final state of eternal life. In this, we can see the beginnings of the tendency, which would become particularly clear in the writings of Thomas Aquinas, to conceive merit *ontologically*, rather than in terms of a personal obligation of God to the individual Christian. Whereas the earlier medieval theologians had understood merit to refer essentially to the obligation of God towards man, the theologians of the early Dominican school tended to understand merit in terms of ontological participation in the divine nature itself. This may be contrasted with the teaching of the early Franciscan school, which retained the older personal understanding of merit.[27]

A significant feature of the medieval understanding of condign merit is that merit and its reward are understood to be proportionally related. Thus Roland of Cremona states that merit *de condigno* is not called merit *de digno* precisely because the initial 'cum' indicates the association between the merit and its reward: ipsum autem cum adiungitur ibi ad notandum associationem meriti cum praemio.[28] This idea can be found stated with particular clarity in the writings of Odo Rigaldi[29] and Bonaventure.[30] Of considerable significance is the assertion, first clearly encountered in the writings of William of Auxerre, that the relation between merit and reward can be established as a matter of *of justice*.[31] This aspect of the matter is taken up by Thomas Aquinas: unde sicut reddere iustum pretium pro re accepta ab aliquo, est actus iustitiae; ita etiam recompensare mercedem operis vel laboris, est actus iustitiae.[32] Thomas, however, emphasises that the term 'justice' is used in this context in a sense significantly different from its normal use.

Although merit *de condigno* is often referred to as 'true' merit, to distinguish it from merit *de congruo*, it must be appreciated that Thomas understands neither type of merit to represent a just claim on man's part before God. Justice, in the strict sense of the term, can only exist among equals. Just as Aristotle excluded animals and gods from his concept of justice on the grounds that there existed too great a dissimilarity between them and men to allow their inclusion in the contracting political community, so Thomas argues that there is too great a dissimilarity between man and God to allow anyone to speak of man having a 'just' claim before God. 'It is obvious that there is the greatest inequality between God and man, for they are infinitely different, and all of man's good comes from God.'[33] Thus one cannot speak of *iustitia secundum absolutam aequalitatem* in this context, but only of *iustitia secundum proportionem quandam*. Although one can speak of justice and merit in terms of the relationship between God and man, it must be appreciated that merit in this context must be understood as merit on the basis of *iustitia secundum praesuppositionem divinae ordinationis*, rather than on the basis of *iustitia secundum absolutam aequalitatem*. The merit in question is thus merit *secundum quid* – a merit before God which is essentially distinct from all human merit. Merit before God is based upon a divine ordination according to which he will reward a particular work with a specified reward. God cannot be thought of as man's debtor – if God is in debt to anyone, he is in debt to himself, as he has ordained that he will reward such acts in this manner.[34] Merit arises from grace, in that God can be said to bestow quality upon his creatures in an act of grace. Merit is therefore not based upon strict justice, but upon *iustitia secundum quid*, 'a sort of justice', which is based upon God's decision to reward his creatures. In effect, Thomas develops Augustine's principle, that merit is based upon the divine promise, to the effect that *all* merit before God is 'improper' merit, in the sense that it is not based upon strict justice between equals.

It is possible to distinguish between an *intellectualist* and a *voluntarist* approach to the relation between the moral and the meritorious. The former, which is particularly associated with the theologians of the twelfth century and the early Dominican and Franciscan schools, recognises a direct correlation between the moral and the meritorious value of an act, the transition between the two being effected by grace or charity. This relationship is frequently indicated by the use of terms such as 'comparabilis', 'associatio', 'aequiparari' or 'proportionalis'. While there was general agreement that the merit of an act *coram Deo* was a consequence of God's graciousness and liberality in accepting it as such, rather than its inherent value, there was division between the early Dominican and Franciscan schools on whether this merit was to be conceived *ontologically* or *personally*. Although the intellectualism of the early Franciscan school stands in contrast to the voluntarism of the later Franciscan school, an essential continuity between the schools is demonstrated in their mutual tendency to conceive merit in *non-ontological categories*.

The voluntarist position is particularly associated with the later Franciscan school and the *via moderna*. Its fundamental and characteristic feature is the recognition of a discontinuity between the moral and the meritorious realms, the latter being understood to rest entirely upon the divine will itself. For Scotus, every created offering is worth exactly what God accepts it for, and nothing more: dico, quod sicut omne aliud a Deo, ideo est bonum, quia a Deo volitum, et non est converso: sic meritum illud tantum bonum erat, pro quanto acceptabatur.[35] The meritorious value of an act need therefore have no relation to its moral value, as it rests upon God's estimation alone. This position is developed with particular clarity in the works of William of Ockham, and we shall illustrate it with reference to these.

For Ockham, the decision as to what may be deemed to be meritorious or demeritorious lies entirely within the scope of the divine will, and no reference whatsoever need be made to the moral act in question. There is a fundamental discontinuity between the moral value of an act – i.e., the act, considered in itself – and the meritorious value of the act – i.e., the value which God chooses to impose upon the act. Moral virtue imposes no obligation upon God, and where such obligation may be conceded, it exists as the purely contingent outcome of a prior uncoerced divine decision. This aspect of Ockham's teaching has been the subject of considerable criticism, as it appears to suggest that the relation between the moral and the meritorious domains is purely arbitrary.[36] Although Ockham insists that an act can only be meritorious if it is performed in a state of grace,[37] it appears that he regards this as merely a *conditio sine qua non*, secondary in importance to the divine acceptation.[38] For Ockham, an act can only be meritorious *de potentia ordinata* (see §11) if it is performed in a state of grace – but the meritorious *value* of that act is determined solely through the divine will. God is not bound by the moral value of an act, but is free to impose whatever meritorious value upon that act which he may deem appropriate. The relationship between the moral and meritorious values of an act is purely contingent, a consequence of the divine will, and not merely a necessary consequence of the nature of the act itself which God is obliged to respect. Ockham's concept of *covenantal causality* (see §13) necessitates his rejection of an *ex natura rei* causal relationship between the moral and meritorious realms. Ockham uses the dialectic between the two powers of God (see §11) to demonstrate that *de potentia absoluta* an act which is now deemed meritorious might have been demeritorious, even though precisely the same act is involved in each case.[39]

Ockham's discussion of the nature of congruous merit is of particular significance, as it appears to underlie the criticisms of Thomas Bradwardine and Gregory of Rimini directed against the 'modern Pelagians'. According to Ockham, God rewards virtuous acts performed outside a state of grace with congruous merit.[40] However, Ockham insists that this 'merit' carries with it no claim to eternal life, which arises only on account of merit *de condigno*.[41] All that Ockham intends to convey by the notion of congruous merit is that man is capable of acting in such a way that God may bestow upon man a habit of grace – which, as we noted earlier, is the general understanding of the concept at the time. The *function* of the concept within the context of Ockham's soteriology is that it forms the necessary (understood as *necessitas consequentiae*, rather than *necessitas consequentis*) bridge between the states of nature and grace, and between the moral and theological virtues. It is often asserted that Ockham's optimism concerning man's abilities leads him into Pelagianism or 'semi-Pelagianism': it may, however, be pointed out that Ockham's optimism concerning man relates solely to his *moral* capacities, and that the radical discontinuity which Ockham recognises between the moral and meritorious values of an act means that man's moral abilities are largely irrelevant, as the ultimate grounds of merit lie outside of man, in the extrinsic denomination of the divine acceptation. As we have pointed out, the meritorious value of an act lies in the divine estimation of that act rather than in its inherent moral value. Ockham's theology of merit allows him to take a favourable view of man's moral capacities, while at the same time totally destroying the theological foundation upon which man's acts might be considered as capable of meriting grace or eternal life. It is one of the most brilliant aspects of Ockham's theology of merit that he permits man's moral acts to have a considerable inherent moral value, while simultaneously establishing that the moral value of an act is irrelevant in determining its meritorious value, by locating the *ratio meriti* in the extrinsic denomination of the *acceptatio divina*. It will be clear that Ockham's teaching on this matter has been subject to a considerable degree of misrepresentation and misunderstanding, both by his contemporaries and by his modern critics.[42]

Of Ockham's contemporary critics, his fellow Englishman Thomas Bradwardine may be singled out for particular comment. Bradwardine totally rejected the concept of congruous merit prior to grace,[43] insisting that merit was the consequence of grace: unless the tree is itself good, it cannot bear good fruit. A similar position is associated with Gregory of Rimini.[44] In response to the opinion which was more associated with Ockham's followers than with Ockham himself, that man can merit justification *de congruo* by an act of contrition,[45] Gregory denies that contrition is a possibility apart from grace. A rather different, and somewhat startling, approach to the question is associated with John Wycliffe, the later English follower of Bradwardine.[46] Wycliffe totally rejected the concept of *condign* merit, even after the bestowal of grace, on the grounds that the concept implied that God rewarded man's acts *de pura iustitia*, as if they were entirely performed by man himself without the assistance of divine grace. Wycliffe defines congruous merit as merit which arises through God rewarding those human acts which result from the influence of divine grace – and hence altogether excludes the concept of condign merit from consideration:

Et est duplex meritum, scilicet de congruo et de condigno: de congruo quando aliquis meretur de pura gracia premiantis, ut puta, quando premians prevenit cooperando omne meritum merentis ... de condigno autem dicitur quis mereri, quando meretur de pura iusticia ab alico premiante, quod fuit quando premians non graciose coagit cum illo.[47]

Unlike Bradwardine, who conceded both congruous and condign merit after justification, Wycliffe conceded *only* congruous merit, and that *only after* justification. A similar position is associated with Huss,[48] who pointed out that *pura iustitia* implied an equality between God and man which simply did not exist, except in the form of *equalitas proportionis*:

Qui ergo dicunt, quod non potest homo mereri vitam aeternam de condigno, attendunt equalitatem quantitatis; qui autem dicunt, quod homo potest mereri de condigno attendunt equalitatem proporcionis.[49]

It is therefore impossible for man to merit eternal life *de condigno*, even when in a state of grace: non potest pura creatura de condigno

117

mereri vitam eternam.[50] It is instructive to recall that Thomas Aquinas made a similar observation concerning the concept of *iustitia* implied by the concept of condign merit, but did not feel that the 'secundum quid' character of the resulting merit was sufficient reason to reject the concept. The criticisms of Wycliffe and Huss appear to be direct against a misunderstanding or misrepresentation of the nature of condign merit which does not correspond to the teaching of any of the theological schools of the period, in that the existence of a proportional relationship between an act and its reward was not held to imply an equality between man and God.[51]

The later *via moderna* may be regarded as continuing the teaching of Ockham on the nature of merit. Gabriel Biel emphasised that the concept of congruous merit is based upon the divine liberality rather than the divine justice. Man's disposition towards justification is regarded as meritorious *non ex debito iusticie sed ex sola acceptantis liberalitate*.[52] As we have noted above, it is clear that the teaching of the *via moderna* concerning congruous merit was criticised in certain quarters as exhibiting Pelagian tendencies. It is therefore of particular interest to note the defence of the doctrine provided by the noted early sixteenth-century Tübingen exegete Wendelin Steinbach. Steinbach points out how the early church was confused concerning the concept of merit, but that the concept was now sufficiently well understood to avoid a Pelagian misunderstanding of the concept of congruous merit: et tamen hodie non est absonum dicere, quod peccator mereatur bonis operibus de genere vel impetret de congruo a Deo iustificari et graciam sibi infundi.[53]

The continuity between the late medieval and Reformation periods may also be demonstrated from John Calvin's teaching concerning the merits of Christ. The later Franciscan school, the *via moderna* and the *schola Augustiniana moderna* regarded the *ratio meriti* as lying in the divine good pleasure; nothing was meritorious unless God chose to accept it as such. This teaching was extended to include the work of Christ: the *merita Christi* were regarded as being grounded in the *acceptatio divina*. There are excellent reasons for suggesting that Calvin himself encountered such a teaching during his formative Paris years.[54] It is therefore of some considerable interest that Calvin reproduces the essential features of this late medieval understanding of the *ratio meriti Christi*. This point can only fully be appreciated by considering the *Institutio* of 1559 (II.17.1–5), a section which is based upon an exchange of letters between Calvin and Laelius Socinus. In 1555, Calvin responded to questions raised by Socinus concerning the merit of Christ and the assurance of faith,[55] and appears to have incorporated these replies into the 1559 *Institutio* without significant modification. In the course of this correspondence, Calvin's strongly voluntarist understanding of the *ratio meriti Christi* becomes apparent. Although the evident similarity between Calvin and Scotus on this question has been noted in the past,[56] it has not been fully appreciated that Scotus merely marks a point of transition in the medieval discussion of the question of the *ratio meriti*, so that the main theological schools of the fourteenth and fifteenth centuries adopted a similarly voluntarist understanding of the criterion of merit. In other words, there has been a tendency in the past to assume that this similarity between Scotus and Calvin *reflects the specific influence of Scotus* upon Calvin, whereas it actually reflects a more general influence of later medieval theology. Calvin insists that 'apart from God's good pleasure, Christ could not have merited anything': nam Christus nonnisi ex Dei beneplacito quidquam mereri potuit.[57] Christ's work is meritorious *pro nobis* for the simple reason that God has ordained that it will be so, and accepted it as such. The fact that Calvin's discussion of the *ratio meriti Christi* is continuous with that of the *via moderna* suggests that Calvin encountered such an opinion at Paris, perhaps through the influence of John Major. Whatever the historical explanation of this continuity with later medieval thought may be, however, it serves to indicate that there is a closer relationship between late medieval theology and that of the Reformation than many have realised.

§11 The dialectic between the two powers of God

From the discussion of merit presented above, it will be clear that the concept of God being under an obligation to justify man if he does *quod in se est* is a commonplace in the later medieval discussion of justification.[1] But in what sense may God be said to be under an *obligation* to man? Is not this a compromise of the divine freedom and omnipotence? It is this question which forms the context of the dialectic between the two powers of God, which is one of the most important and most frequently misrepresented aspects of the late medieval discussion of justification, and which we propose to discuss in the present section.

The problem identified above is recognised by Augustine, who presented the outlines of a solution which would be taken up and developed by the theologians of the medieval period, particularly by those of the *via moderna*. For Augustine, the divine *obligation* to man arises purely from the divine *promises* made to man: non debendo enim, sed promittendo debitorem se deus fecit, id est non mutuo accipiendo.[2] If God is under any obligation to man, it is as a consequence of his non-coerced decision to place himself under such an obligation by means of his promises to mankind. We have already noted the significance of the divine promises to man in relation to Augustine's understanding of *iustitia Dei* (see §§4, 6). It is clear that Augustine understands the concept of divine obligation to man as an expression of the divine sovereignty, as it demonstrates God's ability to limit his own course of action.[3] This point was taken up and developed during the theological renaissance of the twelfth century, but assumed a new significance in the thirteenth century as a consequence of Averroist determinism. Thus Thomas Aquinas points out that, while God is omnipotent, there are many things which he could do which he wills not to do. From an initial set of possibilities, limited only by the condition that the outcome must not involve contradiction, God willed to actualise a specific subset. In that God could have willed a different subset of possibilities, and was not coerced in his selection, the subset selected for actualisation cannot be regarded as resulting from absolute necessity. However, in that God has chosen to act in this particular manner, the subset of unwilled possibilities must be considered to be set aside as only hypothetically possible.[4] These two sets of possibilities represent the two spheres of the power of God. God's *absolute* power refers to the initial set of possibilities which are open to divine actualisation, which is limited only by the condition that their actualisation does not involve contradiction. Of these initial possibilities, only a small number are selected for actualisation. Their actualisation results in the present order as we know it, the realm of God's *ordained* power. This realm represents the subset of possibilities which God chose to actualise – and having chosen them, he abides by them. Thus there is no absolute necessity for God to choose any particular course of action within the context of the ordained order; however, having chosen to establish the present order, God is under a self-imposed obligation to himself to respect it. Such considerations underlie the important distinction between *necessitas consequentis* (a necessity which arises through the inherent nature of things) and *necessitas consequentiae* (a necessity which arises through the establishment of a contingent order of existence). This important distinction between an *absolute* necessity and *self-imposed conditional* necessity is of vital importance to a correct understanding of the medieval discussion of justification.

The thirteenth century saw the rise of Averroist determinism at Paris, posing a serious threat to the concept of the divine freedom. Among the propositions which were condemned at Paris in 1277 were several which denied or seriously questioned the omnipotence and freedom of God.[5] According to Siger of Brabant, God *necessarily* produces everything which proceeds directly from him.[6] The essential problem which these opinions raises may be stated in terms of two propositions:

1.   God is free, and not bound by any external factors in his action.
2.   God acts *reliably* in his dealings with mankind.

The Averroist controversy made it a matter of urgency to develop a conceptual framework within which both these propositions could be maintained simultaneously. In its original form, the dialectic between the two powers of God was conceived as a solution to this dilemma, and is particularly associated with Henry of Ghent and Duns Scotus. For Scotus, the divine freedom may be upheld in connection with his primordial decision as to which of the possibilities open to initial actualisation would subsequently be actualised. God's freedom in this respect is demonstrated by the non-coerced character of this decision, in that God was free from external constraints (save that contradiction must not result) in his decisions concerning the nature of the present established order. Scotus is thus able to reject the idea that God acts of absolute necessity – i.e., *necessitas consequentis*. Once having determined the nature and character of the established order, however, God has placed himself under a contingent, conditional and self-imposed obligation to respect the order which he has established – and which may therefore be regarded as totally reliable. The present obligation to man on the part of God is a consequence of, as well as an expression of, his freedom. By his absolute power (*de potentia absoluta*) God is totally free in his decisions; by his ordained power (*de potentia ordinata*) God is totally reliable in his actions. The two propositions noted above may therefore be maintained simultaneously without contradiction.

The development of this dialectic between the absolute and ordained power of God is particularly associated with William of Ockham.[7] Like Scotus, Ockham uses the tension between what is *de facto* and what might have been *de possibili* to safeguard the divine freedom in the face of Greco-Arabian determinism. Although

Ockham frequently refers to the first article of the Creed, 'credo in deum patrem *omnipotentem*',[8] it is clear that he understands this omnipotence to have been qualified and circumscribed by his decision to become God the creator. It must be stressed that Ockham does not teach that God is currently able to do one thing *de potentia absoluta*, and the reverse *de potentia ordinata*: as he frequently emphasises, there exists only one power in God at present, and that is his ordained power, itself an expression of his contingent decision to create the established order:

Circa primum dico quod quaedam potest Deus facere de potentia ordinata et aliqua de potentia absoluta. Haec distincto non est sic intelligenda quod in Deo sint realiter duae potentiae quarum una sit ordinata et alia absoluta, quia unica est potentia in Deo ad extra, quae omni modo est ipse Deus. Nec sic est intelligenda quod aliqua potest Deus ordinate facere et aliqua potest absolute et non ordinate, quia Deus nihil potest facere inordinate. Sed est intelligenda quod 'posse aliquid' quandoque accipitur secundum leges ordinatas et institutas a Deo; et illa dicitur Deus posse facere de potentia ordinata.[9]

Where Ockham appears to go further than Scotus is in the *use* he makes of the dialectic between the powers of God. For Ockham, the dialectic between the powers of God was a critical tool for theological analysis: we shall illustrate this point with reference to his critique of the necessity of created habits in justification (see §13). Thus while Peter Aureole insisted upon the absolute necessity of a created habit in justification, Ockham pointed out that God was free to choose an alternative mode of justification, had he chosen to do so. Without rejecting their *de facto* implication in justification, Ockham demonstrated that created habits were not involved as a matter of *absolute* necessity.

Ockham's use of the dialectic between the two powers of God as a critical theological tool was misunderstood at an early stage. In 1326 a commission of six theologians censured 51 articles taken from Ockham's writings, including a number of relevance to the doctrine of justification. Some six centuries later, the report of these *magistri* was rediscovered,[10] allowing us to establish both the precise nature of the condemned propositions, as well as the reasons for their condemnation. The four propositions which concern us are the following:

1.   *de potentia Dei absoluta* a man may make good use of his will by his purely natural powers, which God may accept as meritorious.[11] The *magistri* pronounced this to be Pelagian 'or worse', as it overthrew the habit of charity altogether.[12]

2.   *de potentia absoluta* God may accept a man *ex puris naturalibus* as worthy of eternal life without his possessing habitual grace, or damn him without his having sinned.[13]

3.   *de potentia absoluta* God may accept a man *ex puris naturalibus* as worthy of eternal life without his possessing a habit of charity. Taking these two propositions together, the *magistri* pronounced that they were Pelagian, in that they taught that man could be accepted to eternal life by his natural abilities.

4.   *de potentia absoluta* God may remit sin without the infusion of grace.[14] This proposition follows from the others, and the *magistri* duly repeat their charge of Pelagianism.

The text of the condemned propositions makes it explicit that they are intended to be undestood as discarded hypothetical possibilities, pertaining *de potentia absoluta* but not *de potentia ordinata*. The *magistri*, however, insisted that the addition of the phrase *de potentia Dei absoluta* made no difference to the sense of the propositions.[15] It is clear that this amounts to a culpable misunderstanding of Ockham's intentions: Ockham merely exploits the tension between what *might have been* and what *actually pertains* to demonstrate the contingency and reliability of the established order. As we have noted, Ockham insists that there is only one power in God: God only has one course of action open to him at present, irrespective of what his initial options were. If both the absolute and ordained powers of God were understood to pertain now, the charge of Pelagianism against Ockham could be regarded as justified. The fact remains, however, that it is manifestly obvious that this is not what Ockham meant.

That Ockham is not guilty of Pelagianism in these propositions may be confirmed by considering the position of Gregory of Rimini, one of the most ferociously anti-Pelagian theologians of the medieval period, on the same questions. Like Ockham, Gregory emphasises that, while God is not bound by any absolute necessity to accept a man to eternal life if he possesses a habit of charity, he has ordained that *de potentia ordinata* the possession of such a habit will result in the glorification of the *viator*. Gregory thus draws three conclusions:[16]

1.   *De potentia absoluta* God may accept a man as *gratus* without a habit of created grace.

2.   *De potentia absoluta* God is not obliged to accept as *gratus* the *viator* who is in possession of such a habit.

3.   *De potentia absoluta* God may accept an act as meritorious even if it is performed outside a state of grace.

It is clear that these propositions correspond to those of Ockham which were condemned at Avignon, and that they represent hypothetical possibilities *de potentia Dei absoluta* which do not pertain *de facto*. Furthermore, a careful examination of the writings of the *modernus* Pierre d'Ailly suggests that the critique of the necessity of grace is justification, conducted *via* hypothetical speculation *de potentia absoluta*, is specifically aimed at *created habits of grace*, and not the uncreated grace of the Holy Spirit himself.[17] In effect, the necessity of a created infused habit of grace in justification may be regarded as the consequence of the intrusion of Aristotelianism within the sphere of the doctrine of justification, and the application of 'Ockham's Razor' – in this case, supported by a critique based upon the dialectic between the two powers of God – leads to the rejection of the absolute necessity of such a habit. The fact that the Tridentine decree on justification declines to affirm the necessity of a created habit of grace or charity in justification may be regarded as demonstrating that the hypothetical critique of the concept had made its point well.

The soteriological point which theologians of the *via moderna* used the dialectic between the two powers to emphasise is that the present established order of salvation, although radically contingent, is totally reliable. God is not obliged by any external constraints to justify man: however, having determined to do so by a free and uncoerced act of self-limitation, he abides by that decision. By his absolute power, God retains the *ability* to do many things which he does not *will* to do. The established order of salvation, to which scripture and tradition bear witness, is an expression of the divine will, and circumstances under which God would act contrary to his established and revealed will can never arise. To the objection that, because the present order depends upon the divine will, the possibility that God might revoke this order through a further act of will cannot be ignored, the theologians of the *via moderna* responded by appealing to the unity of intellect and will within God: God's actions are always totally consistent and reliable. God always acts justly, not because he acts in accord with generally accepted standards of justice, but because he possesses an inward sense of justice which is manifested in his actions and which is consistent with his nature, even though this lies beyond human knowledge.

The use of the dialectic between the two powers of God within the *via moderna* has often been illustrated with reference to the writings of Gabriel Biel, and it is necessary to challenge a serious and influential misrepresentation of Biel's teaching on the *potentia Dei absoluta*. Carl Feckes argues that Biel used the absolute power of God as a convenient vehicle for conveying his own true theology, while retaining traditional teaching in connection with the ordained power of God. In other words, Biel states *de potentia absoluta* what he would have stated *de potentia ordinata*, were it not for fear of recrimination by the ecclesiastical authorities.[18] This criticism of Biel is impossible to sustain, particularly when it is appreciated that the use to which Biel puts the tool of the dialectic between the two powers of God is that of not merely *defending* the established order of salvation against divine capriciousness, but also of providing a firm theological foundation (in the concept of the *pactum*) upon which the established order of salvation may be more securely grounded. This misrepresentation of Biel's thought has also had considerable influence in connection with the related question of the influence of later medieval theology upon the young Martin Luther: if what Biel *really* meant is to be determined from his statements concerning the *absolute* power of God, then Luther's early opinions should be compared with Biel's opinions *de potentia Dei absoluta*. This inevitably leads to the simplistic and quite unjustifiable conclusion that Luther merely states *de potentia ordinata* what Biel stated *de potentia absoluta* – which is as much a caricature of Luther's thought as it is of Biel's![19] Feckes' interpretation of Biel appeared in 1925; the first significant criticism of his approach appeared in 1934, with the publication of Paul Vignaux' highly influential study on fourteenth-century theology,[20] which included a careful study of Ockham's 'voluntarism'.[21] The established order of salvation is not arbitrary but rational, and its rationality can be demonstrated on the basis of probable, though not necessary, arguments. According to Vignaux, the hypothetical order *de potentia absoluta* represents the order of divine logic, in that the possibilities open to divine actualisation are non-contradictory; the actual order *de potentia ordinata* is the order of divine mercy, in that God has voluntarily made himself a debtor to those who possess divine grace in order that they might be justified. Vignaux developed this point in 1935, in his highly acclaimed study of the young Luther,[22] in which he emphasised that it was a total misrepresentation of Biel's thought to argue that the absolute power pertained to the order of reason and law, while the ordained order pertained solely to the arbitrary *de facto* situation.[23] The established order, Vignaux stressed, demonstrates simultaneously the divine justice and the divine mercy. On the basis of this, subsequent studies have emphasised the innocence of Biel's use of the dialectic between the two powers of God,[24] although criticism has frequently been directed against the amount of theological energy wasted on hypothetical speculation *de potentia Dei absoluta*.[25] Similar criticism was directed against the device in the fifteenth century, as may be seen from Erasmus' comments concerning the theological questions which were perplexing the Paris *théologastres* in the final decade of the century. Two such questions may be noted:

1.   Can God undo the past, such as making a harlot into a virgin?[26]
2.   Could God have become a beetle or a cucumber, instead of man?[27]

In fact, both these questions raised serious theological issues, similar to the question of the necessity of created habits in justification, which could not be resolved without the appeal to the dialectic of the two powers of God.[28]

The understanding of divine self-limitation associated with the *via moderna* is particularly associated with a 'covenant' (*pactum*) between God and man. It must be emphasised that this *pactum* should not be confused with the early form of the social contract theory which is so characteristic a feature of the political thought of Marsilius of Padua. The *pactum* is ordained and instituted unilaterally by God, as an act of kindness and generosity towards man. Strictly speaking, it is necessary to recognise two covenants, one pertaining to the natural order, relating to all mankind, by which God commits himself to upholding the created universe and the laws which govern it; the other pertaining to the theological order, relating to the church, by which God commits himself to the salvation of sinful mankind. It is with this latter covenant that we are chiefly concerned. At the heart of this concept of the covenant lies a major break with the rationalistic limitations of the Aristotelian concept of God, and a return to a more biblical concept of God who, though omnipotent, has entered into a covenant with the descendants of Abraham. The existence of this covenant affirms God's commitment both to the salvation of mankind and the means ordained towards this end, particularly the sacramental system of the church (see §8). It is this *pactum* which forms the fulcrum about which the doctrines of justification associated with the *via moderna* turn.[29]

In his discussion of sacramental causality, Thomas Aquinas notes the following opinion concerning the relationship between the sacraments and grace:

Quidam tamen dicunt quod non sunt causa gratiae aliquid operando: sed quia Deus, sacramentis adhibitis, in anima gratiam operatur. Et ponunt exemplum de illo qui, afferens denarium plumbeum, accipit centum libras ex regis ordinatione: non quod denarius ille aliquid operetur ad habendum praedictae pecuniae quantitatem; sed hoc operatur sola voluntas regis.[30]

Thomas rejected this opinion on the grounds that 'a lead coin is no more than a certain kind of sign of the royal ordination directing that the man who presents it is to receive a sum of money'. However, the opinion rejected by Thomas would become an important feature of later medieval understandings of justification, especially within the *via moderna*. Under the terms of the *pactum* between God and man, God has ordained that he will accept human acts as worthy of eternal life. This act of divine will is completely contingent and uncoerced: nevertheless, it is also totally reliable. The *pactum* encapsulated the general medieval conviction that God had imposed upon himself an obligation to man, and that his decision, though contingent, was totally reliable. We have already noted the characteristic teaching of the *via moderna* concerning the dichotomy between the moral and the meritorious realms (see §10): *de potentia ordinata*, however, the relationship between the moral and the meritorious value of an act was established by the *pactum*. We have already discussed this point in relation to the teaching of the *via moderna* on the meritorious character of the disposition towards justification (see §7). The *pactum* determines the relation between the *bonitas intrinseca* and the *valor impositus* of man's moral actions, and thus provides the foundation for the justification of the sinner. While the divine freedom was safeguarded through the absolute power of God, the divine reliability was safeguarded through the ordained power, as expressed in the *pactum*. The emphasis placed by the theologians of the *via moderna* upon the *contingency* and *reliability* of the established order of salvation is particularly well demonstrated by the young Luther's discussion of the reasons why faith and grace are implicated in justification:

Immo et fides et gratia, quibus hodie iustificamur, non iustificarent nos ex seipsis, nisi pactum Dei faceret. Ex eo enim precise, quia testamentum et pactum nobiscum foecit, ut qui crediderit et baptisatus fuerit, salvus sit, salvi sumus. In hoc autem pacto Deus est verax et fidelis et sicut promisit, servat.[31]

The most important use to which the dialectic between the two powers of God was put in the medieval period was the demonstration of the radical contingency of the rôle of created habits in justification, associated with which is the development of the concept of 'covenantal causality'. This topic will be further explored in §13. Our attention is now claimed by the question of the relationship between predestination and justification.

§12 The relation between predestination and justification

The first systematic discussion of the relation between predestination and justification is encountered in the works of Augustine of Hippo.[1] Although earlier writers appear to have realised that Paul's discussion of the rejection of Israel, contained in Romans 9–11,[2] raised the question of predestination, their chief concern appears to have been the defence of what they understood to be an authentically Christian understanding of free will in the face of astral fatalisms, such as Gnosticism. The confusion between the concepts of predestination and fatalism or determinism unquestionably served to lessen patristic interest in the idea of *divine* predestination, with the inevitable result that the early patristic period is characterised by a theological optimism quite out of character with the Pauline corpus of the New Testament.[3] It is with Augustine that attention is first directed to the idea that God exercises more control over the entire process of salvation than might at first seem to be the case.

As noted earlier (§4), Augustine appears to have first confronted the problem of predestination in the course of his correspondence with Simplicianus of Milan.[4] Around 395, Simplicianus found himself perturbed by several issues arising from his reading of Romans 9–11. Why did God hate Esau? And was the idea that God hardened Pharaoh's heart compatible with the Christian understanding of the nature of God and of human freedom? Simplicianus' attempt to persuade Ambrose of Milan to discuss the problem appear to have resulted in failure: the bishop seems to have considered that the writings of Paul posed no problems which could not be resolved simply by reading him aloud.[5] Simplicianus then turned to Augustine for guidance, and by doing so appears to have occasioned the characteristic theological position generally known as 'Augustinianism', which would have so incalculable an effect upon subsequent western theological speculation concerning the relation between predestination and justification.

The essence of Augustine's position upon this question may be summarised in the statement that man's *temporal* election, or justification, is the consequence of God's *eternal* election, or predestination.[6] Thus Augustine interprets the hardening of Pharaoh's heart as a consequence of divine predestination, understood as a positive action on God's part.[7] However, Augustine totally excludes the possibility of an arbitrary *fiat* on the part of God in this respect by emphasising that predestination is based upon and is ultimately an expression of divine justice. Augustine demonstrates that the hardening of Pharaoh's heart is based upon justice in three ways:

1. The hardening of Pharaoh's heart must be seen as a consequence of his previous sins.[8]

2. The hardening of Pharaoh's heart is not totally a work of God: Pharaoh must be regarded as having contributed to the hardening of his heart by his own free will.[9] Even in his discussion of predestination, Augustine insists upon the reality of the human free will.

3. God's judgement, whether open to public scrutiny or not, is always just.[10] God is just, so that whether he hardens a man's heart is not an arbitrary matter, but a matter of justice.

Even in the famous letter to Sixtus, written at the close of the Pelagian controversy, Augustine insists upon the total justice of divine predestination. God determines the destinies of men on the basis of justice. Augustine frequently emphasises the role of the divine wisdom in predestination, intending by this to draw attention to the distinction between predestination and fatalism.[11] The total sovereignty of God in election is maintained: man's justification is preceded by the stirring of his will by God – and God, in his wisdom, has determined only to prepare the wills of a few.[12] For Julian of Eclanum, any such teaching called into question the divine justice; Julian, however, employed a concept of *iustitia Dei* which Augustine was not prepared to sanction.[13]

Augustine declined to draw from his doctrine of predestination the conclusion that God predestined some to eternal life and others to damnation, or the related conclusion that Christ died only for the elect. These conclusions, however, would be drawn – and opposed! – with considerable frequency thereafter. The first theologian who can legitimately be styled 'predestinarian' is the fifth-century Gallic priest Lucidus, whose views were condemned at the Council of Arles (473). Of particular importance are his assertions that Christ did not die for all men, that the divine grace is irresistible, and that those who are lost, are lost through God's will:

(Lucidus) dicit quod Christus Dominus et Salvator noster mortem non pro omnium salute susceperit; quid dicit quod praescientia Dei hominem violenter impellat ad mortem, vel quod cum Dei pereant voluntate qui pereunt.[14]

This condemnation was endorsed by Orange II (529), which specifically anathematised anyone who believed that some are predestined to evil by God.[15] Although some have argued that the council's condemnation was directed against Augustine, the fact remains that Augustine did not explicitly teach a doctrine of *double* predestination.

The most significant predestination controversy of the medieval period erupted in the ninth century, centring on the Benedictine monk Godescalc of Orbais (often incorrectly referred to as 'Gottschalk').[16] Until recently, our knowledge of this controversy stemmed chiefly from the accounts of Godescalc's supporters and opponents. The original text of Godescalc's chief writings was rediscovered in the first half of the present century,[17] with the result that we are now in a position to assess the significance of the great predestinarian controversy of the ninth century with some accuracy.

Godescalc's doctrine of double predestination, *praedestinatio gemina*, is a logical consequence of a fundamentally Augustinian understanding of the relation between nature and grace. Where Godescalc appears to have differed from Augustine is in the rigour with which he deduced the necessity of double predestination from the prevenience of grace in justification. Every rational creature, whether human or angelic, continually needs divine grace if he is to be acceptable to God.[18] This necessity of grace extends also to the proper functioning of the human free will, which is unable to will or to do good apart from grace.[19] With total fidelity to Augustine, Godescalc asserted that man's free will is only truly free when it has been liberated by grace.[20] So far, Godescalc and Augustine are in agreement – yet Augustine teaches predestination *ad vitam*, whilst Godescalc teaches *praedestinatio gemina*. How does this difference arise, given the evident similarities in premises between the two men?

It seems that the fundamental principle upon which Godescalc based his doctrine of double predestination is that of the divine immutability: credo et confiteor deum omnipotentem et incommutabilem praescisse et praedestinasse angelos sanctos et homines electos ad vitam gratis aeternam.[21] If there is in God no new judgement or decision, then all must be predestined. The possibility of any such new judgements or decisions is excluded on the grounds that 'if God does something which he has not done through predestination, he will have to undergo change'[22] – which is quite unthinkable, given Godescalc's doctrine of the immutability of God. If God damns anyone, he must have determined to do so from all eternity, in that he is otherwise subject to change. Therefore,

Godescalc concluded, both the salvation of the elect and the reprobation of the damned are predestined from all eternity. It is possible
that this radical departure from the teaching of Augustine on this
matter may have been occasioned by the teaching of Isidore of
Seville, who explicitly taught that 'there is a double predestination,
of the elect to rest and of the damned to death. Both are caused by
divine judgement.'[23] Godescalc frequently refers to the great Spanish
bishop with approval in relation to his teaching on predestination.[24]

If some are predestined to evil, it follows that Christ cannot have
died for all men, but only for those predestined to life. This conclusion is unhesitatingly accepted by Godescalc.[25] The text frequently
cited against him in relation to this point was I Timothy 2.4, which
refers to God desiring 'all men to be saved'. Godescalc rejected the
suggestion that this reference implied that God desired all men in
general to be saved, interpreting it instead as an affirmation that
whoever is saved, is saved by divine predestination.[26]

The most sophisticated critique of Godescalc's doctrine of predestination was due to the Irish head of the cathedral school in Paris,
John Scotus Erigena. In his *De divina praedestinatione*, written
c. 850, Scotus criticised Godescalc for his misinterpretation and
improper use of theological language. Terms such as 'predestination'
and 'foreknowledge' are predicated of God metaphorically (*trans-
lative de deo predicari*), so that the precise meaning of the term
'predestine' cannot be assumed to be the same in the following
statements:

1.   God has predestined the elect to salvation.
2.   God has predestined the wicked to damnation.

Although this would not satisfy Prudentius of Troyes,[27] it served to
draw attention to some of the difficulties attending the debate.

The most implacable opponent of the views of Godescalc was
Hincmar of Reims, who accused *isti moderni praedestinatiani* of teaching that 'the necessity of salvation has been imposed upon those who
are saved, and the necessity of damnation upon those who perish'.[28]
This was unacceptable, as it appeared to deny the reality of human
free will, which Hincmar asserted to be real, even if weakened by the
Fall (*per se sufficiens sibi ad malum, languidum autem atque invalidum
ad omne bonum*).[29] Hincmar also asserted that Godescalc's statements
amounted to a contradiction of the teaching of Augustine, and cited
the pseudo-Augustinian treatise *Hypognosticon*[30] in support of his
refutation of the Benedictine:

Praedestinatio quippe a praevidendo et praeveniendo vel praeordinando futurum aliquid dicitur; et ideo Deus cui praescientia non accidens est, sed essentia fuit semper, et est, quidquid antequam sit praescit, praedestinat; et propterea praedestinat, quia quale futurum sit praescit ... Sed non omne quod praescit, praedestinat. Mala enim tantum praescit, bona vero et praescit et praedestinat. Quod ergo bonum est, praescientia praedestinat, id est, priusquam sit in re praeordinat.[31]

Citing this work as 'Augustine's book on predestination', Hincmar insisted that predestination and foreknowledge must be distinguished. As Florus of Lyons – a moderate supporter of Godescalc – pointed out, this restricted predestination to the elect, while allowing the divine foreknowledge to apply to both the elect and damned.[32] Florus himself had no difficulty in rejecting the Augustinian provenance of the treatise in question.[33]

In 849, Hincmar convened a synod at Quiercy, which condemned the opinions of Godescalc, and deprived him of his orders. The synod was reconvened by Hincmar in 853, and issued a renewed censure of predestinarianism in the form of four *capitula*:[34]

1. Predestination is to be distinguished from foreknowledge. God can be said to predestine to eternal life, but he cannot be said to predestine to punishment. A distinction is made between the predestination of punishment, and predestination *to* punishment. In effect, this amounts to a restatement of the teaching of the pseudo-Augustinian *Hypognosticon*, noted above. For Hincmar, 'God had predestined what divine equity was going to render, not what human iniquity was going to commit'[35] – i.e., God has predestined that he will reward evil with punishment, but *not* the evil that will be thus punished.

2. Man's *libertas arbitrii*, which was lost in Adam, has been restored in Christ.[36] This *capitulum* is extremely unsatisfactory, as it manifestly confused *liberum arbitrium* and *libertas arbitrii* – i.e., natural and acquired freedom. A similar weakness may be noted in the first *capitulum*, which asserts that God created man 'righteous, without sin, and endowed with *liberum arbitrium*'.[37] As Florus of Lyons pointed out, this statement of free will was utterly devoid of any reference to divine grace.[38] Florus found a similar weakness in the same *capitulum*, in that it appeared to make grace a mere consequence of divine foreknowledge.[39] The confusion of nature and grace is one of the most striking features of the first two *capitula* of this synod.

3. God wills to save all men, rather than just the elect.[40]

4. Jesus Christ died for *all* men, and not just for a section of

humanity.[41] Again, this amounts to a restatement of Hincmar's position that Christ had suffered and died for all men, even if they refused to accept his gift of redemption.[42] *Sanguis Christi redemptio est totius mundi*.[43] For Hincmar, God was evidently guilty of injustice if Christ was permitted to die for the elect alone.[44] The teaching of this *capitulum* was criticised by Florus of Lyons on the grounds that it implied that the blood of Christ was shed in vain (*esse inane et vacuum*) if it was shed for those who did not believe in it.[45] Florus himself argued that Christ's blood was not shed for all men, but for his church, i.e., 'all believers in Christ who have been or now are or ever will be'.[46]

Florus himself drew upon seven 'rules of faith' in which a careful distinction is made between the concepts of predestination and foreknowledge, and for which he claimed the authority of both scripture and the fathers:[47]

1. The predestination and foreknowledge of God are, like God himself, eternal and unchangeable.

2. There is nothing in all creation which is not foreknown or predestined by God himself.

3. Anything which may be said to have been predestined may also be said to have been foreknown, just as whatever may be said to have been predestined may also be said to have been foreknown. Nothing exists which can be said to have been predestined but not foreknown, and vice versa.

4. The good works of both men and angels may be said to be foreknown and predestined by God, while their evil works may be said to be foreknown, but not predestined, by God. The evident tension between this statement and the previous two is not discussed at any length.

5. God's foreknowledge and predestination cannot be said to impose necessity upon anyone. This point had been made against Hincmar by supporters of Godescalc, such as Ratramnus[48] and Servatus Lupus.[49]

6. These concepts of foreknowledge and predestination are implied by Holy Scripture, even at those points at which they are not explicitly stated.

7. None of those who are elect may ever perish, just as none of those who are damned can ever be saved.

The pronouncements of the Synod of Quiercy were overturned by the Council of Valence (855).[50] Whereas Quiercy had insisted that there is *una Dei praedestinatio tantummodo*, Valence asserted a double predestination, *praedestinatio electorum ad vitam et praedestinatio impiorum ad mortem*.[51] It must be emphasised that the Council understood this latter predestination to be essentially different from the predestination of the elect: in electione tamen salvandorum misericordiam Dei praecedere meritum bonum; in damnatione autem periturorum meritum malum praecedere iustum Dei iudicium.[52] The canons of Valence were reaffirmed four years later at a local synod held in Langues. In that same year, it is reported that Nicholas I issued a declaration endorsing the doctrine of double predestination, and the associated teaching that Christ died only for the elect.[53] It is impossible to confirm this report, as no such papal declaration is known to exist. Hincmar, writing in 866, declared his belief that the alleged declaration was a fraud.[54]

The ninth-century debate on predestination was not continued in subsequent centuries. The tenth century is generally regarded as a period of stagnation or decline,[55] and the theological renaissance of the late eleventh and twelfth centuries saw little attention being paid to the question. In general, two schools of thought concerning the motivation of divine predestination may be discerned:

1. The general opinion, which recognised that there was no basis whatsoever in man for either predestination to glory or reprobation, the difference resting solely in the divine will itself. This opinion was supported by Peter Lombard in his *Sentences*,[56] and in this he was followed by the majority of the theologians of High Scholasticism, and particularly by the theologians of the early Dominican school. Thus Thomas Aquinas taught that the divine decision in man's election was necessarily free and uncoerced, made without reference to man's foreseen merit or demerit.[57]

2. The minority opinion, according to which there is some basis in the man for both predestination and reprobation. This opinion is particularly associated with the early Franciscan school, such as Alexander of Hales and Bonaventure. Predestination is understood as an act of intellect, rather than will: the divine will must be informed by the intellect before the decision to elect or reject, and the information supplied by the intellect relates to the foreseen use of the grace granted to the individual in question.[58]

Duns Scotus departed from the early Franciscan school's teaching on predestination by insisting that predestination was an act of the divine *will* rather than the divine *intellect*. Predestination is understood as an act of will by which God, electing a rational creature, ordains him to grace and glory, or the act of intellection which *accompanies* (and not, as in the case of the earlier Franciscan school, *precedes*) this election.[59] Scotus understands predestination as *praedestinatio ad vitam*, to be distinguished from reprobation. One of the most important aspects of Scotus' doctrine of predestination is the means by which he deduces the gratuity of predestination. Scotus appears to be the first theologian to use the principle *omnis ordinate volens prius vult finem quam ea quae sunt ad finem* to demonstrate the utter gratuity of predestination.[60] Before Scotus, the gratuity of predestination had been deduced from the *datum* of the gratuity of grace. For Scotus, however, the volition of the end itself must precede the volition of the means to that end – i.e., God wills the final glorification of man before he wills the means by which this end may be achieved. As grace is merely the means to the end of predestination, it is improper to deduce the gratuity of predestination from that of grace, in that grace is logically posterior to predestination. Therefore the election of a soul to glory must precede the foreknowledge of merits, and hence be without any foundation outside the divine will. The logical priority of predestination over the means by which it is attained inevitably means that the *ratio praedestinationis* lies in the divine will itself. Predestination is therefore totally gratuitous, in that it represents an act of divine will, uninformed by the intellect's analysis of any *ratio praedestinationis in creatura*. The *processus praedestinationis* is therefore such that eternal life precedes merit in terms of its logical analysis, but is consequent to it in terms of its execution in time.[61]

This analysis runs into difficulty in the case of reprobation. Following the teaching of the early Franciscan school, Scotus refuses to concede that God actively wills reprobation. Citing the axiom *non prius est Deus ultor quam aliquis sit peccator*, Scotus argues that the foreknowledge of sin must precede reprobation.[62] As all good is to be attributed principally to God, and all evil to man, Scotus argues that different processes must be considered to operate in the cases of predestination and reprobation.[63] As predestination is an act of the divine will, rather than the divine intellect, Scotus rejects the opinion that foreknowledge is a cause of predestination: the decision of God to predestine a soul to glory does not depend upon information about the soul in question being made available to the divine will by the divine intellect. It is clear that predestination is thus understood to be an active decision on the part of God, rather than the essentially passive endorsement of a prior human decision. This stands in contrast to Scotus' teaching on reprobation, which is understood to be a passive act of divine permission in regard to human sin. The distinction may be illustrated by considering the cases of Peter and

Judas. The former was predestined by God independent of foreknowledge of his merit: God prepared for Peter the means of grace by which he might be glorified. In the case of Judas, however, God merely recognises his sin and punishes him for it. This points to an important difference between Thomas Aquinas and Scotus: for the former, God predestines first to grace and subsequently to glory; for the latter, God predestines first to glory and then to grace. It also illustrates a significant difference between the intellectualism and the voluntarism of the early and later Franciscan schools respectively. The intellectualist approach to predestination involves the intellect informing the will concerning the foreseen use an individual will make of a gift of grace, thus permitting the will to make an informed decision. The *ratio praedestinationis* and *ratio reprobationis* are both located in the creature. The voluntarist approach, however, necessarily locates the *ratio praedestinationis* in the divine will, and Scotus' fidelity to the teaching of the earlier Franciscan school on the *ratio reprobationis* appears to involve him in a serious contradiction, in that his voluntarist presuppositions dictate that it should also be located in the divine will.

Scotus' doctrine of predestination has important consequences for his soteriology in general. As is well known, Scotus regards the Fall of man and the incarnation of the son of God as being essentially independent of each other. The incarnation did not occur as a consequence of human sin. For Scotus, Christ in his human nature was first in the order of the divine foreknowledge, predestined before all other creatures. The *processus praedestinationis* places the predestination of creatures *after* the predestination of the incarnation, as may be seen from the following *ordo praedestinationis*. First, God, apprehends himself by means of the *summum bonum*; second, he apprehended all other creatures; third, he predestined some to glory and thence to grace; fourth, he performed what might be termed an act of omission, by not predestining the remainder; fifth, he foreknew that they would fall in Adam; sixth, he preordained the remedy for the Fall of man, in that man might be redeemed by the passion and death of the son of God. Thus Christ in the flesh was first predestined to grace and glory, in common with the elect, although prior to them; only after the divine foreknowledge of the Fall of man was his incarnation ordained as a remedy for the sin of man. Scotus supports this teaching by arguing that a physician necessarily wills the health of his patient before he specified the remedy which will cure him.[64] In other words, the elect are predestined to grace and glory *before* (both *logically* and *chronologically*) Christ's passion was ordained as a means to that end. As we have already noted (§10), this has significant consequences for his doctrine of the *meritum Christi*.

This doctrine of predestination was developed in a significant direction by William of Ockham, who also remained faithful to the Franciscan teaching that reprobation is based upon a quality within man, rather than an act of divine will. For Ockham, *praedestinare*, in its active mood, refers to the future bestowal of eternal life upon an individual, just as *reprobare* refers to the infliction of punishment upon him. It is clear that both verbs have a specifically future reference, so that any proposition which contains the verbs must necessarily refer to the future.[65] Thus the proposition *Petrus est praedestinatus* is not necessarily true, as the verb here appears with reference to the past.[66] The statement can only refer to a future instant during which God will bestow eternal life upon Peter – and only at that instant can the proposition be said to be true. Of course, its truth at that instant guarantees its truth in the past, so that the proposition is then recognised always to have been true. However, the fundamentally eschatological orientation of Ockham's concept of predestination prevents any positive statement concerning the truth of the proposition from being made until that point has been reached. For Ockham, predestination signifies three entities: God, man, and eternal life. Ockham rejects any understanding of predestination as a real relation additional to God's own necessary being, or as a *relatio realis* added to man by virtue of his being predestined.[67] Predestination is defined solely in terms of the final gift of eternal life, given by God to man.

Ockham's discussion of the *cause* of predestination is generally regarded as being extremely difficult to follow. First, it may be noted that Ockham's understanding of predestination is such that, strictly speaking, it is impossible to speak of it having a cause in the first place. Ockham is only prepared to discuss predestination in terms of the priority of propositions. Ockham provides the following causal sequence of propositions, apparently in the form of an enthymene, to illustrate this point:[68]

1. This man will finally persevere.
2. Therefore he will be predestined.

The non-syllogistic character of the argument may, of course, be rectified by supplying the assumed major premise: 'a man who finally perseveres will be predestined'. Whilst this constitutes the only permissible statement on the relationship between predestination and human merit which is possible, given Ockham's definitions of the terms, it must be pointed out that there are several passages in which he refers to the relationship between predestination and merit in more traditional terms. On the basis of a careful examination of such passages, it appears that Ockham allows both a general *praedestinatio cum praevisis meritis* and a special and distinct *praedestinatio ex gratia speciali*, both possible *de potentia ordinata*. Some will be saved on account of their merits, as without acting freely they would not merit their salvation. As predestination is equivalent to being given eternal life, these individuals may be said to have merited their predestination, *provided that* the explicitly future reference of this statement is acknowledged. Only when eternal life is finally bestowed upon an individual can he be said to be predestined, and only then can the causality of the matter be properly discussed. In the case of other individuals (St Paul being isolated as a specific example), predestination is regarded as arising for no other reason that that God desires their salvation without merit.

The obscurity surrounding Ockham's pronouncements upon predestination has led to a number of questionable conclusions being drawn in connection with them. Oberman concludes that Ockham taught predestination *post praevisa merita*,[69] which, in addition to being a questionable interpretation of Ockham's teaching in the first place, compounds the confusion still further by introducing the terminology of Protestant Orthodoxy where it is clearly totally out of place and seriously misleading. As we have argued elsewhere,[70] Ockham's doctrine of predestination is best approached through the writings of Gabriel Biel, which may be treated as a commentary upon Ockham. Biel himself pronounced his *Collectorium* to be an attempt *dogmata et scripta venerabilis inceptoris Guilelmi Occam Angli indagatoris acerrimi circa quattuor sententiarum libros abbreviare*. In fact, Biel's discussion of predestination represents a considerable expansion, rather than an abbreviation, of Ockham's statements on the matter.[71] We therefore propose to analyse Biel's doctrine of predestination as an influential late medieval interpretation of Ockham's teaching on the matter.

Oberman's analysis of Biel's doctrine of predestination is confused by his use of the categories of predestination *post praevisa merita* and *ante praevisa merita*. We have already noted this point in relation to his analysis of Ockham's teaching on the matter. Biel, naturally, does not use either phrase,[72] nor the conceptual framework within which

Protestant Orthodoxy discussed the doctrine of justification. Biel, it must be emphasised, is entitled to be interpreted by the standards of, and within the context of his own conceptual framework, rather than an alien framework imposed upon him. Following Ockham, Biel understands the term predestination to have a specifically future reference. If an individual receives eternal life, he may be said to be predestined *at that moment* – but not before. If God chooses to accept the *viator* to eternal life at the end, that man may be said to be predestined from that moment, and from that moment only. Of course, his predestination at that moment demonstrates his predestination at earlier points – but it is impossible to verify the statement until the actual bestowal of eternal life takes place. The statement '"A" is predestined' cannot be verified until 'A' actually has eternal life bestowed upon him by God.[73] Oberman has argued that Biel cannot have a meaningful doctrine of predestination on the grounds that his Pelagian doctrine of justification makes predestination not merely superfluous, but actually destructive.[74] Oberman's criticism of Biel may be rejected, however, for two reasons. First, it is dependent upon Oberman's prior conviction that Biel teaches a Pelagian doctrine of justification, which is questionable (see §7). Second, Oberman misunderstands Biel to refer predestination to *justification*, whereas it is clear that Biel refers it to the final bestowal of eternal life. This misunderstanding appears to have arisen through Oberman's approaching Biel through the later Protestant understanding of the nature of predestination, evident in his unjustifiable use of terms such as *praedestinatio ante praevisa merita*. The justification of the sinner does not demonstrate his predestination, which is only demonstrated by his final glorification. Man's justification does not necessarily imply his future glorification.

A consideration of Biel's discussion of the grounds of merit (*ratio meriti*) makes Oberman's thesis even more improbable. Eternal life cannot be merited *de congruo*, but only *de condigno* by the *viator* in possession of a habit of grace.[75] The ultimate grounds of merit, however, lie in the divine will (see §10), which leads to a hiatus between the moral and the meritorious realms. The *ratio meriti* lies outside of man, in the extrinsic denomination of the divine acceptation. Applying these observations to Biel's doctrine of predestination, we find that we are forced to draw a conclusion very different from that of Oberman. Like Ockham, Biel recognises two modes of predestination, which may be termed *praedestinatio cum praevisis meritis* and *praedestinatio ex gratia speciali*. The former term is to be preferred to Oberman's anachronistic and misleading *praedestinatio post praevisa merita*. It will be evident that if an individual, such as St Paul, is predestined *ex gratia speciali*, the *ratio praedestinationis* will lie outside man. Some commentators, however, appear to assume that the general mode of predestination *cum praevisis meritis* locates the *ratio praedestinationis* within man, so that man may be said to occasion his own predestination. It will be evident that this is not the case. Even in this mode of predestination, the *ratio praedestinationis* lies outside of man, precisely because the *ratio meriti* lies outside of man in the extrinsic denomination of the *acceptatio divina*. If the grounds of man's predestination by this mode is his merit, it must be conceded immediately that the grounds of this merit lie outside of man, in the extrinsic denomination of the *acceptatio divina*. This observation leads to the following important conclusion: predestination *cum praevisis meritis* is itself predestination *ex gratia speciali* mediated through the secondary cause of merit. The two types of predestination are essentially the same, except that one proceeds directly, and the other indirectly through secondary causes. The situation may be represented as follows:

1. Predestination *ex gratia speciali:*
   acceptatio divina → ratio praedestinationis.
2. Predestination *cum praevisis meritis:*
   acceptatio divina → ratio meriti → ratio praedestinationis.

In both cases, the ultimate grounds of predestination lie outside of man, in the extrinsic denomination of the divine acceptation. Viewed from the standpoint of the divine acceptation, the two modes are essentially the same: the essential difference between them is that one proceeds directly, the other indirectly. In both cases, however, the *ratio praedestinationis* is one and the same, the *acceptatio divina*, external to man and outside his control.

A very different understanding of the nature of divine predestination, however, emerged during the fourteenth century, and is particularly associated with the academic Augustinian revival at Oxford, and especially at Paris, usually known as the *schola Augustiniana moderna*.[76] In many respects, the *schola Augustiniana moderna* may be regarded as developing a doctrine of predestination similar to that of Godescalc of Orbais. Although Augustine himself did not explicitly teach a doctrine of double predestination,[77] there were those who argued that it represented the logical outcome of his doctrine of grace, and hence claimed the support of the African bishop for their teaching. The origins of this sterner understanding of predestination are usually considered to lie in the anti-Pelagian polemic of the English secular priest, Thomas Bradwardine.

In his witty caricature of fourteenth century theology, Chaucer derided those who studied

> ... the holy doctor Augustyn
> or Boece, or the bishop Bradwardyn.[78]

This reference to Bradwardine may well reflect a revival of interest in his works, due to the influence of Wycliffe. Bradwardine's chief work, *de causa Dei contra Pelagianum* is a somewhat tedious rambling work aimed at certain unnamed *Pelagiani moderni*, presumably the Oxford circle based upon Merton College in the fourteenth century, noted for their Ockhamism.[79] According to Bradwardine's own account of the history of his religious opinions, he himself was attracted to Pelagianism in his early days as a philosophy student at Oxford.[80] However, this youthful espousal of some form of Pelagianism – and Bradwardine never favours us with an explicit definition of the term – was to evaporate when confronted with Romans 9.16, which was to become the *Leitmotif* of his mature theology. It is quite possible that Bradwardine's conversion to a theocentric doctrine of grace prior to his inception as a theological student exemplifies the Augustinian *cognitio* through *illuminatio*.[81] Whilst Bradwardine's theological sources in *de causa Dei* are primarily scriptural, it is clear that his interpretation of these sources is based upon Augustine, whom he values above all others as their interpreter.[82] Although Bradwardine follows Augustine faithfully in defending the existence of a weakened free will against those, such as *vani astrologi*, who maintained a psychological determinism,[83] he departs significantly from Augustine's teaching in relation to the Fall. For Bradwardine, man's need for grace is a consequence of his creatureliness, rather than of the Fall: even when in Paradise, man was impotent to do good. This departure from Augustine is also evident in connection with his teaching on predestination. Although Bradwardine follows Augustine in discussing predestination within the context of the question of final perseverance, his explicit teaching on *double* predestination at once distinguishes him from the authentic teaching of Augustine. Bradwardine's doctrine of predestination is essentially supralapsarian, although it may be noted that he is careful to locate the origin of evil in secondary causes, so that God may be said to predestine *to* evil, but not to *predestine* evil. It may be noted in this respect that Bradwardine's discussion of contingency appears to contain several novel elements: contingency is understood not merely to include the non-necessary, but also to express the principle that events may occur at random or by chance, apart from God's providential direction. In rejecting this understanding of contingency, Bradwardine appears to teach that all things happen of necessity, in that God may be said to cause and direct them. On the basis of such presuppositions, it may be conceded that Bradwardine's doctrine of double predestination expresses a metaphysical, rather than a theological, principle.

In the nineteenth century, Bradwardine was widely regarded as having prepared the way for the Reformation through the questions which he raised, and through the influence which he mediated through Wycliffe and Huss.[84] This view cannot be maintained in its original form. Thus while Bradwardine emphasised the role of the divine will in predestination, Wycliffe saw predestination as a form of divine truth, known to God by means of the ideas themselves before their actualisation. Thus Wycliffe's doctrine of predestination is not based upon a free decision of the divine will: his understanding of necessity is such that the reprobate are damned by foreknowledge, rather than an unconditional act of divine will.[85] In primis suppono cum doctore secundo, quod omnia quae eveniunt sit necessarium evenire:[86] Wycliffe's determinism, as stated in this celebrated *locus*, may possibly reflect the influence of Bradwardine. It is also quite possible that Wycliffe's determinism is a necessary consequence of his doctrine of real universals and possibilities.[87] The attribution of Wycliffe's form of determinism to the influence of Bradwardine is rendered questionable by two considerations. First, Bradwardine's understanding of *necessitas antecedens* presupposes the real existence of human free will – a freedom which Wycliffe explicitly rejects. Second, Bradwardine explicitly condemns as *heretical* the thesis that everything which occurs, takes place by absolute necessity – yet it is precisely this thesis which some argue Wycliffe derived from Bradwardine. A more realistic estimation of Bradwardine's significance is that he established an academic form of Augustinianism, based primarily upon his anti-Pelagian writings, which eventually became characteristic of the *schola Augustiniana moderna*. Two factors, however, combined to reduce Bradwardine's influence over this school. First, Bradwardine was not a member of a religious order, which would propagate his teaching. By contrast, Gregory of Rimini's teaching was extensively propagated within the Augustinian Order. Second, the Hundred Years War resulted in Oxford becoming isolated as a centre of theological study, with Paris gaining the ascendancy. The *schola Augustiniana moderna* thus came to be based on Paris, even though it is possible to argue that its origins lay at Oxford.

A doctrine of double predestination, similar in respects to that of Bradwardine, is associated with Gregory of Rimini.[88] Predestination is defined as the divine decision to grant eternal life, and reprobation as the decision not to grant it[89] – and *both* are understood to be acts of divine will. Predestination and reprobation are not based upon foreknowledge of the use made of free will, not of whether an obstacle will be placed in the path of grace:

Mihi autem videtur quod ex dictis scripturae et sanctorum sequuntur hae conclusiones cum quarum omnium veritate non state veritas alicuius modi dicendi de praedictis. Harum prima est, quod nullus est praedestinatus propter bonum usum liberi arbitrii quem Deus praescivit eum habiturum qualitercumque considereter bonitas eius.

Secunda, quod nullus est praedestinatus quia praescitus fore finaliter sine obice habituali et actuali gratiae. Tertia, quod quemcumque Deus praedesti- navit gratis tantummodo et misericorditer praedestinavit. Quarta, quod nullus est reprobatus propter malum usum liberi arbitrii quem illum Deus praevidet habiturum. Quinta, quod nullus est reprobatus quia praevisus fore finaliter cum obice gratiae.[90]

The exclusive location of both predestination and reprobation in the divine will runs counter to the general opinion of the period, which tended to locate the cause of reprobation at least partly in man himself. Gregory's views were widely propagated within the Augusti- nian Order, by theologians such as Hugolino of Orvieto,[91] Dionysius of Montina,[92] Johannes Hiltalingen of Basel,[93] Johannes Klenkok[94] and Angelus Dobelinus.[95]

The renewed interest in, and increasing understanding of, August- ine in the fourteenth and fifteenth centuries is reflected in the increasingly critical approach adopted to the *dictum*, widely attri- buted to Augustine: si non es praedestinatus, fac ut praedestineris. 'If you are not predestined, endeavour to be predestined!' Johannes Eck, later to be Luther's opponent at the Leipzig Disputation of 1519, described this *dictum* as a 'teaching of Augustine which is better known than the history of Troy':

Ex data distinctione clare potest haberi verus sensus propositionis divini Augustini, quae est notior alias historia Troiana: 'Si non es praedestinatus, fac ut praedestineris' ... Recipit ergo veritatem, quando intelligitur de praedes- tinatione secundum quid et secundum praesentem iusticiam, et est sensus:

Si non es praedestinatus, scilicet per praesentam gratiam, *fac* poenitendo et displicentiam de peccatis habendo *ut praedestineris* gratiam acquirendo, a qua diceris praedestinatus secundum praesentem iusticiam.[96]

In adopting this approach to the *ratio praedestinationis*, Eck appears to have believed himself to remain faithful to the teaching of the early Franciscan school.[97] For Eck, the *dictum* represented a significant development of the axiom *facienti quod in se est Deus non denegat gratiam* (see §7). The *viator*, by doing *quod in se est*, could ensure that he would receive the grace necessary for him to be 'predestined'. Predestination may therefore be regarded as the divine counterpart to man's doing *quod in se est*,[98] so that the *viator* may reassure himself concerning his predestination by performing good works. It is, of course, significant that Eck refers predestination to justification, rather than to the final future bestowal of eternal life. The non-Augustinian character of this *dictum* was increasingly recognised during the closing years of the medieval period. For example, Johannes Altenstaig's celebrated theological dictionary of 1517 attributes the maxim to an unnamed doctor: unde quidam doctor; si non est praedestinatus, fac ut praedestineris. Unde in potestate tua est damnari vel salvari.[99] In the same year, Johannes von Staupitz published his famous series of lectures on predestination, *Libellus de exsecutione aeternae praedestinationis*, in which he supported his argument to the effect that man's temporal election is posterior to the eternal divine election with a denial of the Augustinian provenance of the maxim.[100]

Finally, it is appropriate to inquire into the *function* of doctrines of predestination within the context of medieval theologies of justification. This function is best demonstrated by considering the profile of Duns Scotus' doctrine of justification. Scotus' doctrine of justification resembles an Iron Age settlement, containing a highly vulnerable central area surrounded by defensive ditches. The two defensive ditches in Scotus' doctrine of justification are his doctrines of absolute predestination and divine acceptation, which emphasise the priority of the divine will in justification. The central area, however, is highly vulnerable to the charge of Pelagianism, in that Scotus insists upon the *activity* of the human will in justification. Any study of Scotus' doctrine of justification which does not take account of the theological context in which it has been placed (i.e., the doctrines of the *acceptatio divina* and absolute predestination) will inevitably conclude that Scotus is guilty of Pelagianism or some kindred heresy. The charges of Pelagianism or 'semi-Pelagianism' brought against Scotus by an earlier generation of scholars are now appreciated to be hopelessly inaccurate,[101] although it is relatively easy to understand how these arose. It will, of course, be evident that a weakening of these outer defences without a concomitant strengthening of the inner structure of the doctrine of justification will make such a doctrine increasingly vulnerable to a Pelagian interpretation. It is the opinion of several scholars of the later medieval period that precisely such a weakening may be detected in the soteriology of the *via moderna*,[102] although we have reservations concerning such conclusions. In effect, the theologians of the *via moderna* appear to have recognised the close interconnection between the doctrines of predestination and divine acceptation, with the result that the two outer ditches have become merged into one, although the basic profile of their doctrines of justification remains similar to that of Scotus.

§13 The critique of the rôle of supernatural habits in justification

We have already noted how justification is invariable understood to involve a real change in the sinner (see §5), and not merely an external pronouncement on the part of God. This change was generally regarded as involving the infusion of a supernatural habit of grace into the soul of man (see §9). It will be clear, however, that there remains an unresolved question concerning the relationship between these aspects of justification. Are these habits infused into man in order that he may be regarded as acceptable by God? Or is man regarded as acceptable by God, as a result of which the supernatural habits are infused? Although these two may be regarded as being essentially simultaneous, there still remains the question of their *logical* relationship. Is the infusion of supernatural habits theologically prior or posterior to the divine acceptation? It is this question which lay at the heart of the fourteenth-century debate on the rôle of supernatural habits in justification, which forms the subject of the present section.

The starting point for this discussion is generally agreed to be Peter Lombard's identification of the *caritas* infused into the soul in justification with the Holy Spirit.[1] For Thomas Aquinas, this opinion is impossible to sustain, as the union of the uncreated Holy Spirit with the created human soul appeared to him to be inconsistent with the ontological distinction which it was necessary to maintain between them.[2] Thomas therefore located the solution to the problem in a created gift which is itself produced within the soul by God, and yet is essentially indistinguishable from him – the supernatural habit.[3] The general teaching of the early Dominican and Franciscan schools is that the immediate or formal cause of justification, and hence of divine acceptation, is the infused habit of grace. This opinion is also characteristic of the *schola Aegidiana*, the early school within the Augustinian Order, as may be illustrated from the position of Thomas of Strasbourg on this matter: nullus potest esse formaliter Deo gratus, nisi sit informatus gratia a Deo creata.[4] The possibility of a purely extrinsic acceptation is rejected on the grounds that a real change must occur in man if he is to be acceptable to God, and that such a change is effected solely by a created habit of grace.[5] Grace is *aliquid creatum in anima*, which alone renders man acceptable to God.[6] The general consensus of the thirteenth century was thus that *gratiae infusio* was prior to *acceptatio divina*.

The fourteenth century saw this consensus shattered through the systematic application of the dialectic between the two powers of God (see §11) and the concept of covenantal causality. The origins of this critique of the role of supernatural habits in justification is generally regarded as owing its origins to Duns Scotus, whose teaching on the matter we shall consider in detail.[7] The terms *acceptatio* or *acceptio*, first extensively employed by Scotus, are of biblical provenance.[8] Scotus notes three general senses of the term: simple contemplation; efficacious volition; and the divine acceptation which not merely wills a thing to be, but also accepts it according to the greater good.[9] It is in this final sense that the term is used in Scotus' analysis of the seventeenth distinction of the first book of the Lombard's *Sentences*. Scotus' interpretation of the Lombard at this point is based upon two explicitly acknowledged presuppositions: the reality of the justification of sinners (*iustificatio impii*), and the real possibility of human merit. It is significant that Scotus regards these as *articuli fidei*, and derives them from the Apostles' Creed.[10] The theological problem which requires resolution is the following: how *can* God justify sinners and permit human merit? The explicit linking of these two questions is of considerable significance, as essentially the same solution emerges to both: the *ratio iustificationis* and *ratio meriti* are identical, in that they must both be located in the extrinsic denomination of the *acceptatio divina*.

Scotus' insistence upon the unity and the simplicity of the divine will leads him to the conclusion that the divine will cannot be altered from within. If God wills to accept something, or if he wills not to accept something else, the reason for the distinction must be regarded as lying outside the divine will itself, if a serious internal contradiction is not to result. That God should choose to save *this* man and to reject *that* man must reflect a fundamental difference between the two men in question, as the divine will is unable, according to Scotus, to move itself to accept one and not the other without external causes. Whether a man is accepted or not must depend upon the man himself. The obvious difficulties which this assertion raises in relation to his teaching on predestination (see §12) are not discussed. Therefore, Scotus argues, there must be a habit within man, by which he can be accepted at a given moment in time, whereas previously he was not regarded as acceptable. This difference, Scotus argues, is the habit of charity.[11] This is the first of four arguments which Scotus brings forward in support of his contention that a habit of charity is required *de potentia ordinata* for justification. His second argument is based upon the immutability of the divine will, and has already been touched upon above. As the divine will is immutable, the diversity apparent in the fact that God accepts some, and not others, must arise on account of a similar diversity within the individuals in question. There must therefore be something inherent within the individual which leads to this diversity of judgement – and Scotus identifies this as the presence, or absence, of the created habit of charity.[12] His third argument is based upon privation. Man is not born in a state of justice, so he is unable to increase in justice unless it is by means of a supernatural habit. If this were not the case, man could be both a friend and enemy of God, both loved and not loved. Therefore there must exist a supernatural habit which can account for this transition from being an enemy of God to being a friend of God – and this is the habit of charity.[13] Finally, Scotus argues that those who deny the necessity of such a habit *de potentia Dei ordinata* must be considered as asserting that an individual is as acceptable to God *before* penitence as it is *afterwards* – which is heretical.[14] Scotus thus insists that a habit of charity is required for justification *de potentia Dei ordinata*.

Having established this conclusion, Scotus begins to employ the dialectic between the two powers of God to qualify his conclusions. By his absolute power, God was not under any compulsion whatsoever to accept a soul to eternal life on account of its possession of a created habit of charity, nor was he obliged to employ such intermediates in justification in the first place. God need not do anything by second causes which he could do directly himself. God has ordained, however, that such a habit of charity is required for acceptation and justification. This necessity, however, does not arise through the nature of divine acceptation itself (*ex natura rei*), but merely arises on account of the laws which God has established by his ordained will (*ex pacto divino*). By God's absolute power, a quite different set of laws might have existed in connection with divine acceptation. Whilst the laws relating to divine acceptation through created habits may be considered to be utterly reliable,[15] they must also be considered to be equally contingent.

This leads to Scotus' important discussion of whether this created habit of charity can be said to be the formal cause of justification, in which the maxim *nihil creatum formaliter est a Deo acceptandum* plays an important rôle. Scotus begins his discussion by citing Augustine in support of the general consensus of the period to the effect that those who are accepted by God are distinguished from those who are not by their possession of a created habit of charity.[16] This does not, however, mean that the habit of created charity may be regarded as the formal cause of divine acceptation, considered from the stand-point of the one who elicits the act of acceptation (i.e., God), as this must be regarded as lying within the divine will itself.[17] A distinction must be made between the primary cause of divine acceptation (i.e., a *necessary* cause, arising out of the nature of the entities in question) and the secondary cause of divine acceptation (i.e., a *contingent* cause, which has its *esse* solely in the divine apprehension). On the basis of this distinction, Scotus argues that the created habit of charity must be regarded as a secondary cause of divine acceptation. God ordained from all eternity that the created habit of charity should be the *ratio acceptandi*, so that its importance in this connection is contingent, rather than necessary, deriving solely from the divine ordination, and not from any universally valid law. In effect, this amounts to an unequivocal statement of the concept of *covenantal causality*, noted earlier (see §11). The inner connection between acceptation and the habit of charity does not lie in either the nature of acceptation or the habit of charity, but solely in the divine ordination that there should be a causal relationship between them, which has now been actualised *de potentia Dei ordinata*.[18]

A further aspect of Scotus' teaching on acceptation which should be noted is his distinction between divine acceptation of a person and divine acceptation of his acts. The *acceptatio personae* takes priority over the *acceptatio actus*.[19] As it is the acceptation of the person which gives rise to the acceptation of his acts, it will be clear that the *ratio meriti* lies outside man in the divine acceptation itself. Furthermore, a distinction must be drawn between acceptation to eternal life and acceptation to grace. The former relates to the *end* of justification, the latter to its *means*. In keeping with the general Scotist principle (see §12) that the end is willed before the means to this end, it follows that acceptation to grace is posterior to acceptation to eternal life. Acceptation to grace is merely *acceptatio secundum quid*, as it presupposes *acceptatio simpliciter* – i.e., acceptation to eternal life.[20] As we noted earlier (see §12), the general profile of Scotus' doctrine of justification is thus such that the fundamental gratuity of justification and predestination are maintained, despite the apparent threat posed to this gratuity by Scotus' insistence upon the activity of the human will.

Scotus' teaching on the secondary and derivative rôle of the created habit in justification was criticised by Peter Aureole,[21] who is generally regarded as being the most important theologian in the period between Scotus and Ockham. He appears to have been dissatisfied with the Aristotelianism of his period, in that both his psychology and his noetic are fundamentally Augustinian in character.[22] It is interesting to note that Peter is heavily dependent upon Durandus of St Pourçain, mediated through the quodlibetal questions of Thomas of Wilton.[23] While Peter's epistemology is characterised by his rejection of any realist understanding of universal concepts,[24] it must be pointed out that it is inaccurate to characterise his epistemology as 'nominalist' in the usual sense of the term: his understanding of the role of *conceptio* in cognition suggests that his particular form of 'nominalism' should be styled *conceptualism*. Peter's theology of justification is of particular interest on account of his explicit and penetrating criticism of Scotus on two matters: the type of denomination required for divine acceptation, and the rôle of the divine will in predestination.

In marked contrast to Scotus, Peter maintains that for a soul to be *accepta Deo*, a habit of charity is necessary. In his rejection of Scotus' maxim *nihil creatum formaliter est a Deo acceptandum*, Peter argues that the necessity of the intrinsic denomination of the habit of charity for divine acceptation is itself the consequence of a primordial divine ordination. His teaching on the matter may be summarised in the three propositions which he advances in support of this contention:[25]

1. divine acceptation is the natural and necessary result of the presence of a created form in the soul;[26]

2. this form is not itself the consequence of divine acceptation, but itself renders the soul acceptable to God by the application of the divine love;[27]

3.   this form, by which the soul is accepted, is some habitual love of
        God, directly infused into the soul by God himself, and which does
        not arise from man's natural powers.[28]

Peter then identifies this *aliqua forma creata* as the habit of charity,
directly infused by God himself into the soul of the *viator*. Thus the
extrinsic denomination of the divine acceptation is itself based upon
the intrinsic denomination of the infused habit of charity.

Peter's criticism of Scotus' doctrine of absolute predestination is
based on related considerations. Scotus had taught that God first
predestined a soul to glory, and then to grace *quasi posterius*. For
Peter, this failed to do justice to the universal saving will of God. The
divine will must extend to the salvation of all men, not merely to those
who are predestined. Peter eliminates this apparent arbitrariness on
the part of God by insisting that the formal cause of divine acceptation
must be considered to be the intrinsic denomination of the habit of
charity. By doing this, he effectively reduces predestination to an act
of divine power, based upon foreknowledge.[29]

It will be clear that the fundamental disagreement between Peter
and Scotus relates to the question of the causality of the supernatural
habit of charity. For Scotus, the causality of the habit in connection
with divine acceptation is *covenantal*, reflecting the divine ordination
that such a causality should exist. For Peter, the causality is *ex natura
rei*, itself a consequence of the nature of the created habit of charity
and the act of divine acceptation. The nature of the entities implicated in the act dictates that such a causal connection is necessary,
independent of any divine ordination concerning it. Once the habit of
charity has been infused into the soul of the *viator*, God is obliged, by
the very nature of things, to accept that *viator*.

Peter's association of the priority of habit over act was rejected by
William of Ockham. After stating Peter's three theses, Ockham
begins his criticism mildly enough: ista opinio non videtur mihi
vera.[30] The first thesis to which he refers is that a created form in the
soul is by its very nature (*ex natura rei*) pleasing to God, so that it
results in divine acceptation and the bestowal of grace. Ockham
immediately demonstrates the *contingency* of this thesis: *de potentia
absoluta*, God may bypass created habits, preparing and accepting the
soul to eternal life in the absence of any such habit. God's granting
eternal life and the beatific vision to an individual is in no way a
consequence of or dependent upon the possession of such a created
habit.[31] To those who object that it is only by virtue of the possession
of such a habit that a *viator* becomes worthy of eternal life, Ockham

replies that all that is actually necessary is that God disposes the *viator* towards eternal life.

Ockham's second argument against Peter is that both being loved and being hated by God are effects of the divine will. To be hated by God, however, does not necessarily result in *aliqua forma creata detestabilis* formally inhering within the soul of the *viator* who is hated by God. It is therefore inconsistent to assert that such a created form is required within the soul of a *viator* if he is to be *loved* by God, while not simultaneously asserting that such a form is required if he is to be *hated* by God. The inconsistency involved is further emphasised by Ockham in connection with the action of the sacrament of baptism. If Peter's thesis is valid, according to Ockham, it must follow that a sinner who is newly converted and baptised would be loved and hated *at the same time*, as the habits of mortal sin and charity would coexist.

Ockham's critique of Peter continues with a strong statement of the priority of acts over habits. The meritorious nature of an act is not located in the fact that the *viator* is in possession of a created habit of charity. Merit has its origin in the uncoerced volition of the moral agent. The criterion of merit or demerit is what God chooses to accept or reject, lying outside the moral agent, and not reflecting any quality (such as a created habit) inherent to the *viator*. God can do directly what he would normally do by a supernatural habit. Although God is *now* obliged to justify man by means of created supernatural habits, this does not reflect the nature of things, but simply the divine ordination. After considering the opinion of Thomas Aquinas on the *ratio meriti*, Ockham concludes:

Ideo dico aliter ad quaestionem, quod non includit contradictionem aliquem actum esse meritorium sine omni tali habitu supernaturali formaliter inform-ante. Quia nullus actus ex puris naturalibus, nec ex quacumque causa creata, potest esse meritorius, sed ex gratia Dei voluntari, et libere acceptante. Et ideo sicut Deus libere acceptat bonum motum voluntatis tamquam merito-rium quando elicitur ab habente caritatem, ita de potentia sua absoluta posset acceptare eundem motum voluntatis etiam si non infunderet caritatem.[32]

De facto, a created habit is implicated in divine acceptation – but this implication arises *ex pacto divino*, not *ex natura rei*. While not questioning the *de facto* necessity of such habits in justification, Ockham demonstrated their radical contingency, and thus under-mined the conceptual foundations upon which the *habitus*-theology had been established in the thirteenth century.

Ockham's basic position was defended by Gabriel Biel,[33] in that the *de facto* necessity of habits in justification was maintained, while their absolute necessity was rejected. That habits are implicated in the divine acceptation is a matter of theological contingency: nihil creatum potest esse ratio actus divini.[34] Biel, however, defends the traditional teaching on the rôle of created habits in justification with considerable skill. Particular attention should be paid to his argument that actual grace is inadequate to cope with the ravages of human sin: as God cannot accept indifferent or sinful acts, the *viator* would be required to avoid these totally at all times – which is clearly an impossibility. Biel stresses the reality of venial sin, and points out that the concept of *habitual* grace allows for a certain degree of indifference of sinfulness to coexist with acceptability.[35] It must be conceded, however, that the precise significance of the concept of created grace within the context of the soteriology of the *via moderna* is open to question, in that the theological foundations of the concept, laid in the earlier medieval period when the concept of ontological (i.e., *ex natura rei*) causality had been regarded as self-evident, appear to have been quite demolished through the application of the dialectic between the two powers of God and the concept of covenantal (i.e., *ex pacto divino*) causality. The arguments for the necessity of created grace originally rested upon the apparent necessity of created habits in effecting the transformation from *homo peccator* to *homo iustus* and his acceptance by God. The new emphasis upon the priority of acts over habits called this presupposition into question.

The theologians of the *schola Aegidiana* (i.e., the early school of theology within the Augustinian Order, based upon the teaching of Giles of Rome) taught that divine acceptation was contingent upon a created habit of grace. We have already noted this point in relation to Thomas of Strasbourg. This teaching is maintained by several later theologians of the Augustinian Order, such as Johannes von Retz: (nullus) potest esse formaliter carus vel gratus nisi informatus gratia a Deo creata.[36] The *schola Augustiniana moderna*, however, followed Scotus and the *via moderna* in teaching the priority of the act of divine acceptation over the possession of created habits. This development is associated with the theologian usually regarded as having established the theological foundations of the *schola Augustiniana moderna*, Gregory of Rimini.

Gregory distinguished two modes by which a soul is accepted by God:[37]

1. An *intrinsic* mode, by a habit of grace informing the soul;
2. An *extrinsic* mode, by which the divine will accepts the soul directly to eternal life.

Grace may therefore be understood either as an intrinsic created gift, or as the extrinsic divine acceptation. The former, however, must be regarded as contingent, in that God must be at liberty to do directly what he would otherwise do indirectly, through created intermediates. Thus God normally accepts the *viator* on the basis of created grace informing the soul: however, as God himself is the prime cause of the secondary cause of acceptation (i.e., the habit of created grace), he must be regarded as at liberty to bypass the intrinsic mode of acceptation altogether. Distinguishing between created and *un*created grace, Gregory argues that the uncreated gift itself (i.e., the Holy Spirit) is itself sufficient for acceptation without the necessity of any created form or habit. Gregory is thus able to maintain the possibility of a purely extrinsic justification by simple acceptation: a habit bestowed upon the *viator* does not bestow any benefits which cannot be attributed to the Holy Spirit himself.[38]

This logico-critical approach to the rôle of created habits in justification was developed by Hugolino of Orvieto, who is distinguished in other respects as being one of the most conservative anti-Pelagian theologians of the Augustinian Order.[39] Like Gregory, Hugolino was concerned to preserve the divine freedom in man's justification, particularly in relation to created habits. The primacy of acts over habits is maintained uncompromisingly: no created grace, whether actual or habitual, can render a man *gratus*, *carus*, or *acceptus ad vitam aeternam* before God as its formal effect. In common with Gregory, Hugolino regards the formal cause of justification to be the extrinsic denomination of the divine acceptation.[40] If the possession of a habit of charity were the formal cause of justification, Hugolino argues that it would follow that a creature (i.e., the created habit) would effect what was appropriate to the uncreated grace of the Holy Spirit, which is unthinkable. Hugolino thus assigns a minimal rôle to created habits in justification, tending to see justification as a direct personal act of God himself. Hugolino's extensive use of the dialectic between the two powers of God has raised the question of the influences of the *via moderna* upon his theology, although it is difficult to demonstrate the positive influence of the *via moderna* upon his theology.[41] Hugolino's views on divine acceptation appear to be derived from Scotus, probably *via* Gregory of Rimini, rather than from Ockham.

A similar critique of the rôle of created habits in justification can be shown to characterise the writings of later theologians of the Augustinian Order. Hugolino's teaching was developed by his junior in the

Order, Dionysius of Montina, who lectured on the *Sentences* at Paris in the academic year 1371–2.[42] A similar critique was developed by Alphonsus of Toledo.[43] Johannes Klenkok insisted that God could undoubtedly remit sin without the necessity for any created qualities within the soul: *immo mihi plus valeret solus Deus me in via dirigens quam quaecumque tales qualitates.*[44] A similar conclusion is drawn by Johannes Hiltalingen of Basel.[45] The position of Angelus Dobelinus is less certain, although he is clearly unhappy about the underlying rationale for the necessity of created habits in justification.[46] Dobelinus himself clearly attached considerably greater importance to the uncreated gift of the Holy Spirit than to created habits. In this, he may be regarded as having been followed by Johannes von Staupitz, who emphasised the priority of *gratia increata* over *gratia creata*: the movement of the soul towards God in justification is effected by none other than the Holy Spirit himself.[47] Indeed, there are grounds for suspecting that Staupitz may have abandoned the concept of a created habit of grace altogether.[48]

This late medieval critique of the rôle of created habits in justification, with an increased emphasis upon the rôle of uncreated grace in the person of the Holy Spirit, constitutes the background against which Luther's early critique of the rôle of habits in justification should be seen.[49] Luther argues that the habit required in justification is none other than the Holy Spirit: *habitus adhuc est spiritus sanctus.*[50] There is every reason to suppose that Luther's critique of the rôle of created habits in justification, and his emphasis upon justification as a personal encounter of the individual with God, reflects a general disquiet concerning the theological foundations of created grace, and a decisive shift away from created grace towards the uncreated grace of the Holy Spirit in the late medieval period.

The question of the nature of the formal, or immediate, cause of justification is of particular significance in three respects.

1. It permits the teachings of the early and later Franciscan schools on justification, which are in other respects very similar, to be distinguished.

2. It allows the *schola Aegidiana* to be distinguished from the *schola Augustiniana moderna*.

3. It emerged as an important issue in its own right at the Council of Trent. The Tridentine discussion of the question can only be understood in the light of the medieval discussion of the question.

4. The medieval schools of thought on justification

Introduction

The late eleventh and early twelfth centuries saw a remarkable advance and consolidation within the church and society as a whole, in literature, science, philosophy and theology.[1] In part, this renaissance must be regarded as a direct consequence of increasing political stability in western Europe, a fact which is recognised by several writers of the period, such as Andrew of St Victor: *ab otiosis enim et in tempore otii et non a discurrentibus et perturbationis tempore sapientia discitur.*[2] The rise of canonical theology had been greatly stimulated by the emergence of the church as a unifying social force during the Dark Ages, and its development was to reach its zenith during the twelfth century, under Gratian of Bologna and Ivo of Chartres. The Berengarian and Investiture controversies[3] further stimulated the need for systematic codification in theology. This need for theological development and codification was met by the monastic and cathedral schools, which quickly became the intellectual centres of a rapidly developing society. It is a simple matter to demonstrate that each of these schools developed its own particular and characteristic stance on theological and spiritual matters, and it is the purpose of the present chapter to document the different interpretations of the doctrine of justification which emerged from such schools in the medieval period.

The ninth century saw the development of St Gall, Reichenau, Tours, Mainz, Corbie, Laon and Reims as theological centres.[4] The rise of the great cathedral schools in the eleventh century appears largely due to the instructions issued in 1079 to his bishops by the reforming pope Gregory VII, to the effect that all bishops should 'cause the discipline of letters to be taught in their churches'.[5] By the year 1197, which witnessed the death of Peter the Chanter,[6] Paris had become established as the theological centre of Europe. During the course of the twelfth century, the Parisian schools of the Ile de la Cité and the abbeys of the Left Bank would far surpass in importance those of Leon, Chartres, Bec, Reims and Orléans, which had dominated the eleventh century. The rise of the Left Bank schools was largely a consequence of the migration of masters from the Ile de la Cité to evade the jurisdiction of the chancellor. The masters' practice of placing themselves under the jurisdiction of the independent congregation of St Geneviève would only receive formal papal authorisation in 1227, but was a widespread practice in the late twelfth century. The second half of the twelfth century was dominated by the schools based upon masters such as Peter Abailard, Gilbert of Poitiers, Peter Lombard and Hugh of St Victor. These schools were, however, of relatively little significance in connection with the development of the doctrine of justification, and as we have already noted their contributions in connection with individual aspects of this development in the previous chapter, we do not propose to discuss them any further.

A development which, though not theological in itself, was to have an incalculable effect upon the development of the medieval understanding of justification was the establishment of the Dominican and Franciscan schools at Paris in the early thirteenth century. The Friars Preachers arrived at Paris in 1218 and the Friars Minor the following year. Until the arrival of the friars at Paris, teaching at the University of Paris had been solely the responsibility of the secular clergy. Neither the Dominicans nor the Franciscans can be regarded as having come to Paris with the object of founding theological schools, which makes subsequent events all the more significant. By the year 1229, both Orders were established at their Parisian houses, at which they carried out teaching, in addition to their other work. Theology was taught at the university by secular masters, who held eight chairs of theology according to the decree of Innocent III of 14 November 1207.[7] By 1229, this number had risen to twelve, of which three were reserved for canons of Notre Dame.[8] In 1229 a dispute arose which led to the 'Great Dispersion' of masters and students between March 1229 and April 1231. Although the masters left Paris for other centres of study, the friars continued their work. As they were not subject to the normal university discipline, they were not obliged to join the general exodus. Among those who left Paris for Cologne was a certain Boniface, who left vacant his chair of theology. His place appears to have been taken by Roland of Cremona, a Dominican student of the secular master John of St Giles. Roland was granted his licence in theology by William of Auvergne, bishop of Paris, over the head of his chancellor. The second Dominican chair was established the following year, when John of St Giles himself entered the Dominican Order on 22 September 1230. This second chair of theology would thereafter be known as the 'external' chair, reserved for Dominican masters from outside Paris. The Franciscan chair was established in 1236 or 1237, when an English secular master, Alexander of Hales, caused a sensation by joining the Friars Minor. By 1237, therefore, three of the twelve chairs in theology at the university of Paris were reserved for members of the Dominican or Franciscan Orders. The establishment of these chairs may be regarded as marking the first phase of the conflict between the friars and the secular masters which was so characteristic a feature of the university during the thirteenth and fourteenth centuries: the secular masters appear to have been convinced that the friars deliberately remained in Paris during the Dispersion to take advantage of their absence.[9]

The significance of the University of Paris to our study may also be illustrated from the later medieval period, in that both the *via moderna* and the *schola Augustiniana moderna* were well represented in its faculties in the fourteenth and fifteenth centuries. The faculty of arts at Paris initially attempted to stem the influence of the *via moderna*: on 29 December 1340, a statute condemning the *errores Ockanicorum* took effect.[10] Henceforth any candidate wishing to supplicate for the degree of Master of Arts at Paris would have to swear that, in addition to being under the age of twenty-one and having studied arts for six years, he would observe the statutes of the faculty of arts *contra scientiam Okamicam*, and abstain from teaching such doctrines to his pupils.[11] The ineffectiveness of these measures may be judged from the career of the noted *modernus* Pierre d'Ailly, who was appointed chancellor of the university in 1389.[12] Paris would remain a stronghold of the *via moderna* until the sixteenth century. During the fourteenth century, the *schola Augustiniana moderna* appears to have become established at the university through the activity of Gregory of Rimini and his followers, such as Hugolino of Orvieto.[13] The historical significance of both these movements, however, is largely due to their influence upon the development of the Reformation in general, and the theology of Martin Luther in particular,[14] with the result that they are usually discussed with relation to the late medieval universities of Germany, rather than Paris itself.[15]

In the following sections, we shall characterise and compare the five main schools of thought on justification during the medieval period. In view of the importance of the *via moderna* and *schola Augustiniana moderna* to the development of the theology of the Reformation, we propose to consider these in more detail than the other three.

§14 The early Dominican school

On 24 June 1316, a decree of the provincial chapter of the Dominican Order in Provence was promulgated, stating that the works of Albertus Magnus, Thomas Aquinas and Peter of Tarantaise were to be regarded as normative in doctrinal matters.[1] Of these three doctors, however, it is clear that Thomas was regarded as pre-eminent: in 1313, the general chapter of the Order ruled that no friar of the Order was to be permitted to undertake theological studies at Paris without three years' study of the works of Thomas, and that no *lector* was to be permitted to mention opinions contrary to his teaching, unless such opinions were refuted immediately.[2] It will be clear, of course, that these rulings were made without apparent reference to the diversity of opinion which may be found within Thomas' writings, which we have noted during the course of the present study. Thus his doctrine of justification as stated in the *Commentary on the Sentences* (1252–6) is quite distinct from that stated in the *prima secundae* of the *Summa Theologiae* (1270), as noted above (see §§7, 9). There appears to have been some confusion within the early Dominican school as to which of these works should be used in ascertaining the authentic position of the Angelic Doctor. It may be pointed out that the distinctive contribution of Johannes Capreolus to the development of the later Thomist school was his insistence that the *Summa* represents the final determination and retraction of Thomas' earlier statements.[3]

Along with other Parisian masters of the period, Roland of Cremona is known to have developed an interest in Aristotle,[4] and this interest is reproduced by his successors within the early Dominican school. Of particular importance in this respect is his ontological interpretation of merit (see §10), and the definition of justification as a *motus* from sin to rectitude. The Aristotelian foundations of Thomas Aquinas' teaching on the *processus iustificationis* (see §5) and the necessity of a disposition towards justification (see §7) are particularly significant examples of the theological influence of the Stagirite over the theology of the early Dominican school. The positive estimation of Aristotle is one of the most prominent features of the early Dominican school, and is particularly evident when contrasted with the strong Augustinianism of the early Franciscan school.

One of the most important aspects of the early Dominican school's teaching on justification relates to the question of 'original justice', *iustitia originalis*. The thirteenth century witnessed considerable discussion of the question of whether the first man was created in a state of grace or a purely natural state. The general consensus in the earlier part of the period was that Adam was created in the integrity of nature, but not in a state of grace. If Adam received the gift of sanctifying grace, he did so voluntarily.[5] In his earlier works, Thomas Aquinas appears to register a hesitant disagreement with the opinion of Albertus Magnus on this question. It seems clear that Thomas favoured the opinion that Adam received grace at the instant of his creation, as judged from his discussion of the matter in the *Commentary on the Sentences*.[6] This opinion is unequivocally stated in the later disputed questions *de malo*,[7] where it is stated that *iustitia originalis*, which Adam received at the moment of his creation, included sanctifying grace (*gratia gratum faciens*).[8] This same view is put forward in the *Summa Theologiae*, in an important discussion of the Old Testament *locus* which usually constituted the point of departure for speculation on this matter: Deus fecit hominem rectum (Ecclesiastes 7.30).[9] What can this mean except that God created man, and then bestowed original justice upon him? The basis of this original justice must be considered to be the supernatural submission of the will to God, which can only be effected through sanctifying grace: radix originalis iustitiae, in cuius rectitudine factus est homo, consistat in subiectione supernaturali rationis ad Deum, quae est per gratiam gratum faciens.[10] This original justice pertains to the essence of the soul, and is inherent within man.[11] Thomas is careful to point out this does not amount to an equation of nature and grace.[12] For Thomas, the *status naturae integrae* is merely an abstraction: not even Adam could ever be said to have existed in this state, for at the instant of his creation he was endowed with the *donum supernaturale* of *gratia gratum faciens*. Although nature must be regarded as being good, it is nevertheless incomplete, and requires ordering towards its principal good (i.e., the enjoyment of God) through the aid of supernatural grace. It therefore follows that original sin may be formally defined as the privation of original righteousness. Although Thomas follows Albertus Magnus in adopting Anselm of Canterbury's definition of original sin as *privatio iustitiae originalis*, it is necessary to observe that he uses the term *iustitia* in a significantly different sense from Anselm.

The prime effect of the first sin, according to Thomas, is thus the instantaneous fall of Adam from the *supernatural* plane to which he had been elevated at the moment of his creation through *gratia gratum faciens* to the purely *natural* plane. The human nature which is transmitted to us from Adam is thus nature deprived of the supernatural gifts once bestowed upon Adam, but capable of receiving such gifts subsequently: anima naturaliter capax gratiae.

The general characteristics of the early Dominican school at Paris, as exemplified by Thomas Aquinas, may be summarised as follows.

1. The possibility of man meriting justification *de congruo* is rejected on the basis of the general principle that all merit presupposes grace. It must be pointed out that this opinion is characteristic of the *Summa Theologiae* but *not* of the earlier *Commentary on the Sentences*, in which a congruously meritorious disposition for justification is upheld. There appears to have been some confusion within the early Dominican school upon this matter.

2. The possibility of man knowing with absolute certitude whether he is in a state of grace is rejected.[13] God is totally beyond man's comprehension, and although the *viator* may know in a conjectural manner whether he has grace – e.g., by observing whether he takes delight in God – he cannot know *beyond doubt* whether he is in a state of grace. It may be noted that this represents the general medieval opinion on this question, rather than the peculiar teaching of the early Dominican school.

3. Original righteousness is understood to include the gift of sanctifying grace, so that the formal element of original sin may be defined as *privatio iustitiae originalis*.

4. The formal cause of justification is defined to be the habit of created grace.

5. The principle of merit is understood to be the habit of created grace.

6. The necessity of a human disposition towards justification is maintained, on the basis of the Aristotelian presupposition that motion implies premotion.

7. A strongly maculist position is adopted in relation to the conception of Mary.[14]

§15 The early Franciscan school

The early Franciscan school of theology owed its origins to its first great Parisian master, Alexander of Hales. The work which is generally known as the *Summa Fratris Alexandri*, long thought to be an authentic work of Alexander's, is now regarded as being compo-site.[1] Alexander's authentic lectures on the *Sentences*, generally considered to date from 1222–9, were discovered in the form of students' notes in 1946.[2] On the basis of these, and a series of disputed questions which antedate his joining the Franciscan Order, it is possible to argue that the main features of the early Franciscan school's teaching on justification are essentially identical with the early teaching of Alexander of Hales. In other words, Alexander does not appear to have modified his theology significantly upon joining the Friars Minor, and subsequent Franciscan masters perpetuated his teachings as the authentic teaching of their Order. This may be illustrated with reference to his teaching on original justice.

Alexander notes that there are two opinions concerning Adam's pristine state: the first is that he was created in a purely natural state; the second that he was created in a state of *gratia gratum faciens*.[3] The opinion adopted is a consequence of the interpretation of Ecclesiastes 7.30, *Deus fecit hominem rectum*. Alexander draws a distinction between natural and gratuitous justice, and argues that the verse in question clearly refers to a state of natural justice.[4] In this, he was followed by Odo Rigaldi, who taught that Adam was created in a state of purely natural justice and innocence, relying upon actual grace (*gratia gratis data*), rather than *gratia gratum faciens*.[5] Bonaventure similarly states that man was not endowed with *gratia gratum faciens* at his creation,[6] while recognising his endowment with *gratia gratis data*.

The characteristic features of the early Franciscan school's teaching on justification are the following.

1. The possibility of man meriting justification *de congruo* is upheld.
2. The possibility of absolute certitude of grace is rejected.
3. Original righteousness is understood to include the gift of actual grace; the opinion that the gift included *gratia gratum faciens* is rejected.
4. The formal cause of justification is understood to be a created habit of grace.
5. The formal principle of merit is understood to be a created habit of grace.
6. The necessity of a human disposition towards justification is maintained upon Augustinian psychological grounds.
7. A maculist position is adopted in relation to the conception of Mary.

The early Franciscan school can be shown to have found itself in difficulty towards the end of the thirteenth century in relation to its understanding of the relationship between nature and grace. The Augustinianism of the early school is not restricted to its soteriology and psychology, but extends also to its epistemology. The early Franciscan school adopted the Augustinian doctrine of divine illumination,[7] which is actually an elaboration of a metaphor which Augustine himself used in an attempt to explain how God makes himself understood to man. God is to the human mind what the sun is to the physical world. Just as a physical object cannot be seen without the light of the sun, so the mind is unable to perceive spiritual truths without divine illumination. Just as the sun is the source of the light by which man is able to see physical objects, so God is the course of the spiritual light by which man is able to apprehend divine truth. It will be evident that this concept betrays considerable affinity with the Platonic notion of the Good as the sun of the intelligible world. The fundamental difficulty which faced the early Franciscan proponents of divine illumination was that it was far from clear as to whether this illuminating influence of God was to be considered as a *natural* or *supernatural* light: was it *naturalia* or *gratuita*? Scotus' radical criticism of Henry of Ghent's illuminationism[8] led to the characteristically abstractionist epistemology of the later Franciscan school, and considerable unease concerning illuminationism may be detected in the final years of the early Franciscan school. Thus Peter Olivi stated that he supported the doctrine of divine illumination merely because it happened to be the traditional teaching of his order, while even Matthew of Aquasparta was unable to decide whether divine illumination counted as a 'somewhat general influence' or a 'special influence' of God. The essential problem underlying this question is that of the relationship between nature and grace, and it is precisely this difficulty which emerged from the early Franciscan discussion of the nature and necessity of a human disposition for justification. The essential difficulty facing the early Franciscan theologians was that the transition from nature to grace was *prima facie* impossible. The transition between opposites was held to be impossible without an intervening stage – but how is this *tertium quid* to be understood? The concept of *gratia gratis data* did not appear to resolve the difficulty, as the ontological chasm between nature and grace remained. It must be emphasised that this difficulty arises through the early Franciscan understanding of *iustitia originalis*: for the early Dominican school, man was *naturally* capable of grace, having been created with this facility; for the Franciscans, however, the possession of *gratia gratum faciens* was not included in the original endowment of nature. The problem of the ontological transition implicit in justification had not been resolved by the time Richard of Middleton's *Commentary on the Sentences* appeared at some point shortly after 1294. The period of the early Franciscan school may be regarded as closing at this point, in that a new approach to the problem was being developed which would avoid this difficulty. The solution of this difficulty, however, involved the abandonment of much of the earlier Franciscan pre-suppositions concerning the nature of grace and its rôle in justification, and the period of the later Franciscan school may thus be regarded as beginning at this point.

§16 The later Franciscan school

The early Franciscan school looked to Bonaventure for its inspiration and guidance; the latter Franciscan school substituted for him the colossal figure of Duns Scotus. Although there are undoubtedly Augustinian elements in Scotus' theology, it is quite clear that there has been a decisive shift away from Augustinianism towards a more Aristotelian metaphysics, particularly in connection with epistemological matters. Furthermore, Scotus' discussion of justification is quite distinct from that of Bonaventure at points of major importance, among which may be noted his teaching on the relationship between the elements of the *processus iustificationis* (see §5), on the possibility of extrasacramental justification (see §8), on the cause of predestination (see §12) and on the formal principle of merit and justification (see §13). This latter is of particular significance in relation to the major difficulty we noted in the previous section in connection with the early Franciscan school's teaching on the relationship between nature and grace. For Scotus, the volition of the end necessarily precedes the volition of the means to that end, so that the precise means by which justification occurs is of secondary importance to the fact that God has ordained that it *will* occur. The increasing emphasis upon the priority of the extrinsic denomination of the divine acceptation (see §13) over the possession of a habit of grace inevitably led to a marked reduction in interest in the question of how such a habit came about in the soul. Furthermore, Scotus' concept of covenantal causality eliminated the ontological difficulty felt by the theologians of the early Franciscan school over the possibility of the transition from nature to grace: for Scotus, God had ordained that this transition could be effected through a congruously meritorious disposition towards justification, so that there was no difficulty in abolishing the hiatus between the states of nature and grace. Scotus' approach to the question which posed such difficulties for his predecessors in the Franciscan Order may therefore be said to have resolved the problem in two ways. First, the question was discussed in a significantly different context: for Scotus, the divine acceptation was prior to the possession of a habit of grace, whereas the theologians of the early Franciscan school regarded divine acceptation as posterior to, and contingent upon, the possession of a habit of grace. Second, the *ex natura rei* concept of causality, which posed such difficulties for the theologians of the early Franciscan school, was replaced with an *ex pacto divino* concept, which eliminated the difficulty at once. These alterations, however, resulted in significant changes in Franciscan teaching on justification, which will be noted below.

Scotus' theology of justification, which may be regarded as characteristic of the later Franciscan school, has already been discussed at some length in terms of its individual aspects. There remains, however, one aspect of his teaching which was the subject of considerable confusion in the medieval period itself, and which requires further discussion. This is the question of the possibility of the certitude of grace. The Council of Trent witnessed a significant debate among the assembled prelates[1] over Scotus' teaching on this matter, reflecting the considerable difficulty in interpreting Scotus' pronouncements concerning it. This difficulty chiefly arises from the fact that Scotus never treats the matter *ex professo*, although he comments upon it briefly in his discussion of the possibility of extrasacramental justification (see §9). In general, however, it is clear that Scotus rejects the possibility of such certitude. A man who is conscious of having elicited an act of love for God is not able to conclude that he is in possession of an infused habit of charity as a result. He cannot deduce this from either the substance or the intensity of the act itself, nor from the pleasure or ease with which he elicits the act. If such a conclusion were possible, the *viator* could know for certain that he was in a state of charity.[2] It is, however, impossible for the *viator* to know whether he is worthy of love or hate. The impossibility of such certitude is particularly emphasised by Scotus in connection with the reception of the sacraments.[3] It may be concluded that Scotus adopts the general position of the twelfth and thirteenth centuries by declining to allow the *viator* anything other than *conjectural* certainty, and rigorously excluding the possibility of *absolute* certitude, of grace.

A development of major importance within the later Franciscan schools concerns the doctrine of the Immaculate Conception.[4] This doctrine is of subsidiary importance in relation to the development of the doctrine of justification, in that it relates to the extent of Christ's redeeming work. Prior to Scotus, there appears to have been a general maculist consensus. Thomas Aquinas states this consensus as follows: sanctificatio beatae virginis non potuit esse decenter ante infusionem animae quia gratiae capax nondum fuit, sed nec etiam in ipso instanti infusionis.[5] The most devastating argument against the concept of the Immaculate Conception, as used by the theologians of the early Dominican school, such as Albertus Magnus and Thomas Aquinas, is that the exemption of Mary from sin would limit the perfection of the work of Christ, who must be considered to have died for *all* mankind without exception. It is a reflection of Scotus' subtlety that he is able to turn this argument *against* the doctrine into an argument *for* it. If Christ is the most perfect redeemer, it must be conceded that he is able to redeem at least one person in the most perfect manner possible. As it is more perfect to preserve someone from sin than to liberate them from it, it follows that the most perfect mode of redemption is preservation from sin. Turning his attention to the pressing question of who that single person might be, Scotus argues that it is appropriate that the person concerned should be the mother of the redeemer himself.[6] Scotus' second argument in defence of the Immaculate Conception is the Anselmian principle that the highest possible honour consistent with scripture and tradition should be ascribed to Mary.[7]

Scotus' influence within the Franciscan Order was such that the doctrine of the Immaculate Conception had become the general teaching of the Order by the middle of the fourteenth century,[8] and rapidly became accepted within the *via moderna* and *schola Augustiniana moderna*. The doctrine is particularly useful in distinguishing the later Franciscan and Dominican schools of theology, although Dominican theologians associated with the *via moderna* – such as Robert Holcot – appear to have experienced some difficulty in accommodating the tension between the teaching of their *Orders* and their *schools*.[9]

The leading features of the later Franciscan school's teaching on justification may be summarised as follows:

1.   The possibility of man meriting justification *de congruo* is upheld.
2.   The possibility of absolute certitude of grace is rejected.

3.   Original righteousness is understood to refer to the gift of actual, rather than habitual, grace.

4.   The formal cause of justification is understood to be the extrinsic denomination of the divine acceptation. The intrinsic denomination of the created habit of charity is relegated to the status of a *secondary* formal cause of justification.

5.   The formal principle of merit is understood to be the extrinsic denomination of the divine acceptation. Every act of man is worth precisely what God chooses to accept it for.

6.   The necessity of a preparation for justification is upheld. The psychological justification for this preparation, associated with the earlier Franciscan school, appears to be abandoned.

7.   Mary must be regarded as exempt from the common human condition of original sin, and thus as standing outside the scope of Christ's normal mode of redemption. This does not, however, mean that Scotus denies that Christ redeemed Mary, as some have suggested: rather, a different mode of redemption is envisaged in this specific case.

§17 The *via moderna*

In the present study, the term *via moderna* has been employed to refer to the theological school based upon the teachings of William of Ockham, including such theologians as Pierre d'Ailly, Robert Holcot, Gabriel Biel and Wendelin Steinbach. The term 'Nominalism' has frequently been employed in the past to designate this school, and we therefore propose to indicate the reasons for preferring the term *via moderna*.

Until recently, it was generally considered that pre-Reformation catholicism had been captured by a single school of 'Nominalism', which was everywhere in control of the teaching of Christian doctrine.[1] In part, the assertion of the dominance of this 'crippled parody of true scholasticism'[2] has arisen through the questionable presuppositions and methods of an earlier generation of Reformation historians, who tended to base their estimations of the nature of pre-Reformation catholicism solely upon studies of German academic theologians of the late fifteenth century, such as Gabriel Biel, in an attempt to elucidate the background against which the emergence of the theology of the young Luther must be understood. Unfortunately, the results of these early studies were applied uncritically to catholicism throughout Europe, on the unjustified and inherently unjustifiable assumption that the situation in the German universities accurately reflected late medieval theology in general.

This situation, however, is rapidly being remedied. A series of seminal studies have drawn attention to the astonishing diversity of theological opinion within the movement originally known as 'Nominalism', so that it is now recognised that it is quite improper to speak of a homogeneous 'Nominalist' theology in the first place. A series of studies published in the third and fourth decades of the present century drew attention to the existence of two diametrically opposed trends within 'Nominalism' in relation to the powers of human nature and the dynamics of grace.[3] Hence William of Ockham, Robert Holcot and Gabriel Biel came to be seen as promoting an optimistic view of human nature, allowing man a positive rôle in his own justification, while others, such as Marsilius of Inghen, Gregory of Rimini and Heinrich Totting von Oyta were critical of such views, asserting a doctrine of grace which must be considered to be more Augustinian in character. The most important monograph to appear during this early period was Cardinal Ehrle's justly celebrated study *Der Sentenzenkommentar Peters von Candia* (1925), in which the multiplicity of opinions within the allegedly homogeneous 'Nominalist' school of the fourteenth and fifteenth centuries was adequately demonstrated for the first time. On the basis of his studies, Ehrle argued that the term 'Nominalism' was sufficiently ill-defined as to be misleading.[4] This point was further emphasised by Lang, who pointed out that many of those who accepted Ockham's *philosophy* were considerably more sceptical concerning his *theology*,[5] so that the fact that a thinker of the fifteenth century held an Ockhamist epistemology could be not regarded as implying that he held a 'Nominalist' doctrine of justification. In a highly significant study, Hochstetter drew attention to the fact that it was improper to equate 'Nominalism' and 'Ockhamism' in the first place,[6] in that the term 'Nominalist' tended to be applied to the followers of Ockham *by their opponents*.

The term 'Nominalism' was first used in the twelfth century to refer to the anti-realist position on the question of universals, otherwise known as 'Terminism', and is used to designate an epistemological, rather than a theological, aspect of a writer's doctrine. As such, the term should be applied primarily to thinkers of the twelfth century: as Vignaux has pointed out, when a writer of the thirteenth century refers to the *nominales*, he has the logicians of the previous century in mind.[7] The term is not generally used to refer to Ockham by his contemporaries, although Ehrle notes that a condemnation of 1472 includes Ockham among the *nominales*.[8] It is, however, quite absurd to assume that Ockham's position on the question of universals should dictate the remainder of his philosophical and theological system, so that the epithet 'Nominalist' may be considered a convenient means of encapsulating his entire thought in a single term. The fundamental contention of nominalism or terminism, in its strict and proper epistemological sense, is that all things which exist to the mind are merely particulars: there is no genuine or objective identity in things which are not in themselves identical. This may be contrasted with the realist position, which concedes the existence of universals, arguing that the apparent situation is the real situation. It should be noted, of course, that realism and nominalism are not directly opposed, in that realism is effectively the *via media* between nominalism and universalism.[9] Thus Ockham's rejection of a 'common nature' and his emphasis upon the knowledge of the particular indicate a nominalist epistemology. But what, it may reasonably be asked, are the theological consequences of such an epistemology?

Elsewhere, we have shown how Ockham's nominalism is of significance in relation to his Christology.[10] Whereas the theologians of the *via antiqua* – such as the Albertists, Thomists and Scotists – found no difficulty with the concept of *humanitas* denoting a universal human nature, Ockham's nominalism required him to hold that it denotes individual *homines*. The point is well made by Martin Luther, who shares Ockham's terminism in this respect:

Terministen hieß man eine secten in der hohen schulen, unter welchen ich auch gewesen. Die selbigen haltens wider die Thomisten, Scotisten und Albertisten und hießen auch Occamisten von Occam, ihrem ersten anfenger, und sein die aller neuesten secten, und ist die mechtigste auch tzu Paris. Der hader war, ob *humanitas* und dergleichen wordt eine gemeine menscheit heiße, die in allen menschen were, wie Thomas und die andern halten. Ja, sagen die Occamisten oder Terministen, es sey nichtes mit solcher gemeiner menschheit, sondern der Terminus 'homo' oder menschheit heist alle menschen insonderheit, gleichwie ein gemalt menschen bilde alle menschen deutet.[11]

It is not, however, clear that such logical considerations in relation to the signification of terms has any bearing on the doctrine of justification. Thus Martin Luther, Gregory of Rimini,[12] Hugolino of Orvieto,[13] William of Ockham, Robert Holcot and Gabriel Biel may all be regarded as nominalists on the basis of the sole acceptable criterion – their position on the question of universals. It will, however, be evident that the six writers have very different doctrines

168

of justification, the first three adopting radically Augustinian positions, and the remainder positions which approach, although do not strictly constitute, Pelagianism. This point serves to illustrate the general conclusion of modern late medieval scholarship, that there were many doctors who shared common nominalist epistemological presuppositions who otherwise had little, if anything, in common. The publication of an increasing number of theological treatises by *moderni* has made it abundantly clear that a nominalist epistemology (i.e., Terminism) can be associated with such an astonishing variety of theological positions that it conveys no useful information concerning a given 'Nominalist's' theology. Just as the theologians of an earlier period (such as the early Dominican and Franciscan schools) were generally realist, those of the later medieval period were generally nominalist. It is therefore necessary to find an acceptable alternative designation for theologians such as Ockham, Holcot and Biel.

How then, may the distinctive school of thought traditionally known as 'Nominalism' be designated? One possible way of avoiding the difficulties noted above is to define 'Nominalism' as the characteristic theological position of Ockham *cum suis*,[14] and ignore the fundamentally epistemological reference of the term. This pragmatic approach to the difficulty is, however, quite unacceptable, not least because it means that it inevitably perpetuates the myth of the homogeneity of late medieval thought. In addition, it will be clear that the specific meaning of the word 'Nominalism' will alter with each successive study of the thought of Ockham and his circle. Furthermore, it is important to establish whether writers who have traditionally been designated as 'Nominalists' through the questionable presuppositions and research methods of earlier generations of scholars actually merit the description in the first place, which evidently requires that some criterion be accepted for the purpose other than the loose descriptive definition suggested. Recent research, however has discredited this approach for a rather different, and totally unexpected, reason. In an important study, Schepers demonstrated that Oxford radical 'Nominalism' *was a specifically anti-Ockhamist movement*.[15] Robert Holcot and Adam Wodeham have now been identified as the chief proponents of Ockham's system after his departure from England in 1324, and the Dominican William of Crathorn and the Franciscan Walter Chatton as their radical opponents.[16] There is thus every reason to suppose that Ockhamism was a non-radical system, with Ockham being regarded as a reactionary by those who wished to develop his nominalism fully. If the term 'Nominalism' is employed to refer to the teachings of Ockham *cum suis*, it will therefore be clear that there were others with at least as great, and almost certainly a considerably greater, claim to represent a 'Nominalist' theology.

For reasons such as those we have outlined above, we refuse to employ the term 'Nominalist' in the present study, preferring to adopt the increasingly common alternative *via moderna*,[17] which refers primarily to a theological method, based on the application of the dialectic between the two powers of God and the concept of covenantal causality, rather than the *corpus* of doctrines resulting from its application. Although the theologians of the *via moderna* generally adopted a nominalist epistemology, in common with their contemporaries, their characteristic soteriological opinions were quite independent of this nominalism. The characteristic features of the doctrines of justification associated with the theologians of the *via moderna* are similar to those of the later Franciscan school. Despite the nominalism of the former and the realism of the latter, their doctrines of justification are substantially identical. Where differences exist between the two schools, they are primarily concerned with the *conceptual framework* within which the justification of the *viator* was discussed, rather than the *substance* of their teaching on justification. Indeed, the *via moderna* may be regarded as having exploited the dialectic between the two powers of God and the concept of the *pactum* (see §11) to place the teaching of the later Franciscan schools upon a firmer conceptual foundation. Furthermore, the differences which exist between the later Franciscan school and the *via moderna* in relation to the conceptual framework within which justification was discussed do not appear to have any *direct* bearing upon the epistemological differences between the schools.

The context within which the question of the possibility of the justification of the *viator* is set by the theologians of the *via moderna* is that of the *pactum* between God and man. God has ordained to enter into covenantal relationship with man by virtue of which he will accept human acts as being worthy of salvation, even though their intrinsic value is negligible. This distinction between the *intrinsic* and *imposed* value of moral acts is of decisive importance, as it permits the axiom *facienti quod in se est Deus non denegat gratiam* (see §7) to be interpreted in a sense which allows a man to play a positive rôle in his own justification, without elevating that rôle to Pelagian proportions. In this way, the theologians of the *via moderna* were able to maintain the teaching of both the early and later Franciscan schools concerning man's meritorious disposition towards justification, while establishing a conceptual framework within which this teaching could be safeguarded from the charge of Pelagianism. Linked with this was the related concept of *covenantal causality*, by which the theologians of the *via moderna* were able to avoid the ontological difficulties experienced by the early Franciscan school concerning the transition from nature to grace.

One aspect of the soteriology of the *via moderna* which is of particular interest is the Christological lacuna within their understanding of the economy of salvation.[18] It is quite possible to discuss the justification of the *viator* within the terms set by the theologians of the *via moderna* without reference to the incarnation and death of Christ. This point is best seen by considering the following question: what, according to the theologians of the *via moderna*, is the difference between the justification of man in the period of the Old Testament and in the period of the New? Biel's understanding of the covenant between God and man is such that God rewards the man who does *quod in se est* with grace, irrespective of whether this pertains under the old or new covenants. The Old Testament character of the ethics of the *via moderna* has frequently been noted:[19] it does not appear to have been fully appreciated, however, that this arises from the simple fact that the Old Testament scheme of justification is essentially the same as the New. Both the Old and the New Testaments hold out the promise of rewards to those who do good.[20] Whilst the new covenant abrogates the ceremonial aspects of the old, the moral law of the Old Testament remains valid.[21] Christ is therefore more appropriately described as *Legislator* than *Salvator*: Christ has fulfilled and perfected the law of Moses in order that he may be imitated by Christians.[22] Caritatem precipuit Christus legislator noster et tamquam signum suae legis ac discipulatus praestituit.[23] The justice which is required of man in order that he may be justified is the same in the Old and New Testaments: ubera hec due sunt partes iustitiae, declinare scilicet a malo et facere bonum.[24]

The characteristic features of the doctrines of justification associated with the *via moderna* may be summarised as follows. It must be emphasised that the following features pertain *de potentia Dei ordinata*.

1. The necessity of man meriting justification *de congruo* is maintained, this being regarded as effecting the transition between the moral and the meritorious planes within the terms of the *pactum*.

2.   The possibility of man knowing with absolute certitude whether he is in possession of grace is rejected, although various degrees of conjectural certainty are conceded. In view of the total reliability of the *pactum*, however, the uncertainty is understood to arise through man's inability to know whether he has done *quod in se est*.[25]

3.   Original righteousness is understood to include the gift of actual, but not sanctifying grace. The state of pure nature is thus understood to include the *influentia Dei generalis* alone.[26]

4.   The formal cause of justification is defined as the extrinsic denomination of the divine acceptation. It is not clear what rôle created habits play within the soteriology of the *via moderna* (see §13).

5.   The formal principle of merit is defined as the extrinsic denomination of the divine acceptation.

6.   The necessity of a human disposition towards justification is maintained, on the grounds that it constitutes the contracted link between the realms of nature and grace within the terms of the *pactum* – i.e., within the context of *ex pacto divino* causality, it functions as the cause of the infusion of grace. The difficulties associated with the early Franciscan school – which arise from an *ex natura rei* understanding of causality – are thus avoided.

7.   A strongly immaculist approach is generally adopted to the question of the conception of Mary.

§18 The medieval Augustinian tradition

In the previous section, we noted how the questionable presuppositions and methods of earlier generations of Reformation historians led to a distorted understanding of the nature and influence of the *via moderna*. A distorted impression of the 'medieval Augustinian tradition' has also arisen for similar reasons. The tendency on the part of an earlier generation of historians to approach the late medieval period with the concerns and presuppositions of the Reformation itself (particularly in relation to Martin Luther) resulted in the identification of 'Nominalism' and 'Augustinianism' as two theological movements within the later medieval period which were totally and irreconcilably opposed. In particular, the conflict between the 'Nominalism' of Gabriel Biel and the 'Augustinianism' of Johannes von Staupitz was assumed to be a general feature of the period between the death of Duns Scotus and Luther's revolt against the theology of Gabriel Biel in 1517. A study of the interaction between 'Nominalists' and 'Augustinians' in the fourteenth and fifteenth centuries, however, indicates that this dichotomy is more easily suggested than demonstrated. The highly questionable methods of earlier Reformation historiographers thus resulted in an estimation of pre-Reformation catholicism being deduced which reflects solely or largely the interests, concerns and presuppositions of modern Luther scholars.

Recently, this trend has been reversed, with increasing attention being paid to the theology of the later medieval period as a subject of importance in its own right, independent of its relation to the Reformation, with a considerable number of important studies being published on medieval Augustinian theologians.[1] As a result, we are now in a position to evaluate the nature and influence of the 'medieval Augustinian tradition'. In the present section, we propose to consider whether any 'medieval Augustinian tradition' can be identified with a coherent teaching on justification.

As noted in the previous section, there is a growing tendency to reject the idea of 'Nominalism' as a homogeneous school of thought during the later medieval period. It is not generally appreciated, however, that this has important consequences for the definition of 'Augustinianism' during the same period, in that the latter was usually *defined in relation to 'Nominalism'*. Once the idea of a homogeneous school of 'Nominalism' is rejected, the point of reference for the definition of 'Augustinianism' is removed. The vast amount of research undertaken on theologians of the Augustinian Order during the present century has made it clear that a dichotomy between 'Augustinianism' and 'Nominalism' is quite untenable. A phenomenally wide spectrum of theological opinions existed at the time, so that the use of the terms 'Nominalist' and 'Augustinian' *as correlatives* is now obviously inappropriate.

The situation has been still further confused by the variety of interpretations placed upon the term 'Augustinian' by historians and theologians alike. At least four senses of the term may be distinguished in writings of contemporary medieval scholarship.[2]

1. The theology of the Latin west in general, in so far as it represents a refraction of that of Augustine.
2. The theology of the Augustinian Order (i.e., the Order of the Hermits of St Augustine), whether this theology may happen to correspond to the teaching of Augustine or not. As used in this sense, the term 'Augustinian' has the same significance as 'Franciscan' or 'Dominican' (see §§14–16): an 'Augustinian' theology need therefore bear no relation to that of Augustine, just as that of

the early Franciscan school bears no relation to that of Francis or
that of the early Dominican school to Dominic.

3. The theology of a specific group within the Augustinian Order,
which corresponds to a greater extent with the teaching of
Augustine.

4. A theology which corresponds to that of Augustine, particularly in
relation to his teaching on original sin and predestination, irrespective of whether the theologian in question belonged to the Augustinian Order.

This confusion is particularly well illustrated by the attempt of A. V.
Müller to demonstrate that Luther stood within a school of theo-
logians which represented a theology more Augustinian than that of
Thomas Aquinas or Bonaventure.[3] In particular, Müller argued that
Luther's concept of *iustitia duplex* could be traced back to a theological school which included Simon Fidati of Cascia (d. 1348),
Hugolino of Orvieto (d. 1373), Agostino Favaroni (d. 1443) and
Jacobus Perez of Valencia (d. 1490).[4] A similar thesis was defended,
although for rather different reasons, by Eduard Stakemeier, who
argued that the doctrine of double justification associated with
Girolamo Seripando during the Tridentine proceedings on justification represented an Augustinian theological tradition which could
only be properly understood when set within the context of the
theological tradition of the Augustinian Order – to which both
Seripando and Luther belonged.[5] It is, however, quite impossible to
sustain the thesis that both Luther and Seripando represent possible
variations on a basically Augustinian theology of justification, in
Stakemeier's sense of the term.[6] Not only does Luther's implacable
hostility to the doctrine of double justification exclude such a thesis
from the outset:[7] the important study of Henninger demonstrated
that Augustine himself knew nothing of such a doctrine of double
justification,[8] so that the use of the epithet 'Augustinian' was quite
inappropriate to characterise Seripando's doctrine of justification.
There are, in fact, serious difficulties attending *any* attempt to
characterise the theology of any later medieval thinker as 'Augustinian' (in the sense of 'corresponding to the thought of Augustine
himself'), as we shall make clear in what follows.

It is necessary to make a clear distinction between the *dogmatic
content* of Augustine's theology, and the *terms and concepts* which he
originally employed to express this content. In particular, it may be
emphasised that Augustine's theological vocabulary was frequently
developed in a polemical context, in conscious opposition to his

Pelagian or Donatist opponents, so that the form of his responses was frequently determined by the prior questions or objections of his opponents. An excellent example of this is provided by his distinction between operative and cooperative grace, which met the needs of the moment, but proved less valuable to his later interpreters. The theological renaissance of the twelfth century was almost entirely based upon the works of Augustine, as we have already noted. It soon became clear, however, that this involved the introduction of terms and concepts unknown to Augustine (such as the distinction between congruous and condign merit) in an attempt to preserve the *dogmatic content* of his theology, while expressing it in a more systematic form.

The essential point which we wish to make is the following: by the close of the thirteenth century, the dogmatic content of Augustine's theology had become expressed in terms and concepts unknown to Augustine himself. Once such developments had taken place, there was no real possibility of abandoning them. Thus the only theologians of the later medieval period who can lay claim to be 'Augustinian' in the strict sense of the term are those who were sufficiently reactionary, not merely to retain the dogmatic context of Augustine's theology, but also the terms in which he himself expressed it. However, as theologians who wished to express opinions closer to those of Augustine than their contemporaries were obliged to use the theological vocabulary of their day if they wished to engage in dialogue with their contemporaries, it will be evident that few, if any, 'Augustinian' theologians can be adduced.

The term 'Augustinian' must therefore be used in a qualified sense, signifying 'retaining the *dogmatic content*, if not the *conceptual forms*, of Augustine's theology'. There are, however, serious objections even to this modified definition of the term. For example, we have already drawn attention to the numerous pseudo-Augustinian works in circulation in the medieval period (see §7), many of which were clearly opposed to the teaching of Augustine on justification. Furthermore, the general tendency of the age to use collections of Augustinian 'sentences', rather than the original works of Augustine, inevitably led to Augustinian citations being used out of context, with an inevitable distortion in their meaning. An excellent example of this phenomenon has been noted in the cases of Duns Scotus and Gabriel Biel, who both manage to achieve a complete inversion of Augustine's teaching on the relation between grace and free will by confusing an image used by Augustine himself with a similar image found in the pseudo-Augustinian *Hypognosticon*.[9] Most significantly of all, the criterion of the 'Augustinianism' of a theologian usually employed in this context is his teaching on predestination and related matters, as noted above. This is open to question, as it appears to rest upon the presupposition that Augustine's doctrine of predestination is more characteristically 'Augustinian' than the remainder of his teaching, such as his doctrine of the church. Thus John Huss, usually identified as a late medieval 'Augustinian', may well justify this epithet in relation to his soteriology – yet his ecclesiology is radically non-Augustinian. It is this fundamental point which underlies the famous epigram: 'The Reformation, inwardly considered, was just the ultimate triumph of Augustine's doctrine of grace over Augustine's doctrine of the church.'[10]

The criterion usually employed in establishing the 'Augustinianism' of a theologian is whether he taught that anything in man himself could be said to cause his subsequent justification. The rejection of any such *ratio iustificationis ex parte creaturae* is usually taken as evidence of a theologian's 'Augustinianism'. This criterion, however, is open to question, as such a rejection may arise for thoroughly non-Augustinian reasons. This may be illustrated with reference to Thomas Bradwardine, who rejects the thesis that anything in man is the cause of his justification for the following reasons:

Prima, quod nihil potest quicquam movere sine Deo idem per se et proprie commovente. Secunda, quod nihil potest quicquam movere sine Deo immediate idem movente. Tertia, quod nihil potest quicquam movere sine Deo idem movente immediatius alio motore quocunque. Quarta, quod nulla propositio tribuens quodcunque creatum cuicunque causae secundae, est immediata simpliciter.[11]

God is the efficient, formal and final cause of everything which occurs concerning his creatures, so that the creature has no rôle to play in the causal sequence whatsoever. The reasons for Bradwardine's rejection of any *ratio iustificationis ex parte creaturae* are thus Aristotelian in nature, rather than Augustinian, and clearly raise questions relating to the rôle of the Fall in this theology. Man's need for grace is a consequence of his creatureliness, rather than his sinfulness as a result of the Fall. There is thus no fundamental difference between man's pristine and fallen states in this respect, as in both he is a creature. It is difficult to see how such a theologian can be deemed to be 'Augustinian', in view of the critical rôle of the Fall and human sin in Augustine's theology. It is almost certain that Gregory of Rimini, the great fourteenth-century theologian of the

Augustinian Order, singles out Bradwardine for special criticism for his un-Augustinian views on the Fall.[12] A more sustained critique of Bradwardine upon this point may be illustrated from the writings of other members of the Augustinian Order at the time, such as Johannes Klenkok, who studied at Bradwardine's university, Oxford, in the decades following the appearance of de causa Dei.[13] Klenkok's critique of Bradwardine is very similar to that of his fellow-Augustinian Hugolino of Orvieto:[14] both Augustinian theologians regarded Bradwardine as perpetrating a metaphysical determinism which owed nothing to Augustine. Similar criticisms were made by the later Augustinians Johannes Hiltalingen of Basel[15] and Angelus Dobelinus, the first professor of theology at the university of Erfurt.[16]

A more significant approach to the 'medieval Augustinian tradition' is to study theological currents prevalent within the Augustinian Order during the later medieval period. When this is done, it is possible to distinguish two main schools of thought within the Order during the period: the schola Aegidiana and the schola Augustiniana moderna. We shall consider these two schools individually.

The school of thought which developed during the fourteenth century, based upon the writings of Giles of Rome, was known as the schola Aegidiana,[17] suggesting that Giles was regarded as a theological authority by those who followed in his footsteps within the Order. Although the theory that members of the Augustinian Order were obliged to swear fidelity to the teachings of Giles of Rome at the time of their profession has not stood up to critical examination,[18] it is nevertheless clear that a school of thought developed within the Order which remained faithful to his teaching. This fidelity is particularly clear in relation to his teaching on original righteousness.[19] Thus Dionysius de Burgo regarded Giles of Rome and Thomas Aquinas as being theological authorities of equal importance, although his occasional preference for doctor noster Aegidius is noticeable.[20] Thomas of Strasbourg refers to Giles as doctor noster, and cites him with sufficient frequency to suggest that he regards him as a theological authority of some considerable weight.[21] Johannes von Retz, the second member of the Augustinian Order to become professor of theology at Vienna, cited both Giles of Rome and especially his follower Thomas of Strasbourg extensively.[22] Johannes Hiltalingen of Basel considered that the theologians of the Augustinian Order could be regarded as constituting a distinct theological school, although he neglected to mention which particular features were characteristic of this putative 'school'.[23] It seems, however, that the characteristic features of the *schola Aegidiana* are due to Giles of Rome himself, the strongly Augustinian character of his theology being slightly modulated with Thomism at points.[24] The strongly Augustinian cast of the *schola Aegidiana* may be particularly well seen in the emphasis placed upon the priority of *caritas* and *gratia* in man's justification.[25]

It seems, however, that the *schola Aegidiana* gave way to the *schola Augustiniana moderna* during the fourteenth century. It is generally accepted that the period of medieval Augustinian theology can be divided into two periods: the first encompassing the period between Giles of Rome and Thomas of Strasbourg, and the second the period between Gregory of Rimini and the early sixteenth century. The theologians of the Augustinian Order appear to have been significantly influenced by theological currents from outside their Order, as may be seen from their changing understandings of the nature of the conception of Mary. The earlier theologians of the *schola Aegidiana*, such as Giles of Rome, Albert of Padua, Augustinus Triumphus of Ancona and Gregory of Rimini were strongly maculist in their Mariological persuasions.[26] However, from the late fourteenth century onwards, the theologians of the Augustinian Order came to adopt the immaculist position. Thus beginning with Johannes Hiltalingen of Basel, Henry of Freimar,[27] and Thomas of Strasbourg, and continuing into the fifteenth and early sixteenth centuries with Jacobus Perez of Valencia, Johannes de Paltz[28] and Johannes von Staupitz,[29] the theologians of the Augustinian Order moved away from the teaching of the *schola Aegidiana* in this respect. Although similar divergences from other characteristic teachings of the *schola Aegidiana*, such as their understanding of *iustitia originalis*,[30] may also be detected, the most fundamental difference relates to the method employed in theological speculation.

In the previous section, we noted the emergence of the logico-critical attitudes of the *via moderna* within the German universities of the late fourteenth and early fifteenth centuries, and the resulting polarisation between *antiqui* and *moderni*. In the late fourteenth century, precisely such a polarisation between the methods and presuppositions of the *via antiqua* and *via moderna* took place within the Augustinian Order itself.[31] While the *antiqui* were primarily concerned with establishing accurately the opinions of writers such as Augustine on the basis of historico-critical studies, the *moderni* employed the logico-critical device of the dialectic between the two powers of God (see §12) to 'correct' such opinions.[32] One such 'correction' was the critique of the role of created habits in justification (see §13). Although the theologians of the *schola Aegidiana* held that the formal cause of justification was the created habit of grace, the theologians of the *schola Augustiniana moderna* adopted the characteristic position of the later Franciscan school and the *via moderna* – that the *ratio iustificationis* was the extrinsic denomination of the divine acceptation.[33] By the late fifteenth century, a theology of justification had developed within certain sections of the Augustinian Order which can only be regarded as a hybrid species, retaining much of the authentic theological emphases of Augustine (e.g., the emphasis upon man's depravity, and the priority of *caritas* in justification), while employing methods (such as the dialectic between the two powers of God) which owed more to the *via moderna*.[34] This point serves to emphasise the total futility of attempting to make a sharp distinction between 'Augustinian' and 'Nominalism' in the later medieval period: not only did many Augustinians adopt a nominalist epistemology (such as Gregory of Rimini and Hugolino of Orvieto) – they also incorporated significant elements of 'Nominalism' into their discussion of justification. Indeed, it may be argued that it is precisely this variation between individual 'Augustinian' theologians in relation to the extent to which they appropriated elements of 'Nominalism' which has caused such confusion in the present century concerning the characteristics of a putative school of 'Augustinian' theology in the medieval period.

It will therefore be clear that it is impossible to speak of a single homogeneous 'medieval Augustinian tradition' during the Middle Ages in relation to the doctrine of justification. Two such traditions may be identified:

1. The school of thought, often referred to as the *schola Aegidiana*, which is based upon the teaching of Giles of Rome, which understood the created habit of grace to be the *ratio iustificationis*.

2. The later school of thought, usually referred to as the *schola Augustiniana moderna*, mediated through Gregory of Rimini and Hugolino of Orvieto, which had serious reservations concerning the rôle of created habits in justification, and which placed increasing emphasis upon the uncreated grace of the Holy Spirit and the extrinsic denomination of the divine acceptation. It is within this latter tradition that Martin Luther's early critique of the rôle of created habits in justification should be understood.[35]

5. The transition from the medieval to the modern period

§19 Forerunners of the Reformation doctrines of justification?

It is clearly of considerable interest to establish the relationship between the doctrines of justification associated with the emerging churches of the Reformation of the sixteenth century and those associated with earlier periods in the history of doctrine. The historical importance of this question will be self-evident, in that the character, distinctiveness and final significance of any movement in intellectual history is invariably better appreciated when its relationship to comparable movements which preceded it are positively identified. It is for this reason that considerable attention is currently being directed towards establishing the precise relationship between the thought of the late medieval period and that of the Reformation. It must be appreciated, however, that scholarly interest in the *historical* aspects of the question concerning the continuity of the late medieval and Reformation periods has tended to obscure the theological aspect of the question, which was considered to be more significant at the time of the Reformation itself. The fundamental theological question which is thus raised is the following: can the teachings of the churches of the Reformation be regarded as truly catholic?[1] In view of the centrality of the doctrine of justification to both the *initium theologiae Lutheri* and the *initium Reformationis*,[2] this question becomes acutely pressing concerning the doctrine of justification itself. If it can be shown that the central teaching of the Lutheran Reformation, the fulcrum about which the early Reformation turned, the *articulus stantis et cadentis ecclesiae*,[3] constituted a theological *novum*, unknown within the previous fifteen centuries of catholic thought, it will be clear that the Reformers' claim to catholicity would be seriously prejudiced, if not totally discredited.

The question of the historical continuity between the teaching of the churches of the Reformation and that of earlier periods in relation to justification thus became acutely pressing. For the Roman Catholic opponents of the Reformation, such teachings represented theological innovations. For Bossuet, the Reformers had significantly altered the common teaching of the catholic church upon this central doctrine and by doing so, had forfeited their claims to orthodoxy and catholicity:

The church's doctrine is always the same ... the Gospel is never different from what it was before. Hence, if at any time someone says that the faith includes something which yesterday was not said to be of the faith, it is always *heterodoxy*, which is any doctrine different from *orthodoxy*. There is no difficulty about recognising false doctrine: there is no argument about it: it is recognised at once, whenever it appears, merely because it is new.[4]

This was such a serious charge that the theologians of the Reformation were obliged to meet it, which they did in two manners.

1. The claim was rejected out of hand, it being asserted that the Reformation represented a long-overdue return to the truly catholic teaching of the church, which had become distorted and disfigured through the questionable theological methods of later medieval theology. Particular emphasis was laid upon the alleged concurrence of the Reformation teachings on justification with those of Augustine.[5]

2. The claim was conceded, to varying extents, but was qualified in an important respect. The doctrines of justification associated with the Reformation only represent innovations if orthodoxy is determined by the decrees of the corrupt late medieval church. A dichotomy was posited between the corrupt official teaching of the church, and the faithful catholic teaching of individual 'proto-Reformers', which would eventually triumph at the time of the Reformation.[6] It is this thesis which is usually stated in terms of the existence of 'Forerunners of the Reformation'.[7] In the present section, we are particularly concerned with the historical task of establishing areas of continuity and discontinuity between the late medieval period and that of the Reformation. In view of the theological importance of the question, however, we shall examine both of the positions identified above.

From the analysis of the late medieval schools of thought on justification presented in the present study, it will be clear that there existed considerable diversity of opinion on the matter during the later medieval period. This diversity represents a particular instance of the general pluralism of late medieval religious thought, which is usually argued to originate from the fourteenth century.[8] The

Tridentine decree on justification may be regarded as an attempt to define the limits of this pluralism, if not to impose a unity upon it.[9] But are the characteristic features of the Reformation doctrines of justification foreshadowed in the doctrinal pluralism of the late medieval period? Before attempting to answer this question, the characteristic features of such teachings must first be identified.

The first era of the Reformation witnessed a broad consensus emerging upon both the *nature* of justification and the *context* in which it was set. The following three features are characteristic of Protestant understandings of the *nature* of justification over the period 1530–1730:[10]

1. Justification is understood to be the forensic declaration that the Christian is righteous, rather than the process by which he is made righteous, involving a change in his *status* before God, rather than his *nature*.

2. A deliberate and systematic distinction is made between the concept of *justification* itself (understood as the extrinsic divine pronouncement of man's new status) and the concept of *sanctification* or *regeneration* (understood as the intrinsic process by which God renews the justified sinner).

3. The formal, or immediate cause, of justification is understood to be the alien righteousness of Christ, imputed to man in justification, so that justification involves a *synthetic* rather than an *analytic* judgement on the part of God.

In defining these features as characteristic of Protestant understandings of justification, it must be emphasised that neither Martin Luther nor Huldrych Zwingli understood justification in precisely this manner. The consolidation of these features as characteristics of Protestantism appears to have been achieved through the considerable influence of Philip Melanchthon. It is nevertheless clear that Luther's doctrine of the *iustitia Christia aliena* laid the conceptual foundation for such a doctrine of forensic justification.[11] In effect, Luther must be regarded as a figure of transition, standing at the junction of two rival understandings of the nature of justification. As we demonstrated earlier (see §5), the medieval theological tradition was unanimous in its understanding of justification as both an act and a process, by which both man's status *coram Deo* and his essential nature underwent alteration. Although Luther regarded justification as an essentially unitary process, he nevertheless introduced a decisive break with the western theological tradition as a whole by insisting that, through his justification, man is *intrinsically* sinful yet *extrinsically* righteous.[12] It is at this point that it is possible to distinguish the otherwise similar teachings of Luther and Johannes von Staupitz on justification.[13]

It must be emphasised that it is totally unacceptable to characterise the doctrines of justification associated with the Reformation solely with reference to their anti-Pelagian character, or their associated doctrines of predestination. Although an earlier generation of scholars argued that the Reformation resulted from the sudden rediscovery of the radical anti-Pelagianism of Augustine's soteriology, it is clear that this judgement cannot be sustained. The emergence of the *schola Augustiniana moderna* (see §18) in the fourteenth century was essentially an academic movement based upon the anti-Pelagian writings of Augustine,[14] and the possibility that both Calvin and Luther, as well as other Reformers such as Peter Martyr Vermigli, demonstrate continuity with this late medieval Augustinian school calls this judgement into question.[15] In its radical anti-Pelagianism, the Reformation, in its first phase, demonstrated a remarkable degree of continuity with well-established currents in late medieval thought. This is not, of course, to say that the Reformation was *typical* of the late medieval period, but merely to observe that the Reformation demonstrates strong affinities with one of the many theological currents which constituted the flux of late medieval theology. Equally, the Reformers unhesitatingly rejected the necessity of created habits of grace in justification, a tendency which is evident from Luther's *Randbemerkungen* of 1509–10 onwards.[16] By doing so, they reflected the general tendency of the period, particularly within the *via moderna* and *schola Augustiniana moderna*, to locate the *ratio iustificationis* primarily in the extrinsic denomination of the divine acceptation (see §13). The covenantal, rather than ontological, and voluntarist, rather than intellectualist, foundations of late medieval theology may also be argued to have passed into the theology of the first phase of the Reformation. It will therefore be clear that many of the fundamental presuppositions of the soteriology of the late medieval period passed into the early theology of the Reformation. Within the flux of late medieval theology, currents may easily be identified which demonstrate various degrees of continuity with the emerging theologies of justification associated with the first phase of the Reformation.

These areas of continuity, nevertheless, relate to the *mode* of justification, rather than to its *nature*. Despite the disagreement within the various theological schools concerning the manner in which justification came about, there was a fundamental consensus on what the term 'justification' itself signified. Throughout the entire medieval period, justification continued to be understood as the process by which a man is made righteous, subsuming the concepts of 'sanctification' and 'regeneration'. *Iustificare* was understood to signify *iustum facere* throughout the period. Albrecht Ritschl is thus correct when he states that:

We shall ... search in vain to find in any theologian of the Middle Ages the Reformation idea of justification – the deliberate distinction between justification and regeneration ... Their deliberate treatment of the idea of justification proceeds rather on the principle that a real change in the sinner is thought of as involved in it – in other words, the Reformation distinction between the two ideas is at the outset rejected.[17]

The significance of the Protestant distinction between *iustificatio* and *regeneratio* is that a fundamental discontinuity has been introduced into the western theological tradition *where none had existed before*. Despite the astonishing theological diversity of the late medieval period, a consensus relating to the *nature* of justification was maintained throughout. The Protestant understanding of the *nature* of justification represents a theological *novum*, whereas its understanding of its *mode* does not. It is therefore of considerable importance to appreciate that the *criterion employed in the sixteenth century* to determine whether a particular doctrine of justification was Protestant or otherwise was *whether justification was understood forensically*. The fury surrounding the Osiandrist controversy only served to harden the early Protestant conviction that any doctrine of justification by inherent righteousness was inherently anti-Protestant.[18] The history of the Reformation itself, especially as it concerns Osiander and Latomus, demonstrates that the criterion employed *at the time* to determine whether a given doctrine was Protestant or otherwise primarily concerned the manner in which justifying righteousness was understood. It would therefore appear to be historically unsound to use any other criterion in this respect.

Once this point is conceded, we may return to a consideration of the two main lines of defence of the catholicity of Protestant doctrines of justification encountered during the first phase of the Reformation. The first such approach, which is particularly associated with Philip Melanchthon, is to argue that the Reformation understandings of justification represent a legitimate interpretation of the theology of Augustine, so that the Lutheran Reformation may be regarded as recovering the authentic teaching of the African bishop from the distortions of the medieval period.[19] However, it will be clear that the medieval period was astonishingly faithful to the teaching of Augustine on the question of the nature of justification, where the Reformers departed from it. Melanchthon himself appears to have been unaware of this point, as Latomus pointed out with some force.[20] A more forceful statement of the same position is associated with the Scottish Protestant polemicist James Buchanan (1804–70), who declared his intention to:

prove as a matter of FACT . . . that the Protestant doctrine of justification was not a 'novelty' introduced for the first time by Luther and Calvin . . . and that there is no truth in the allegation that it had been unknown for fourteen hundred years before the Reformation.[21]

Thus he indignantly rejects any suggestion that the Reformers were theological innovators, or that 'Augustine knew nothing of a forensic justification by faith', teaching instead 'the opposite doctrine of a "moral" justification by infused or inherent righteousness'.[22]

If the catholicity of Protestant understandings of the nature of justification is to be defended, it is therefore necessary to investigate the possible existence of 'Forerunners of the Reformation doctrines of justification' – i.e., writers from the later medieval period itself who, in conscious opposition to what they deemed to be the corrupt teaching of the contemporary church, foreshadowed the teaching of the Reformers on the point at issue. Although this approach yields valuable results in the area of sacramental theology and ecclesiology, particularly in connection with the opinions of Wycliffe and Huss, it fails in relation to the specific question of the nature of justification and justifying righteousness. It is, of course, possible to argue that later medieval teaching on *predestination* establishes the case for 'Forerunners of the Reformation doctrines of justification'.[23] However, as we shall indicate below, this appears to rest upon a fallacy.

In an important study, Oberman argued that Dettloff was unable to distinguish the 'nominalistic' and 'scotistic' traditions on justification (i.e., the teachings of the *via moderna* and the late Franciscan school)

because he concentrated on the doctrine of justification, which in the late medieval sources is always associated and connected with a discussion of predestination. These differences do not appear in an analysis of the *content* of statements on justification, but rather in the different *context* of justification, namely, in the diverging ways of understanding the doctrine of predestination.[24]

This point is unquestionably valid: precisely because there was a fundamental continuity within the medieval tradition concerning the *content* of justification, differences between theologians had to be sought elsewhere, in their discussion of its *context*. It may, however, be noted that analysis of the doctrine of predestination does not exhaust an analysis of a writer's views on the context of justification, which must also be regarded as including his statements concerning the possibility or otherwise of extrasacramental justification. Nevertheless, this cannot be regarded as an adequate scholarly foundation for dealing with the relationship between the doctrines of justification of the late medieval period and the Reformation – precisely because there exist such significant differences between their understandings of the *nature* of justification that an inquiry into its *mode* is no longer necessary. The appeal to writers' statements concerning *predestination* in an attempt to elucidate their doctrines of *justification* is legitimate *only when their statements are otherwise indistinguishable*. In the case of the later Franciscan school and the *via moderna*, such statements are near-identical (see §§16, 17), so the appeal is proper. Nevertheless, in the case of late medieval theology and the theology of the first phase of the Reformation, statements concerning justification are immediately distinguishable without the necessity of appealing to their statements concerning predestination. In this case, there is a remarkable degree of continuity between the statements of certain strands of late medieval thought (e.g., the *schola Augustiniana moderna*) and that of the Reformation, despite the fact that their statements pertaining to the *content*, as opposed to the *context*, of justification (to use Oberman's terms) are grossly different. It will therefore be clear that the application of this method to study the continuity between the thought of the later medieval period and the first phase of the Reformation is seriously misleading, as well as being unjustifiable.

The essential feature of the Reformation doctrines of justification is that a deliberate and systematic distinction is made between *justification* and *regeneration*. Although it must be emphasised that this distinction is purely notional, in that it is impossible to separate the two within the context of the *ordo salutis*, the essential point is that a notional distinction is made where none had been acknowledged before in the history of Christian doctrine. A fundamental discontinuity was introduced into the western theological tradition where none had ever existed, or ever been contemplated, before. The Reformation understanding of the *nature* of justification – as opposed to its *mode* – must therefore be regarded as a genuine theological *novum*.

Like all periods in the history of doctrine, the Reformation demonstrates both continuity and discontinuity with the period which immediately preceded it. Chief among these discontinuities is the new understanding of the nature of justification, whereas there are clearly extensive areas of continuity with the late medieval theological movement as a whole, or well-defined sections of the movement, in relation to other aspects of the doctrine, as noted above. That there are no 'Forerunners of the Reformation doctrines of justification' has little theological significance today, given current thinking on the nature of the development of doctrine, which renders Bossuet's static model, on which he based his critique of Protestantism, obsolete. Nevertheless, the historical aspects of the question continue to have relevance. For what reasons did the Reformers abandon the catholic consensus on the nature of justification? We shall take up this matter in the following volume.

APPENDIX
A glossary of medieval soteriological terms

acceptatio divina
The divine act by which God grants man eternal life. In later medieval theology, the term is used to emphasise the fact that man's salvation is ultimately dependent upon the divine decision to accept him, rather than any quality (such as a created habit) which man himself may possess. See §13. It should be emphasised that *acceptatio divina* should not be confused with *acceptio personarum*: this latter term is used by Julian of Eclanum and others to refer to the idea of divine favouritism, which is rejected in favour of the divine *aequitas*. See §6.

amor amicitiae
The pure love of another for the sake of love itself, without any ulterior motive. The term is frequently employed by the theologians of the *via moderna* in discussing the preconditions of justification.

attritio
An imperfect natural form of repentance for sin, which arises out of fear of divine punishment. See §§7, 8. To be distinguished from *contritio*.

concursus generalis
The natural influence of God upon his creation, also referred to as the *influentia generalis*. The concept is usually discussed in terms of Aristotelian physics, where the general *concursus* of the first cause (i.e., God) is understood to be essential if the potentiality of second causes is to be actualised. See §7.

contritio
A perfect form of repentance for sin arising out of love for God (*amor amicitiae*), to be distinguished from *attritio*. *Contritio* is usually regarded as being possible only with the assistance of divine grace. See §§7, 8.

ex natura rei – ex pacto divino
Two fundamentally different concepts of causality underlying the medieval discussion of justification. Ontological, or *ex natura rei*, causality is based upon the presupposition that an inherent connection exists between the

causally related entities or processes which necessitates their causal relationship; covenantal, or *ex pacto divino*, causality is based upon the presupposition that whatever connection exists between the causally related entities or processes exists solely on account of a divine ordination that such a relationship shall exist. See §§7, 11, 13.

ex puris naturalibus
The abilities of man in his purely natural state, without any special assistance of God, except the *concursus generalis*. This should not be confused with the concept of *natura pura* introduced later by Cajetan.

facere quod in se est
The requirement laid upon man by God if he is to dispose himself towards the reception of the gift of grace. See §7.

gratia gratis data
A transitory gift of grace to the *viator* which may coexist with a state of sin. See §9.

gratia gratum faciens
A habitual gift of grace which renders the *viator* acceptable to God, and which may not coexist with a state of mortal sin. See §9.

habitus
A permanent state or disposition within the *viator*, to be distinguished from a transitory act. The habit of grace is understood to be a created form within the soul of the *viator*, intermediate between the divine and human natures, through whose influence the *viator* is changed to become more like God. See §9. The *habitus gratiae* is often referred to as *gratia creata*, to distinguish it from the uncreated grace (*gratia increata*) of the Holy Spirit himself. See further §13.

meritum de condigno
Merit in the strict sense of the term – i.e., a moral act performed in a state of grace, and worthy of divine acceptation on that account. See §10.

meritum de congruo
Merit in a weak sense of the term – i.e., a moral act performed outside a state of grace which, although not meritorious in the strict sense of the term, is considered an 'appropriate' ground for the infusion of justifying grace (*gratia prima*). See §10. The concept is generally discussed in relation to the axiom *facienti quod in se est Deus non denegat gratiam*: see §7.

pactum
The 'covenant' between God and man which governs the theology of the *via moderna*. See §§7, 11, 17.

Appendix: medieval soteriological terms

potentia Dei absoluta
The absolute power of God – i.e., the possibilities open to God before he entered into any decisions concerning his course of action which led him to establish the ordained order through creation and subsequently redemption. It refers primarily to God's ability to do anything, subject solely to the condition that the outcome should not involve logical contradiction. See §11.

potentia Dei ordinata
The ordained power of God – i.e., the established order of salvation, which although contingent, is totally reliable. See §11. The dialectic between the absolute and ordained powers of God was used by the theologians of the later Franciscan school, the *via moderna* and the *schola Augustiniana moderna* to demonstrate the contingency of the implication of created habits of grace in justification. See §13.

viator
Literally, 'wayfarer' or 'pilgrim'. The traditional medieval term used to refer to the believer on his way to the heavenly Jerusalem.

Abbreviations

Bibliographical abbreviations follow S. Schwertner, *Internationales Abkür-zungsverzeichnis für Theologie und Grenzgebiete* (Berlin, 1974).

AThA	*Année théologique augustinienne*
ARG	*Archiv für Reformationsgeschichte*
CChr	Corpus Christianorum Series Latina
CFr	*Collectanea Franciscana*
CSEL	Corpus Scriptorum Ecclesiasticorum Latinorum
D	*Enchiridion Symbolorum*
DThC	*Dictionnaire de théologie catholique*
EThL	*Ephemerides Theologicae Lovanienses*
FS	*Franziskanische Studien*
FrS	*Franciscan Studies*
HThR	*Harvard Theological Review*
MGH.Ep	*Monumenta Germaniae historica: Epistolae*
MGH.SRG	*Monumenta Germaniae historica: Scriptores rerum Germanicarum*
PG	Patrologiae cursus completus, Series Graeca
PL	Patrologiae cursus completus, Series Latina
REAug	*Revue des études augustiniennes*
RSPhTh	*Revue des sciences philosophiques et théologiques*
RSR	*Revue des sciences religieuses*
RThAM	*Recherches de théologie ancienne et médiévale*
SJTh	*Scottish Journal of Theology*
ZKG	*Zeitschrift für Kirchengeschichte*
ZKTh	*Zeitschrift für katholische Theologie*
ZThK	*Zeitschrift für Theologie und Kirche*

Notes

Notes to §1

1 F. Loofs, 'Der articulus stantis et cadentis ecclesiae', *Theologische Studien und Kritiken* 90 (1917) 323–400; A. E. McGrath, 'Der articulus iustificationis als axiomatischer Grundsatz des christlichen Glaubens', *ZThK* 81 (1984) 383–94.

2 J. Gross, *La divinisation du chrétien*; H. Merki, *Homoiosis Theoi von der platonischen Angleichung an Gott zur Gottähnlichkeit bei Gregor von Nyssa* (Freiburg, 1952).

3 V. N. Lossky, 'Rédemption et déification', in *A l'image et ressemblance de Dieu* (Paris, 1967) 95–108.

4 H. F. Dondaine, *La corpus dionysien de l'Université de Paris au XIIIe siècle* (Rome, 1953).

5 See G. A. Hadjiantoniou, *Protestant Patriarch. The Life of Cyril Lucaris, Patriarch of Constantinople* (Richmond, Va., 1961).

Notes to §2

1 P. Stuhlmacher, *Gerechtigkeit Gottes bei Paulus* (Göttingen, 1966); G. Herold, *Zorn und Gerechtigkeit Gottes. Eine Untersuchung zu Röm. 1, 16–18* (Bern/Frankfurt, 1973). A detailed discussion of the findings of contemporary scholarship on the Pauline doctrine of justification is beyond the scope of the present study: for excellent introductions and further references, see E. Käsemann, 'Gottesgerechtigkeit bei Paulus', *ZThK* 58 (1961) 367–78; E. Jüngel, *Paulus und Jesus* (Tübingen, 1962); K. Kertelge, *Rechtfertigung bei Paulus. Studien zur Struktur und zum Bedeutungsgehalt des paulinischen Rechtfertigungsbegriffs* (Tübingen, 1966); Käsemann, *An die Römer*, 2nd edn (Tübingen, 1974) 84–240; U. Wilkens, *Rechtfertigung als Freiheit: Paulusstudien* (Neukirchen, 1974); Subilia, *La giustificazione per fede*, 7–29.

2 McGrath, 'Justice and Justification'; idem, '"The Righteousness of God"'.

3 M. Cohen, *Essai comparatif sur le vocabulaire et la phonétique du Chamito-Sémitique* (Paris, 1947).

4 For example, the use of the Canaanite *saduk* in the Tel el-Amarna texts to indicate that the king had acted 'correctly' when dealing with the 'Kasi'

192

(= Cushite?) people. See D. Hill, *Greek Words and Hebrew Meanings. Studies in the Semantics of Soteriological Terms* (Cambridge, 1967) 82–98, esp. 82–6. The following studies should be consulted: H. Cazelles, 'A propos de quelques textes difficiles relatifs à la justice de Dieu dans l'Ancien Testament', *Revue Biblique* 58 (1951) 169–88; A. Dünner, *Die Gerechtigkeit nach dem Alten Testament* (Bonn, 1963); O. Kaiser, 'Dike und Sedaqa. Zur Frage nach der sittlichen Weltordnung. Ein theologische Präludium', *Neue Zeitschrift für systematische Theologie und Religionsphilosophie* 7 (1965) 251–75; H. H. Schmid, *Gerechtigkeit als Weltordnung. Hintergrund und Geschichte des alttestamentlichen Gerechtigkeitsbegriffs* (Tübingen, 1968). It is significant that the findings of these modern studies were foreshadowed in the study of Ludwig Diestel, 'Die Idee der Gerechtigkeit, vorzüglich im Alten Testament, biblisch-theologisch dargestellt', *Jahrbuch für deutsche Theologie* 5 (1860) 173–204, and thence in the seminal study of Albrecht Ritschl, *Die christliche Lehre von der Rechtfertigung und Versöhnung* (3 vols: Bonn, 1870–74) 2.102 n.1.

5   W. Eichrodt, *Theology of the Old Testament* (2 vols: Philadelphia, 1975) 1.239–49; G. von Rad, *Old Testament Theology* (2 vols: London, 1975) 1.370–83. It may be noted that there are two Hebrew words usually translated as 'righteousness', the masculine ṣedeq and the feminine ṣeḏāqâ. Until recently, it was assumed that these were synonymous. The recent study of A. Jepsen, '*sdq* und *sdqh* im Alten Testament', in *Gottes Word und Gottes Land* ed. H. G. Reventloh (München, 1965) 78–89, calls this into question, for two reasons. First, it is philologically improbable that two different words should bear exactly the same meaning at the same time. Second, ṣedeq is used as a characterising genitive, especially for weights and measures, as in Leviticus 19.36. ṣeḏāqâ is not used in this manner.

6   On ṛtá, see Heinrich Lüders, *Varuṇa* I: *Varuṇa und die Wasser* (Göttingen, 1951) 13–27, especially 27 (on the relation between the Vedic ṛtá and the Avestic aša); idem, *Varuṇa* II: *Varuṇa und das Ṛta* (Göttingen, 1959) 402–654. The complex nuances of the Iranian term aša are well brought out by Christian Bartholomae, *Altiranisches Wörterbuch* (Strassburg, 1905) 229–38. The Caucasian term äcäg, deriving from the Iranian, should also be noted in this context: see H. Hommel, 'Wahrheit und Gerechtigkeit. Zur Geschichte und Deutung eines Begriffspaars', *Antike und Abendland* 15 (1969) 159–86; 182–3 n.86. Note also the functions of the Egyptian deity *Ma'at* (ibid., 165 n.24) and the relationship of the Babylonian *kittu* and *mesaru* (ibid., 165 n.25).

7   J. Barr, *The Semantics of Biblical Language* (Oxford, 1961) 107–60; 107. The studies of G. Weiler, 'A Note on Meaning and Use', *Mind* 76 (1967) 424–7, and J. M. E. Moravcsik, 'How do Words get their Meanings?', *Journal of Philosophy* 78 (1981) 5–24, are of relevance here.

8   G. Wildeboer, 'Die älteste Bedeutung des Stammes *sdq*', *Zeitschrift für die alttestamentliche Wissenschaft* 22 (1902) 167–9.

9   e.g., I Samuel 12.7; Micah 6.5.

10 Judges 5.11.

11 e.g., Judges 11.27; cf. also II Samuel 18.31.

12 Schmid, op. cit., 67; Cf. von Rad, op. cit., 1.370.

13 H. Cremer, *Die paulinische Rechtfertigungslehre im Zusammenhang ihrer geschichtlichen Voraussetzungen* (Gütersloh, 1899). The German term 'Gemeinschaftstreue' has subsequently become increasingly used as a translation of ṣᵉḏāqâ.

14 Isaiah 46.13; cf. 56.1. See C. F. Whitley, 'Deutero-Isaiah's Interpretation of *sedeq*', *Vetus Testamentum* 22 (1972) 469–75.

15 Thus J. F. A. Sawyer, *Semantics in Biblical Research. New Methods of Defining Hebrew Words for Salvation* (London, 1972) 50. For a penetrating criticism of Sawyer's work, see the review by P. Wernberg-Møller, *Journal of Theological Studies* 24 (1973) 215–17.

16 S. Öhmann, 'Theories of the "Linguistic Field"', *Word* 9 (1953) 123–34; N. C. W. Spence, 'Linguistic Fields, Conceptual Spheres and the *Weltbild*', *Transactions of the Philological Society* (1961) 87–106.

17 P. Guiraud, 'Les champs morpho-sémantiques', *Bulletin de la Societé Linguistique de Paris* 52 (1956) 265–88.

18 e.g., H. Chadwick, *Early Christian Thought and the Classical Tradition* (Oxford, 1984).

19 See R. A. Kraft, 'Jewish Greek Scriptures and Related Topics', *New Testament Studies* 16 (1970) 384–96; 17 (1971) 488–90.

20 M. Salomon, *Der Begriff der Gerechtigkeit bei Aristoteles* (Leiden, 1927); P. Trude, *Der Begriff der Gerechtigkeit in der aristotelischen Rechts- und Staatsphilosophie* (Berlin, 1955). For a useful general survey, see E. A. Havelock, 'DIKAIOSUNE. An Essay in Greek Intellectual History', *Phoenix* 23 (1969) 49–70.

21 For the difficulties they faced, see H. S. Gehman, 'The Hebraic Character of LXX Greek', *Vetus Testamentum* 1 (1951) 81–90; H. M. Orlinsky, 'The Treatment of Anthropomorphisms and Anthropopathisms in the Septuagint of Isaiah', *Hebrew Union College Annual* 27 (1956) 193–200; C. Rabin, 'The Translation Process and the Character of the Septuagint', *Textus* 6 (1968) 1–26.

22 e.g., Psalm 24.5; 33.5; 103.6. The problem is evident in Deutero-Isaiah: see J. W. Olley, *'Righteousness' in the Septuagint of Isaiah: A Contextual Study* (Missoula, Mont. 1979) 65–78.

23 For a survey of the knowledge of Hebrew in the Middle Ages, see B. Smalley, 'Andrew of St Victor, Abbot of Wigmore: A Twelfth Century Hebraist', *RThAM* 10 (1938) 358–74; idem, *The Study of the Bible in the Middle Ages*, 2nd edn (Notre Dame, 1970) 112–95.

24 Cicero, *Rhetoricum libro duo* II, 53. Cf. Justinian, *Institutio* I, 1 'Iustitia est constans et perpetua voluntas suum unicuique tribuens'.

25 For details of the two translations, see J. N. D. Kelly, *Jerome: his Life, Writings and Controversies* (London, 1975).

26 H. Bornkamm, 'Iustitia Dei in der Scholastik und bei Luther', *ARG* 39 (1942) 1–46.

27 See N. M. Watson, 'Some observations concerning the use of δικαιόω in the Septuagint', *Journal of Biblical Literature* 79 (1960) 255–66.

28 e.g., Polybius III.xxxi.9; cited Olley, op. cit., 38.
29 In apocryphal works, the secular Greek sense of the term is usually encountered, as at Ecclesiasticus 42.2. Here the term 'justification of the ungodly' (δικαιοῦσθαι τοῦ ἀσηβῆ), so profound in its Pauline sense, merely means 'the punishment of the wicked'.
30 *Nicomachean Ethics* V 1136ᵃ30.
31 *de civ. Dei* VII, 14; CSEL 40.322.10–17.
32 For what follows, see McGrath, 'Justice and Justification', 412–13.
33 *de Trin.* xi, 19; CChr 62A.549.16–17 'Mereri enim eius est, qui sibi ipse meriti adquierendi auctor existat'. See further Peñamaria de Llano, *La salvación por la fe*, 191–7.

Notes to §3

1 B. Gerhardsson, *Tradition and Transmission in Early Christianity* (Lund/Copenhagen, 1964).
2 J. K. Mozley, *The Impassibility of God* (Cambridge, 1926); R. B. Edwards, 'The Pagan Doctrine of the Absolute Unchangeableness of God', *Religious Studies* 14 (1978) 305–13. For a criticism of this doctrine, see J. Moltmann, *Der gekreuzigte Gott. Das Kreuz Christi als Grund und Kritik christlicher Theologie* (München, 1981⁴) especially 256–8; W. McWilliams, 'Divine Suffering in Contemporary Theology', *SJTh* 33–54; K. Surin, 'The Impassibility of God and the Problem of Evil', *SJTh* 35 (1982) 97–119.
3 For its classic statements, see A. von Harnack, *History of Dogma*; idem, *Grundriß der Dogmengeschichte* (Freiburg, 1889). See also J. Rivière, *La propagation du christianisme dans les trois prèmiers siècles d'après les conclusions de M. Harnack* (Paris, 1908); A. Grillmeier, 'Hellenisierung-Judaisierung des Christentums als Deuteprinzipien der Geschichte des kirchlichen Dogmas', *Scholastik* 33 (1958) 321–55; 528–58; W. Panneberg, 'Die Aufnahme des philosophischen Gottesbegriffs als dogmatisches Problem der frühchristlichen Theologie', *ZKG* 70 (1959) 1–45.
4 Oberman, *Werden und Wertung*, 133–4 n. 179.
5 Loofs, *Leitfaden*, 229–32; M. F. Wiles, *The Making of Christian Doctrine. A Study in the Principles of early Doctrinal Development* (Cambridge, 1978) 94–113.
6 Beck, *Vorsehung und Vorherbestimmung*.
7 Wörter, *Verhältnis von Gnade und Freiheit*.
8 For an introduction to the questions involved, see S. Lyonnet, 'Le sens de ἐφ᾽ ᾧ en Rom v.12 et l'exégèse des pères grecs', *Biblica* 36 (1955) 436–57; idem, 'Le péché originel et l'exégèse de Rom v.12–14', *RSR* 44 (1956) 63–84; idem, 'Le péché originel en Rom v.12–14', *RSR* 44 (1956) 63–84; idem, 'Le péché originel en Rom v.12. L'exégèse des pères grecs et les décrets du Concile de Trente', *Biblica* 41 (1960) 325–15.
9 K. Stendahl, *Paul among Jews and Gentiles* (Philadelphia, 1983) 83.
10 A. von Harnack, *Marcion. Das Evangelium von fremden Gott* (Leipzig, 1924) is useful here.

11 Thus O. Cullmann, *The Early Church* (London, 1956) 96.

12 Edition in PG 65.929–66. It is possible that this tract is part of the larger work *de lege spirituali*: see J. Quasten, *Patrology* (3 vols: Philadelphia, 1963) 3.505–6.

13 See Wörter, op. cit.; T. F. Torrance, *The Doctrine of Grace in the Apostolic Fathers* (Edinburgh, 1948).

14 e.g. see *LThK* 4.984–8.

15 *I Apol.* 43–4.

16 D. Amand, *Fatalisme et liberté dans l'antiquité grecque* (Louvain, 1945) 195–207.

17 ibid., 86–7; J. Daniélou, *Philon d'Alexandria* (Paris, 1958) 175–81.

18 H. Jonas, *The Gnostic Religion* (Boston, 1958) 46–7; 270–7.

19 Theophilus of Antioch, *Epist. ad Autol.* ii, 27. For a discussion of the use of the term αὐτεξουσία in early Pauline exegesis, see Schelkle, *Paulus Lehrer der Väter*, 439–40.

20 The controversy is particularly associated with Macarius the Egyptian: see Davids, *Bild vom neuen Menschen.* See also I. Hausherr, 'L'erreur fondamentale et la logique de la messalianisme', *Orientalia Christiana Periodica* I (1935) 326–60; F. Dorr, *Diadochus von Photike und die Messalianer* (Freiburg, 1937); H. Dörries, *Symeon von Mesopotamia. Die Überlieferung der messalianischen "Makarios" Schriften* (Leipzig, 1941). The relationship between Gregory of Nyssa and the movement is intriguing: R. Staats, *Gregor von Nyssa und die Messalianer* (Berlin, 1968).

21 Macarius of Egypt, *de custodia cordis* xii; PG 34.836A.

22 ibid.; PG 34.834D.

23 John of Damascus, *de fide orthodoxa* ii, 30.

24 John Chrysostom, *In epist. ad Rom.*, Hom. xix, 6. It is significant that the Latin translations of Chrysostom's sermons were the work of the Pelagian Anianus of Celeda: see B. Altaner, 'Altlateinische Übersetzungen von Chrysostomusschriften', *Kleine patristische Schriften*, Texte und Untersuchungen 83 (1967) 416–36. Cf. PL 48.626–30.

25 Schelkle, op. cit., 248–52.

26 J. Gaïth, *La conception de la liberté chez Gregoire de Nysse* (Paris, 1953) 79–81.

27 E. Dobler, *Nemesius von Emesa und die Psychologie des menschlichen Aktes bei Thomas von Aquin* (Freiburg, 1950).

28 See C. C. J. Webb, *God and Personality* (London, 1919) 44–5.

29 *de anima* 21; CSEL 20.334.27–9 'Haec erit vis divinae gratiae, potentior utique natura, habens in nobis subiacentem sibi liberam arbitrii potestatem, quod αὐτεξούσιον dicitur'.

30 See F. Ricken, 'Nikaia als Krisis des altchristlichen Platonismus', *Theologie und Philosophie* 44 (1969) 333–9.

31 Text in PL 17.45–508. See A. Souter, *The Earliest Latin Commentaries on the Epistles of St Paul* (Oxford, 1927).

32 Souter, op. cit., 65; 72–3; 80.

33 e.g., H. von Campenhausen, *Fathers of the Latin Church* (London, 1964).

34 e.g., A. Nygren, *Agape and Eros* (Philadelphia, 1953) 343–8.

35 *de paenitentia* 2; CChr 1.323.44–6.
36 *de paenitentia* 5; CChr 1.328.32–329.25. It may, of course, be argued that there are grounds for suggesting the 'ingenuous use of *mereri* and *meritum*' in the pre-Augustinian tradition: see Bakhuizen van den Brink, 'Mereo(r) and meritum'. For an excellent study of Hilary of Poitiers' understanding of the relationship between merit and faith, see Peñamaria de Llano, *La salvación por la fe*, 191–247.
37 A. Beck, *Römisches Recht bei Tertullian. Eine Studie zur frühen Kirchen-rechtslehre* (Aalen, 1967); P. Vitton, *I concetti giuridici nelle opere di Tertulliano* (Roma, 1971) 50–4.

Notes to §4

1 *Carmina S. Isidora ascripta* 5; PL 83.1109A.
2 *Monologion*, praefatio; ed. Schmitt, 1.8.9.
3 *de praed. sanct.* iii, 7; *Retractiones* I, xxiii, 3–4.
4 *de praed. sanct.* iv, 8; PL 44.966A 'Nam si curassent, invenissent istam quaestionem secundum veritatem divinarum scripturarum solutam in primo libro duorum, quos ad beatae memoriae Simplicianum scripsi episcopum Mediolanensis ecclesiae ... in ipso exordio episcopatus mei.'
5 See Salguerio, *Doctrine de Saint Augustin*, for an excellent analysis.
6 P. Brown, *Augustine of Hippo* (London, 1967) 151. It is perhaps mislead-ing for Brown to suggest that Augustine 'interpreted Paul as a Platonist' in his early period: to his dying day, Augustine never ceased to interpret Paul as a Platonist, and even died with a quotation from Plotinus on his lips. Presumably Brown intends us to understand that Augustine approached Paul with *different* Platonist presuppositions in his later period. (Thus it could be argued, for example, that his development of the doctrine of predestination reflects *Platonic* determinism as much as Pauline, in that the neo-Platonic tradition was never lacking in sympathy for determinist turns of thought, or for the attribution of human actions to transcendent forces and powers.)
7 e.g., *de serm. Dom. in monte* I, xviii, 55; *Expos. quar. prop. ex Epist. ad Rom.* 44.
8 *ad Simpl.* I, ii, 6.
9 *ad Simpl.* I, ii, 12. Augustine here remarks that Paul 'ostendit etiam ipsam bonam voluntatem in nobis operante Deo fieri': CChr 44.36.324–5.
10 *ad Simpl.* I, ii, 21. 'Liberum voluntatis arbitrium plurimum valet, immo vero est quidem, sed in venundatis sub peccato, quid valet?' CChr 44.53.740–2.
11 Nygren, *Das Prädestinationsproblem*, 47–8. This is not to exclude further development of significance prior to 396: thus, for example, his initial opinion that Paul was referring to unbelievers in Romans 7 later gave way to the insight that he was referring to believers.
12 For a chronological list, see E. TeSelle, *Augustine the Theologian* (London, 1970) 11–14.

13 Others in Augustine's circle of acquaintances held 'Augustinian' views before Augustine himself – see *de lib. arb.* III, iii, 7, where Evodius is mentioned as linking the divine will and necessity.

14 *contra Iul.* II, viii, 23 'Sed vos festinatis et praesumptionem vestram festinando praecipitatis. Hic enim vultis hominem perfici, atque utinam Dei dono et non libero, vel potius servo proprie voluntatis arbitrio'.

15 An important exception, noted by Nygren, op. cit., 41, is his rejection of the opinion that the initiative to respond to God's offer of salvation belongs to man's *liberum arbitrium* – compare *de lib. arb.* III, xvi, 45 with *Retractiones* I, 9, or *Epist.* 143.

16 *de spir. et litt.* v, 7 '. . . homini Deus dedit liberum arbitrium sine quo nec male nec bene vivitur' CSEL 60.159.12–13. For a more detailed analysis of Augustine's doctrine of *liberum arbitrium*, see Ball, 'Libre arbitre et liberté'; idem., 'Développements de la doctrine de la liberté'; G. R. Evans, *Augustine on Evil* (Cambridge, 1982) 112–49.

17 *de spir. et litt.* xxxiii, 58 '. . . (omnibus) adimat liberum arbitrium, quo vel bene vel male utentes iustissime iudicentur' CSEL 60.216.20–1.

18 *de spir. et litt.* xxx, 52 'Liberum ergo arbitrium evacuamus per gratiam? Absit; sed magis liberum arbitrium statuimus . . . quia gratia sanat voluntatem, qua iustitia libere diligatur' CSEL 60.208.16–27.

19 *de nat. et grat.* lxvi, 77. See E. Gilson, *Introduction à l'étude de S. Augustine*, 3rd edn (Paris, 1949) 185–216; M. T. Clark, *Augustine Philosopher of Freedom* (New York, 1958), especially 45 n.1; Gilson, *History of Christian Philosophy in the Middle Ages* (London, 1978) 78–9. It may be noted that Gilson tends to over-systematise Augustine's thought, and that it is possible that the distinction he here detects is less significant than might at first appear to be the case.

20 *contra duas epist. Pelag.* III, viii, 24 'Et liberum arbitrium captivatum non nisi ad peccatum valet, ad iustitiam vero nisi divinitus liberatum adiutumque non valet' CSEL 60.516.24–6.

21 e.g., see the medical image employed in *de nat. et grat.* iii, 3. Cf. n.18.

22 *de grat. et lib. arb.* ii, 4.

23 *Epist.* 214, 2.

24 *Serm.* 169, 13.

25 e.g., the somewhat unperceptive discussion in N. P. Williams, *The Grace of God* (London, 1930) 19–43.

26 *de grat. et lib. arb.* xvii, 33 'Ut ergo velimus, sine nobis operatur; cum autem volumus, et sic volumus ut faciamus, nobiscum cooperatur.' For an earlier distinction between 'operation' and 'cooperation', see *ad Simpl.* I, ii, 10 'ut velimus enim et suum esse voluit et nostrum: suum vocando, nostrum sequendo. Quod autem voluerimus, solus praestat, id est, posse bene agere et semper beate vivere' CChr 44.35.298–301.

27 See the seriously inaccurate statements of J. I. Packer and O. R. Johnston, *The Bondage of the Will* (London, 1957) 49.

28 See J. Rivière, art. 'Mérite', *DThC* 10.642–51.

29 e.g., *Epist.* 194, 19. On this, see Bakhuizen van den Brink, 'Mereo(r) and Meritum'.

30 See §1.
31 For an excellent discussion, see Burnaby, *Amor Dei*, 219–52.
32 *Enarr. in Ps. 109,1*; CChr 40.1601.11–13. Cf. *Sermo* 110, iv, 4 'Promissorum suorum nobis chirographum fecit. Non debendo enim sed promittendo debitorum se deus fecit, id est non mutuo accipiendo' PL 38.641A. For an excellent discussion of this concept of self-obligation, see Hamm, *Promissio, pactum, ordinatio*, 8–25.
33 *Epist.* 194, 5, 19; CSEL 57.190 'cum Deus coronat merita nostra, nihil aliud coronat quam munera sua'.
34 As suggested by R.-C. Dhont, *Le problème de la préparation à la grâce* (Paris, 1946), on the basis of texts such as *de div. quaest. lxxxiii* 68, 4 'Praecedit ergo aliquid in peccatoribus, quo, quamvis nondum sint iustificati, digni efficiantur iustificatione: et item praecedit in aliis peccatoribus quod digni sunt obtunsione' CChr 44A.180.126–9.
35 K. Holl, 'Die iustitia dei in der vorlutherischen Bibelauslegung des Abendlandes', in *Gesammelte Aufsätze zur Kirchengeschichte* (Tübingen, 1928) 3. 171–88; McGrath, '"The Righteousness of God"'.
36 Studer, 'Jesucristo, nuestra justicia', 266–70.
37 *de spir. et litt.* xi, 18.
38 The fullest discussion is *de Trin.* XIII. See J. Rivière, *Le dogme de la rédemption chez Saint Augustin*, 3rd edn (Paris, 1933). The later dogmatic distinction between the 'person' and 'work' of Christ is unknown to Augustine.
39 Burnaby, op. cit., 168–72.
40 e.g., *de grat. Christi et pecc. orig.* II, xxviii, 33.
41 e.g., *Serm.* 152, 9.
42 e.g., *Serm.* 163, 1.
43 Particularly in relation to the virtue of humility: e.g., *Enarr. in Ps. 31, 18*; CChr 38.239.41–54.
44 *de corr. et grat.* viii, 18. See Nygren, op. cit.; F.-J. Thonnard, 'La prédestination augustinienne. Sa place en philosophie augustinienne', *REAug* 10 (1964) 97–123.
45 e.g., *Epist.* 98, 2. Elsewhere, Augustine criticised the Pelagians for making the grace of Christ consist solely in his example, and asserting that men are justified by imitating him, where they are in fact justified by the Holy Spirit who *subsequently* leads them to imitate him: *Opus imp. contra Iul.* II, 46.
46 Burnaby, op. cit., 173.
47 *Serm.* 297, 1.
48 *de Trin.* XV, xvii, 31.
49 *de Trin.* XV, xviii, 32.
50 Augustine frequently treats *dilectio* and *caritas* as synonymous – e.g., *de Trin.* XV, xviii, 32; xix, 33–7.
51 *de Trin.* XV, xviii, 32.
52 *in Johan. tr.* xxix, 6; xxv, 12; *Serm.* 164, 2; *Enarr. in Ps. 31.1–8.* The Vulgate translates the verse as '... per fidem, quae per caritatem operatur'.

53 For Augustine's concept of faith as intellectual adherence to revealed truth, see A. Dorner, *Augustinus. Sein theologisches System und seine religions-philosophische Anschauung* (Berlin, 1873) 194–7; M. Löhrer, *Der Glaubensbegriff des hl. Augustinus in seiner ersten Schriften* (Einsiedeln, 1955). J. Hessen, *Augustins Metaphysik der Erkenntnis* (Leiden, 1960) provides useful background material.

54 *in ep. Johan. tr.* v, 7; *Serm.* 90, 6; 93, 5; 165, 4; *Epist.* 183, i, 3; *de spir. et litt.* xxxii, 56.

55 Burnaby, op. cit., 78 'It cannot be denied that faith, in Augustine's general usage of the term, has the predominantly intellectual connotation of the definition which he gave at the end of his life – 'to believe means simply to affirm in thought, *cum assensione cogitare'*. The reference is to *de praed. sanct.* ii, 5. See also n.53.

56 Bavaud, 'La doctrine de la justification d'après Saint Augustin', 31–2.

57 Burnaby, op. cit., 78.

58 e.g., *Exp. quar. prop. ex Ep. ad Rom* 22; *ad Simpl.* I, ii, 3; *Serm.* 131, 9; 292, 6; *Epist.* 160, xxi, 52; *de grat. et lib. arb.* vi, 13. Other expressions used include *efficitur iustus* (e.g., *de spir. et litt.* xxxii, 56) and *fit pius* (e.g., *Serm.* 160, 7; *in John. tr.* iii, 9).

59 *de grat. et lib. arb.* xvii, 33.

60 *Ench.* I, 44.

61 See the important conclusions reached by J. Henninger, *S. Augustinus et doctrina de duplici iustitia* (Mödling, 1935) 79 'i. Existit aliqua iustitia, qua homo vere, intrinsecus, coram Deo iustus est; ii. Haec iustitia consistit in aliquo dono permanenti, quo homo elevatur ad aliquem statum, altiorem, ita ut sit particeps Dei, deificatus.'

62 J. A. Stoopio, *Die deificatio hominis in die Sermones en Epistulae van Augustins* (Leiden, 1952); Capánaga, 'La deificación en la soteriología agustiniana'. The theme appears to be more pronounced in Augustine's sermons than in his specifically doctrinal works.

63 Burnaby, op. cit., 141–53; 168–77.

64 G. Philips, 'Saint Augustin a-t-il connu une "grâce créée"?', *EThL* 47 (1971) 97–116; P. G. Riga, 'Created Grace in St. Augustine', *Augustinian Studies* 3 (1972) 113–30.

65 *Serm.* 192, 1 – possibly a direct citation from the Cappadocians. For Augustine's relation to the Cappadocians, see B. Altaner, 'Augustinus, Gregor von Nazianz und Gregor von Nyssa', *Revue Bénédictine* 61 (1951) 54–62; idem, 'Augustinus und die griechische Patristik. Eine Zusammen-fassung und Nachlese zu den quellenkritischen Untersuchungen', *Revue Bénédictine* 62 (1952) 201–15.

66 *de Trin.* XIV, xii, 15.

67 *Enarr. in Ps. 49*, 2; *Serm.* 192, 1.

68 *contra Iul.* I, ix, 45.

69 *de spir. et litt.* xxix, 50.

70 *contra duas epist. Pelag.* III, v, 14. The entire section at III, v, 14–vii, 23 merits careful study.

71 *Serm.* 349, i, 1.

72 *de grat. et lib. arb.* xvii, 36; *de spir. et. litt.* xxvii, 48. The excellent study of J. Wang Tch'ang-Tche, *Saint Augustin et les vertus des païens* (Paris, 1938) should be noted.

73 *contra Iul.* IV, iii, 19.

74 *contra Iul.* IV, iii, 31.

75 *de civ. Dei* II, 21. On the theme of the 'two cities', see A. Lauras and H. Rondet, 'Le thème des deux cités dans l'œuvre de saint Augustin', *Etudes Augustiniennes* 28 (1953) 99–160; Y. Congar, '"Civitas Dei" et "Ecclesia" chez S. Augustin', *REAug* 3 (1957) 1–14.

76 *de civ. Dei* XI, 17. See also *de lib. arb.* I, v, 11 '... iustum est, ut omnia sint ordinatissima'. The Platonic conception of justice as the right ordering of the parts of the soul is also evident in Augustine's definition of justice as *amor amato serviens et propterea recte dominans: de moribus ecclesiae* xv, 25.

77 Gilson, op. cit., 77–81.

78 R. A. Markus, *Saeculum: History and Society in the Theology of St. Augustine* (Cambridge, 1970) 72–104.

79 On this see McGrath, 'Justice and Justification'; idem., '"The Righteousness of God"'.

80 e.g., *de lib. arb.* xviii, 27; *Enarr. in Ps. 83, 11*. For Augustine's relation to Cicero, see M. Testard, *Saint Augustin et Cicéron* (2 vols: Paris, 1958).

81 See McGrath, 'Divine Justice and Divine Equity' for a more detailed analysis.

82 Lactantius, *Divinae Institutiones* V, vii, 2; CSEL 19.419.12–14.

83 Cicero, *de rep.* I, 39 'Est igitur, inquit Africanus, res publica, res populi; populus autem non omnis hominim coetus quoquo modo congregatus, sed coetus multitudinis iuris consensu et utilitatis communione societatis.' See Testard, op. cit., 2.39–43.

84 *de civ. Dei* XIX, 23. Cf. XIX, 21.

85 *de lib. arb.* I, vi, 15.

86 On this whole question, see P. A. Schubert, *Augustins Lex-Aeterna-Lehre nach Inhalt und Quellen* (Münster, 1924). See also J. Rief, *Der Ordobegriff des jungen Augustinus* (Paderborn, 1962).

87 *de div. quaest. lxxxiii* 83, 2 '... quia omnis ista hominum iustitia, quam et tenere animus humanus recte faciendo potest et peccando amittere, non imprimeretur animae, nisi esset aliqua incommutabilis iustitia, quae integra inveniretur a iustis, cum ad eam converterenter, integra relinqueretur a peccantibus, cum ab eius lumine averterentur' CChr 46A.245.31–6. See also *ad Simpl.* I, ii, 16. Cf. F. J. Thonnard, 'Justice de Dieu et justice humaine selon Saint Augustin', *Augustinus* 12 (1967) 387–402.

88 *de spir. et. litt.* xxvi, 45.

Notes to introduction

1 Julian of Toledo, *Antikeimenon* II, 69; PL 96.697C. Cf. Augustine, *de civ. Dei* XI, 1, where he refers to living 'in an intermediate age' (*in hoc interim*

saeculo) in a similar context. See further H.-I. Marrou, *L'ambivalence du temps de l'histoire chez saint Augustin* (Montréal, 1950); idem, 'Civitas Dei, civitas terrena: num tertium quid?', *Studia Patristica* 2 (Berlin, 1957) 342–50.

2 See J. J. Contreni, *The Cathedral School of Laon from c. 850–c. 1000* (Munich, 1978); J. Marenbon, *From the Circle of Alcuin to the School of Auxerre. Logic, Theology and Philosophy in the Early Middle Ages* (Cambridge, 1981) and references therein.

3 D. M. Cappuyns, 'Le premier représentant de l'augustinisme médiévale', *RThAM* 1 (1929) 309–37.

4 G. R. Evans, *The Language and Logic of the Bible. The Earlier Middle Ages* (Cambridge, 1984) 133–9.

5 e.g., Isidore of Seville, *Sententiae*: PL 83.537–738; Burchard of Worms, *Decretum*: PL 140.338–1058.

6 Grabmann, *Geschichte der scholastischen Methode*, 2.385–6.

7 Oberman, *Werden und Wertung der Reformation*, 82–140.

8 G. Aulén, *Christus Victor* (London, 1934). On the development of the idea of the 'Harrowing of Hell', see J. M. Usteri, *Hinabgefahren zur Hölle* (Zürich, 1886).

9 D. M. de Clerk, 'Droits du démon et nécéssité de la rédemption. Les écoles d'Abélard et de Pierre Lombard', *RThAM* 14 (1947) 32–64.

10 Thus A. B. Ritschl, *Die christliche Lehre von der Rechtfertigung und Versöhnung* (Bonn, 1870) §4, begins his discussion of the doctrine with reference to Anselm of Canterbury.

11 Landgraf, *Einführung in die Geschichte* 29; 39–40.

12 C. Spicq, *Esquisse d'une histoire de l'exégèse latine au moyen âge* (Paris, 1944).

13 W. Affeld, 'Verzeichnis der Römerbriefkommentare der lateinischen Kirche', *Traditio* 12 (1957) 396–406. For an exhaustive list of medieval biblical commentaries, see F. Stegmüller, *Reportorium Biblicum Medii Aevii* (7 vols: Barcelona, 1950–61).

14 e.g., Robert of Melun, *Questiones de epistolis ad Romanos*, ed. Martin, 80.14–81.20.

15 e.g., Hervaeus of Bourg Dieu, *Comm. in ep. divi Pauli*, PL 181.644B–47A.

16 See H. Cloes, 'La systématisation théologique pendant la première moitié du XIIe siècle', *EThL* 34 (1958) 277–329, who illustrates this point with particular reference to Hugh of St Victor's *de sacramentis*. See also H. Köster, *Die Heilslehre des Hugo von Sankt Viktor* (Emsdetten, 1940); V. Marcolino, *Das alte Testament in der Heilsgeschichte. Untersuchung zum dogmatischen Verständnis des alten Testaments als heilsgeschichtliche Periode nach Alexander von Hales* (Münster, 1970).

Notes to §5

1 On the medieval theories of signification, see G. R. Evans, *The Language and Logic of the Bible. The Earlier Middle Ages* (Cambridge, 1984) 72–122.

2 e.g., Luke 1.6.

3 e.g., Atto of Vercelli, *Exp. epist. Pauli*, PL 134.149C; Haimo of Auxerre, *Expos. in divi Pauli epist.*, PL 119.381A.

4 e.g., Sedulius Scotus, *Coll. in omnes Pauli epist.*, PL 103.41C '... aliud est iustificari coram Deo, aliud coram hominibus'.

5 See McGrath, 'Forerunners of the Reformation?'.

6 See E. Dietrich, 'Die Lehren der angelsächsischen Kirchen, nack Ælfriks Schriften', *Zeitschrift für die historische Theologie* 25 (1855) 550–94; M. M. Gatch, *Preaching and Theology in Anglo-Saxon England* (Toronto, 1977) for further details.

7 See H. MacGillivray, *The Influence of Christianity on the Vocabulary of Old English* (Studien zur englischen Philologie 8: Halle, 1902) 148–58; N. O. Halvorsen, *Doctrinal Terms in Ælfric's Homilies* (University of Iowa Studies: Humanistic Studies 5/1: 1932) 56–7; M.-M. Dubois, *Ælfric sermonnaire, docteur et grammarien* (Paris, 1943). It may be noted that Wulfstan's vocabulary is limited compared with Ælfric's: see L. H. Dodd, *A Glossary of Wulfstan's Homilies* (New York, 1908).

8 *The Pearl*, ed. E. V. Gordon (Oxford, 1953) ll. 699–700.

9 See his translation of Romans 8.30: B. Thorpe, *The Homilies of the Anglo-Saxon Church* (2 vols: London, 1864–6) 2.367.1–3.

10 e.g., see *The Gothic and Anglo-Saxon Gospels, with the Versions of Wycliffe and Tyndale* ed. J. Bosworth (London, 1865) 10.29; *Libri Psalmorum versio antiqua Latina cum paraphrasi Anglo-Saxonica* ed. B. Thorpe (Oxford, 1835) 18.8, where '... iustificati sunt...' is translated 'Hi synt gerihtwisode...'. See also *Homilies* 2.430.2; 472.2–3.

11 *Homilies* 2.286.2–5.

12 *Die gotische Bibel*, ed. W. Streitberg (2 vols: Heidelberg, 1965).

13 Thus Romans 1.1–6.22 are missing, as well as other important sections.

14 See Streitberg's edition for full notes on the manuscript giving this translation.

15 The best translation of *wairthan* in modern German is *werden*, which can be justified on philological grounds. The Gothic term is frequently used to translate γίνεσθαι – see Streitberg, op. cit., 2.167.

16 *contra Iul.* II, viii, 23; PL 44.689B.

17 *Exp. in Psalmos*, PL 152.1087A 'Notandum quod haec beneficia non narrat ordine; prius enim fuit a captivitate per fidem averti, postea vero peccata operiri, et sic post iniquitatem remitti; et ad ultimum in bonis operibus et virtutibus benedici.'

18 *Comm. in epist. Pauli*, PL 181.642D.

19 For an excellent discussion of the *processus iustificationis* in the early medieval period, see Landgraf, *Dogmengeschichte der Frühscholastik*, I/1 287–302. The reference is to Cod. Paris Nat. lat. 15269 fol. 44, cited Landgraf, op. cit., 291 n.11.

20 Peter Comestor, *Sermo* 17; PL 198.1769B 'Iustificatio etiam in tribus consistit, vel notatur; in gratia infusione, in liberi arbitrii cooperatione, tandem in consummatione; primum est incipientium, secundum proficientium, tertium pervenientium.'

21 Cod. Vat. lat. 1174 fol. 83v; Cod. Vat. lat. 1098 fol. 151v, 157; cited Landgraf, op. cit., 299. Cf. 298 n.41 and 299 n.45.

22 *Sententiarum libri quinque* III, 2; PL 211.1044A–B. Peter of Poitiers was a pupil of Peter Lombard, upon whose *Sentences* his own work was modelled: see P. S. Moore, *The works of Peter of Poitiers* (Notre Dame, 1936) 1–24. He must not be confused with Peter of Poitiers of St Victor or Peter of Poitiers of Cluny: see J. W. Baldwin, *Masters, Princes and Merchants* (2 vols: Princeton, 1970) 1.32–4; J. Kritzeck, *Peter the Venerable and Islam* (Princeton, 1964) 31–4.

23 *Summa Aurea* lib. III tr. ii q.1; fol. 121v.

24 Alexander of Hales, *In IV Sent.* dist. xvii n.7; Albertus Magnus, *In IV sent.* dist. xviiA a. 10; ed. Borgnet, 29.673 'Dicitur ab omnibus, quod quattuor exiguntur ad iustificationem impii, scilicet infusio gratiae, motus liberi arbitrii in peccatum sive contritio, quod idem est, motus liberi arbitrii in Deum, et remissio peccati'; Bonaventure, *In II Sent.* dist. xxvi a.1 dub. 3; Thomas Aquinas, *In IV Sent.* dist. xvii q.1 a.4; ed. Mandonnet, 4.843; idem, *Summa Theologiae* IaIIae q.113 a.6; Odo Rigaldi, *In II Sent.* dist xxvi membr. 1 q.2 a.3 (ed. Bouvy, 331.48–32.68). Matthew of Aquasparta redefines the four elements as *satisfactio, conversio, reformatio, vivificatio*: *In II Sent.* dist. xxviii a.1 q.1.

25 See McGrath, 'The Influence of Aristotelian Physics upon St Thomas Aquinas' Discussion of the "Processus Iustificationis"'. See also Flick, *L'attimo della giustificazione*, 104–54.

26 *In IV Sent.* dist. xviiA a.15.

27 G. Grunwald, *Geschichte der Gottesbeweise im Mittelalter* (Münster, 1907) 107–10.

28 IaIIae q.113 a.8.

29 IaIIae q.113 a.6.

30 IaIIae q.113 a.6 ad 1um.

31 IaIIae q.113 a.8 ad 2um.

32 IaIIae q.113 a.5.

33 IaIIae q.113 a.6 3um.

34 IaIIae q.113 a.8 ad 3um 'Philosophus dicit, in *II Physic.*, in motibus animi omnino praecedit motus in principium speculationis, vel in finem actionis ... Et quia motus liberi arbitrii est motus animi, prius naturae ordine movetur in Deum sicut in finem, quam ad removendum impedimentum peccati.'

35 IaIIae q.113 a.8.

36 *de veritate* q.28 a.8; ed. Spiazzi, 1.549 'et ideo inter gratiae infusionem et culpae remissionem nihil cadet medium'. An identical opinion is encountered earlier: *In IV Sent.* dist. xvii q.1 a.4; ed. cit., 4.847.

37 IaIIae q.113 aa.1, 2.

38 IaIIae q.63 a.4.

39 IIaIIae q.58 a.5.

40 IaIIae q.113 a.1.

41 IaIIae q.100 a.12.

42 IaIIae q.100 a.12 ad 3um.

43 IaIIae q.83 a.4.
44 IaIIae q.113 a.1 ad 2um 'Iustitia importat generaliter totam rectitudinem ordinis. Et ideo magis denominatur huiusmodi transmutatio a iustitia quam a caritate vel fide.' On the significance of 'rectitude', see McGrath, 'Rectitude: The Foundations of Anselm of Canterbury's Soteriology'. Thomas is aware of Anselm's definition of *iustitia* as 'rectitudo voluntatis propter se servata', and cites it with approval on occasion. For the relation between *rectitudo* and *iustitia* according to Thomas, see IaIIae q.21 a.3; q.46 a.7 ad 2um; q.55 a.4 ad 4um; q.100 a.2 ad 2um; q.113 a.1. The essential distinction being made is between *iustitia proprie* as *rectitudo actus* and *iustitia metaphorice* as *rectitudo ordinis in partibus hominis*.
45 IaIIae q.109 a.8.
46 IaIIae q.113 a.1 ad 2um.
47 See McGrath, 'The Influence of Aristotelian Physics'.
48 *Itinerarium mentis in Deum* IV, 3.
49 On this, see the brilliant study of R. Guardini, *Systembildende Elemente in der Theologie Bonaventuras. Die Lehren vom Lumen Mentis, von der Gradatio Entium and der Influentia Sensus et Motus* (Leiden, 1964).
50 *Quaestiones disputatae de gratia* q.2; ed. Doucet, 45–9.
51 *Quaestiones disputatae de gratia* q.7; ed. Hödl, 63.
52 e.g., *Glossa in Decretum Gratianis*, Cod. Bamberg Can. 13, cited Landgraf, op. cit., I/1 210 'Talis est gratia, quia nec virtus nec opus vel motus mentis. Et secundum hoc nichil ponit.' See Alszeghy, *Nova Creatura*, for further references and discussion.
53 *Alexandri de Hales Summa Theologica* pars I inq. I tr. ii q.3 tit.3 membr. 2 cap. 1. sol; ed. Quaracchi, 2.77 'Dicendum quod "Deus esse per gratiam" ponit necessario gratiam creatam in creatura.'
54 *I Sent* dist. xxxvii cap. 1.
55 See Oberman, 'Wir sind pettler'; Courtenay, 'Covenant and Causality'; Hamm, *Promissio, pactum, ordinatio*; McGrath, 'Anti-Pelagian Structure'.
56 *Opus Oxoniense* IV dist. xvi q.2.
57 Thomas Aquinas, *Summa Theologiae*, IIIa 1.56 a.2 ad 4um.
58 e.g., IaIIae q.113 a.1 'Remissio peccatorum est iustificatio'.
59 McGrath, 'Forerunners of the Reformation?'.
60 *Canonis Missae Expositio* 31B; ed. Oberman/Courtenay, 1.314–5.
61 See McGrath, op. cit., for details.

Notes to §6

1 See H. Denifle, *Luther und Luthertum. Die abendländischen Schriftausleger bis Luther über iustitia Dei und iustificatio* (Mainz, 1905); Holl, *Iustitia Dei in der vorlutherischen Bibelauslegung*; H. Bornkamm, 'Iustitia Dei in der Scholastik und bei Luther', *ARG* 39 (1942) 1–46; McGrath, '"The Righteousness of God"'.
2 Ambrosiaster, *Comm. in epist. Pauli*, PL 17.56B. See also 17.74B; 80A–B.

3 e.g., Atto of Vercelli, *Expos. epist. Pauli*, PL 134.160B. See also 134.161B; 162A. On Augustine himself, see §4.

4 'Hieronymus', *Brev. in Psalm.* 70.2, PL 26.1025D.

5 *Brev. in Psalm. 30.1*; PL 26.906B 'Quia nisi a Deo iustificemur, per nos non possumus iustificari.'

6 On this, see McGrath, 'Divine Justice and Divine Equity in the Controversy between Augustine and Julian of Eclanum'.

7 Augustine, *Opus imperf. contra Iul.* III, 2; CSEL 85/1.352.6–7.

8 Augustine, *Opus imperf. contra Iul* I, 38; CSEL 85/1.28.10–35.

9 PL 131.291D 'Mea iustitia est malum pro malo reddere. Tu solus iustus, quam circa nos ostendisti, reddens bonum pro malo, qua de impio facis bonum.'

10 Atto of Vercelli, *Exp. epist. Pauli*, PL 134.137A–8B.

11 e.g., Sedulius Scotus, *Coll. in omnes Pauli epist.*, PL 103.18D 'Iustitia Dei est, quia quod promisit, dedit'; Haimo of Auxerre, *Expl. in Psalmos* PL 116.295A; Bruno of Würzburg, *Expos. Psalm.*, PL 140.132D; 265C. This understanding of *iustitia Dei* is reproduced in the 14th century vernacular poem *The Pearl*: see A. D. Horgan, 'Justice in *The Pearl*', *Review of English Studies* 32 (1981) 173–80; McGrath, 'Divine Justice and Divine Equity' 317–18; idem. '"The Righteousness of God"', 70–1.

12 See G. Paré, A. Brunet and P. Tremblay, *La renaissance du XIIe siècle* (Paris, 1933).

13 A. von Harnack, *History of Dogma*, 3.310. Cf. H. Rashdall, *The Idea of Atonement in Christian Theology* (London, 1920) 355 'Anselm appeals to justice ... but his notions of justice are the barbaric ideals of an ancient Lombard king or the technicalities of a Lombard lawyer rather than the ideas which would have satisfied such a man as Anselm in ordinary human life.' For a similar misunderstanding, see G. Aulén, *Christus Victor* (London, 1934) 100–9.

14 On this, see McGrath, 'Rectitude. The Moral Foundations of Anselm of Canterbury's Soteriology'.

15 *Proslogion*, 9; ed. Schmitt, 1.106.18–107.3.

16 *Proslogion*, 10; ed. cit., 1.109.4–5.

17 *Cur Deus homo* I, 12.

18 For this concept as developed by the medieval canonists, see E. Wohlhauper, *Aequitas Canonica. Eine Studie aus dem kanonischen Recht* (Paderborn, 1931); H. Lange, 'Die Wörter aequitas und iustitia auf römischen Münzen', *Zeitschrift der Savigny-Stiftung für Rechtsgeschichte*, Romanistische Abteilung, 52 (1932) 296–314.

19 *Cur Deus homo* I, 23.

20 *de veritate* 12; *de casu diaboli* 9.

21 *de veritate* 4; ed. cit., 1.181.6–8.

22 *de veritate* 12; ed. cit., 1.192.6–8. Our interpretation is supported at this point by the study of G. Söhngen, 'Rectitudo bei Anselm von Canterbury als Oberbegriff von Wahrheit und Gerechtigkeit', in *Sola Ratione* ed. H. Kohlenberger (Stuttgart, 1970) 71–7.

23 See H. Hommel, 'Wahrheit und Gerechtigkeit. Zur Geschichte und Deutung eines Begriffspaares', *Antike und Abendland* 15 (1969) 159–86.

24 *Cur Deus homo* I, 11.

25 *de casu diaboli* 16; *de conceptu virginali et originali peccato* II, 22–3. On this, see Blomme, *La doctrine du péché*. The earlier work of R. M. Martin, *La controverse sur le péché originel au début du XIVe siècle* (Louvain, 1930) is also useful. It may be noted that the influence of Anselm's concept of original sin appears to have been insignificant until Albertus Magnus defined the formal element of original sin as *privatio iustitiae*, although the same concept may be found in Odo of Cambrai, *de peccato originali*, PL 160.1071–1102. In particular, the school of Laon maintained the older Augustinian understanding of original sin as concupiscence: William of St Thierry, *Disp. adv. Abael.* 7; PL 180.275A; Robert Pullen, *Sententiarum libri octo* II, 27; PL 186.754B–5C.

26 *Cur Deus homo* I, 12.

27 *Aliquot quaestionum liber XV*, PL 93.471–8. On this, and other aspects of the *ius diaboli*, see Rivière, *Le dogme de la rédemption*.

28 Gregory, *Moralium libri XXXIII*, xv, 31; PL 76.692D–3C.

29 For an excellent analysis, see F. Hammer, *Genugtuung und Heil. Absicht, Sinn und Grenzen der Erlösungslehre Anselms von Canterbury* (Wien, 1966).

30 Anselm of Laon, *Sententiae* 47; ed. Lottin, *Psychologie et Morale* 5.144; *Sententiae Atrebatenses*, ed. Lottin, 5.414; *Sententie divine pagine*, ed. Bliemetzrieder, 41. See also note 25.

31 Anselm of Laon, *Sententiae* 47–8, ed. Lottin, 5.44–7; the School of Laon, *Sententiae* 354–5, ed. Lottin, 5.269–70. Cf. Peter Lombard, *III Sent.* dist. xviii, 5.

32 Abailard, *Exp. in Epist. ad Rom.*, PL 178.834D. See de Clerck, *Droits du démon*; R. E. Weingart, *The Logic of Divine Love. A Critical Analysis of the Soteriology of Peter Abailard* (Oxford, 1970) 84–8.

33 Hugh of St Victor, *de sacramentis* I, viii, 4; PL 176.308A–B.

34 De Clerk, op. cit., 39–45. It must be conceded that the *Epitome theologiae Christianae* departs considerably from the 'received view' when it denies that man was *ever* subject to the power of the devil: *Epitome* 23; PL 178.1730D–31A 'constat hominem sub potestate diaboli non fuisse, nec de eius servitute redemptum esse'.

35 *de erroribus Abaelardi* V, 13–14; PL 182.1063D–65B.

36 *Sententiarum libri quinque* IV, 19; PL 211.1212A. See also de Clerck, op. cit., 56–7.

37 *Exp. in epist. ad Rom*, PL 178.864A; 868B; *Sermo* 30; PL 178.567D; *Dialogus*, PL 178.1653A; 1654C; 1656D–57A. See Weingart, op. cit., 141–2.

38 e.g. *Epitome theologiae Christianae* 32; PL 178.1750C. See Lottin, *Le concept de justice*, 512–13. A similar definition is due to Stephen Langton: ibid., 513–14.

39 Lottin, op. cit., 514 n. 1.

40 Lottin, op. cit., 514 n. 2.

41 Lottin, op. cit., 515 nn. 1–2.

42 Text as established by Lottin, op. cit., 517.13–18, from Paris Nat. lat. 14891 and 15952, and Brussels Bibl. roy. 12042–9.

43 *de sacramentis* I, viii, 8; PL 176.310D.

44 *de sacramentis* I, viii, 8–9; PL 176.311A–D.

45 Lottin, op. cit., 521 n. 1. See also A. H. Chroust, 'The Philosophy of Law from St. Augustine to St. Thomas Aquinas', *New Scholasticism* 20 (1946) 26–71; 64–70, esp. 64 n.141.

46 Lottin, op. cit., 521 n. 2.

47 Thomas Aquinas, *de veritate* q.23 a.6; ed. Spiazzi, 1.426 'Dicero autem quod ex simplici voluntate dependeat iustitia, est dicere quod divina voluntas non procedat secundum ordinem sapientiae, quod est blasphemum.'

48. O. Lottin, *L'ordre morale et l'order logique d'après St. Thomas* (Louvain, 1924); idem, 'L'intellectualisme de la morale Thomiste', *Xenia Thomistica* I (1925) 411–27.

49 *Summa Theologiae* IIIa q.46 a.3.

50 IIIa q.46 a.2 ad 3um.

51 See G. Stratenwerth, *Die Naturrechtslehre des Johannes Duns Scotus* (Göttingen, 1951), where it is argued that Scotus thereby drove a conceptual wedge between the realms of natural and divine law. On Ockham, see W. Kölmel, 'Das Naturrecht bei Wilhelm Ockham', *FS* 35 (1953) 39–85; for Biel's in relation to Ockham's, see idem, 'Von Ockham zu Gabriel Biel. Zur Naturrechtslehre des 14. und 15. Jahrhunderts', *FS* 37 (1955) 218–59.

52 Biel, *Canonis missae expositio* 23 E; ed. Oberman/Courtenay 1.212. Cf. *In I Sent.* dist. xliii q.1 a.4 cor.; ed. Werbeck/Hoffmann 1.746.5–7 'Deus potest aliquid facere, quod non est iustum fieri a deo; si tamen faceret, iustum esset fieri. Unde sola voluntas divina est prima regula omnis iustitiae, et eo quod vult aliquid fieri, iustum est fieri.'

53 *Opus Oxoniense* III dist. xix q.1 n.7.

54 See M. M. Menges, *The Concept of Univocity regarding the Predication of God and Creatures according to William of Ockham* (New York/Louvain, 1952).

55 e.g. *Alexandri de Hales Summa Theologica*, pars I inq.1 tr.4 q.1 membr.2 cap.2 ad 4um; ed. Quaracchi, 1.207 'Dicendum quod iustitia dicitur dupliciter. Uno modo retributio unicuique secundum merita: et sic non omnia facit de iustitia; Alio modo condecentia bonitatis; et sic omnia facit de iustitia nec aliquid facit nisi quod condecet iustitiae'; Thomas Aquinas, *In IV Sent.* dist. xlvi q.1 a.1 sol.1; idem, *Summa Theologiae* Ia q.21 a.1 ad 3um. Philip the Chancellor, *Summa*, cited Lottin, op. cit., 518–19; Odo Rigaldi, cited Lottin, op. cit., 518–19; Albertus Magnus, *Summa de bono*, cited Lottin, op. cit., 519–21.

56 *Summa Theologiae* Ia q.21 a.3 ad 2um; cf. idem, *In IV Sent.* dist. xlvi q.2 a.2 sol.2.

57 *Opus Oxoniense* IV dist. xlvi q.1 n.7.

58 *Opus Oxoniense* IV dist. xlvi q.1 nn.2–4. It must be pointed out that

Scotus elsewhere notes that it is not *contrary* to justice to forgive sin: *Opus Oxoniense* IV dist. xlvi q.4 n.17 'dare bonum indebitum non est contra iustitiam, quia est liberalitatis et actus unius virtutis non repugnat alteri'.

59 Bornkamm, op. cit., 20.

60 See McGrath, 'Mira et nova diffinitio iustitiae'; idem, *Luther's Theology of the Cross* (Oxford, 1985) 95–113.

61 *In I Sent.* dist. xli q.1 a.3 dub.3 summ.3; ed. Werbeck/Hoffmann, 1.732.16–18.

62 *In II Sent.* dist. xxvii q.1 a.3 dub.4; ed. cit., 2.253.7–9.

63 Hamm, *Promissio, Pactum, Ordinatio*, 462–6.

64 *Missae canonis expositio* 59S; ed. Oberman/Courtenay, 2.446. For the possibility that *iustitia Dei* is thus understood to be purely arbitrary, see McGrath, '*Righteousness of God*', 72; idem, 'Some Observations concerning the Soteriology of the *Via Moderna*', *RThAM* 52 (1985) 182–93.

65 *In II Sent.* dist. xxxvi q. unica a.1 nota 3; ed. cit., 2.622.5–3.10.

66 WA 55 II.108.15–109.11 for the full text; for the gloss, see WA 55 I.70.9–11.

67 WA 4.262.4–5. For Luther's concept of conventual causality, see McGrath, *Luther's Theology of the Cross*, 85–90.

68 On this, see McGrath, op. cit., 93–161.

69 See G. R. Evans, *The Language and Logic of the Bible. The Earlier Middle Ages* (Cambridge, 1984) 101–22.

70 *Theologia Christiana* I, 7.

71 *Theologicae Regulae* 26; PL 210.633D. See G. R. Evans, *Alan of Lille. The Frontiers of Theology in the Later Twelfth Century* (Cambridge, 1983) 29–33.

72 G. R. Evans, 'The Borrowed Meaning. Grammar, Logic and the Problems of Theological Language in Twelfth-Century Schools', *Downside Review* 96 (1978) 165–75.

73 See Evans, *Alan of Lille*, 41–51.

74 *Tract. in Hexam.* I, 12; PL 192.1252B.

75 See McGrath, '"The Righteousness of God"'. What follows is based on Ockham, *In I Sent.*, dist. ii q.3; *Opera Theologica* 2.50–74.

76 See Menges, op. cit.; G. Leff, *William of Ockham. The Metamorphosis of Scholastic Discourse* (Manchester, 1977) 400–11.

77 Ockham, *In I Sent.* dist. ii q.3; *Opera Theologica*, 2.61–2.

Notes to §7

1 Augustine, *Sermo* 169, 13.

2 The term 'axiom' is, of course, being used in a loose sense, rather than in the Euclidian or Boethian senses of the term: see G. R. Evans, 'Boethian and Euclidian Axiomatic Method in the Theology of the Later Twelfth Century', *Archives Internationales d'Histoire des Sciences* 103 (1980) 13–29.

3 Recent studies have emphasised Pelagius' orthodox intentions: R. F. Evans, *Pelagius: Inquiries and Reappraisals* (New York, 1968); G. Greschat, *Gnade als konkrete Freiheit. Eine Untersuchung zur Gnadenlehre des Pelagius* (Mainz, 1972). The older study of G. de Plinval, *Pélage, ses écrits,*

sa vie et sa réforme (Lausanne, 1943) is still helpful. On the reforming nature of Pelagianism, see the two excellent studies of Peter Brown: 'Pelagius and His Supporters: Aims and Environment', *Journal of Theological Studies* 19 (1968) 93–114; 'The Patrons of Pelagius: The Roman Aristocracy between East and West', *Journal of Theological Studies* 21 (1970) 56–72. Particular attention is drawn to the fact that the ascetic discipline and aims of Pelagianism are now regarded as the *least* original aspects of the movement, being regarded as part of the general western reception of oriental monastic traditions through the translations of Rufinus in the late fourth century (on which see F. Winkelmann, 'Spätantike lateinische Übersetzungen christlicher griechischer Litera-tur', *Theologische Literaturzeitung* 95 (1967) 229–40).

4 *de dono persev.* xx, 53. Cf. *Confessiones* X, xxix, 40 'da quod iubes et iube quod vis'.

5 Cf. Harnack, *History of Dogma* 5.245 n.3. The alternative 'synergism' is similarly unacceptable: Williams, *Grace of God*, 44.

6 *de praed. sanct.* i, 2.

7 *Commonitorium* 2; Pl 50.640B 'In ipsa item catholica ecclesia magnopere curandum est, ut id teneamus, quod ubique, quod semper, quod ad omnibus creditum est; hoc est etenim vere proprieque catholicum.'

8 D. J. MacQueen, 'John Cassian on Grace and Free Will'. Cf. A. Hoch, *Die Lehre des Johannes Cassianus von Natur und Gnade* (Freiburg, 1894). The two general studies of Chéné, 'Que significiaent ''initium fidei'' and 'Le sémipelagianisme du Midi de la Gaule' provide valuable background material.

9 *de incarnat.* VII, i, 2.

10 Both this council and Orange II (q.v.) were *local*, rather than ecumenical. For the difficulties this raises, see *Problems of Authority. An Anglo-French Symposium* ed. J. M. Todd (London, 1964), 63–4.

11 D. 105.

12 C. Gore, 'Our Lord's Human Example', *Church Quarterly Review* 16 (1883) 298. A similar link between Nestorius and Pelagius is identified by John Cassian (*de incarnat.* I, iii, 5). See also the somewhat scurrilous poem of Prosper of Aquitaine, *Epitaphium Nestorianae et Pelagianae haeresos*, PL 51.153.

13 Cap. 1; D. 130.

14 Cap. 3; D. 132.

15 Cap. 9; D. 141 'Non aufertur liberum arbitrium, sed liberatur'.

16 Can. 1; D. 174. The reference here appears to be to freedom from sin, rather than *liberum arbitrium*. See also n.10.

17 Can. 5; D. 178. For the terms *initium fidei* and *affectus credulitatis*, as they occur in this canon, see the studies of Chéné cited in n.8.

18 Can. 8; D. 181 '. . . per liberum arbitrium, quod in omnibus, qui de praevaricatione primi hominis nati sunt, constat esse vitiatum . . . omnium liberum arbitrium per peccatum primi hominis asserit infirma-tum'. This is made especially clear in the 'profession of faith' appended to the canons (D. 199).

19 This remarkable fact appears first to have been noticed by Bouillard, *Conversion et grâce chez Thomas d'Aquin*, 98–102; 114–21. See also M. Seckler, *Instinkt und Glaubenswille nach Thomas von Aquin* (Mainz, 1961) 90–133.

20 *II Sent.* dist. xxviii 4. See further J. N. D. Kelly, *Jerome* (London, 1975) 309–23. The attitude of Thomas Bradwardine and Gregory of Rimini to the *Epistula ad Demetriadem*, allegedly due to Jerome, is significant: Oberman, *Werden und Wertung*, 87.

21 M. de Kroon, 'Pseudo-Augustin im Mittelalter', *Augustiniana* 22 (1972) 511–30. For the problems this raises, see McGrath, '"Augustinianism"?' 253–4.

22 D. 348 'Gratiam Dei praevenire et subsequi hominem credo et profiteor, ita tamen, ut liberum arbitrium rationali creaturae non denegem.'

23 Anselm, *de lib. arb.* 3. Cf. F. Bäumker, *Die Lehre Anselms von Canterbury über dem Willen und seine Wahlfreiheit* (Münster, 1912).

24 See Mitzka, 'Anfänge einer Konkurslehre'. For this concept in the early Augustinian school, see Trapè, *Il concorso divino del pensiero di Egidio Romano*. On the development of the concept in High Scholasticism, see Auer, *Entwicklung der Gnadenlehre*, 2.113–45.

25 Mitzka, op. cit., 175.

26 *II Sent.* dist. xxv 8–9.

27 See L. Grane, *Contra Gabrielem. Luthers Auseinandersetzung mit Gabriel Biel in der Disputatio contra scholasticam theologiam (1517)* (Gyldendal, 1972); Ernst, *Gott und Mensch am Vorabend der Reformation*.

28 For an analysis of these theses, see Grane, op. cit., 369–73.

29 *In II Sent.* dist xxv q. unica a.3 dub.2.

30 *In II Sent.* dist. xxv q. unica a.1 not.1.

31 For an excellent analysis, see Ernst, op. cit., 325–8.

32 e.g., *In II Sent.* dist. xxviii q. unica a.2 concl.1.

33 *In II Sent.* dist. xxviii q. unica a.2 conc.3.

34 *In II Sent.* dist. xxviii q. unica a.2 conc.2.

35 *In II Sent.* dist. xxvii q. unica a.3 dub.2 prop.1.

36 *In II Sent.* dist. xxviii q. unica a.2 conc.1.

37 Thus Oberman, *Harvest of Medieval Theology*, 176–7; H. J. McSorley, 'Was Gabriel Biel a Semi-Pelagian?', in *Wahrheit und Verkündigung* ed. L. Scheffczyk *et al.* (2 vols: München, 1967) 2.1109–20; J. E. Biechler, 'Gabriel Biel on "liberum arbitrium"', *The Thomist* 34 (1970) 114–27. For replies, see F. Clark, 'A New Appraisal of Late Medieval Nominalism', *Gregorianum* 46 (1965) 733–65; Ernst, op. cit.; McGrath, 'The Anti-Pelagian Structure of "Nominalist" Doctrines of Justification'.

38 e.g., Biechler, op. cit., 125 'Biel's own doctrine of justification, clearly Pelagian though it was, apparently provoked little or no pre-Lutheran opposition'. It may be pointed out that the list of forbidden books published after Trent makes no reference to Biel or other theologians of the *via moderna*: indeed, Biel was still highly regarded by the German Roman Catholic church in the late sixteenth century: Oberman, op. cit., 427.

39 For an excellent study of Biel's attitude to tradition, see Oberman, op. cit., 365–408.

40 The conciliar collections of the period, however, generally attributed the canons of the Council of Carthage (418) to the Council of Mileve (416).

41 *Sententiarum libri quinque* III, 2; PL 211.1047A–B.

42 *Quaestiones disputatae 'antequam esset frater'* q.53 membr.3; ed. Quaracchi, 2.1020.24–22.7.

43 *Quaestiones disputatae de gratia* q.7; ed. Hödl, 64; cf. *Tractatus de gratia* q.2 membr.1 a.2; ed. Hödl, 72.

44 *In II Sent.* dist. xxvi membr.1 q.1; ed. Bouvy, 308.89–92. See also B. Pergamo, 'Il desiderio innato del soprannaturále nelli questioni inediti di Oddone Rigaldo', *Studi Francescani* 32 (1935) 414–46; 33 (1936) 76–108.

45 *In II Sent.* dist. xxvi membr.1 q.1 ad 1um; ed. cit., 308.95–105. It may be noted at this point that Thomas Aquinas never seems to use the term *gratia creata* at all, although he appears to demonstrate familiarity with the term at one point (*In II Sent.* dist. xxvi q.1 a.1).

46 See E. Gössmann, *Metaphysik und Heilsgeschichte. Eine theologische Untersuchung der Summa Halensis* (München, 1964); G. Philips, 'La théologie de la grâce dans la "Summa Fratris Alexandri"', *EThL* 49 (1973) 100–23. This work is composite, and does not stem from Alexander of Hales: J. Auer, 'Textkritische Studien zur Gnadenlehre des Alexander von Hales', *Scholastik* 15 (1940) 63–75. For the origins of the distinction between *gratia creata* and *gratia increata*, see Auer, *Entwicklung der Gnadenlehre*, 1.86–123.

47 *Summa Fratris Alexandri* pars III inq.1 tract.2 q.1 cap.1 and the following sections; *Alexandri de Hales Summa Theologica*, 4.1023–60.

48 *Summa Fratris Alexandri* pars III inq.1 tract.1 q.2 cap. 1 a.2 sol.; ed. cit., 4.959. On this whole question, see Dhont, *Le problème de la préparation à la grâce*.

49 *Summa Fratris Alexandri* pars II inq.2 tract.3 sect.2 q.2 tit.3 cap.4 a.1 ad 3um; ed. cit., 1.729. For a more detailed study of this question, see G. Philips, *L'Union personelle avec le Dieu vivant*.

50 See Mitzka, *Die Lehre des hl. Bonaventura von der Vorbereitung auf die heiligmachenden Gnade*.

51 *Breviloquium* V, ii, 2.

52 *In IV Sent.* dist. xvii pars 1 a.2 q.2 ad 1.2.3um.

53 On this point, see Mitzka, op. cit., 64.

54 *Quaestiones disputatae de gratia* q.3; ed. Douchet, 69–72. The argument is based on the maxim 'naturaliter est anima gratiae capax', which will be shown to be characteristic of the early Dominican school.

55 *Quaestiones* q.4; ed. cit., 94–6.

56 *Quaestiones* q.4; ed. cit., 97.

57 *Quaestiones* q.4; ed. cit., 98–9 'Gratia enim gratis data quasi medium tenet inter naturam vel voluntatem et gratiam gratum facientem.'

58 *In II Sent.* dist. xxix a.1 q.1. The important study of Heynck, 'Die aktuelle Gnade bei Richard von Mediavilla', should be consulted.

59 *In II Sent.* dist. xxviii a.1 q.2.

60 Hocedez, *Richard de Middleton*, 277.

61 *Quaestiones disputatae de statu naturae lapsae* q.2; ed. cit., 178.

62 See M. Grabmann, *Die philosophische und theologische Erkenntnislehre des Kardinals Matthaeus ab Aquasparta* (Wien, 1906); E. Gilson, 'Roger Marston, un cas d'Augustinisme avicennisant', *Archives d'histoire doctrinale et littéraire du moyen âge* 8 (1952) 37–42.

63 Thomas Aquinas, *Summa Theologiae* IaIIae q.113 a.10. It is interesting to compare this with Tertullian's assertion that the soul is 'anima naturaliter Christiana': see H. Chadwick, *Early Christian Thought and the Classical Tradition* (Oxford, 1984) 3.

64 See McGrath, 'Influence of Aristotelian Physics'.

65 Doms, *Die Gnadenlehre des Albertus Magnus*, 163–8.

66 *In II Sent.* dist. xxviii q.1 a.4, ed. Mandonnet, 2.726–30.

67 *In II Sent.* dist. xxviii q.1 a.4, ed. Mandonnet, 2.728.

68 *Summa Theologiae* IaIIae q.109 a.6.

69 loc. cit.: Cf. J. Stufler, *Gott der erste Beweger aller Dinge* (Innsbruck, 1936).

70 *In II Sent.* dist. xxviii q.1 a.4, ed. Mandonnet, 2.728. See Stufler, 'Die entfernte Vorbereitung auf die Rechtfertigung nach dem hl. Thomas'.

71 *de veritate* q.24 a.15, ed. Spiazzi, 1.467.

72 For details of this work, which is actually an extract from the *Eudemian Ethics*, see A. Pelzer, 'Les versions des ouvrages de morale conservés sous le nom d'Aristote en usage au XIIIᵉ siècle', *Revue néo-scholastique de philosophie* 23 (1921) 37–9; T. Deman, 'Le "Liber de bona fortuna" dans la théologie de S. Thomas d'Aquin', *RSPhTh* 17 (1928) 41–50.

73 See Bouillard, *Conversion et grâce*, 114–21.

74 *Summa contra Gentiles* III, 149, 8.

75 *Summa contra Gentiles* III, 149, 1. For a discussion of the axiom which so influenced Thomas, see Stufler, 'Der hl. Thomas und das Axiom "omne quod movetur ab alio movetur"'.

76 *Summa contra Gentiles* III, 149. 1.

77 *Quodl.* q.1 a.7. A similar opinion may be found in the Romans *Reportatio* cap. 10 lect. 3.

78 *Summa Theologiae* IaIIae q.112 a.2 ad 3um 'nulla praeparatio exigitur quam ipse non faciat'.

79 IaIIae q.112 a.3.

80 IaIIae q.112 a.2 ad 2um. See J. Stufler, 'Zur Kontroverse über die praemotio physica', *ZKTh* 47 (1927) 533–64.

81 See Steinmetz, *Misericordia Dei*, 93–5.

82 Literally, 'God does not deny grace to the man who does what is in him.'

83 Irenaeus, *adv. haer.* IV, xxxix, 2. Cf. Origen, *contra Celsum* VII, 42. See J. Rivière, 'Quelques antécédents patristiques de la formule "facienti quod in se est"', *RSR* 7 (1927) 93–7.

84 For an excellent discussion of the axiom in this period, see Landgraf, *Dogmengeschichte* I/1 249–64.

85 *Homiliae de sanctis* 2; PL 155.1496B.

86 e.g., in his Romans commentary, cited Landgraf, op. cit., 251 nn.14, 15. Cf. n.16 'Facite, quod vestrum est, quia Deus faciet, quod suum est.' On his concept of merit, which is closely related, see Hamm, *Promissio, pactum, ordinatio*, 109–18.

87 Cod. Erlangen lat. 353 fol. 84; cited Landgraf, op. cit., 252.

88 *Sententiarum libri octo* VI, 49; PL 186.893B. See Courtney, *Robert Pullen*, 226–33.

89 *contra Hereticos* I, 51; PL 210.356B. Cf. 356A 'Nec poenitentia est causa efficiens remissionis peccati, sed tantum gratuita Dei voluntas.' See also *Theologicae Regulae* 87; PL 210.666A–C.

90 Cod. Vat. lat. 1098 fol. 155v; cited Landgraf, op. cit., 260.

91 *Quaestiones de gratia* q.6; ed. Hödl, 55–6. See also *Tractatus de gratia* q.3 membr.2 a.2 sol.; ed. Hödl, 61.

92 *Tractatus de gratia* q.3 membr.2 a.2 sol.; ed. cit., 60 'Concedo igitur quod si homo faciat quod in se est, Deus necessario, id est immutabiliter dat ei gratiam.'

93 *In II Sent.* dist. xxvi membr.1 q.2 a.3; ed. Bouvy, 331.48–332.68.

94 *In II Sent.* dist. xxviii membr.1 q.4 a.2 ad 3um; ed. cit., 86.49–52.

95 *Summa Halensis* Inq.4 tr.3 q.3 tit.1; ed. Quaracchi, 2.730–1.

96 *Summa Halensis* Inq.4 tr.3 q.3 tit.1; ed. cit., 2.731.

97 *In IV Sent.* dist. xiv pars 1 a.2 q.2; dist. xvii pars 1 a.1 q.2. This point is emphasised by G. Božitkovič, *S. Bonaventurae doctrina de gratia et libero arbitrio* (Marienbad, 1919).

98 e.g., *Breviloquium* V, iii, 4 'Rursus, quoniam Deus sic reformat, quod leges naturae inditas non infirmat; ideo sic hanc gratiam tribuit libero arbitrio, ut tamen ipsum non cogat, sed eius consensus liber maneat.'

99 *In II Sent.* dist. xxviii q.1 a.4.

100 *In II Sent.* dist. xxviii q.1 a.4 ad 4um.

101 *In IV Sent.* dist. xvii q.1 aa.3–4.

102 Thus Roger of Marston, *Quaestiones disputatae de statu naturae lapsae* q.1 ad 11um; ed. cit., 195.

103 Cod. Paris Nat. lat. 14551 fol. 103r; Cod. Paris Nat. lat. 15690 fol. 228v; Klosterneuburg Cod. 322; cited Grabmann, *Mittelalterliches Geistesleben* 2.453–5.

104 *Summa Theologiae* IaIIae q.112 a.3 'Praeparatio ad hominis gratiam est a Deo sicut a movente, a libero autem arbitrio sicut a moto.'

105 IaIIae q. 109 a.6 ad 2um. See also *in Hebr.* cap. 12 lect. 3 nn. 688–0.

106 Dhont, op. cit., 267–8. See also L. Capéran, *Le problème du salut des infidèles* (2 vols: Tolouse, 1934) 2.49–57.

107 *In II Sent.* dist. xxvii q.2 a.4 ad 3um. Peter allows that man may dispose himself remotely, but not proximately, to justification through his unaided powers: *In II Sent.* dist. xxviii q.1 aa.2, 3.

108 *In II Sent.* dist. xxviii q.1 a.4; ed. cit., 2.728–9.

109 *de veritate* q.29 a.6; ed. cit., 1.564.

110 *Summa Theologiae* IaIIae q.114 a.6.

111 IaIIae q.114.a.5 Cf. IaIIae q.112 aa.2, 3; q.114 aa.3, 5.

112 *In II Sent.* dist. xxvii q.2 a.2. 'Meritum impetrativum' is synonymus with 'meritum de congruo'.

113 *In II Sent.* dist. xxviii, xxix q.1 a.4.

114 *Textbeilage* 119; cited Zumkeller, 'Der Wiener Theologieprofessor Johannes von Retz'.

115 *In II Sent.* dist. xxvi, xxvii q.1 a.3, conc.2.

116 *Textbeilage* 117. Here, as above, Retz is heavily dependent upon Thomas of Strasbourg – cf. *In II Sent.* dist. xxviii, xxix q.1.

117 Oberman, *Archbishop Thomas Bradwardine*, 155–9; Gregory of Rimini, *In II Sent.* dist. xxvi q.1 aa.1, 2; Zumkeller, 'Johannes Klenkok', 240–52; idem, 'Erfurter Augustinertheologen' 46–8; idem, 'Johannes von Dorsten', 32–6; 44–8; 184–6. On the role of the *auxilium speciale Dei* in Gregory's theology of justification, see Burger, 'Das auxilium speciale Dei in der Gnadenlehre Gregors von Rimini'.

118 Steinmetz, op. cit., 94–97; 114–22.

119 Zumkeller, 'Erfurter Augustinertheologen', 54–5. For a fuller study of his theology, see M. Ferdigg, 'De vita et operibus et doctrina Ioannis de Palz', *Analecta Augustiniana* 30 (1967) 210–321; 31 (1968) 155–318. See also Steinmetz, op. cit., 94–7; 114–22.

120 On this, see Courtenay, 'Covenant and Causality'; idem., 'The King and the Leaden Coin'; Oberman, *Werden und Wertung*, 161–200. On token coins, see W. J. Courtenay, 'Token Coinage and the Administration of Poor Relief during the Late Middle Ages', *Journal of Interdisciplinary History* 3 (1972–3) 275–95.

121 *In IV Sent.* dist. q.1 C 'Sicut si rex ordinaret quod quicumque acciperet denarium plumbeum haberet certum donum, et tunc denarius plumbeus esset causa sine qua non respectu illius doni.'

122 *Super libros Sapientiae* III, 35.

123 See McGrath, ' "The Righteousness of God" ', 113–17.

124 *In II Sent.* dist. xxvii q. unica a.3 dub.4.

125 *In II Sent.* dist. xxvii q. unica a.2 conc.4; ed. Werbeck/Hoffmann, 2.517.1–8.

126 *In II Sent.* dist. xxvii q. unica a.3 dub.4.

127 On Geiler, see Douglass, *Justification in Late Medieval Preaching*.

128 *Orat. Domini* 9B; cited Douglass, op. cit., 144 n.2.

129 *Nav. fat.* 22S; cited Douglass, op. cit., 145 n.1.

130 *Nav. pen.* 28v 1, cited Douglass, op. cit., 139 n.3.

131 *Nav. pen.* 18r 1; cited Douglass, op. cit., 143 n.1.

132 See McGrath, *Luther's Theology of the Cross*, 72–92.

133 WA 4.262.4–7. Cf. WA 3.288.37–289.4. See further L. Grane, *Contra Gabrielem. Luthers Auseinandersetzung mit Gabriel Biel in der Disputatio contra scholasticam theologiam 1517* (Gyldendal, 1968), 296–301; R. Schwarz, *Vorgeschichte der reformatorischen Bußtheologie* (Berlin, 1968), 249–59; O. Bayer, *Promissio. Geschichte der reformatorischen Wende in Luthers Theologie* (Göttingen, 1971), 115–43.

Notes to §8

1 J. de Ghellinck, 'Un chapitre dans l'histoire de la définition des sacrements au XIIe siècle', in *Mélanges Mandonnet* (Paris, 1930) 2.79–96; N. M. Haring, 'Berengar's Definitions of *Sacramentum* and Their Influence upon Medieval Sacramentology', *Medieval Studies* 10 (1948) 109–46; D. van den Eynde, 'Les définitions des sacrements pendant la première période de la théologie scolastique (1050–1235)', *Antonianum* 24 (1949) 183–228; 439–88; 25 (1950) 3–78.

2 Cassiodorus, *Exp. S. Pauli epist. ad Rom.*; PL 68.417B; Sedulius Scotus, *Coll. in omnes B. Pauli epist.*; PL 103.42D. The central significance of baptism to the Pelagian soteriology should be noted here: see T. Böhlin, *Die Theologie des Pelagius und ihre Genesis* (Uppsala, 1957), especially 29–43. The controversy surrounding the views of Jovinian on the relationship between baptism and membership of the church called this theology into question (e.g., Jerome, *Dialog. contra Pelag.* III, 1; PL 23.595B) – but see S. Prete, 'Lo scritto pelagiano 'de castitate' è di Pelagio?', *Aevum* 35 (1961), 315–22.

3 Jerome, *Epist.* 130, 9; CSEL 56.189.4–5.

4 *Regula canonicorum* 14; PL 89.1104A–05B.

5 O. D. Watkins, *A History of Penance* (2 vols: London, 1920). Cf. B. Poschmann, *Penance and the Anointing of the Sick* (New York, 1954).

6 Harnack, *History of Dogma* 5.325.

7 See J. F. McNeill and H. M. Gamer, *Medieval Handbooks of Penance* (New York, 1938). The older edition of H. J. Schmitz, *Die Bußbücher und die Bußdisziplin der Kirche. Die Bußbücher und das kanonische Bußverfahren* (2 vols: Düsseldorf, 1883–98) is still invaluable.

8 L. Wallach, *Alcuin and Charlemagne. Studies in Carolingian History and Literature* (Ithica, NY, 1959); J. Marenbon, *From the Circle of Alcuin to the School of Auxerre. Logic, Theology and Philosophy in the Early Middle Ages* (Cambridge, 1981).

9 *Liber de divinis officiis* 55; PL 101.1284B. See also *de virtutibus et vitiis* 12; PL 101.622A; *de confessione peccatorum*, PL 101.652B 'Dic tu prior iniustitias tuas, ut iustificeris.'

10 It occurs, in various forms, throughout the period: see Alcuin, *de virtutibus et vitiis* 13; PL 101.623A; Eadmer, *Liber de S. Anselmi similitudinibus* 175; PL 159.695A; Ivo of Chartres, *Decretum* XV, 26; PL 161.862D; Bruno of Asti, *Comm. in Ioannem* II, 11; PL 165.545A; Honorius of Autun, *Speculum ecclesiae*; PL 172.881C; *Summa Sententiarum* V, 7; PL 176.133A; Hugh of St Victor, *de sacramentis* II, xiv, 8; PL 176.567A; Werner of St Blasien, *Deflorationes* 2; PL 157.1184A; Zacharias Chrysopolitanus, *In unum ex quattuor* III, 99–100; PL 186.315D; Richard of St Victor, *de potestate ligandi* 19; PL 196.1171C; Ermengaudus, *contra Waldenses* 13; PL 204.1261A; Alan of Lille, *contra Hereticos* I, 55; PL 210.358B; Peter Lombard, *IV Sent.* dist. xx 1, 5.

11 In fact, Rabanus quotes Alcuin at some length, without acknowledge-

ment: compare Alcuin, PL 101.621D–22B with Rabanus, PL 101.102D–3A; and Alcuin, PL 101.622B–3A with Rabanus, PL 101.103A–4A.

12 *Exp. in epist. S. Pauli*; PL 117.391C.

13 *Exp. in omnes epist. Pauli*; PL 153.55B–C.

14 e.g., that of Hugh of St Cher, cited Landgraf, *Dogmengeschichte*, I/1 298 n.41, where the fifth element is *peccati remissio quoad penam temporalem*.

15 For an excellent discussion, see Landgraf, op. cit., III/1 279–345.

16 *de conceptu virginali* 29; ed. Schmitt, 2.173.1–3 'Quare si sic moriuntur: quia non sunt iniusti, non damnantur, sed et iustitia Christi qui se dedit pro illis, et iustitia fidei matris ecclesiae quae pro illis credit quasi iusti salvantur.'

17 *Tractatus de baptismo* II, 9; PL 182.1037D.

18 Cod. Paris Nat. lat. 15269 fol. 151v; cited Landgraf, op. cit., III/1 289 n.22.

19 *Exp. in epist. ad Rom.* II, 3; PL 178.838B.

20 Leipzig Universitätsbibliothek Cod. lat. 427, cited Landgraf, op. cit., I/2 50.

21 *Theologiae Regulae* 86; PL 210.667B 'Habentur ergo virtutes in habitu, quando homo per illas potentias quamdam habet habilitatem, et pronitatem ad utendum eis, si tempus exigerit.'

22 D. 410.

23 A. Landgraf, 'Die frühscholastischen Definition der Taufe', *Gregorianum* 27 (1946) 200–19; 353–83. See also Haring, op. cit., 131–8.

24 *de sacramentis* I, ix, 2; PL 176.317D 'Sacramentum est corporale vel materiale elementum foris sensibiliter propositum ex similitudine repraesentans, et ex institutione significans, et ex sanctificatione continens aliquam invisibilem et spiritualem gratiam.'

25 *IV Sent.* dist. i 1–4. See E. F. Rogers, *Peter Lombard and the Sacramental System* (New York, 1917); van den Eynde, op. cit., 222–8. On the significance of the number seven, see B. Geyer, 'Die Siebenzahl der Sakramente in ihrer historischen Entwicklung', *Theologie und Glaube* 10 (1918) 324–48.

26 *Speculum ecclesiae*; PL 172.1061C.

27 *Homilia* 13; PL 158.622B–C.

28 *Comm. in Lucam*; PL 165.427C–D.

29 Honorius of Autun, *Elucidarum* II, 20; PL 172.1050C–D.

30 e.g., Anselm of Canterbury, *de concordia praescientiae* III, 6.

31 Anciaux, *La théologie du sacrement du penance* 164–274. For the necessity of penance in justification, see Alger of Liège, *Liber de misericordia et iustitia*; PL 180.888D; Richard of St Victor, *Sermo* 53; PL 177.1051C; Bernard of Clairvaux, *Tractatus de interiori domo*; PL 184.509B; Peter of Blois, *Liber de confessione*; PL 207.1081D; Philip of Harvengt, *In cantica canticorum*; PL 203.552B; Peter Lombard, *IV Sent.* dist. xiv 1. In his *Decretum*, Gratian appears to leave open the question of the necessity of confession in justification, although he notes the strong case which can be made in its favour: e.g., PL 187.1532A.

32 Cap. 21; D. 437.
33 On this, see G. J. Spykman, *Attrition and Contrition at the Council of Trent* (Kampen, 1955) 17–89.
34 See McGrath, 'Rectitude', 211–12.
35 *Ethica* 18; PL 178.661A.
36 *Ethica* 24–26; PL 178.668C–74A.
37 *I Sent.* dist. xviii 6.
38 *Sententiarum libri quinque* III, 2; PL 201.1047C.
39 *Quaestio* 78; ed. Warichez, 205.
40 *contra Hereticos* I, 51; PL 210.356A–C.
41 *contra Hereticos* I, 51; PL 210.354A–B.
42 Thomas Aquinas, *Summa Theologiae* IIIa q.90 a.2.
43 *Purgatori* IX.94–102.
44 *Opus Oxoniense* IV dist. i q.6 nn.10–11.
45 *Opus Oxoniense* IV dist. xiv q.4 n.14.
46 e.g., N. Krautwig, *Der Grundlagen der Bußlehre des Joh. Duns Scotus* (Freiburg, 1938). For a reply, see J. Klein, 'Zur Bußlehre des seligen Joh. Duns Scotus', *FS* 27 (1940) 104–13; 191–6, especially 108.
47 *Opus Oxoniense* IV dist. xiv q.4 n.14.
48 *Opus Oxoniense* IV dist. xiv q.4 n.14.
49 This point has been well brought out by V. Heynck, 'A Controversy at the Council of Trent concerning the Doctrine of Duns Scotus', *FrS* 9 (1949) 181–258.
50 Feckes, *Rechtfertigungslehre des Gabriel Biel*, 66 n.189.
51 *In IV Sent.* dist. xiv q.2 a.2 concl.4.
52 See Oberman, *Harvest of Medieval Theology*, 146–60.
53 *In IV Sent.* dist. xiv q.2 a.2 concl.4. Biel uses the traditional appeal to the leper-cleansing ritual (Luke 17.14 – cf. Leviticus 14) to illustrate the need for confession; see *Sermones dominicales de tempore* (Hagenau, 1510) 76.
54 *In IV Sent.* dist. xiv q.2 a.1 nota. 2.
55 *In IV Sent.* dist. xiv q.2 a.1 nota. 2; cf. *Canonis Missae expositio* 26F.
56 *Canonis Missae expositio* 31C.
57 Valla, *Adnotationes*; in *Monumenta politica et philosophica rariora* (Torino, 1959–) 5.807 (on Matthew 3.2); 5.824 (on Mark 1.14); 5.872 (on II Corinthians 7.9–10). It is interesting to note that the opinion of Isidore of Seville, that there exists an etymological connection between *punire* and *poenitere* (*Etymologiae* VI, xix, 71; PL 82.258C), was generally rejected during the twelfth century. However, a close link between *poenitentia* and fear of punishment was presupposed by certain theologians, such as Anselm of Laon, possibly on the basis of this alleged etymological association: see Anciaux, op. cit., 155–7.
58 Biel's linking of justification and the eucharist should be noted here: Oberman, op. cit., 271–80.
59 Cf. Augustine, *de baptismo* IV, xvii, 24 'Salus extra ecclesiam non est.'
60 e.g., see the use made of this text by Astesanus of Asti: Schmitz, op. cit., 1.800.

Notes to §9

1 See Alszeghy, *Nova Creatura*; Auer, *Entwicklung der Gnadenlehre*; Beumer, *Gratia supponit naturam*; Doms, *Die Gnadenlehre des sel. Albertus Magnus*; Gillon, *La grâce incréée*; Hervé de l'Incarnation O.C.D., 'La grâce dans l'œuvre de S. Léon le grand', *RThAM* 22 (1955) 193–212; Heynck, *Die aktuelle Gnade bei Richard von Mediavilla*; R. Javelet, *Image et ressemblance au XIIᵉ siècle de S. Anselme à Alain de Lille* (2 vols: Paris, 1967); Landgraf, *Dogmengeschichte* I/1 51–140; 141–201; Molteni, *Roberto Holcot*; Philips, 'La théologie de la grâce chez les préscolastiques'; idem, 'La théologie de la grâce dans la "Summa Fratris Alexandri"'; Schupp, *Die Gnadenlehre des Petrus Lombardus*; Stoeckle, '*Gratia supponit naturam*'; Vanneste, 'Nature et grâce dans la théologie du XIIᵉ siècle'; idem, 'Nature et grâce dans la théologie de Saint Augustin'.
2 Cf. H. de Lubac, *Surnaturel: Etude historique* (Paris, 1946).
3 See Vanneste, op. cit.
4 *Comm. in Iohan.*, PL 122.325C; *de divisione naturae* III.3, PL 122.631D.
5 *de divisione naturae* V.23, PL 122.904B.
6 *de divisione naturae* V.30, PL 122.939A.
7 e.g., Hervaeus of Bourg Dieu, *Comm. in epist. divi Pauli*, PL 181.1446C–D; Hugh of St Victor, *de sacramentis* I, vi, 17; PL 176.237D–8A; Hugh of Amiens, *Dialogi* IV, 6; PL 192.1184A.
8 *Quaestio* 64; ed. Warichez, 179.
9 *Sententiarum libri quinque* II, 20; PL 211.1025A. Cf. also here the anonymous Cod. Paris Nat. lat. 686 fol. 40v, cited Landgraf, op. cit., I/1 180 n.76 'quod dicitur natura quantum ad creationem, dicitur gratia quantum ad recreationem vel reformationem'.
10 *Summa*, Cod. Erlangen 353 fol. 32, cited Landgraf, op. cit., 180 'Fides mea est supra rationem et ratione nullum naturale bonum est homine excellentius. Ergo fides supra omnia naturalia.' Praepositinus was associated with a group of scholars upon whom the strongest influence was Peter Lombard, including Peter of Poitiers, Peter of Capua and Stephen Langton: see J. W. Baldwin, *Masters, Princes and Merchants* (2 vols: Princeton, 1970).
11 *Summa Aurea* lib. II tr. xiv cap 2; fol. 69.
12 *Summa de bono*, Cod. Vat. lat. 7669 fol. 12, cited Landgraf, op. cit., I/1 198–99 n.84.
13 *Summa Theologiae* IaIIae q.110 a.1 'Sic igitur per hoc quod dicitur homo gratiam Dei habere, significatur quiddam supernaturale in homine a Deo proveniens.' For the relation between grace and supernature in High Scholasticism, see Auer, *Entwicklung der Gnadenlehre*, 2.219–50.
14 *II Sent.* dist. xxvii 7.
15 Bonaventure, *In II Sent.* dist. xxvii dub.1; ed. Quaracchi, 2.669 'Accipitur enim gratia uno modo largissime, et sic comprehendit dona naturalia et dona gratuita ... Alio modo accipitur gratia minus communiter, et sic comprehendit gratiam gratis datam et gratum facientem.'
16 Doms, op. cit., 167–8.

17 *In II Sent.* dist. xxviii a.2 q.3; ed. cit., 2.689.

18 *In II Sent.* dist. xxviii a.2 q.1; ed. cit., 2.682.

19 Thomas, *In II Sent.* dist. xxviii q.1 a.4; ed. Mandonnet, 2.728. See Stufler, 'Die entfernte Vorbereitung auf die Rechtfertigung nach dem hl. Thomas'; P. de Vooght, 'A propos de la grâce actuelle dans la théologie de Saint Thomas', *Divus Thomas* (Piacenza) 31 (1928) 386–416. Thomas elsewhere appears to regard it as a *charism* – i.e., a gift to help *others*: *Summa Theologiae* IaIIae q.111 a.1.

20 e.g., Bonaventure, *In II Sent.* dist. xxvii a.1 qq.1–5; Thomas, *In II Sent.* dist. xxvi q.1 aa.1–6. The systematic use of the term *habitus* in this context appears to be due to the influence of Philip the Chancellor: see P. Fransen, 'Dogmengeschichtlichen Entfaltung der Gnadenlehre', in *Mysterium Salutis* ed. J. Feiner and M. Löhrer (Einsiedeln, 1973) 4/2.631–722; 672–9. The first magisterial reference to grace as a *habitus* is encountered in the decisions of the Council of Vienne of 1312 (D 483: 'et virtutes ac informans gratia infunduntur quoad habitum'), although the term is used earlier (1201) in relation to the virtues (D 410 'et virtutes infundi . . . quoad habitum').

21 See Albertus Magnus, *In II Sent.* dist. xxvi aa.6–7.

22 *In II Sent.* dist. xxvi q.1 a.6; ed. cit., 2.682–6. For what follows, see the excellent study of Lonergan, *Grace and Reason*.

23 *de veritate* q.27 a.5; ed. Spiazzi, 1.524–8.

24 *Summa Theologiae* IaIIae q.111 a.2.

25 Ia q.62 a.2 ad 3um; *Quodl.* 1 a.7.

26 *In II Sent.* dist. xxvi q.1 a.6 ad 2um; ed. cit., 2.685.

27 Cited in *In III Sent.* dist. xxiii q.1 a.1; ed. cit., 3.698.

28 *de veritate* q.27 a.5 ad 3um; ed. Spiazzi, 1.526.

29 *de veritate* q.27 a.5 ad 3um; ed. cit., 1.526–7. Thomas emphasises that this arises 'non quidem propter defectum gratiae, sed propter infirmitatem naturae'. Cf. q.24 a.7.

30 For an introduction to the problem, see D. Janz, 'A Reinterpretation of Gabriel Biel on Nature and Grace', *Sixteenth Century Journal* 8 (1977) 104–8.

Notes to §10

1 Augustine, *de grat. et lib. arb.* vi, 15. See also *Epist.* 194. 19.

2 Bakhuizen van den Brink, 'Mereo(r) and meritum in some Latin Fathers'; Peñamaria de Llano, *La salvación por la fe*, 191–211. See also the earlier study of K. H. Wirth, *Der 'Verdienst'-Begriff in der christlichen Kirche* I. *Der 'Verdienst'-Begriff bei Tertullian* (Leipzig, 1892); II. *Der 'Verdienst'-Begriff bei Cyprian* (Leipzig, 1901).

3 Augustine, *Sermo* 111, iv, 4; PL 38.641A. For an excellent discussion of this aspect of Augustine's theology, see Hamm, *Promissio, pactum, ordinatio*, 11–18.

4 Augustine, *Epist.* 130, 14.

5 e.g. Hervaeus of Bourg-Dieu, *Comm. in epist. Pauli*; PL 181.1052B–D;

Anselm of Canterbury, *de casu diaboli* 17; *de veritate* 12; Peter Abailard, *Exp. in Epist. ad Rom.*, PL 178.903A, 919B, 920A–B; Bernard of Clairvaux, *de grat. et lib. arb.* vi, 16; PL 182.1010C; Honorius of Autun, *Elucidarum* II, 3; PL 172.1135D; Robert Pullen, *Sententiarum libri octo* V, 9; PL 186.837B–C; Peter of Poitiers, *Sententiarum libri quinque* III, 2; PL 211.1045A–D; Alan of Lille, *Theologicae Regulae* 86; PL 210.665C–6A; Hugh of St Victor, *de sacramentis* I, vi, 17; PL 176.247C–D; Richard of St Victor, *In apoc. Ioann.* VII, 8; PL 196.883C–D; Peter Lombard, *II Sent.* dist. xxvii, 7.

6 The remark of Magister Martinus is typical of many: 'Cum Deus coronat nostra merita, quid aliud coronat quam sua munera.' (Cod. Paris Nat. lat. 14556 fol. 314, cited Landgraf, *Dogmengeschichte* I/1 185. 'Master Martin' (i.e., Martin of Fougères) was one of the theologians, such as Alan of Lille and Simon of Tournai, who owed a particular debt to Gilbert de la Porrée: see J. W. Baldwin, *Masters, Princes and Merchants* (2 vols: Princeton, 1970) 1.44. Cf. the Augustinian *loci* referred to in note 1.

7 See Landgraf, 'Untersuchungen zu den Eigenlehren Gilberts de la Porrée'; idem, 'Mitteilungen zur Schule Gilberts de la Porrée'; idem, 'Neue Funde zur Porretanerschule'; idem, 'Der Porretanismus der Homilien des Radulphus Ardens'.

8 e.g. Alan of Lille, *Theologicae Regulae* 82; PL 210.663C 'Solus Christus proprie nobis meruit vitam aeternam': cf. Hamm, op. cit., 32–4. Cardinal Laborans' critique of the theological application of *civil* concepts of merit should be noted here (Hamm, op. cit., 47–66), along with Hamm's excellent discussion of the general teaching of the *Porretani*: op. cit., 26–40.

9 Cod. British Museum Harley 957 fol. 179v; cited Landgraf, op. cit., I/1 271.

10 e.g. Cod. British Museum Royal 9 E XII fol. 95v; Cod. Vat. lat. 4297 fol. 24; cited Landgraf, op. cit., I/1 272 nn.17, 18.

11 e.g. as used in Geoffrey of Poitiers' *Summa*: Brugge Bibliothèque de la Ville Cod. lat. 220 fol. 114v; cited Landgraf, op. cit., 276 n.35 'Et ita patet, quod non meretur de congruo. Et certum est, quod nec de condigno.'

12 Landgraf, op. cit., I/1 238–302.

13 Most notably by Harnack, *History of Dogma*, 6.275–317.

14 *In II Sent.* dist. xxvii q.2.

15 Auer, *Entwicklung der Gnadenlehre*, 2.85 'Es war das religiöse und vielleicht seelsorgliche Bedürfnis, aus der Güte Gottes die Möglichkeit einer wirksamen Vorbereitung auf die Gnade zu erweisen.'

16 Auer, op. cit., 2.86 'Daß diese Lehre nichts mit den von Harnack aus tiefem innerem Unverständnis für die Hochscholastik geborenen Vorwürfen eines Neosemipelagianismus zu tun hat, ist ganz selbstverständlich, wenn man das ganz auf Gottes Barmherzigkeit gebaute interpretative Verdienst (das mit Harnacks menschlich-bürgerlichem Verdienstbegriff nichts zu tun hat) und die ganz in Gottes Gnade gesetzte Betätigung des Menschen überhaupt und die eigens vorausgesetzten

aktuellen göttlichen Anregungen für diese Bereitung des Menschen für Gott ins Auge faßt.'

17 *De tropis loquendi*, Cod. Vat. lat. 1283 fol. 38r, cited Landgraf, op. cit., I/1 270 n.5. On this work, see G. Evans, 'Peter the Chanter's *De Tropis Loquendi*: The Problem of the Text', *New Scholasticism* 55 (1981) 95–103.

18 *Theologicae Regulae* 82; PL 210.663B–C.

19 Cod. Salzburg St Peter a. X 19 fol. 25; cited Landgraf, 'Untersuchungen zu den Eigenlehre Gilberts de la Porrée', 201–2 n.7.

20 *Summa*, Cod. Paris Nat. lat. 15747 fol. 42v; cited Landgraf, *Dogmengeschichte* I/1 276 n.37.

21 *De meritis*; in *Opera Omnia* 1.310 aF.

22 This point is emphasised by Hamm, who distinguishes two distinct senses in which the concept of self-limitation was understood: an *absolute* sense (Hamm, op. cit., 41–103) and a *restricted* sense (ibid., 104–249). This useful distinction permits much of the earlier confusion on this matter to be resolved.

23 *In II Sent.* dist. xxviii q.4 a.1 arg.1; ed. Bouvy, 82.10.

24 *In III Sent.* dist. xviii a.1 q.2 resp.

25 *Summa Aurea* lib. III tr.2 q.6 arg.1; fol. 136d 'Mereri ex condigno est facere de indebito debitum vel de debito magis debitum.'

26 *Summa* 35, 2; ed. Cortesi, 117.

27 cf. Thomas Aquinas, *In II Sent.* dist. xxvi q.1 a.3.

28 Roland of Cremona, *Summa* 347, 66; ed. Cortesi, 1050.

29 Auer's distinction between *Würdigkeit* (i.e., 'worth') and *Verdienst* (i.e., 'merit') is valuable here: Auer, op. cit., 2.150.

30 *In II Sent.* dist. xxvii a.2 q.2.

31 *Summa Aurea* lib. III tr.16 q.2 arg.7; fol. 221c.

32 *Summa Theologiae* IaIIae q.114 a.1. Cf. *In II Sent.* dist. xxvii q.1 a.3; *In III Sent.* dist. xviii a.2.

33 IaIIae q.114 a.1.

34 IaIIae q.114 a.1 ad 3um. This important section is frequently overlooked by Thomas' critics.

35 *Opus Oxoniense* III dist. xix q.1, 7. This view should be contrasted with that of Peter Aureoli, *In I Sent.* dist. xvii q.1 a.2 'ex quo patet quod ex divino amore debetur actibus nostris ut habeant meriti rationem *intrinsice et ex natura rei*'. (Our italics: note the assertion of *ex natura rei* causality).

36 e.g., Iserloh, *Gnade und Eucharistie* 64–7.

37 It may be noted that Ockham actually notes two solutions to the problem of the relation between grace and merit, without actually committing himself to either: see Leff, *William of Ockham*, 498–9.

38 Iserloh, op. cit., 111.

39 *In III Sent.* q.12.

40 *In IV Sent.* q.9.

41 *In IV Sent.* q.9 'Et dico quod respectu gratie nullus actus est meritorius de condigno nisi ille qui est respectu eterne beatitudinis.'

42 An excellent example of this is provided by Leff's early study of Bradwardine, in which he seriously misrepresents Ockham: G. Leff,

Bradwardine and the Pelagians: A Study of 'De Causa Dei' and its Opponents (Cambridge, 1957) 188–210. His later *William of Ockham* acknowledges and corrects these misunderstandings: see especially *William of Ockham*, 470 n.85.

43 *De Causa Dei* I, 39. Cf. Oberman, *Archbishop Thomas Bradwardine*, 155–9; Leff, *Bradwardine and the Pelagians*, 75–7. Leff is incorrect when he states that Bradwardine denied congruous merit *totally*.

44 *In II Sent.* dist. xxvi, xxvii, xxviii q.1 a.1.

45 e.g. Robert Holcot, *In IV Sent.* q.1 a.8 'Nam peccator meretur de congruo iustificationem per motum contritionis.'

46 For the relation between the two theologians, see Laun, 'Die Prädestination bei Wiclif und Bradwardine'.

47 *De sciencia Dei*, cited J. A. Robson, *Wyclif and the Oxford Schools* (Cambridge, 1961) 209 n.1. It is, of course, possible that Wycliffe means that congruous merit results from God's prevenient grace *prior to* justification.

48 *In II Sent.* dist. xxvii q.5; ed. Flajshans, 2.308–9.

49 *In II Sent.* dist. xxvii q.5; ed. cit., 307.

50 *In II Sent.* dist. xxvii q.5; ed. cit., 308.

51 Even Durandus of St Pourçain's discussion of the questions appears innocent of this assumption: *In II Sent.* dist. xxvii q.2; fol. 177r–8r.

52 *In II Sent.* dist. xxvii q.1 a.1 nota 3.

53 Steinbach, *Opera exegetica* 1.136.4–6.

54 On this, see A. E. McGrath, 'John Calvin and Late Medieval Thought: A Study in Late Medieval Influences upon Calvin's Theological Development', *ARG* 77 (1986) forthcoming.

55 The replies are incorporated into the 1559 edition of the *Institutio* at the following points: II.17.1–5; III.2.11–12. See the marginal notes in *Ioannis Calvini Opera Selecta* ed. P. Barth and G. Niesel (München, 1926–36) 3.509; 4.20–22.

56 e.g., A. Gordon, 'The Sozzini and their School', *Theological Review* 16 (1879) 293–322.

57 *Institutio* II.17.1; ed. cit., 3.509.

Notes to §11

1 For the best study of this concept, see Hamm, *Promissio, pactum, ordinatio*. See also §§7, 10.

2 *Sermo* 110, iv, 4; PL 38.641A.

3 Hamm, op. cit., 15 'Der promissio-Begriff hat somit im Zusammenhang der Vorstellung von Gott als Schuldner die spezifische Funktion, Gottes Selbstverpflichtung als Ausdruck seiner Souveränität zu interpretieren.'

4 *Summa Theologiae* Ia q.25 a.5 ad 1um.

5 For a useful discussion, see E. Gilson, *History of Christian Philosophy in the Middle Ages* (London, 1978) 406–8.

6 For the thesis in question, see P. Mandonnet, *Siger de Brabant de*

l'Averroisme latin au XIIIe siècle (2 vols: Louvain, 1908–11) 2.195. The example noted is the twentieth on the published list.

7 See M. A. Pernoud, 'Innovation in William of Ockham's References to the *Potentia Dei*', *Antonianum* 65 (1970) 65–97; Bannach, *Die Lehre von der doppelten Macht Gottes bei Wilhelm von Ockham.*

8 *Quodl.* VI q.6; *Opera Theologica* 9.604.13–16 'Credo in deum patrem omnipotentem. Quem sic intelligo quod quodlibet est divine potentiae attribuendum quod non includit manifestam contradictionem.'

9 *Quodl.* VI q.1; ed. cit., 9.585.14–586.24.

10 See A. Pelzer, 'Les 51 articles de Guillaume d'Occam censurés en Avignon en 1326', *Revue d'histoire ecclesiastique* 18 (1922) 240–70. A second, briefer version of the list of articles is now known: J. Koch, 'Neue Aktenstücke zu dem gegen Wilhelm von Ockham in Avignon geführten Prozess', *RThAM* 8 (1936) 168–97. The list of 56 articles drawn up by John Lutterell, along with his appended comments, has been edited by F. Hoffmann, *Die Schriften des Oxforder Kanzlers Johannes Lutterell* (Leipzig, 1959) 3–102.

11 Pelzer, op. cit., 250–1.

12 ibid., 251 'Dicimus quod iste longus processus in predicto articulo contentus est erroneus et sapit heresim Pelagianam vel peius.'

13 ibid., 253.

14 ibid., 253.

15 ibid., 252 'Nec potest excusari per illam addicionem, quam ponit: de potentia Dei absoluta, quia argumentum suum eque procedit absque illa condicione sicut cum illa. Propositio autem, quam assumit, est heretica et conclusio heretica.'

16 Gregory of Rimini, *In I Sent.* dist. xvii q.1 a.2.

17 See Courtenay, 'Covenant and Causality in Pierre d'Ailly', 107–9.

18 Feckes, *Rechtfertigungslehre des Gabriel Biel*, 12 'Darum retten sich die Nominalisten gern auf das Gebiet der potentia absoluta hinüber, wenn die Konsequenzen ihrer Prinzipien mit der Kirchenlehre in Konflikt zu geraten drohen.' On the basis of this presupposition, Feckes argues that Biel developed two essentially independent doctrines of justification, one according to God's absolute power (which represents Biel's own teaching), and one according to God's ordained power (which represents the teaching of the church): ibid., 22.

19 On the question of Luther's relationship to the theology of the *via moderna*, see McGrath, *Luther's Theology of the Cross*, 72–147.

20 Vignaux, *Justification et prédestination.*

21 ibid., 127–40. Particular attention should be paid to the comments made concerning Seeberg and Feckes: 132 n.1.

22 Vignaux, *Luther Commentateur des Sentences.*

23 ibid., 78 'La *potentia absoluta* ne représente pas la raison et le droit, ni la *potentia ordinata*, une pure donnée de fait: toute interprétation de ce genre trahirait la pensée de Gabriel Biel ... (L'ordre établi) est un ordre fait de libéralité à la fois et de la justice.'

24 e.g., R. Weijenborg, 'La charité dans la première théologie de Luther', *Revue d'histoire ecclesiastique*, 45 (1950) 615–69; 617.
25 Iserloh, *Gnade und Eucharistie*, 137–46. It may be noted that Oberman's early emphasis upon the priority of the *potentia absoluta* (e.g., see H. A. Oberman, 'Some Notes on the Theology of Nominalism with Attention to its Relation to the Renaissance', *HThR* 53 (1960) 47–76 is later replaced by a much more balanced approach in *The Harvest of Medieval Theology*, 30–47.
26 Erasmus, *Opera Omnia*, 6.927B.
27 Erasmus, *Opera Omnia*, 6.927B–C.
28 See W. J. Courtenay, 'John of Mirecourt and Gregory of Rimini on whether God can undo the past', *RThAM* 39 (1972) 244–56; 40 (1973) 147–74; A. E. McGrath, '*Homo assumptus*? A Study in the Christology of the *Via Moderna*, with Particular Reference to William of Ockham', *EThL* 61 (1985) 283–97.
29 On this, see Oberman, 'Wir sind pettler'; Courtenay, 'The King and the Leaden Coin'; McGrath, 'The Anti-Pelagian Structure of "Nominalist" Doctrines of Justification'.
30 *Summa Theologiae* IIIa q.62 a.1. See W. Lampen, *De causalitate sacramentorum iuxta scholam Franciscanum* (Bonn, 1931).
31 WA 3.289.1–5. Cf. WA 4.261.32–39; 4.262.2–7. See McGrath, *Luther's Theology of the Cross*, 72–92.

Notes to §12

1 We follow Nygren, *Das Prädestinationsproblem in der Theologie Augustins*, 294, in distinguishing between the *doctrine* and the *problem* of predestination. While the former is stated in the Pauline corpus, the latter is first recognised in the writings of Augustine.
2 e.g., Schelkle, *Paulus Lehrer der Väter*, 336–53; 436–40.
3 See §3 for a consideration of the issues involved.
4 For a careful analysis, see Nygren, op. cit., 41–8.
5 Ambrose, *Epist.* 37, 1.
6 *ad Simplic.* I, ii, 6; CChr 44.30.165–31.198.
7 *de grat. et lib. arb.* xxi, 42–3.
8 *de grat. et lib. arb.* xx, 41; xxi, 43; xxiii, 45.
9 *de grat. et lib. arb.* xxiii, 45 'et deus induravit per iustum iudicium, et ipse Pharao per liberum arbitrium'.
10 *de grat. et lib. arb.* xx, 41 'sicut ipse iudicat, occultissimo quidem iudicio, sed sine ullo dubitatione iustissimo'. Augustine's tendency to refer to the reprobate as *non praedestinati* appears to result from his reluctance to make God the author of sin. This is clearly stated in *de praed. sanct.* x, 19 'Praedestinatione quippe Deus ea praescivit quae fuerat ipse facturus . . . Praescire autem potens est etiam quae ipse non facit, sicut quaecumque peccata; quia etsi sunt quaedam quae ita peccata sunt ut poena sint etiam peccatorum, unde dictum est "Tradidit illos Deus in reprobam mentem

ut faciant quae non conveniunt", non ibi peccatum est, sed iudicium. Quocirca praedestinatio Dei quae in bono est, gratiae est, ut dixi, praeparatio; gratia vero est ipsius praedestinationis effectus.' This tendency to use the term *praedestinatio* solely *in bono* represents, in our opinion, the final position of Augustine on this matter. However, it is possible to point to earlier phases in his thinking on the question. Initially, Augustine appears to have regarded predestination simply as an aspect of the doctrine of justification, and refers to the operation of grace upon man in a purely positive sense. There appears, however, to have been a middle period, corresponding broadly to the greater part of the Pelagian controversy, in which Augustine occasionally speaks of *praedestinatio ad aeternam mortem* – e.g., *de an. et orig.* IV.xi.16 'qui est et illis quos praedestinavit ad aeternam mortem iustissimus supplicii retributor'; *Ench.* 100, 26 '. . . bene utens et malis, tamquam summe bonus, ad eorum damnationem quos iuste praedestinavit ad poenam, et ad eorum salutem quos benigne praedestinavit ad gratiam'. Augustine appears to have later realised the difficulties attending such a concept, not least in the realm of theodicy, and abandoned it. Although it is clearly possible to argue that the concept logically follows from Augustine's doctrine of grace, the fact remains that Augustine chose to exercise a terminological reserve at this point in order to avoid compromising other aspects of his theology.

11 Augustine makes it clear that wisdom is to be understood as the antithesis of fate: *Epist.* 194, ii, 5. It is interesting to note Ælfric's rejection of the fatalist associations of the Old English term *wyrd* in precisely the same context: *The Homilies of the Anglo-Saxon Church* ed. B. Thorpe (2 vols: London, 1864–6) 1.114.13; cf. N. O. Halvorsen, *Doctrinal Terms in Ælfric's Homilies* (University of Iowa Studies: Humanistic Studies 5/1, 1932) 11; 52–3.

12 e.g., *Epist.* 194, ii, 3–4. Cf. A. Sage, 'Praeparatur voluntas a Deo', *REAug* 10 (1964) 1–20.

13 See McGrath, 'Divine Justice and Divine Equity in the Controversy between Augustine and Julian of Eclanum'.

14 D. 160a. Cf. E. Amman, art. 'Lucidus', *DThC* 9.1020–40. Both the date and the status of this council are open to question: it may date from 475, and it appears to represent the private judgement of a group of individuals, rather than that of the church.

15 D. 200. See also the confirmation of the pronouncements of Orange II on this matter by Boniface II in 531: D. 200a–b.

16 The best study is that of K. Vielhaber, *Gottschalk der Sachse* (Bonn, 1956), especially 68–82. For useful studies of the intellectual spirit of the period, see L. M. de Rijk, 'On the Curriculum of the Arts of the Trivium at St. Gall from c.850–c.1000', *Vivarium* 1 (1963) 35–86; J. J. Contreni, *The Cathedral School of Laon from 850–930* (Munich, 1978).

17 G. Morin, 'Gottschalk retrouvé', *Revue Bénédictine* 43 (1931) 302–12. The contents of MS Berne 83 were published by Lambot, *Œuvres théologiques et grammaticales de Godescalc d'Orbais*.

18 *de praedestinatione* 13; ed. Lambot, 234.

19 *Responsa de diversis* 6; ed. cit., 148.
20 *de praedestinatione* 15; ed. cit., 242.
21 *Confessio brevior*; ed. cit., 52.
22 *Responsa de diversis* 7; ed. cit., 157. Cf. *Confessio prolixior*; ed. cit., 56.
23 Isidore of Seville, *Sent.* II, vi, 1; PL 65.656A.
24 e.g., Godescalc, *Confessio brevior*; ed. cit., 54 'Unde dicit et sanctus Isidorus: Gemina est praedestinatio sive electorum ad requiem, sive reproborum ad mortem'; *Responsa de diversis* 7; ed. cit., 154–5.
25 *Opuscula theologica* 20; ed. cit., 279–82.
26 *de praedestinatione* 14; ed. cit., 238. The same conclusion was expressed more forcefully by Servatus Lupus, *Quaest.*, PL 119.646A–B.
27 See G. R. Evans, 'The Grammar of Predestination in the Ninth Century', *Journal of Theological Studies* 33 (1982) 134–45; idem, *The Language and Logic of the Bible: The Earlier Middle Ages* (Cambridge, 1984), 111–13.
28 *de praedestinatione* 26; PL 125.270B.
29 *de praedestinatione* 23; PL 125.209C.
30 The work is also known as *Hypomnesticon* or *Commonitorium contra Pelagianos et Coelestianos*, probably written by Marius Mercator. For the impact of pseudo-Augustinian literature in the Middle Ages, see M. de Kroon, 'Pseudo-Augustin im Mittelalter', *Augustiniana* 22 (1972) 511–30.
31 *Hypognosticon* VI, ii, 2; PL 45.1657D. Hincmar cites this work in *Epist.* 37b; *MGH.Ep* 8.17–18.
32 *Liber de tribus epistolis* 34; PL 121.1043C.
33 *Liber de tribus epistolis* 35; PL 121.1044–47. The *Liber de tribus epistolis* is of considerable importance in connection with our knowledge of the Synod of Quiercy.
34 D. 316–19.
35 Hincmar, *Epist.* 37b; *MGH.Ep* 8.19.
36 D. 317.
37 D. 316 'Deus omnipotens hominem sine peccato rectum cum libero arbitrio condidit'.
38 Florus of Lyons, *de tenenda scriptura veritate* 3; PL 121.1087C–D.
39 *de tenenda scriptura veritate* 4; PL 121.1091B–92B.
40 D. 318. This point was never seriously questioned.
41 D. 319.
42 Hincmar, *Recl.*; ed. Gundlach, 290–1.
43 Hincmar, *de praedestinatione* 32; PL 125.309B.
44 *de praedestinatione* 34; PL 125.350A.
45 Florus of Lyons, *Liber de tribus epistolis* 16; PL 121.1015C.
46 *Liber de tribus epistolis*; PL 121.1129A.
47 *Liber de tribus epistolis* 1–6; PL 121.989–98.
48 Ratramnus, *de praedestinatione* 2; PL 121.54D; 69B–C.
49 Servatus, *Epist. Add.* 3, 4; *MGH.Ep* 6.110–12.
50 D. 320–5.
51 Can. 3; D. 322.
52 Can. 3; D. 322.

53 The report may be found in the *Annals of Saint-Berlin* 859, as cited in *MGH.SRG* 31.53.

54 Hincmar, *Epist.* 187; *MGH.Ep* 8.196.

55 M. Grabmann, *Die Geschichte der katholischen Theologie* (Darmstad 1961) 28.

56 *I Sent.* dist. xl, xli.

57 *de veritate* q.6 a.1; ed. Spiazzi, 1.114 'Praeexigitur etiam et electio, per quam ille qui in finem infallibiliter dirigitur ab aliis separatur qui non hoc modo in finem diriguntur. Haec autem separatio non est propter diversitatem aliquam inventam in his qui separantur quae possit ad amorem incitare: quia antequam nati essent aut aliquid boni aut mali fecissent, dictum est: Iacob dilexi, Ezau odio habui.' However, predestination includes *propositum, praeparatio* and *praescientia exitus* (*In I Sent.* dist. xl q.1 a.2; ed. Mandonnet, 1.945), whereas reprobation is merely *praescientia culpae et praeparatio poenae* (*In I Sent.* dist. xl q.4 a.1; ed. cit., 1.954). Cf. *de veritate* q.6 a.3; *Summa Theologiae* Ia q.23 aa.3, 5.

58 Pannenberg, *Die Prädestinationslehre des Duns Skotus*, 30–3, 77–9. For a reliable summary of the two main medieval traditions on the *ratio praedestinationis*, see Johannes Eck, *Chrysopassus Praedestinationis* I, 2.

59 *Opus Oxoniense* I dist. xl q. unica n.2. For an excellent analysis of Scotus' doctrine of predestination, see Pannenberg, op. cit., 54–68; 90–119; 125–39.

60 Lennerz, 'De historia applicationis principii "omnis ordinate volens prius vult finem quam ea quae sunt ad finem"'. As Lennerz notes (op. cit., 245), there is no hint in the text (*Opus Oxoniense* I dist. xli q. unica n.11) to suggest that Scotus accepted this on the basis of an earlier authority.

61 Pannenberg, op. cit., 90–3.

62 Pannenberg, op. cit., 95–100. The discussion of the question in the later Paris *Reportata* is significantly different: ibid., 103–11.

63 *Opus Oxoniense* I dist. xli q. unica n.12.

64 *Opux Oxoniense* III dist. xix q. unica n.6.

65 *Tractatus de praedestinatione* q.1 N; ed. Boehner, 13 'Quarta suppositio: Quod omnes propositiones in ista materia, quantumcumque sint vocaliter de praesenti vel de praeterito, sunt tamen aequivalenter de futuro, quia earum veritas dependet ex veritate propositionum formaliter de futuro.' Cf. Boehner's analysis of this text: ed. cit., 49.

66 *Tractatus de praedestinatione* q.1 M; ed. cit., 12–13.

67 op. cit., 50–1 for the argument, which is rather obscure. A better statement of the same principle may be found elsewhere: *In I Sent.* dist. xli q.1 F.

68 *Tractatus* q.4 B; ed. cit., 36.

69 Oberman, *Harvest of Medieval Theology*, 211. In taking this stand, Oberman finds himself in conflict with Seeberg and Vignaux, both of whom correctly find a concept of predestination in the strict sense in Ockham's thought: op. cit., 206–11.

70 McGrath, 'The Anti-Pelagian Structure of "Nominalist" Doctrines of Justification', 108–10.

71 On Biel's relation to Ockham, see M. L. Picascia, *Un Occamista quattrocentesco Gabriel Biel* (Firenze, 1971) 37–41. Cf. *In I Sent.* dist. xli q. unica a.2 conc.3.

72 As pointed out by F. Clark, 'A New Appraisal of Late Medieval Nominalism, *Gregorianum* 46 (1965) 733–65. Oberman appears to be dependent upon Feckes at this point: cf. Feckes, *Die Rechtfertigungslehre des Gabriel Biel*, 88 n. 268.

73 *In II Sent.* dist. xxvii q. unica a.3 dub. 4; ed. Werbeck/Hoffmann, 2.523.11–16.

74 Oberman, op. cit., 196.

75 *In II Sent.* dist. xxvii q. unica a.1 nota. 1.

76 See Oberman, *Werden und Wertung*, 81–90; M. Schulze, '"Via Gregorii" in Forschung und Quellen', in *Gregor von Rimini. Werk und Wirkung bis zur Reformation* ed. H. A. Oberman (Berlin, 1981) 1–126; 25–64.

77 As W. von Loewenich points out, doctrines such as double predestination or irresistible grace are 'tätsachlich bedenkliche Elemente in Augustins Gnadenlehre': *Von Augustin zu Luther* (Witten, 1959) 111. Oberman labours under the mistaken apprehension that Augustine's most characteristic teaching on predestination is *praedestinatio gemina*, which goes some considerable way towards explaining his simplistic designation of Bradwardine's theology as 'Augustinian': Oberman, *Archbishop Thomas Bradwardine*, 145 n.1.

78 *The Nonne Preestes Tale* 421–2; Group B 4431–2.

79 For details of this important group based on Merton, see W. J. Courtenay, *Adam Wodeham: An Introduction to his Life and Writings* (Leiden, 1978).

80 *De causa Dei* I, 35.

81 *De causa Dei* I, 35.

82 *De causa Dei* II, 31.

83 For an excellent discussion, see Oberman, op. cit., 65–70.

84 e.g., Harnack, *History of Dogma* 6.169–70. Harnack is totally dependent upon the earlier study of G. Lechler, *Johann von Wiclif und die Vorgeschichte der Reformation* (Leipzig, 1873).

85 See Laun, 'Die Prädestination bei Wiclif und Bradwardin'.

86 *de domino divino* I, 14, apparently making reference to *de causa Dei* III, 1 '... omnia quae eveniunt de necessitate eveniunt'. This thesis, however, is condemned by Bradwardine as heretical: *de causa Dei* III, 12. For the important distinction between *antecedent* and *absolute* necessity, as used by Bradwardine, see Oberman, op. cit., 70–5. Wycliffe's thesis, that everything happens by absolute necessity, was condemned by the Council of Constance on 4 May 1415, and again in papal bulls of 22 February 1418: D. 607.

87 S. H. Thomson, 'The Philosophical Basis of Wyclif's Theology', *Journal of Religion* 11 (1931) 86–116; 113.

88 See M. Schüler, *Prädestination, Sünde und Freiheit bei Gregor von Rimini* (Stuttgart, 1934) 39–69; Vignaux, *Justification et prédestination*, 141–75.

89 *In I Sent.* dist. xl, xli q.1 a.2.

90 *In I Sent*. dist. xl, xli q.1 a.2; ed. Trapp, 3.326.17–26.
91 See Zumkeller, 'Hugolin von Orvieto'.
92 See Zumkeller, *Dionysius de Montina*, 77–8.
93 See Zumkeller, 'Johannes Hiltalingen von Basel', 81–98.
94 See Zumkeller, 'Johannes Klenkok', 259–66.
95 See Zumkeller, 'Angelus Dobelinus', 77–91.
96 Eck, *Chrysopassus praedestinationis* I, 66. On the circumstances surrounding the composition of this work, see J. Greving, *Johann Eck als junger Gelehrter. Eine literatur- und dogmengeschichtlich Untersuchung über seinen Chrysopassus praedestinationis aus dem Jahr 1514* (Münster, 1906) 16–19.
97 Eck, *Chrysopassus praedestinationis* IV, 13 'nam multis flectibus et undosis ventis agita carina nostra, doctoribus hincinde in diversa euntibus, tandem ad divi Eustachii Bonaventureae portum applicuimus'.
98 Cf. Eck, *Chrysopassus praedestinationis* III, 51. This point is made especially clear in the later *annotatiunculae* on the first book of the Sentences; *In I Sent*. dist. xli; ed. Moore, 120.27–8 'Deus nunquam deest homini facienti quod in se est. Et haec est ratio praedestinationis.' It is, however, clear that Eck is aware of a different interpretation of the axiom *facienti quod in se est* which excludes it being the *ratio praedestinationis*: *In I Sent*. dist. xli; ed. cit., 120.19–24 '... Hoc modo facere quod in se est est malum et damnabile.'
99 Johannes Altenstaig, *Vocabularius theologiae* (Hagenau, 1517), art. 'Praedestinatio'.
100 The sermons were preached during Advent 1516, and were published in Latin and in German translation the following year. See Steinmetz, *Misericordia Dei*, 79–97.
101 As first demonstrated by P. Minges, *Die Gnadenlehre des Johannes Duns Scotus auf ihren angeblichen Pelagianismus und Semipelagianismus geprüft* (Münster, 1906). See further W. Dettloff, 'Die antipelagianische Grundstruktur der scotischen Rechtfertigungslehre.'
102 e.g. Oberman, *Harvest of Medieval Theology*, 196.

Notes to §13

1 *I Sent*. dist xvii 6.
2 Thomas Aquinas, *In I Sent*. dist. xvii q.1 a.1.
3 See Iserloh, *Gnade und Eucharistie*, 81 'Besonders Thomas hatte noch betont, daß das Prinzip des übernatürlichen Handelns dem Menschen innerlich zu eigen sein muß, damit die Handlung freiwillig und verdienstlich ist. Deshalb könne sie nicht vom Heiligen Geist unmittelbar hervorgebracht sein, sondern müße einer dem Menschen inhärierenden Form entspringen.' Cf. T. Bonhoeffer, *Die Gotteslehre des Thomas von Aquin* (Tübingen, 1961) 87–97.
4 *In II Sent*. dist. xvii q.1 a.1.
5 *In II Sent*. dist. xvii q.1 a.1.

6 *In II Sent.* dist. xvii q.1 a.1 'Quantum ad primum ponam duas conclusiones. Prima est, quod gratia gratificans nos Deo, vel per quam nos grati sumus Deo, est aliquid creatum in anima. Secunda est, quod naturali cognitione nullus potest certitudinaliter in se cognoscere huiusmodi, quamviscunque realiter creatus sit in anima sua.'

7 We here follow Dettloff, *Die Lehre von der acceptatio divina bei Johannes Duns Skotus.*

8 Dettloff, op. cit., 3 nn.6–21 for examples.

9 *Reportata Parisiensis* I dist. xvii q.2 n.4.

10 *Reportata Parisiensis* I dist. xvii q.1 n.3.

11 *Reportata Parisiensis* I dist. xvii q.1 n.3.

12 *Reportata Parisiensis* I dist. xvii q.1 n.4.

13 For the full text, see Dettloff, op. cit., 56 n.204. A fuller version of the previous argument may also be found at n.202.

14 *Reportata Parisiensis* I dist. xvii q.1 n.4.

15 *Reportata Parisiensis* I dist. xvii q.1 n.7.

16 *Reportata Parisiensis* I dist. xvii q.2 n.2 'sed per solam caritatem distinguitur acceptus Deo a non accepto'.

17 *Reportata Parisiensis* I dist. xvii q.2 n.5.

18 *Reportata Parisiensis* I dist. xvii q.2 n.6.

19 Dettloff, op. cit., 159.

20 ibid., 160.

21 See Vignaux, *Justification et prédestination*, 43–95.

22 R. Schmücker, *Propositio per se nota. Gottesbeweise und ihr Verhältnis nach Petrus Aureoli* (Werl, 1941).

23 A. Maier, 'Literarhistorische Notizen über Petrus Aureoli, Durandus und den "Cancellarius"', *Gregorianum* 29 (1948) 213–51.

24 R. Dreiling, *Der Konzeptualismus in der Universalienlehre des Franziskanerbischofs Petrus Aureoli* (Münster, 1913).

25 For an excellent analysis, see Dettloff, *Die Entwicklung der Akzeptations- und Vedienstlehre*, 29–36.

26 *In I Sent.* dist. xvii p.1 a.2; 408 bD 'Quod est aliqua forma creata a Deo quae ex natura rei et de necessitate cadit sub Dei complacentia et cuius existentiam in anima ipsa gratificetur et sit Deo accepta et dilecta aut cara.'

27 *In I Sent.* dist. xvii p.1 a.2; 410 aD 'Quod huiusmodi forma qua ex natura rei redditur anima Deo grata non profluit ex divina acceptatione in anima.'

28 *In I Sent.* dist. xvii p.1 a.2; 410 bG 'Quod forma qua anima sit accepta est quaedam habitualis dilectio, quae ab ipso infunditur nec ex puris naturalibus generatur.'

29 *In I Sent.* dist. xl a.1.

30 *In I Sent.* dist. xvii q.1; *Opera Theologica* 3.445.13. For what follows, see 445.13–466.21.

31 *In I Sent.* dist. xvii q.1. On this, see Vignaux, op. cit., 99–118.

32 *In I Sent.* dist. xvii q.2; *Opera Theologica* 3.471.15–472.5.

33 On this, see Vignaux, *Luther Commentateur des Sentences*, 45–86; Oberman, *Harvest of Medieval Theology*, 160–84.

34 *In I Sent.* dist. xvii q.3 a.3 dub.2; ed. Werbeck/Hoffmann, 1.433.5.
35 *In II Sent.* dist. xxvii q. unica a.1 nota 1.
36 Zumkeller, 'Johannes von Retz', Textbeilage 48. Cf. Thomas of Strasbourg, *In II Sent.* dist. xxvi, xxvii q.1 a.1.
37 *In I Sent.* dist. xvii q.1 a.2. On this, see Vignaux, *Justification et prédestination*, 142–53.
38 *In I Sent.* dist. xvii q.1 a.2 'alioquin ... caritas creata natura sua aliquam dignitatem in respectu ad vitam aeternam tribueret animae quam nullo modo posset sibi per seipsum tribuere Spiritus sanctus'.
39 Zumkeller refers to him as 'der Vertreter eines ausgesprochenen Augustinianismus': Zumkeller, 'Hugolin von Orvieto', 110.
40 Zumkeller, op. cit., 120–1.
41 ibid., 144.
42 Zumkeller, *Dionysius de Montina*, 76–81.
43 Zumkeller, 'Johannes Klenkok', 256.
44 ibid., 255 n.8.
45 Zumkeller, 'Johannes Hiltalingen', 136 n.246.
46 Zumkeller, 'Angelus Dobelinus', 118–19.
47 Steinmetz, *Misericordia Dei*, 106.
48 ibid., 106–7.
49 See Vignaux, *Luther Commentateur des Sentences*; R. Schwarz, *Fides, Spes und Caritas beim jungen Luther* (Berlin, 1962); 13–40 McGrath, *Luther's Theology of the Cross*, 81–5.
50 WA 9.44.1–4; cf. WA 9.43.2–8.

Notes to introduction

1 M. D. Chenu, *La théologie au XIIe siècle* (Paris, 1957); J. de Ghellinck, *Le mouvement théologique de XIIe siècle* (Bruxelles, 1969²). For more general studies, see C. Haskins, *The Renaissance of the Twelfth Century* (Cambridge, Mass., 1927); G. Paré, A. Brunet and P. Tremblay, *La renaissance du XIIe siècle* (Paris, 1933); W. A. Nitze, 'The so-called Twelfth Century Renaissance', *Speculum* 23 (1948) 464–71; E. M. Sandford, 'The Twelfth Century: Renaissance or Proto-Renaissance?', *Speculum* 26 (1951) 635–42.
2 MS 45, Pembroke College, Cambridge; cited B. Smalley, *The Study of the Bible in the Middle Ages* (Notre Dame, Ind., 1970²) 116 n.1.
3 On this, see A. Fliche, *La querelle des investitures* (Paris, 1946).
4 See J. J. Contreni, *The Cathedral School of Laon from c.850–c.1000* (Munich, 1978); J. Marenbon, *From the Circle of Alcuin to the School of Auxerre* (Cambridge, 1981).
5 'Ut omnes episcopi artes litterarum in suis ecclesiis docere faciant': cited P. Delhaye, 'L'organisation des écoles au XIIe siècle', *Traditio* 5 (1947) 240.
6 See A. Clerval, *Les écoles de Chartres au Moyen-Age* (Chartres, 1895); F. Bliemetzrieder, 'Robert von Melun und die Schule Anselms von Laon', *ZKG* 53 (1934) 117–70; R. Klibansky, 'The School of Chartres',

in *Twelfth Century Europe and the Foundations of Modern Society* ed.
M. Clagett *et al.* (Wisconsin, 1961) 3–14; J. W. Baldwin, *Masters, Princes
and Merchants. The Social Views of Peter the Chanter and his Circle* (2 vols:
Princeton, 1970).

7 *Chartularium Universitatis Parisiensis* ed. H. Denifle and E. Chatelain (4
vols: Paris, 1889–97) 1.65 n.5.

8 *Chartularium Universitatis Parisiensis* 1.85 n.27. The number of chairs
over the period were as follows: 1200–1218 – 8; 1218–19 – 10; 1219–21 –
11; 1221 onwards – 12. For details, see P. Glorieux, *Répertoire des Maîtres
en théologie de Paris au XIIIe siècle* (2 vols: Paris, 1933).

9 H. Rashdall, *The Universities of Europe in the Middle Ages*, ed. F. M.
Powicke and A. B. Emden (3 vols: London, 1935) 1.370–6; P. R.
McKeon, 'The Status of the University of Paris as *Parens Scientiarum*: An
Episode in the Development of its Autonomy', *Speculum* 39 (1964)
651–75; M.-M. Dufeil, *Guillaume de Saint-Amour et la polémique universi-
taire parisienne 1250–1259* (Paris, 1972) 146–282.

10 For the text, see R. Paqué, *Das Pariser Nominalistenstatut. Zur Entstehung
des Realitätsbegriffs der neuzeitlichen Naturwissenschaft* (Berlin, 1970)
8–12.

11 C. E. du Boulay, *Historia Universitatis Parisiensis* (6 vols: Paris, 1665–75)
4.273–4. A minimum age of thirty-five was specified elsewhere: *Chartularium Universitatis Parisiensis* 1.79.

12 d'Ailly was granted his *magisterium* in theology at Paris on 11 April 1381,
being then four years under the minimum age laid down by statute:
Chartularium Universitatis Parisienses 3.259 n.33.

13 For a list of the doctors of this school, see A. Zumkeller, 'Die Augustinerschule des Mittelalters: Vertreter und philosophisch-theologische Lehre',
Analecta Augustiniana 27 (1964) 167–262; 174–6. The close association of
the school with Paris will be evident.

14 See McGrath, *Luther's Theology of the Cross*, 27–40; 53–71.

15 Of course, Calvin's period of study at Paris raises the fascinating question of the influence of these schools upon his thought: see A. E.
McGrath, 'John Calvin and Late Medieval Thought. A Study in Late
Medieval Influences upon Calvin's Theological Thought', *ARG* 77 (1986)
forthcoming.

Notes to §14

1 *Fontes vitae Sancti Thomae Aquinatis* ed. M.-H. Laurent (Toulouse, 1934)
Fasc. 6 *Documenta* c.52; 662.

2 *Acta capitulorum generalium Ordinis Praedicatorum* ed. B. M. Riecherd
(Romae, 1898) 2.64.

3 See M. Grabmann, 'Johannes Capreolus O.P. der "Princeps Thomi-
starum" und seine Stellung in der Geschichte der Thomistenschule', in
Mittelalterliches Geistesleben ed. L. Ott (München, 1955) 3.370–410.

4 E. Gilson, *History of Christian Philosophy in the Middle Ages* (London,
1978) 260. The study of F. J. Roensch, *Early Thomistic School* (Dubuque,

Iowa, 1964) contains an invaluable discussion of the early English and French followers of Thomas' noetic.

5 This is the position of Peter Lombard, Alexander of Hales, Albertus Magnus and Bonaventure: see R. Garrigou-Lagrange, *La synthèse Thomiste* (Paris, 1947) 305–11.

6 *In II Sent.* dist. xx q.1 a.3 appears to avoid any firm statement on the matter. A more definite statement may be found later: *In II Sent.* dist. xxix q.1 a.2.

7 Dating from 1268(?).

8 *de malo* q.4 a.2 ad 17um.

9 *Summa Theologiae* Ia q.95 a.1.

10 Ia q.100 a.1 ad 2um.

11 IaIIae q.83 a.2 ad 2um.

12 Ia q.100 a.1 ad 2um.

13 IaIIae q.112 a.5. This article is of considerable importance. Thomas elsewhere teaches that the grace of final perseverance is a further gift of God to the elect, which cannot be merited: IaIIae q.114 a.9.

14 IIIa q.27 a.2 ad 3um. This question is discussed further in §16.

Notes to §15

1 J. Auer, 'Textkritische Studien zur Gnadenlehre des Alexander von Hales', *Scholastik* 15 (1940) 63–75.

2 Published as *Glossa in Quatuor Libros Sententiarum Petri Lombardi*. For an excellent introduction, see *Glossa* 4.18*–44*. Alexander is of particular significance in that it was through him that Peter Lombard's *Sentences* was divided into its present divisions, and became the standard text in the schools: see I. Brady, 'The Distinctions of the Lombard's Book of Sentences and Alexander of Hales', *FrS* 25 (1965) 90–116.

3 *In II Sent.* dist. xxiv n.1; ed. cit., 2.206.9–11.

4 *In II Sent.* dist. xxiv n.1; ed. cit., 2.207.14–19.

5 *In II Sent.* dist. xxix q.1; ed. Bouvy, 90.57–88.

6 *In II Sent.* dist. xxxiv pars 2 a.3 q.2 ad 3um. For a useful summary of the differences between Bonaventure and Thomas, see Bruch, 'Die Urgerechtigkeit als Rechtheit des Willens nach der Lehre des hl. Bonaventuras', especially 193–4. See further Kaup, 'Zum Begriff der iustitia originalis in der älteren Franziskanerschule'.

7 See M. Grabmann, 'Zur Erkenntnislehre des älteren Franziskanerschule', *FS* 4 (1917) 105–18; E. Gilson, 'Sur quelques difficultes de l'illumination augustinienne', *Revue néoscolastique de philosophie* 36 (1934) 321–31; idem., 'Roger Marston, un cas d'Augustinisme avincennisant', *Archives d'histoire doctrinale et littéraire du moyen-âge* 8 (1952) 37–42; P. A. Faustino Prezioza, 'L'attività del soggeto pensante della gnoseologia di Matteo d'Acquasparte e di Ruggerio Marston', *Antonianum* 25 (1950) 259–326.

8 *Opus Oxoniense* I dist. iii q.4 aa.1–3. For an outstanding study of Scotus' critique of Henry of Ghent's illuminationism, see P. C. Vier, *Evidence*

and Its Function According to John Duns Scotus (New York, 1951). The early Dominican school, it may be noted, was also critical of Augustine's illuminationism: see the classic study of E. Gilson, 'Pourquoi S. Thomas a critiqué S. Augustin', *Archives d'histoire doctrinale et littéraire du moyen âge* 1 (1926–7) 5–127.

Notes to §16

1 See V. Heynck, 'A Controversy at the Council of Trent concerning the Doctrine of Duns Scotus', *FrS* 9 (1949) 181–258.
2 *Opus Oxoniense* IV dist. xvii q.3 n.21.
3 *Reportata Parisiensis* IV dist. ix q. unica n.2.
4 See H. Ameri, *Doctrina theologorum de Immaculata B.V.M. Conceptione tempore Concili Basiliensis* (Roma, 1954); I. Brady, 'The Development of the Doctrine of the Immaculate Conception in the Fourteenth Century after Aureoli', *FrS* 15 (1955) 175–202; K. Balic, 'Die Corredemptrixfrage innerhalb der franziskanischen Theologie', *FS* 39 (1957) 218–87; M. Mückshoff, 'Die mariologische Prädestination im Denken der franziskanischen Theologie', *FS* 39 (1957) 288–502.
5 *In III Sent.* dist. iii q.1 ad 2um. Cf. *Summa Theologiae* IIIa q.27 a.2 ad 3um.
6 *Opus Oxoniense* III dist. iii q.1 n.4. Cf. K. Balic, *Duns Scoti Theologiae Marianae elementa* (Sibenici, 1933).
7 *Opus Oxoniense* III dist. iii. q.1 n.10.
8 For a survey of opinions, see F. de Guimarens, 'La doctrine des théologiens sur l'Immaculée Conception de 1250 à 1350', *Etudes Franciscains* 3 (1952) 181–203; 4 (1953) 23–51; 167–87; A. di Lella, 'The Immaculate Conception in the Writings of Peter Aureoli', *FrS* 15 (1955) 146–58; E. M. Buytaert, 'The Immaculate Conception in the Writings of Ockham', *FrS* 10 (1950) 149–63.
9 *Super libros Sapientiae* lect. 160C.

Notes to §17

1 e.g., G. H. Tavard, *Protestantism* (London, 1950) 20. For similar understandings of 'Nominalism' as that of Tavard, see R. M. Torelló, 'El Ockhamismo y la decadencia escolástica en el siglo XIV', *Pensamiento* 9 (1953) 199–228; J. R. Gironella, 'Para la historia del nominalismo y de la reacción antinominalista de Suárez', *Pensamiento* 17 (1961) 279–310.
2 See H. Grisar, *Luther* (6 vols: London, 1913–17) 1.130.
3 Ritter, *Marsilius von Inghen und die okkamistische Schule in Deutschland*; Feckes, *Die Rechtfertigungslehre des Gabriel Biel*; A. Lang, *Heinrich Totting von Oyta. Ein Beitrag zur Entstehungsgeschichte der ersten deutschen Universitäten und zur Problemsgeschichte der Spätscholastik* (Münster, 1937); N. Häring, *Die Theologie der Erfurter Augustiner-Eremiten Bartholomäus Arnoldi von Usingen* (Limburg, 1939).

4 Ehrle, *Der Sentenzenkommentar Peters von Candia*, 106–7. For his discussion of 'Nominalist' diversity, see ibid., 108–251.
5 A. Lang, *Die Wege der Glaubensbegründung bei den Scholastikern des 14. Jahrhunderts* (Münster, 1931) 131.
6 Hochstetter, 'Nominalismus?'.
7 P. Vignaux, art. 'Nominalisme', *DThC* 11.717–18. On 'Terminism', see L. M. de Rijk, *Logica Modernorum. A Contribution to the History of Early Terminist Logic* (2 vols: Assen, 1962–7).
8 Cited Ehrle, op. cit., 323.
9 See D. M. Armstrong, *Nominalism and Realism. Universals and Scientific Realism* (2 vols: Cambridge, 1978) 1.12–57.
10 A. E. McGrath, '*Homo Assumptus?* A Study in the Christology of the *Via Moderna*, with Particular Reference to William of Ockham', *EThL* 61 (1984) 283–97.
11 WATr 5.633.1–18; cited Oberman, *Werden und Wertung*, 425.
12 J. Würsdorfer, *Erkennen und Wissen nach Gregor von Rimini* (Münster, 1917).
13 A. Zumkeller, *Hugolino von Orvieto und seine theologische Erkenntnislehre* (Würzburg, 1941) 257–61.
14 Thus P. Vignaux, *Nominalisme au XIVᵉ siècle* (Paris, 1948).
15 M. Schepers, 'Holkot contra Crathorn', *Philosophisches Jahrbuch* 77 (1970) 320–54; 79 (1972) 106–36.
16 On the latter, see G. Gál, 'Gaulteri de Chatton de Guillelmi de Ockham controversia de natura conceptus universalis', *FrS* 27 (1967) 191–212; N. Fitzpatrick, 'Walter Chatton on the Univocity of Being. A Reaction to Peter Aureoli and William Ockham', *FrS* 31 (1971) 88–177.
17 See Ritter, *Via antiqua und via moderna auf deutschen Universitäten des XV. Jahrhunderts*; R. R. Post, *De via antiqua en de via moderna bij vijftiende eeuwse Nederlandse theologen* (Nijmegen, 1964); K.-H. Gerschmann, '"Antiqui-Novi-Moderni" in den "Epistolae obscurorum Virorum"', *Archiv für Begriffsgeschichte* 11 (1967) 23–36; A. G. Weiler, art. 'Antiqui/moderni (via antiqua/via moderna)', in *Historisches Wörterbuch der Philosophie* ed. J. Ritter (Basel, 1971) 1.407–10; A. L. Gabriel, '"Via antiqua" and "via moderna" and the Migration of Paris Students and Masters to the German Universities in the Fifteenth Century', in *Antiqui und Moderni. Traditionsbewußtsein und Fortschrittsbewußtsein im späten Mittelalter* ed. A. Zimmermann (Berlin/New York, 1974) 439–83; Oberman, *Werden und Wertung der Reformation*, 28–55; W. Urban, 'Die "via moderna" an der Universität Erfurt am Vorabend der Reformation', in *Gregor von Rimini. Werk und Wirkung bis zur Reformation* ed. H. A. Oberman (Berlin/New York, 1981) 311–30. It may be noted that the *via moderna* was known by various names at different universities; at Paris, it was referred to as the *via nominalium* (R. G. Villoslada, *La Universidad de Paris durante los estudios de Francisco de Vitorio O.P. 1507–1522* (Roma, 1938) 76; 118); at Heidelberg, as the *via Marsiliana* (after Marsilius of Inghen: Ritter, *Marsilius von Inghens*, 46); at Wittenberg, as the *via*

Gregorii (apparently after Gregory of Rimini: McGrath, *Luther's Theology of the Cross*, 31–4.)

18 See McGrath, '*Homo Assumptus?*'; idem., 'Some Observations concerning the Soteriology of the *Via Moderna*', *RThAM* 52 (1986) 182–93.

19 e.g., Oberman, *Harvest of Medieval Theology*, 108–11; McGrath, *Luther's Theology of the Cross* 110–11.

20 Oberman, op. cit., 112–13.

21 Biel, *In III Sent.* dist. xl q. unica a.2 conc.

22 Oberman, op. cit., 118 n.92. It is this understanding of Christ's function which appears to underlie Luther's early theological difficulties: see WA 38.148.12; 40 I.298.9; 40.I.326.1; 41.653.41; 45.482.16; 47.590.1.

23 Biel, *In III Sent.* dist. xl q. unica a.3 dub.3; ed. Werbeck/Hoffmann, 3.704.18–19.

24 *Sermones Dominicales de tempore* 32D.

25 Biel, *In II Sent.* dist. xxvii q. unica a.3 dub.5; ed. cit., 2.525.11–14 'Homo non potest evidenter scire se facere quod in se est, quia hoc facere includit in se proponere oboedire Deo propter Deum tamquam ultimum et principalem finem, quod exigit dilectionem Dei super omnia, quam ex naturalis suis homo potest elicere.'

26 Biel, *In II Sent.* dist. xxviii q. unica a.1 nota.2; ed. cit., 2.536.1–537.9 'Secundo notandum quod, cum loquimur de puris naturalibus, non excluditur generalis Dei influentia ... Sed per "pura naturalia" intelligitur animae natura seu substantia cum qualitatibus et actionibus consequentibus naturam, exclusis habitibus ac donis supernaturaliter a solo Deo infusis.'

Notes to §18

1 e.g., Zumkeller, 'Hugolin von Orvieto'; Toner, 'The Doctrine of Justification according to Augustine of Rome'; Werbeck, *Jacobus Perez von Valencia*; Ferdigg, 'De vita et operibus et doctrina Joannis de Paltz'; Steinmetz, *Misericordia Dei*; Zumkeller, 'Johannes von Retz'; idem, 'Johannes Klenkok'; idem, 'Johannes von Dorsten'; idem, 'Johannes Hiltalingen von Basel'; idem, 'Erbsünde, Gnade und Rechtfertigung im Verständnis der Erfurter Augustinertheologen des Spätmittelalters'; idem, 'Angelus Dobelinus'; McGrath, '"Augustinianism"? A Critical Assessment of the so-called "Medieval Augustinian Tradition" on Justification'.

2 Cf. D. C. Steinmetz, *Luther and Staupitz. An Essay in the Intellectual Origins of the Protestant Reformation* (Durham, N.C., 1980) 13–16. Steinmetz distinguishes five senses of the term.

3 A. V. Müller, *Luthers theologische Quellen. Seine Verteidigung gegen Denifle und Grisar* (Giessen, 1912).

4 idem, 'Agostino Favorini e la teologia di Lutero', *Bilychnis* 3 (1914) 373–87; idem, 'Giacomo Pérez di Valenza, O.S. Aug., Vescovo di Chrysopoli e la teologia di Lutero', *Bilychnis* 9 (1920) 391–403; idem,

'Una fonte ignota del sistema di Lutero. Il beato Fidati da Cascia e la sua teologia', *Bilychnis* 10 (1921) fasc. 2; idem, 'Il Dr. Paulus di Monaco, il beato Fidati e Lutero', *Bilychnis* 12 (1922) 247–57.

5 E. Stakemeier, *Der Kampf um Augustin. Augustinus und die Augustiner auf dem Tridentinum* (Paderborn, 1937).

6 H. Jedin, *History of the Council of Trent* (2 vols: Edinburgh, 1957–61) 2.258.

7 W. von Loewenich, *Duplex Iustitia. Luthers Stellung zu seiner Unionsformel des 16. Jahrhunderts* (Wiesbaden, 1972).

8 J. Henniger, *S. Augustinus et doctrina de duplici iustitia* (Mödling, 1935).

9 Auer, *Entwicklung der Gnadenlehre in der Hochscholastik* 2.200, with reference to Scotus, *Lectura Prima* I, 17; Oberman, *Harvest of Medieval Theology*, 160–5, with reference to Biel, *Canonis Missae Expositio* 59L.

10 B. Warfield, *Calvin and Augustine* (Philadelphia, 1956), 322.

11 *de causa Dei*, 174.

12 Gregory refers critically to (an unnamed) *unus modernus doctor* in this context: *In II Sent.* dist. xxxix q.1 a.1. The name 'Bradwardine' is inserted in the margins to two manuscripts (Paris Nat. lat. 15891 and Mazarin 914).

13 Zumkeller, 'Johannes Klenkok', 266–90.

14 Zumkeller, 'Hugolin von Orvieto über Urstand und Erbsünde', 175–82.

15 Zumkeller, 'Johannes Hiltalingen von Basel', 115–18.

16 Zumkeller, 'Angelus Dobelinus', 97–103.

17 K. Werner, *Der Augustinismus in der Scholastik des später Mittelalters* (Wien, 1883) 234–300; Zumkeller, 'Die Augustinerschule des Mittelalters'.

18 C. Stange, 'Über Luthers Beziehungen zur Theologie seines Ordens', *Neue kirchliche Zeitschrift* 11 (1900) 574–85; especially 578. For the refutation of this opinion, see McGrath, *Luther's Theology of the Cross*, 36–8.

19 A. V. La Valle, *La giustizia di Adamo e il peccato originale secondo Egidio Romano* (Palermo, 1939); G. Díaz, *De peccati originalis essentia in schola Augustiniana praetridentina* (El Escorial, 1961); idem, 'La escuela agustiniana pretridetina y el problema de la concupiscencia', *La Ciudad de Dios* 174 (1961) 309–56.

20 Trapp, 'Augustinian Theology of the Fourteenth Century', especially 156–7.

21 e.g. *In I Sent.* dist. xvii q.2.

22 e.g., see Zumkeller's edition of Retz, in *Augustiniana* 22 (1972) 540–82; Textbeilage 126, citing Thomas of Strasbourg *In II Sent.* dist. xxviii, xxix q.1 a.3.

23 Trapp, op. cit., 248.

24 J. Beumer, 'Augustinismus und Thomismus in der theologischen Prinzipienlehre des Aegidius Romanus', *Scholastik* 32 (1957) 542–60.

25 Zumkeller, 'Augustinerschule des Mittelalters', 193–5.

26 Oberman, *Harvest of Medieval Theology*, 286–92.

27 Werbeck, *Jacobus Perez von Valencia*, 214–15, n.1.

28 R. Weijenborg, 'Doctrina de immaculata conceptione apud Ioannem de Paltz O.E.S.A., magistrum Lutheri novitii', *Virgo Immaculata* (Roma, 1957) 160–83.

29 Steinmetz, op. cit., 146–7.

30 e.g., compare Johannes Hiltalingen of Basel with Thomas of Strasbourg: Zumkeller, 'Johannes Hiltalingen von Basel', 68–9.

31 As documented by Trapp, op. cit., *passim*.

32 Trapp makes the important point that no theologian of the Augustinian Order uses the dialectic between the two powers of God in the unorthodox manner associated with *moderni* such as John of Mirecourt and Nicholas of Autrecourt: Trapp, op. cit., 265.

33 For documentation of this transition, see McGrath, '"Augustinianism"?'.

34 This does not, of course, imply that the *schola Augustiniana moderna* derived these methods from the *via moderna*: it seems that both schools ultimately derived them from Duns Scotus, the former *via* Gregory of Rimini and the latter *via* William of Ockham.

35 See McGrath, *Luther's Theology of the Cross*, 81–5.

Notes to §19

1 On this, see G. Aulén, *Reformation och Katolicitet* (Stockholm, 1959).

2 See E. Wolf, 'Die Rechtfertigungslehre als Mitte und Grenze reformatorischer Theologie', *Evangelische Theologie* 9 (1949–50) 298–308. There is, of course, a genuine difficulty in establishing the precise causal relationship between the origins of Luther's own theology and that of the Reformation as a whole: see H. A. Oberman, 'Headwaters of the Reformation: *Initia Lutheri – Initia Reformationis*', in *Luther and the Dawn of the Modern Era* ed. H. A. Oberman (Leiden, 1974) 40–88; McGrath, *Luther's Theology of the Cross*, 24 n.45; 52–3; 142.

3 For the sense and origins of this celebrated phrase, see F. Loofs, 'Der articulus stantis et cadentis ecclesiae', *Theologische Studien und Kritiken* 90 (1917) 323–400. It is necessary to challenge Loofs upon several points, particularly his suggestion that the phrase is first used in the eighteenth century by the Lutheran theologian Valentin Löscher in his famous anti-Pietist essay *Timotheus Verinus* (Wittenberg, 1718). For example, the *Reformed* theologian Johann Heinrich Alsted uses the phrase a century earlier, opening his discussion of man's justification *coram Deo* as follows: 'articulus iustificationis dicitur articulus stantis et cadentis ecclesiae' (*Theologia scholastica didacta* (Hanoviae, 1618) 711). Precursors of the phrase may, of course, be found in the writings of Luther himself – e.g., WA 40 III.352.3 '...quia isto articulo stante stat Ecclesia, ruente ruit Ecclesia'.

4 Bossuet, *Première Instruction pastorale* xxvii; cited O. Chadwick, *From Bossuet to Newman. The Idea of Doctrinal Development* (Cambridge, 1957) 17.

5 Thus Philip Melanchthon, *Corpus Reformatorum (Melanchthon)* 2.884

'So man nun fragt, warum sondert ich euch denn von der vorigen Kirchen? Antwort: wir sondern uns nicht von der vorigen rechten Kirchen. Ich halte es eben das, welches Ambrosius und Augustinus gelehret haben.' For the early Protestant understanding of history entailed in such statements, see the suggestive study of H. Rückert, 'Das evangelische Geschichtsbewußtsein und das Mittelalter', in *Mittelalterliches Erbe – Evangelische Verantwortung. Vorträge und Ansprachen zum Gedenken der Gründung des Tübinger Augustinerklosters 1262* (Tübingen, 1962) 13–23.

6 Thus Flacius Illyricus, initially in his *Catalogus testium veritatis* (1556), and subsequently in his celebrated *Magdeburg Centuries* (1559–74).

7 The most important interpretation of the 'Forerunners' is due to Karl H. Ullmann, *Reformatoren vor der Reformation vornehmlich in Deutschland und den Niederlanden* (2 vols: Hamburg, 1841–2). For a critical assessment of this work, see H. A. Oberman, *Forerunners of the Reformation. The Shape of Late Medieval Thought* (Philadelphia, 1981) 3–49, especially 32–43.

8 H. A. Oberman, 'Fourteenth Century Religious Thought. A Premature Profile', *Speculum* 53 (1978) 80–93.

9 See H. A. Oberman, 'Das tridentinische Rechtfertigungsdekret im Lichte spätmittelalterlichen Theologie', *ZThK* 61 (1964) 251–82; idem, 'Duns Scotus, Nominalism and the Council of Trent', in *John Duns Scotus 1265–1965* ed. J. K. Ryan and B. M. Bonansea (New York, 1965), 311–44.

10 See McGrath, 'Forerunners of the Reformation?', 223–8. These features will be documented and discussed further in Volume 2 of the present study.

11 See McGrath, *Luther's Theology of the Cross*, 133–6.

12 WA 56.270.9–11; 343.16–23; 351.23–352.7. It is this principle which underlies Luther's maxim *simul iustus et peccator*: see R. Hermann, *Luthers These 'Gerecht und Sünder zugleich'* (Gütersloh, 1930).

13 As pointed out by Oberman, *Werden und Wertung*, 110–12.

14 Oberman, op. cit., 82–140, especially 83–92.

15 McGrath, *Luther's Theology of the Cross*, 36–40; 63–71; idem, 'John Calvin and Late Medieval Thought. A Study in Late Medieval Influences upon Calvin's Theological Development', *ARG* 77 (1986) forthcoming.

16 P. Vignaux, *Luther Commentateur des Sentences* (Paris, 1934) 5–44; McGrath, *Luther's Theology of the Cross*, 81–5.

17 A. B. Ritschl, *The Christian Doctrine of Justification and Reconciliation* (Edinburgh, 1872) 90–1.

18 This point will be discussed further in Volume 2. See W. Niesel, 'Calvin wider Osianders Rechtfertigungslehre', *ZKG* 46 (1928) 410–30; W. Koehler, *Dogmengeschichte als Geschichte des christlichen Selbstbewusstseins* (Zürich, 1951) 354. Cf. the celebrated statement of Richard Hooker, *Works* ed. J. Keble (3 vols: Oxford, 1845³) 3.486 '... that grand question, which hangeth yet in controversy between us and the Church of Rome, about the matter of justifying righteousness'.

19 See McGrath, 'Forerunners of the Reformation?', 228–36.

20 Latomus, *Duae Epistolae* (Antwerp, 1544) 38.
21 J. Buchanan, *The Doctrine of Justification. An Outline of Its History in the Church and of Its Exposition from Scripture* (Edinburgh, 1867; reprinted Edinburgh, 1961) 94.
22 ibid., 104. In common with many nineteenth-century polemicists, Buchanan appears to confuse 'justification by inherent righteousness' with 'justification by works'. This fact alone is sufficient to indicate the poverty of their understanding of Augustine's teaching on the matter.
23 It is interesting to note that Oberman's case for 'Forerunners' of the Reformation doctrines of justification is nowhere stated explicitly, but appears to rest upon certain writings pertaining to predestination: Oberman, *Forerunners of the Reformation*, 121–41.
24 H. A. Oberman, '"Iustitia Christi" and "Iustitia Dei". Luther and the Scholastic Doctrines of Justification', *HThR* 59 (1966) 1–26; 4. Cf. idem, *Harvest of Medieval Theology*, 185–7, especially 185 'It is a reliable rule of interpretation for the historian of Christian thought that the position taken with respect to the doctrine of predestination is a most revealing indicator of the understanding of the doctrine of justification'.

Bibliography

I. Primary literature

a. Collected works

Corpus Christianorum Series Latina (Turnholt, 1953–)
Corpus scriptorum ecclesiasticorum Latinorum (Vienna, 1866–)
J. P. Migne, *Patrologia cursus completus series Latina* (221 vols: Paris, 1844–64)
    Patrologia cursus completus series Graeca (162 volumes: Paris, 1857–66)
Henricus Denzinger, *Enchiridion Symbolorum Definitionum et Declarationum de Rebus Fidei et Morum* (Barcelona, 1948²⁴⁻²⁵)

b. Biblical

Biblia Hebraica, ed. R. Kittel (Stuttgart, 1972¹⁷)
Septuaginta, ed. A. Rahlfs (Stuttgart, 1975⁹)
Biblia Sacra iuxta Vulgatam versionem (Stuttgart, 1975)

c. Medieval Authors

Aegidius Romanus *Commentarius in secundum librum sententiarum* (2 vols: Venetiis, 1581)
Albertus Magnus *Opera Omnia* ed. S. C. A. Borgnet (38 vols: Paris, 1890–9)
Alexander of Hales *Glossa in IV libros sententiarum* (4 vols: Quaracchi, 1951–7)
    Quaestiones disputatae 'antequam esset frater' (3 vols: Quaracchi, 1960)
Alexander of Hales (attributed) *Summa Theologica* (4 vols: Quaracchi, 1924–48)
Anselm of Canterbury *Opera Omnia* ed. F. S. Schmitt (6 vols: Stuttgart, 1968)
Anselm of Laon *Anselms von Laon systematische Sentenzen* ed. F. P. Bliemetzrieder (Münster, 1919)
Biel, Gabriel *Collectorium circa quattuor libros sententiarum* ed. W. Werbeck and U. Hofmann (4 vols: Tübingen, 1973–84)

Bibliography

Canonis missae expositio ed. H. A. Oberman and W. J. Courtenay (4 vols: Wiesbaden, 1963–67)

Sermones dominicales de tempore (Hagenau, 1510)

Bonaventure *Opera Omnia* (10 vols: Quaracchi, 1882–1902)

Bradwardine, Thomas *De causa Dei contra Pelagium* (Londoni, 1618)

Dante Aligheri *La divina commedia* ed. D. Mattalia (3 vols: Milano, 1975)

Duns Scotus *Opera Omnia* ed. C. Balić (Roma, 1950–)

Commentaria Oxoniensia (2 vols: Quaracchi, 1912–14)

Durandus of St Pourçain *In Petri Lombardi sententias theologicas commentariorum* (2 vols: Venetiis, 1571)

Eck, Johannes *Chrysospassus praedestinationis* (Augsburg, 1514)

In primum librum sententiarum annotatiunculae ed. W. L. Moore (Leiden, 1976)

Erasmus, Desiderius *Opera Omnia*, ed. J. Clericus (10 vols: Lugduni Batavorum, 1703–06)

Novum Instrumentum omne (Basileae, 1516)

Godescalc of Orbais *Œuvres théologiques et grammaticales* ed. C. Lambot (Louvain, 1945)

Gregory of Rimini *Lectura super primum et secundum sententiarum* ed. A. D. Trapp (6 vols: Berlin/New York, 1979–84)

Hincmar of Reims 'Zwei Schriften des Erzbischofs Hinkmar von Reims', ed. W. Gundlach, *ZKG* 10 (1889) 92–145; 258–310

Holcot, Robert *Quaestiones super IV libros sententiarum* (Lugduni, 1497)

Opus super sapientiam Salomonis (Hagenau, 1494)

Huss, John *Opera Omnia* ed. V. Flajshans (3 vols: Praha, 1903–8)

John of La Rochelle *Die neuen Quästionen der Gnadentheologie des Johannes von Rupella* ed. L. Hödl (München, 1964)

Matthew of Aquasparta *Quaestiones disputatae de gratia* ed. V. Doucet (Quaracchi, 1935)

Odo Rigaldi *In II Sent.* dist. xxvi–xxix, ed. J. Bouvy, in 'Les questiones sur la grâce dans le Commentaire des Sentences d'Odon Rigaud', *RThAM* 27 (1960) 305–43; 'La nécessité de la grâce dans le Commentaire des Sentences d'Odon Rigaud', *RThAM* 28 (1961) 69–96

Peter Aureoli *Commentarorium in primum librum sententiarum* (Romae, 1596)

Peter of Bergamo *Summa Aurea* (Venetiis, 1593)

Peter Cantor *Summa de sacramentis et animae consiliis* ed. J.-A. Dugauquier (5 vols: Louvain/Lille, 1954–67)

Peter Lombard *Libri IV Sententiarum* (2 vols: Quaracchi, 1916²)

Peter of Tarantaise *In IV libros sententiarum commentaria* (4 vols: Tolosae, 1649–52)

Richard of Middleton *Supra quattuor libros sententiarum* (4 vols: Bresciae, 1591)

Robert of Melun *Questiones theologice de epistolis Pauli* ed. R. M. Martin (Louvain, 1938)

Roger of Marston *Quaestiones disputatae de statu naturae lapsae* (Quaracchi, 1932)

Bibliography

Roland of Cremona *Summae magistri Rolandi Cremonensis* ed. A. Cortesi (Bergamo, 1962)

Simon of Tournai *Les disputations de Simon de Tournai* ed. J. Warichez (Louvain, 1932)

Steinbach, Wendelin *Opera Exegetica quae supersunt omnia* ed. H. Feld (Wiesbaden, 1976)

Thomas Aquinas *Opera Omnia* (31 vols: Romae, 1882–1947)
> *Scriptum super libros sententiarum Magistri Petri Lombardi* ed. P. Mandonnet and F. Moos (4 vols: Paris, 1929–47)
> *Quaestiones quodlibetales* ed. R. Spiazzi (Roma, 1956⁹)
> *Quaestiones disputatae* ed. R. Spiazzi (2 vols: Roma, 1949⁸)

Thomas of Strasbourg *Commentaria in IIII libros sententiarum* (Veneṭiis, 1564)

William of Auvergne *Opera Omnia* (2 vols: Paris, 1674)

William of Auxerre *Summa Aurea in quattuor libros sententiarum* (Paris, 1500)

William of Ockham *Commentaria in quattuor libros sententiarum* (Lugduni, 1495)
> *Opera philosophica et theologica* (9 vols: New York, 1966–)
> *Tractatus de praedestinatione et de praescientia Dei et de futuris contingentibus* ed. P. Boehmer (New York, 1945)

2. Secondary literature

Alzeghy, S. *Nova creatura. La nozione della grazia nei commentari medievali di S. Paolo* (Roma, 1956)

Amand, D. *Fatalisme et liberté dans l'antiquité grecque* (Louvain, 1945)

Anciaux, P. *La théologie du sacrement du penance au XIIe siècle* (Louvain, 1949)

Auer, J. *Die menschliche Willensfreiheit im Lehrsystem des Thomas von Aquin und Johannes Duns Skotus* (München, 1938)
> *Die Entwicklung der Gnadenlehre in der Hochscholastik* (2 vols: Freiburg, 1942–51)

Bakhuizen van den Brink, J. N. '*Mereo(r)* and *meritum* in some Latin Fathers', *Studia Patristica* 3 (Berlin, 1961) 333–40

Ball, D. 'Libre arbitre et liberté dans Saint Augustin', *AThA* 6 (1945) 368–82
'Les développements de la doctrine de la liberté chez Saint Augustin', *AThA* 7 (1946) 400–30

Bannach, K. *Die Lehre von der doppelten Macht Gottes bei Wilhelm von Ockham* (Wiesbaden, 1975)

Bavaud, G. 'La doctrine de la justification d'après Saint Augustin et la Réforme', *REAug* 5 (1959) 21–32

Beck, H. *Vorsehung und Vorherbestimmung in der theologischen Literatur der Byzantiner* (Rom, 1937)

Beumer, J. 'Gratia supponit naturam. Zur Geschichte eines theologischen Prinzips', *Gregorianum* 20 (1939) 381–406; 535–52

Blomme, R. *La doctrine de la péché dans les écoles théologiques de la première moitié du XIIe siècle* (Louvain, 1958)

Bibliography

Bouillard, H. *Conversion et grâce chez S. Thomas d'Aquin* (Paris, 1944)

Bruch, R. 'Die Urgerechtigkeit als Rechtheit des Willens nach der Lehre des hl. Bonaventuras', *FS* 33 (1951) 180–206

Burger, C. P. 'Das auxilium speciale Dei in der Gnadenlehre Gregors von Rimini', in *Gregor von Rimini. Werk und Wirkung bis zur Reformation* ed. H. A. Oberman (Berlin, 1981) 195–240

Burnaby, J. *Amor Dei. A Study of the Religion of St. Augustine* (London, 1947)

Capánaga, V. 'La deificacíon en la soteriología agustiniana', *Augustinus Magister* (Paris, 1954) 2.745–54

Chéné, J. 'Que significiaient 'initium fidei' et 'affectus credulitatis' pour les sémipelagiens?', *RSR* 35 (1948) 566–88

'Le sémipelagianisme du Midi et de la Gaule d'après les lettres de Prosper d'Aquitaine et d'Hilaire à Saint Augustin', *RSR* 43 (1955) 321–41

Courtenay, W. J. 'Covenant and Causality in Pierre d'Ailly', *Speculum* 46 (1971) 94–119

'The King and the Leaden Coin. The Economic Background of Sine Qua Non Causality', *Traditio* 28 (1972) 185–209

Adam Wodeham. An Introduction to his Life and Writings (Leiden, 1978)

Courtney, F. *Cardinal Robert Pullen. An English Theologian of the Twelfth Century* (Rome, 1954)

Davids, E. A. *Das Bild vom neuen Menschen. Ein Beitrag zum Verständnis des Corpus Macarianum* (Salzburg/München, 1968)

Dettloff, W. *Die Lehre von der acceptatio divina bei Johannes Duns Scotus mit besonderer Berücksichtigung der Rechtfertigungslehre* (Werl, 1954)

Die Entwicklung der Akzeptations- und Verdienstlehre von Duns Scotus bis Luther mit besonderer Berücksichtigung der Franziskanertheologen (Münster, 1963)

'Die antipelagianische Grundstruktur des scotischen Rechtfertigungslehre', *FS* 48 (1966) 266–70

Dhont, R.-C. *Le problème de la préparation à la grâce. Débuts de l'école franciscain* (Paris, 1946)

Doms, H. *Die Gnadenlehre des sel. Albertus Magnus* (Breslau, 1929)

Douglass, E. J. D. *Justification in Late Medieval Preaching. A Study of John Geiler of Strassburg* (Leiden, 1966)

Ehrle, F. *Der Sentenzenkommentar Peters von Candia des pisanerpapstes Alexander V* (Münster, 1925)

Ernst, W. *Gott und Mensch am Vorabend der Reformation. Eine Untersuchung zur Moralphilosophie und -theologie bei Gabriel Biel* (Leipzig, 1972).

Feckes, C. *Die Rechtfertigungslehre des Gabriel Biel und ihre Stellung innerhalb der nominalistischen Schule* (Münster, 1925)

Flick, M. *L'attimo della giustificazione secondo S. Tomasso* (Roma, 1947)

Gillon, B. 'La grâce incréée chez quelques théologiens du XIVe siècle', *Divinitas* 11 (1967) 671–80

Grabmann, M. *Mittelalterliches Geistesleben. Abhandlungen zur Geschichte der Scholastik und Mystik* (3 vols: München, 1926–56)

Die Geschichte der scholastischen Methode (2 vols: Darmstadt, 1956)

Gross, J. *La divinisation du chrétien d'après les pères grecs* (Paris, 1938)

Bibliography

Häring, N. *Die Theologie der Erfurter Augustiner-Eremiten Bartholomäus Arnoldi von Usingen* (Limburg, 1939)

Hamm, B. *Promissio, pactum, ordinatio. Freiheit und Selbstbindung Gottes in der scholastischen Gnadenlehre* (Tübingen, 1977)

von Harnack, A. *History of Dogma* (7 vols: Edinburgh, 1894–9)

Heynck, V. 'Die aktuelle Gnade bei Richard von Mediavilla', *FS* 22 (1935) 297–325

Hocedez, E. *Richard de Middleton: sa vie, ses œuvres, sa doctrine* (Louvain, 1925)

Hochstetter, E. 'Nominalismus?', *FrS* 9 (1949) 370–403

Iserloh, E. *Gnade und Eucharistie in der philosophischen Theologie des Wilhelm von Ockham. Ihre Bedeutung für die Ursachen der Reformation* (Wiesbaden, 1956)

Kaup, J. 'Zum Begriff der iustitia originalis in der älteren Franziskanerschule', *FS* 29 (1942) 44–55

Landgraf, A. M. 'Untersuchungen zu den Eigenlehren Gilberts de la Porrée', *ZKTh* 54 (1930) 180–213

'Mitteilungen zur Schule Gilberts de la Porrée', *CFr* 3 (1933) 185–208

'Neue Funde zur Porretanerschule', *CFr* 6 (1936) 354–63

'Der Porretanismus der Homilien des Radulphus Ardens', *ZKTh* 64 (1940) 132–48

Einführung in die Geschichte der theologischen Literatur der Frühscholastik (Regensburg, 1948)

Dogmengeschichte der Frühscholastik (8 vols: Regensburg, 1952–56)

Laun, J. F. 'Die Prädestination bei Wiclif und Bradwardin', in *Imago Dei. Festschrift für G. Krüger* ed. H. Bornkamm (Gießen, 1932) 63–84

Leff, G. *William of Ockham. The Metamorphosis of Scholastic Discourse* (Manchester, 1975)

Lennerz, H. 'De historia applicationis principii "omnis ordinate volens prius vult finem quam ea quae sunt ad finem" ad probandam gratuitatem praedestinationis ad gloriam', *Gregorianum* 10 (1929) 238–66

Lindbeck, G. 'Nominalism and the Problem of Meaning as illustrated by Pierre d'Ailly on Predestination and Justification', *HThR* 52 (1959) 43–60

Lonergan, B. J. F. *Grace and Reason. Operative Grace in the Thought of St. Thomas Aquinas* (London, 1971)

Loofs, F. *Leitfaden zum Studien der Dogmengeschichte* (Halle, 1906[4])

Lottin, O. 'Le concept de justice chez les théologiens du moyen âge avant l'introduction d'Aristote', *Revue Thomiste* 44 (1938) 511–21

Psychologie et morale au XIIe et XIIIe siècles (8 vols: Louvain/Gembloux, 1942–60)

McGrath, A. E. 'The Anti-Pelagian Structure of "Nominalist" Doctrines of Justification', *EThL* 57 (1981) 107–19

'Rectitude: The Moral Foundations of Anselm of Canterbury's Soteriology', *Downside Review* 99 (1981) 201–13

'"Augustinianism"? A Critical Assessment of the so-called "Medieval Augustinian Tradition" on Justification', *Augustiniana* 31 (1981) 247–67

Bibliography

'Forerunners of the Reformation? A Critical Examination of the Evidence for Precursors of the Reformation Doctrines of Justification', *HThR* 75 (1982) 219–42

'"The Righteousness of God" from Augustine to Luther', *Studia Theologica* 36 (1982) 63–78

'Justice and Justification. Semantic and Juristic Aspects of the Christian Doctrine of Justification', *SJTh* 35 (1982) 403–18

'Divine Justice and Divine Equity in the Controversy between Augustine and Julian of Eclanum', *Downside Review* 101 (1983) 312–19

'The Influence of Aristotelian Physics upon St. Thomas Aquinas' Discussion of the "Processus Iustificationis"', *RThAM* 51 (1984) 223–29

MacQueen, D. J. 'John Cassian on Grace and Free Will, with Particular Reference to *Institutio* XII and *Collatio* XII', *RThAM* 44 (1977) 5–28

Martin, R. M. *La controverse sur le péché originel au début du XIVᵉ siècle* (Louvain, 1930)

Mitzka, F. 'Die Lehre des hl. Bonaventura von der Vorbereitung auf die heiligmachende Gnade', *ZKTh* 50 (1926) 27–72; 220–52

'Die Anfänge der Konkurslehre im 13. Jahrhundert', *ZKTh* 54 (1930) 161–79

Molteni, P. *Roberto Holcot O.P. Dottrina della grazia e della giustificazione* (Pinerolo, 1968)

Müller, O. *Die Rechtfertigungslehre nominalistischer Reformationsgegner, Bartholomäus Arnoldi von Usingen und Kaspar Schatzgeyer über Erbsünde, erste Rechtfertigung und Taufe* (Breslau, 1940)

Nygren, G. *Das Prädestinationsproblem in der Theologie Augustins* (Göttingen, 1956)

Oakley, F. 'Pierre d'Ailly and the Absolute Power of God. Another Note on the Theology of Nominalism', *HThR* 56 (1963) 59–73

Oberman, H. A. *Archbishop Thomas Bradwardine. A Fourteenth Century Augustinian* (Utrecht, 1957)

'Facientibus quod in se est Deus non denegat gratiam. Robert Holcot O.P. and the Beginnings of Luther's Theology', *HThR* 55 (1962) 317–42.

The Harvest of Medieval Theology. Gabriel Biel and Late Medieval Nominalism (Cambridge, Mass., 1963)

'"Iustitia Christi" and "Iustitia Dei". Luther and the Scholastic Doctrines of Justification', *HThR* 59 (1966) 1–26

Forerunners of the Reformation. The Shape of Late Medieval Thought illustrated by Key Documents (New York, 1966)

'Wir sind pettler. Hoc est verum. Bund und Gnade in der Theologie des Mittelalters und der Reformation', *ZKG* 78 (1967) 232–52

'Headwaters of the Reformation: *Initia Lutheri – Initia Reformationis*', in *Luther and the Dawn of the Modern Era* ed. H. A. Oberman (Leiden, 1974) 40–88

Werden und Wertung der Reformation. Vom Wegestreit zum Glaubenskampf (Tübingen, 1977)

Pannenberg, W. *Die Prädestinationslehre des Duns Skotus in Zusammenhang der scholastischen Lehrentwicklung* (Göttingen, 1954)

Bibliography

Peñamaria de Llano, A. *La salvación por la fe. La noción 'fides' in Hilario de Poitiers. Estudio filológico-teológico* (Burgos, 1981)

Pesch, O. H. *Die Theologie der Rechtfertigung bei Martin Luther und Thomas von Aquin* (Mainz, 1967)

Philips, G. 'La théologie de la grâce chez les préscholastiques', *EThL* 48 (1972) 479–508

'La théologie de la grâce dans la "Summa Fratris Alexandris"', *EThL* 49 (1973) 100–23.

L'union personelle avec le Dieu vivant. Essai sur l'origine et le sens de la grâce créée (Gembloux, 1974)

Ritter, G. *Studien zur Spätscholastik I Marsilius von Inghen und die okkamistischen Schule in Deutschland* (Heidelberg, 1921)

Studien zur Spätscholastik II Via Antiqua und Via Moderna auf den deutschen Universtitäten des XV. Jahrhunderts (Heidelberg, 1922)

Rivière, J. *Le dogme de la rédemption au début du moyen âge* (Paris, 1934)

'Le dogme de la rédemption au XIIᵉ siècle d'après les dernièrnes publications', *Revue du Moyen Age Latin* 2 (1946) 101–12.

Salguiero, T. *La doctrine de Saint Augustin sur la grâce d'après le traité à Simplicien* (Porto, 1925)

Schelkle, K. H. *Paulus Lehrer der Väter. die altkirchliche Auslegung von Römer I–II* (Düsseldorf, 1959²)

Schupp, J. *Die Gnadenlehre des Petrus Lombardus* (Freiburg, 1932)

Siewerth, G. *Thomas von Aquin. Die menschliche Willensfreiheit* (Düsseldorf, 1954)

Steinmetz, D. C. *Misericordia Dei. The Theology of Johannes von Staupitz in its Late Medieval Setting* (Leiden, 1968)

Stoeckle, B. *'Gratia supponit naturam.' Geschichte und Analyse eines theologischen Axioms* (Rom, 1962)

Studer, B. 'Jesucristo, nuestra justicia, según san Augustín', *Augustinus. Revista Trimestral* 26 (1981) 253–82

Stufler, J. 'Die entfernte Vorbereitung auf die Rechtfertigung nach dem hl. Thomas', *ZKTh* 47 (1923) 1–23; 161–83

'Der hl. Thomas und das Axiom omne quod movetur ab alio movetur', *ZKTh* 47 (1923) 369–90

Subilia, V. *La giustificazione per fede* (Brescia, 1976)

Toner, N. 'The Doctrine of Justification according to Augustine of Rome (Favaroni)', *Augustiniana* 8 (1958) 164–89; 229–327; 497–515

Trapè, A. *Il concorso divino nel pensiero di Egidio Romano* (Tolentino, 1942)

Trapp, D. 'Augustinian Theology of the Fourteenth Century', *Augustiniana* 6 (1956) 146–274

Vanneste, A. 'Nature et grâce dans la théologie du XIIᵉ siècle', *EThL* 50 (1974) 181–214

'Nature et grâce dans la théologie de Saint Augustin', *Recherches Augustiniennes* 10 (1975) 143–69

Bibliography

Vignaux, P. *Justification et prédestination au XIVᵉ siècle* (Paris, 1934)

Vulfila oder die gotische Bible ed. W. Streitberg (Heidelberg, 1965)

Weingart, R. E. *The Logic of Divine Love. A Critical Analysis of the Soteriology of Peter Abailard* (Oxford, 1970)

Weisweiler, H. 'L'école de Laon et de Guillaume de Champeaux', *RThAM* 4 (1932) 237–69; 371–91

Werbeck, W. *Jacobus Perez von Valencia. Untersuchungen zu seiner Psalmen-kommentar* (Tübingen, 1959)

Wörter, F. *Die christliche Lehre über das Verhältnis von Gnade und Freiheit von den apostolischen Zeiten bis zu Augustinus* (2 vols: Freiburg, 1855–60)

Zumkeller, A. *Dionysius de Montina. Ein neuentdeckter Augustinertheologe des Spätmittelalters* (Würzburg, 1948)

'Hugolin von Orvieto über Urstand und Erbsünde', *Augustiniana* 3 (1953) 35–62; 165–93; 4 (1954) 25–46

'Hugolin von Orvieto über Prädestination, Rechtfertigung und Verdienst', *Augustiniana* 4 (1954) 109–56; 5 (1955) 5–51

'Der Wiener Theologieprofessor Johannes von Retz und seine Lehre von Urstand, Erbsünde, Gnade und Verdienst', *Augustiniana* 22 (1972) 118–84; 540–82

'Johannes Klenkok O.S.A. im Kampf gegen den "Pelagianismus" seiner Zeit. Seine Lehre über Gnade, Rechtfertigung und Verdienst', *Recherches Augustiniennes* 13 (1978) 231–333

'Die Lehre des Erfurter Augustinertheologen Johannes von Dorsten über Gnade, Rechtfertigung und Verdienst', *Theologie und Philosophie* 53 (1978) 27–64; 127–219

'Der Augustinertheologe Johannes Hiltalingen von Basel über Erbsünde, Gnade und Verdienst', *Analecta Augustiniana* 43 (1980) 57–162

'Erbsünde, Gnade und Rechtfertigung im Verständnis der Erfurter Augustinertheologen des Spätmittelalters', *ZKG* 92 (1981) 39–59

'Der Augustiner Angelus Dobelinus, erster Theologieprofessor der Erfurter Universität, über Gnade, Rechtfertigung und Verdienst', *Analecta Augustiniana* 44 (1981) 69–147

Index of names

(A full index is provided at the end of volume II)

Index

early Franciscan school, 47–8, 77,
78–80, 81, 84–5, 86, 89, 113,
114, 134, 136, 160–3
Eck, Johannes, 143–4
Erasmus, Desiderius, 99, 126
Erigena, Johannes Duns, 101, 131

Faustus of Riez, 72, 75
Favaroni, Agostino, 174
Florus of Lyons, 132–4

Geiler, Johannes, of Keisersberg,
89–90
Gilbert de la Porrée, 93
Giles of Rome, 152, 177–8, 179
Godescalc of Orbais, 130–1, 140
Godfrey of Fontaines, 68
Godfrey of Poitiers, 62
Gratian of Bologna, 155
Gregory the Great, 58, 91
Gregory of Nyssa, 32
Gregory of Rimini, 87, 116, 117,
123, 142–3, 152–3, 157, 167,
168, 176–7, 178, 179

Haimo of Auxerre, 92
Henry of Friemar, 178
Henry of Ghent, 68, 121, 162
Hervaeus of Bourg-Dieu, 43, 93
Hilary of Poitiers, 15
Hiltalingen, Johannes, of Basel, 87,
143, 154, 177, 178
Hincmar of Reims, 131–4
Holcot, Robert, 88, 165, 166, 167,
169
Honorius of Autun, 93
Hugh of Rouen, 67
Hugh of St Cher, 67
Hugh of St Victor, 61, 62, 93, 102,
156
Hugolino of Orvieto, 87, 143, 153,
157, 168, 174, 179
Huss, Johann, 117, 142, 176, 185

Irenaeus of Lyons, 20, 83
Isidore of Seville, 23, 131
Ivo of Chartres, 155

Jacobus Perez of Valencia, 174, 178

Jerome, 11, 74, 75
John of La Rochelle, 48, 62, 78–9,
84–5
John of St Giles, 156, 157
Julian of Eclanum, 25, 26, 34, 35,
53–4, 129
Julian of Toledo, 37
Justin Martyr, 20

Klenkok, Johannes, 143, 154, 177

Laborans, Cardinal, 110
Lactantius, 35
later Franciscan school, 115, 118,
136, 163–6, 186
Latomus, Jacobus, 184
Lucaris, Cyril, 4
Lucidus, 129
Luther, Martin, 3, 11, 25, 27, 29,
66–7, 76, 90–1, 125, 143, 154,
157, 168, 172, 179, 182, 183

Macarius of Egypt, 21
Major, John, 119
Mark the Hermit, 20
Marsilius of Inghen, 167
Marsilius of Padua, 126
Matthew of Aquasparta, 48, 80
Melanchthon, Philip, 182, 185

Nemesius of Emessa, 21

Ockham see William of Ockham
Odo of Ourscamp, 110
Odo Rigaldi, 79, 85, 113
Osiander, Andreas, 184

Paltz, Johannes de, 87, 178
Paulinus of Aquileia, 91
Pelagius, 22, 23, 53, 71–2, 74,
75
Peter Abailard, 60–1, 62, 67, 92,
95, 156
Peter Aureole, 122, 149–50, 151
Peter the Chanter, 112, 155
Peter Lombard, 11, 38, 49, 75, 93,
94, 96, 98, 102, 134, 145, 156
Peter Manducator, 43, 92
Peter Olivi, 162

Index

Peter of Poitiers, 43, 61, 78, 95, 101
Peter of Tarantaise, 86, 87, 158
Philip the Chancellor, 85, 102
Praepositinus of Cremona, 101–2
Prosper of Aquitaine, 37, 72, 74
Prudentius of Troyes, 131

Rabanus Maurus, 92
Radulphus Ardens, 83, 110
Ratramnus, 133
Remigius of Auxerre, 54
Retz, Johannes von, 87, 152, 177
Richard of Middleton, 80, 163
Robert Pullen, 84
Roger of Marston, 80
Roland of Cremona, 113, 156, 158

schola Aegidiana 146, 152, 177–9
schola Augustiniana moderna 87, 118, 140–1, 143, 152–4, 157, 178–9, 183
Scotus, Duns *see* Duns Scotus, Johannes
Sedulius Scotus, 91
Seripando, Girolamo, 174
Servatus Lupus, 133
Siger of Brabant, 121
Simon Fidati of Cascia, 174
Simon of Hinton, 62
Simon of Tournai, 95
Simplicianus of Milan, 24, 25, 128

Staupitz, Johannes von, 83, 87, 144, 154, 172, 178
Steinbach, Wendelin, 166
Stephen Langton, 62, 83, 112

Tertullian, 14, 22–3, 28
Thomas Aquinas, 4, 44–7, 63–4, 65, 75, 81–2, 85–7, 97, 103–9, 113–4, 120, 126–7, 134, 145–6, 151, 158, 159, 165
Thomas of Strasbourg, 87, 146, 152, 177, 178

Valla, Lorenzo, 99
via moderna, 49–50, 65–6, 76–8, 87–9, 90, 112, 118, 124–7, 153, 157, 165, 166–72, 183, 185, 186
Vincent of Lérins, 72–3

Walter Chatton, 169
William of Auvergne, 112, 157
William of Auxerre, 44, 62, 102, 113
William of Crathorn, 169
William of Ockham, 68–9, 88, 115–17, 121–3, 137–8, 139, 150–1, 167, 168, 169
Wulfstan, 41
Wycliffe, John, 117, 142, 185

Zwingli, Huldrych, 182

D